From Luababa to Polk County

Zora Neale Hurston Plays
from the Library of Congress

edited by
Jean Lee Cole, Ph.D.
Charles Mitchell, Ph.D.

From Luababa to Polk County

Zora Neale Hurston Plays
from the Library of Congress

edited by
Jean Lee Cole, Ph.D.
Charles Mitchell, Ph.D.

apprentice
house

Edited by Jean Lee Cole, Ph.D. and Charles Mitchell, Ph.D.
Project manager: Kerri Reilly '05
Cover design by Lindsay Miller '05

First printing
10 9 8 7 6 5 4 3 2 1

ISBN: 1-934074-05-5
13-Digit ISBN: 978-1-934074-05-3

apprentice
house
Baltimore, Maryland
www.apprenticehouse.com

Contents

Acknowledgements

This project was shaped by many hands. We would first like to acknowledge the students from Andy Ciofalo's course in book publishing at Loyola College, who worked quickly and intelligently in transcribing the text and performing initial edits. Kerri Reilly, the project manager, and Lindsay Miller, the designer of the cover, deserve special thanks, as does Kevin Atticks, whose thoughtful and elegant design of the book's interior makes for a truly usable edition of Hurston's plays. We should note that without the innovative pedagogy of Professors Ciofalo and Atticks, this book would not exist: their Book Publishing course demonstrates how teaching, scholarship, and professional development can work together.

We also would like to thank Mark Osteen, from Loyola's English Department; Shirley Basfield Dunlap, from the Morgan State University Theatre Department; and Benny Russell, from the Maryland Conservatory of Music, for their work on creating a dramatic reading, with original music, of *Lawing and Jawing* and several of the plays from *Cold Keener* at McManus Theatre on the Loyola campus on March 2, 2005. Discussions held in preparation for this performance gave us important cues regarding our treatment of the typescripts, and the enthusiasm of Mark, Shirley, and Benny for the material inspired us during the sometimes frustrating and tedious editing process. And of course, this performance would not have been possible without the efforts of the students, faculty, and staff of both Morgan State University and Loyola College who performed as actors and musicians. It is our hope that this book, in conjunction with the performance, will further contribute toward the reawakening of interest in Hurston's work.

Finally, we would like to express our appreciation to Loyola College, and especially, the College's Center for the Humanities, for providing the funding to make this project possible. Dan Schlapbach, the organizer of the Humanities Symposium which made Hurston's *Their Eyes Were Watching God* this year's text, provided initial encouragement and suggestions for making it a truly collaborative event. And as always, Patty Ingram of the Center for the Humanities greased the wheels as things moved along.

Jean Lee Cole
Charles Mitchell

Foreword

by Charles Mitchell, Ph.D.

This collection of plays and sketches by Zora Neale Hurston represents the most complete collection of her dramatic writing to date. Fortunately, the Library of Congress rescued these pieces from obscurity in 1997 when a retired librarian discovered them stored in various locations throughout their vast holdings. This treasure-trove of material provides a clear picture of Hurston's theatrical output ranging from 1925 to 1945 and brings us closer to one of the most dynamic figures of the Harlem Renaissance.

The occasion of this publication arises from Loyola College in Maryland's 2005 Humanities Symposium, a week-long series of events related to a particular text sponsored by the National Endowment for the Humanities. When Hurston's *Their Eyes Were Watching God* was chosen, various departments sought ways of exploring her worldview. In a collaborative venture, the English and Communication departments produced this collection of previously unpublished plays, excerpts of which were presented in a reading by the Morgan State University theatre department and Loyola's theatre program.

We hope this volume will help to illuminate Hurston's dramatic writing in the same way that Alice Walker's efforts brought Hurston's novels to the attention of a new generation. With few exceptions, most critics and historians have overlooked Hurston's playwriting. Often, her theatrical pursuits are treated as diversionary or supplementary material for understanding her novels. The most attention given to her dramatic aspirations centers on the controversial and contentious collaboration with Langston Hughes on *Mule Bone*, detailed in Henry Louis Gates' excellent 1991 edition of the play. Here, we have included *De Turkey and De Law*, Hurston's version excised of Hughes' alterations, to show readers her uncompromised version. Although there is evidence that Hurston continued to revise the play as late as 1934, unless some new document is found, *De Turkey and De Law* may stand as her last word on the authorship debate.

It should never be assumed that theatre was any less important to Hurston than her fiction. Hurston was no dilettante – she was a serious and ambitious practitioner. Even while struggling with poverty, she dedicated much of her energy in the 1930s to producing plays with little hope of financial compensation. She also maintained a passionate belief that the precious oral culture collected in her life and fieldwork found its fullest expression on the stage. It was a musical vision, an easy blend of song and dialogue, not the structured scenes with abrupt interpolations found in the white musicals of commercial Broadway. As a folklorist, she wanted to preserve the richness of black culture; as an enthusiast, she wanted to share it with the world.

Although it has been assumed by many that Hurston's theatrical writing began with *Mule Bone*, overwhelming evidence suggests that it began much earlier. Playwriting was Hurston's calling card when she arrived in New York City in 1925. When *Opportunity*, an important black magazine, held a literary contest, two of her three award-winning submissions were plays (*Color Struck* and *Spears*). As the only black student at Barnard College, she listed drama as her primary interest and immediately threw her support behind the Krigwa Players, a New York theatre company formed by W.E.B. Du Bois, the then-editor of *Crisis*. Hurston put forward two pieces for his consideration, a lost play called *The Lilac Bush* and possibly *The First One*. The first was rejected on merit; the second clashed with Du Bois' position on Negro art -- " I do not care a damn for any art that is not used for propaganda."

With characteristic drive, Hurston continued to pursue other opportunities. In 1931, the Gilpin Players, an influential African-American theatre in Cleveland, produced her monologic play, *Sermon in the Valley*, and revived it in 1934 and 1949. The same year that *Sermon* opened, Hurston got her first Broadway credit. *Fast and Furious* opened at the New Yorker Theatre but ran only seven performances. This collection contains her four contributions among the thirty-seven sketches that made up this musical revue: *The Football Game* (copyrighted as *Forty Yards*), *The Poker Game* (copyrighted as *Poker!*), *The Courtroom* (copyrighted as *Lawing and Jawing*) and a version of *Woofing* which was used as a curtain-raiser. Never shy about the spotlight, Hurston and comedienne Jackie (later "Moms") Mabley played two cheerleaders in *The Football Game*.

The critics were not kind to Hurston's first Broadway outing. *New York Times* critic Brooks Atkinson wrote of the production: "In quantity and in toothsome exuberance the minstrels give full measure" but when "the material is hackneyed, when the performers are fat and clumsy, the animalisms of Negro entertainment is lumpish and unwieldy." The critic of *The New York American*, no fan of African-American entertainment, wrote that he "failed to appreciate the geniality and animal humor and vital athletics of their jumbles." During this time, Hurston was tapped to write the book for another revue entitled *Jungle Scandals*, no doubt a riff on the popular all-white Broadway revue, *George White's Scandals*, but the project was cancelled before it got off the ground.

After *Fast and Furious*, Hurston did not have to wait long to get back on the boards. In 1932, *The Great Day*, "a program of original Negro folklore," was performed at the John Golden Theatre in New York in hopes that a producer would pick it up. By all accounts, the show was an artistic success but the 1920s vogue for black musicals was considered over and no offer materialized. It is highly likely that *Railroad Camp* (copyrighted as part of *Cold Keener* [1930] in this volume) was included in this production.

After the show closed, her white benefactor, Charlotte Osgood Mason, barred her from using the folklore material that she had found while under contract. Hurston, still dedicated to the project, revised it by adding a one-act entitled *The Fiery Chariot*, and renamed the show *From Sun to Sun*. Months later, it was presented at the New School for Social Research in New York.

In 1933, Hurston continued to rework her folklore material. She assembled a troupe of actors, dancers, and singers and assembled two concert-like shows, *From Sun to Sun* and *All De Live Long Day*, which were presented in a number of venues throughout Florida: her home town of Eatonville, Rollins College (to a whites-only audience), the Municipal Auditorium in Orlando, and Bethune-Cookman College in Daytona Beach. Another incarnation of this review, *Singing Steel*, was performed at the Chicago Women's Club Theater and the University of Chicago in 1934. The next recorded performance of one of her creations does not surface until 1939 when *The Fire Dance*, a scripted Bahamian dance, was performed in Orlando as part of the Works Progress Administration's "National Exhibition of Skills." Try as she might, lack of interest or lack of funds perpetually frustrated Hurston's theatrical ambitions.

Atkinson's labeling of black performers as "minstrels" speaks directly to the accepted standard by which black representation in the theatre was judged in 1930s: the minstrel show, the only native American theatrical form, was a hodgepodge of musical acts and sketch comedy born of northern racial prejudice and loomed large in the cultural consciousness. White actors (and later black actors seeking work) painted their faces with burnt cork and exaggerated white lips, and thus adorned, populated the stage with horrific stereotypes. Among them was the ignorant and slothful Jim Crow, longing for the "carefree" days of slavery and Zip Coon, the urban figure whose dandyish clothes and high-hat manner demonstrated he had risen above his proper station. By the time Hurston arrived in New York, the minstrel show was dead but its traditions survived as a staple vaudeville act with no social taboo attached. Some of the finest black performers of the age, many of whom rejected these negative images, were sometimes forced to wear ragged minstrel-like costumes or appear in front of sets with painted backdrops depicting watermelon patches or plantation vistas.

It is small wonder that Hurston's use of dialect and frank portrayals of the best and worst of African-American life would be linked to this cultural wallpaper by whites. These depictions also raised the ire of black intellectuals such as Richard Wright. In his review of *Their Eyes Were Watching God*, Wright accused Hurston of perpetuating the minstrel tradition, the technique "that makes the 'white folks' laugh" and echoing Du Bois' point of view, derided her for having no "message." But Hurston's plays were not intended as treatises on race relations. If anything, they exist as celebrations of what she considered the performative nature of black culture. By centering on African-American communities with little white presence, writes Hurston biographer Valerie Boyd, she "protests white oppression by stripping it of its potency, by denying its all-powerfulness in black people's lives."

As for dialect, Hurston always made it clear that accurately duplicating the vernacular of black culture was of the utmost importance. In "The Characteristics of Negro Expression," she wrote: "If we are to believe the majority of writers of Negro dialect and the burnt-cork artists,

Negro speech is a weird thing, full of "arms" and "Ises." Fortunately, we don't have to believe them. We may go directly to the Negro and let him speak for himself."

During the 1920s and 30s, the apex of her theatrical output, black representation was a white affair. The only Broadway shows with black themes were limited to (1) a handful of musical revues that often indulged in exoticism or caricature or (2) well-meaning but demeaning pieces by white playwrights such as Eugene O'Neill (*The Emperor Jones*), Paul Green (*In Abraham's Bosom*), Marc Connelly (*The Green Pastures*) and the Gershwins (*Porgy and Bess*). Hurston's frustration with these portrayals led her to work on *Polk County* in 1944, the last play in this collection. She wrote in a letter that she wanted to "show what can be done with our magnificent imagery instead of fooling around with bastard drama that can't be white and is too lacking in self respect to be gorgeously Negro." She completed the play with what appears to be minor assistance from Dorothy Waring, a white woman and wife of theatrical producer Stephen Kelen-d'Oxylion. Announcements were made concerning a summer opening with Hurston's friend Ethel Waters in a major role but by November, the production fell through.

Among the plays offered here, *Polk County* was the first to be embraced by the theatre community. In 2001, several concert readings at the Library of Congress were scheduled to bring attention to their rediscovery. In 2004, Arena Stage, Washington DC's premiere regional theatre, revived the play. Changes were made: the script was edited for length, music was added, and the number of characters was reduced from 26 to 17. Enormously well received by critics and audiences, it won the Charles MacArthur Award for Outstanding New Musical and moved on to runs at the McCarter Theater Center in Princeton and the Berkeley Repertory Theatre.

Without production, plays are inert -- incomplete blueprints for a live experience. We reproduce these plays in playscript format in the hope that the recent interest in *Polk County* is only the beginning of a journey of rediscovery on the part of theatres everywhere. Hurston always dreamed of building "a Negro theatre" that would be "talked of around the world." Perhaps the availability of these plays can contribute to that ideal.

NOTES ON THE TEXT

The typescripts of the plays held at the Library of Congress American Memory site (http://memory.loc.gov/ammem) were used as the copy text; plays are arranged chronologically by copyright date. Handwritten emendations to the typescripts have been incorporated except where noted. Editing with potential production in mind, character names have been made consistent, grammatical and typographical errors silently corrected, and punctuation normalized. Songs appended at the ends of plays have been incorporated within the text and stage directions edited accordingly.

SPEARS

The X-Ray: The Official Publication of Zeta Phi Beta Sorority (December 1925).

COLOR STRUCK

Fire!! (1 November 1926): 7-15. This periodical is also available in *Negro Periodicals in the United States* (Westport, CT: Negro Universities Press, 1970) and *Black Writers Interpret the Harlem Renaissance* (New York: Garland Publishing, 1996).

Black Female Playwrights: An Anthology of Plays Before 1950. Ed. Kathy Perkins. Bloomington, IN: Indiana University Press, 1989.

The Portable Harlem Renaissance Reader. New York:

Penguin Books, 1995.

Zora Neale Hurston, Eulalie Spence, Marita Bonner, and Others: The Prize Plays and Other One-Acts Published in Periodicals. Ed. Henry Louis Gates, Jr. New York: G.K. Hall, 1996.

Double-Take: A Revisionist Harlem Renaissance Anthology. Ed. Venetria K. Patton and Maureen Honey. New Brunswick, NJ: Rutgers University Press, 2001.

THE FIRST ONE

Ebony and Topaz. Ed. Charles S. Johnson. New York: National Urban League, 1927.

Black Female Playwrights: An Anthology of Plays Before 1950. Ed. Kathy Perkins. Bloomington, IN: Indiana University Press, 1989.

Roots of African American Drama. Ed. Leo Hamalian and James V. Hatch. Detroit, MI: Wayne State University Press, 1991.

The Politics and Aesthetics of "New Negro" Literature. Ed. Cary D. Wintz. New York: Garland Publishing, 1996.

Zora Neale Hurston, Eulalie Spence, Marita Bonner, and Others: The Prize Plays and Other One-Acts Published in Periodicals. Ed. Henry Louis Gates, Jr. New York: G.K. Hall, 1996.

Black Theatre USA: Plays by African Americans from 1847 to Today. Ed. James V. Hatch and Ted Shine. New York: Free Press, 1996.

MULE BONE

Zora Neale Hurston and Langston Hughes. *Mule Bone: A Comedy of Negro Life*. Ed. George Houston Bass and Henry Louis Gates, Jr. New York: HarperPerennial, 1991.

THE FIERY CHARIOT

Typescript. George A. Smathers Libraries Special Collections,

Univ. of Florida, "Stories, Essays, Miscellaneous," vol. 12. Typescript. Schomburg Center for Research in Black Culture, Playscript Collection, New York Public Library.

Short Plays by Zora Neale Hurston

Foreword

FROM "SPEARS" TO THE GREAT DAY:
ZORA NEALE HURSTON'S VISION OF A REAL NEGRO THEATER
by Barbara Speisman

On 12 April 1926, in a letter to Langston Hughes, Zora Neale Hurston asked Hughes a question: "Did I tell you before I left about the new, the REAL Negro art theater I Plan? Well I shall, or rather we shall act out the folk tales, however short with the abrupt angularity and naivete of the primitive 'bama Nigger. ... What do you think?" (Hemenway 115). From 1927 to 1930 Hurston had the opportunity to interpret what "had gone unseen for three hundred years" (113), and she shared many of her discoveries with Hughes, her colleague and friend. Traveling to isolated, rural African American communities, such as Magazine Point, Alabama, as well as her home village of Eatonville, Florida, Hurston came to realize that the folktales and songs she heard during her travels were not creations of the past, but of the everchanging present.

Pretending to be a gangster's girlfriend on the run in a Loughman, Florida, turpentine camp, she had become friends with Big Sweet, a "jook" woman who could out-talk, out-fight, and out-love her male counterparts in the camp. Big Sweet had been instrumental in teaching Hurston the importance of the jook in the development of the "real Negro theater," the theater of "the people farthest down." Hurston came to believe that the real Negro theater was in the "jooks" of the South "where women, like Big Sweet, could hoist a jook song from her belly and lam it against the front door of the theater" ("Characteristics" 254). Hurston was persuaded that only theater could truly convey the mercurial nature, as well as cultural richness, of the folklife, tales, and songs she learned. She wanted to share not only her subject matter with Langston Hughes, but also her vision of a script that would not follow the standard two or three-act format. Hurston also advanced the concept that the real Negro play should be angular in structure, which was similar to African dance ("Characteristics" 247). Thus, at the beginning of her professional career as a folklorist, Hurston was forming a totally different concept of the type of play that she hoped to write; one that would be radically different, not only in theme and subject matter, but in structure as well.

Hughes shared Hurston's enthusiasm for an authentic folk theater in which African Americans would write, direct, and perform their own material. Like Hurston, Hughes believed that "The Negro outstanding characteristic is drama" ("Characteristics" 247), and he proposed to coauthor a folk play with Hurston that would be a real departure in the drama. Hurston's dream of a "real Negro art theater" (Hemenway 115) was one that she would hold onto for much of her creative life. It was, however, one that brought her great frustration and disappointment and even caused her to be alienated from Hughes, a sharer of her dream.

Although Hurston's published work has received much critical attention, her role as a playwright still needs more investigation. Perhaps one of the chief reasons her plays have not received the attention they deserve is that so few of her manuscripts are in published form. Lynda Marion Hill points out in her ground-breaking study *Social Rituals and the Verbal Art of Zora Neale Hurston:*

> Hurston's theatrical career is virtually a lost segment of Hurston's work, and that having available documentation of her staged productions is essential

not only to be able to write a thorough historical account but to reproduce the play, in writing or on stage. (201)

During the spring and summer of 1997, however, several of Hurston's play manuscripts have surfaced. Wyatt Hourston Day, an African American manuscript collector, discovered "Spears" which was first published in Hurston's sorority yearbook, the Zeta Phi Beta *X RAY* for 1925. Alice L. Birney, historian of American literature at the Library of Congress, has discovered three full-length plays and several dramatic skits copyrighted by Hurston from 1925 to 1944. The plays include *Meet the Mamma*, a musical play, copyrighted 12 July 1925, less than three months after the Opportunity Award Banquet at which Hurston won second prize for her play Color Struck and an honorable mention for *Spears*. *Cold Keener*, a musical revue, and *De Turkey and de Law*, a comedy in three acts, were both copyrighted 29 October 1930, shortly before an argument between Hurston and Langston Hughes over authorship of *Mule Bone*. On 21 July 1931, Hurston copyrighted four comical sketches: *Poker!*, *Lawing and Jawing*, *Woofing*, and *Forty Yards*. Hurston did not copyright another play until 15 June 1935, when she copyrighted *Spunk*. With Hurston's permission, Josephine Van Dolzen Pease copyrighted, on 7 April 1936, *Three Authentic Folk Dances from the Deep South*, which are dances to be performed by children. These dances consist of "Rabbit Dance," "Chick-Ma-Chick," Cranney Crow," and "Sissie in the Barn." The final play, and one familiar to Hurston scholars, was *Polk County* which Hurston coauthored with Dorothy Waring; its copyright date was 9 December 1944.[1]

Collectively these manuscripts are over three hundred pages in length, and provide the reader a rich selection with which to analyze Hurston's conviction that the folklife material she had collected in the South would best reach a greater audience "as the product of folk performance"

(Abrahams and Kalcik 229). Hurston came to her definition of a real Negro art theater after the three years she spent researching in the South, but her odyssey as a playwright began several years earlier.

Hurston's first association with drama probably came in 1915 to 1916 while she was employed as a maid in the Gilbert and Sullivan troupe which introduced her to professional actors and musicians. Although she did not actively participate in any of the performances, she certainly had the opportunity to explore the structure of plays, acting, and directing techniques Later, from 1916 to 1919, Hurston moved to Baltimore where her sister Sarah had a rooming house near Pennsylvania Avenue2 which was renowned for its theaters. Here well-known African American performers, like Ethel Waters, often performed. Hurston, therefore, had ample opportunity to observe the then current African American stage drama and musical entertainment. In 1919 Hurston graduated from Morgan Academy and was encouraged by Mae Miller, a young Washington playwright and poet, to enter Howard University's drama department (Perkins 77). This fact suggests Hurston's early interest in the theater.

Her formal study of drama and, in particular, African American drama was at Howard University. Hurston's initial concept of theater was formed under the tutelage of Thomas Montgomery Gregory who had organized the Howard Players to perform plays about Negro life. Gregory had been a member of Professor Baker's famous English 47 Workshop at Harvard University that had served as the dramatic training ground for Thomas Woolf and Eugene O'Neill. Gregory was friends with O'Neill, and O'Neill visited Howard's drama department in 1923 while Hurston was a student. O'Neill and his Provincetown Players took an active interest in the Howard Players and Gregory's hope of developing a national Negro theater.3 Gregory was also unique in that he believed that African American women were capable of writing plays, and encouraged his women students to become playwrights (Perkins 78). Although Hurston wrote Color Struck, "Spears," and "Meet the Mamma" while studying with Gregory, no record has been located that would indicate whether or not Hurston had any of her plays produced while a member of the Howard Players. Gregory kept excellent files, but Hurston's only mention is as a violinist for the Howard orchestra.

However, Gregory was one of the judges for the Opportunity Award Banquet, held on 1 May 1925, which formally ushered in the Harlem Renaissance. There Hurston won second prize for her play *Color Struck* and honorable mention for *Spears*. These plays, African American in content, followed the traditional one and two-act structure. No mention was made of *Meet the Mamma*, her blues musical. Not long after the Opportunity presentation, the Negro Art Theater of Harlem opened with her play, *Color Struck*.4 With this formal production, Hurston began to make a name for herself as a playwright.

Color Struck, a play about miscegenation, has received much critical attention, but Spears has yet to be examined. It appears that in writing *Spears* Hurston was influenced by the Tarzan craze that was sweeping the country at the time-- her characters are dressed in lion skins and loin cloths, with bone jewelry and rings in their noses and ears. Hurston was gambling that she could capitalize on the myth of Africa popular in white America's imagination. Although the characters in the play are unbelievable, the plot contrived, and the ending expected, Hurston's sense of humor and satirical style are evident. *Spears* was not part of Hurston's efforts to establish an authentic American Negro theater, but was rather an attempt to satirize the white concept of what they thought African primitivism to be,5 and perhaps to produce a commercial success.

The play centers on the Luallaba tribe who have been unable to find food and are starving, making them vulnerable to their enemies, the Wahehes. Monanga, King of the Luallabas, meets with Bombay, his old counselor, to debate their predicament. Bombay, like Polonius in Shakespeare's *Hamlet*, provides bombastic, silly advice. Bombay tells his chief that their problem may be solved by "selling our young women to the Wahehes for good." Zaida, the King's beautiful daughter, appears on the scene to announce that she and the other women are hungry, and to ask what her father means to do about it. Uledi, a warrior in love with her, has hidden food and provides Zaida with something to eat. As Zaida eats, the rest of the tribe follows each morsel of meat from the girl's hand to her mouth with their eyes and mimic swallowing when she does. Act 1 ends when the King demands that his medicine man "make medicine for rain" which will solve their problem. The Medicine Man and his accomplices, the Witch Woman and a chicken, participate in a rain dance and, as the drums beat furiously, the dancing grows wilder and Hurston's stage directions are "that this will continue for nine minutes."

In Act 2, a Wahehe warrior accuses Uledi of stealing food and, as a result, Uledi must die or the tribe will fight the Luallabas. When presented with this decision, Monanga quickly agrees that Ulede must perish in order that the tribe may be preserved. However, in Pocohantas style, Saida begs her father to save Ulede's life. Monanga's answer is "that women were not made to counsel men but to serve them." Zaida's reply is that "we women have no minds at all. We know nothing ... what we saw yesterday is today forgotten." She then cleverly reminds her father of Uledi's many heroic adventures, how he saved her life, and "How he is first to hear your voice always. If Uledi has done wrong let me be killed in his place. Your slave has spoken." The play ends with the Luallaba tribe overcoming their enemies and Uledi and Saida in each other's arms. Although *Spears* was published, we do not know if Hurston ever managed to have it performed.

From 1926 to 1930, Hurston may not have written plays, but she was developing ideas about what should constitute the real Negro art theater, and shared with Hughes much of the folk material she had collected. For financial reasons, both Hurston and Hughes had entered into an agreement with Charlotte Osgood Mason, a wealthy patron of the arts, which allowed her to have a great measure of control over their lives and writings. In particular, Hurston had signed a contract with Mason on 8 December 1927 which gave Mason complete ownership of Hurston's collected material and the methods by which it would be presented and published (Hemenway 109). Although Mason informed Hurston that she should not consider using her folk material for theatrical purposes, Hurston persevered in her desire for the "glorious ... departure in the drama" (Hemenway 115).

Upon her return to New York in the winter of 1930, Mason insisted that Hurston complete the manuscript that would become *Mules and Men*. At the same time, Hughes lived nearby and was finishing his novel *Not Without Laughter*. During the spring of 1930, the two friends were finally able to begin writing a play which they believed would change the course of African American theater. Hurston wisely selected "The Bone of Contention," a story she had written while a student at Howard, to avoid Mason's wrath if she found out about the project.

The folktale tells the story of Dave Carter, the best hunter in Eatonville, who, after capturing a wild turkey, is hit over the head with a mule bone by Jim Weston, the town's bully. Dave wants Jim arrested and complains to Mayor Joe Clark: "He can't lam me over mah head wid no mule bone and steal mah turkey and go braggin' about it!" The community divides into Baptists who support Carter, and Methodists who support Weston. The Baptists win and Jim is banished from Eatonville for two years.

Hurston wanted to shape "The Bone of Contention" into a new form that would eliminate the minstrel concept of the African American theater which, even in plays such as *Shuffle Along*, still controlled white audiences' attention. A common form of the minstrel show had two male characters fighting over a girl with the comedy generated through short or even one liners. Hurston wanted to present a full theatrical environment in which the isolated "punch lines" would be produced in a natural manner.6 Hurston became alarmed, however, when Hughes replaced the turkey as the central figure of conflict and instead, in a stereotypical manner, has Dave and Jim fight over a girl (Hemenway 138). Hurston had not intended her tale to be that of two men fighting over their sexual prowess, but rather that they would prove who was the better hunter and man. Dave and Jim's conflict over a woman is closer to the minstrel theme and jokes which Hurston wanted to avoid. In Hughes's version the two men are the best of friends; whereas, in Hurston's folktale, Jim is disliked by Dave, as well as the majority of Eatonville's people.

The structure of Hurston's folktale is simple with few characters, but in adapting the folktale into a play, Hughes included nineteen major characters and twenty-two minor ones. Undoubtedly, Hurston came to believe that Hughes's additions were contrary to her original folktale and that he was changing her story to such an extent that it no longer seemed her own. Hughes was later to say that at the time Hurston appeared to be happy with their joint authorship of *Mule Bone*, and he was totally surprised when she claimed complete ownership (Hemenway 138).

In May 1930, still supported by Mason, Hurston left Hughes to return to the South supposedly to complete the trial scene of Act 2. However, during that time Hurston not only rewrote the play so that it more closely resembled "The Bone of Contention" in its original form, but it appears that she also completed *Cold Keener*.

Hurston's first major change from the jointly written play was to alter the title from *Mule Bone* to *De Turkey and De*

Law, so that there would be no doubt that the fight over the turkey was the main conflict in the play and that Dave and Jim were enemies. By emphasizing Dave's superior hunting abilities, he becomes more a folk hero than a stereotypical minstrel character. We do not know whose idea it was to structure Hurston's folktale into a three-act play, but it was a form that she used only once more, that we know of, and that was in *Polk County*, another cooperative effort with a coauthor.7 Although Hurston did retain the three-act form in *De Turkey and De Law*, she simplified and changed much of the structure of the first act.

In *Mule Bone* the play begins with several Eatonville natives gathering on the front porch of Joe Clark's store. Several of the characters whom Hurston included in her *Eatonville Anthology* (1926) are introduced, for example, Mrs. Roberts, the begging woman who pleads for food for her hungry children. Hurston begins *De Turkey and De Law*, however, with a group of Eatonville children playing "Chick-Ma Chick" in which a young girl pretends to be a mother hen protecting her children from a hawk. One of the children, Essie, a tomboy, leads the group and seems to resemble Hurston as a child in Eatonville. Like young Hurston, she flaunts grown-up authority, and when a voice offstage calls, "If you don't come here wid dat soap you better!", the child tearfully replies, "Soon's I git grown I'm gointer run away. Every time a person gits to havin' fun, it's come here." A page later one of the men on Joe Clarke's store porch refers to her as a "sassy lil birch who needs her guts stomped out." It appears that Hurston was becoming an active participant in the action of the play, a technique she would later use in *Mules and Men*.

Hurston retained Hughes's addition of Daisy as a central character in the play. But, where Hughes interjected Daisy as the major source of conflict between the two rivals, Hurston's Daisy chooses the man who is the better hunter and consequently the better provider. Thus, in Hurston's version, Daisy's character is truer to the folk quality that she intended, rather than to Hughes's minstrel concept.

Hurston returned to Florida to write the second scene of the second act in which the Baptists and the Methodists have the trial which will determine whether Jim or Dave is at fault, and she is sole author of this part of the play.

Act 3 in both *Mule Bone* and *De Turkey and De Law* are the same except that Hurston includes the turkey episode as the central conflict. Daisy informs Jim that she knows Dave is the better shot and killed the turkey to give to her and that Jim "couldn't hit de side of a barn wid uh bass fiddle." Dave answers, "'Course I kilt it, and it for you." The resolution of both plays is with Daisy insisting that the man of her choice must work for a living. Jim and Dave agree, however, that no woman is worth working for; they become friends and decide to return to Eatonville together. Only the stage directions at the end of the plays differ. In *Mule Bone* the stage directions are: "They start back together towards the town, Jim picking a dance tune on his guitar, and Dave cutting back on the ties besides him, singing, prancing, and happily they exist." After the final line of dialogue in *De Turkey and De Law,* Hurston's stage direction is simply "Curtain."

We do not know if Hughes ever read a copy of *De Turkey and De Law*, nor why after Hurston copyrighted it as sole author, she never attempted to have it produced or published. Whatever the personal relations between the two authors and their competition for Mason's support, Zora Neale Hurston and Langston Hughes lost not only their friendship, but the chance to have either version of their coauthored plays produced. In Hughes's autobiography, *The Big Sea*, he admits that "the story was her story, the dialogue her dialogue, and the play her play--even if I had put it together" (158).

In a letter to Mason dated 17 May 1932, Hurston was still bitter about Hughes's claim of authorship. She writes:

"I have a most ungracious letter from Langston Hughes in which he renounces his claim upon the play. His manner of doing so is one of the most unworthy things he ever did." Hurston and Hughes gave up any attempt for a stage production of either *De Turkey and De Law* or *Mule Bone*. However, the question remains as to why Hurston did not then focus her attention on *Cold Keener*, the musical revue that she had copyrighted on the same day as *De Turkey and De Law*.

In *Cold Keener* she experimented with a concept of a real Negro theater as being built upon the folktales, music, and dances of the "primitive Negroes" whose daily lives had so inspired her. *Cold Keener* is possibly Hurston's first attempt at dramatizing some of the material that would later be more fully developed in her fiction, *Mules and Men*, and later in the successful musical revue, *The Great Day*. Before this, Hurston's correspondence had not mentioned *Cold Keener* or her hopes for its success. As Kathy A. Perkins in her study of *Black Female Playwrights Before 1950* noted, "Between 1930 and 1935, Hurston became preoccupied with making a name for herself in the theater. She wrote over twelve plays during this period" (77).

Hurston's legal agreement with Mason may have been the reason that she never actively attempted to interest theatrical producers in producing *Cold Keener*. Since it is the only complete manuscript of one of Hurston's revues, however, it deserves particular attention.

Cold Keener consists of nine skits that have no relationship to one another either in character, theme, or setting. Thus, the sharp "primitive" angularity that Hurston desired as her ideal dramatic form is obtained. The skits have no dramatic thread, such as a narrator or music, to relate to one another, but are linked mainly by their very differences. Even the unusual grammatical forms seem to stress the sharp contrasts of the folktales. The title appears to be another way of portraying the links of orality that bound the folktales and folklife she had researched in the South to their relationship to her research in Harlem and the Bahamas. The daily life of a "pimp" on Lenox Avenue might be totally different from that of Joe Wiley who lives in Magazine Point, Alabama, but their verbal skills unite them. Although blacks in the Bahamas were exposed to a completely different daily environment, they, like southern African Americans, used song as a common thread of communication. Thus, the structure of *Cold Keener* offered Hurston a chance to present the variety of her folk experience in the South, Harlem, and the Bahamas.

Facing the title page of the script of *Cold Keener*, Hurston lists the nine skits which make up the revue: *Filling Station, Cock Robin, Heaven, Mr. Frog, Lenox Avenue, The House that Jack Built, Bahamas, Railroad Camp,* and *Jook.* A summary of the individual skits will help to appreciate Hurston's "journey structure" and her knowledge of the orality that united the different communities.

Filling Station begins "Time: Present. Place: A Point on the Alabama-Georgia line. Setting: A filling station upstage center." Named "The State Line Filling Station," it stretches nearly across the stage. The road passes before and through it. A line down the center of the stage to the footlights divides the left side, "Alabama State Line," from the right, "Georgia State Line." A Model T Ford rattles up and wakes the proprietor:

PROPRIETOR: *(Sleepily)* How many?
FORD FRIVER: Two.
PROPRIETOR: Two what?

> *(The Proprietor gets a quart cup and measures the gas and rings the hose to be sure to get it all, then he pours it in the tank.)*

FORD DRIVER: You better look at my water and air, too.

(He has a very expensive and ornate cap on the radiator, but otherwise the car is most dilapidated. As the Proprietor pours the water into the radiator, the driver gets out of the car and stands off from it looking it over.)

FORD DRIVER: Say, Jimpson, they tells me you got a new mechanic 'round here that's just too tight.

PROPRIETOR: That's right. He kin do more wid 'em than the man that made 'em.

FORD DRIVER: Well, looka here. My car kinda needs overhauling and maybe a little pain't. Look her over and tell me just what you could do to make her look like a brand new car for.

(Proprietor lifts the hood and looks. Walks around and studies the car from all angles. Then stops at the front and examines the radiator cap.)

PROPRIETOR: Well, I tell yo. You see it's like this. This car needs a whole heap of things done to it. But being as you're a friend of mine – tell you what I'll do. I'll just jack that radiator cap up and run a brand new Ford under it for four hundred and ninety-five dollars.

FORD DRIVER: *(Indignantly)* Whut de hen-fire you think I'm goin' tuh let you rob me of my car? That's a good car.

The skit continues as a good looking girl who has had a flat tire drives up to the filling station and says, "I had a flat down the road and I changed it, but it's not fixed. Do you vulcanize?" The Proprietor answers, "We do everything but the buzzard lope--and that's gone outa style." When both the Proprietor and the Ford Driver fail in correctly placing the tire back on the car, the girl kicks it into place herself. The Proprietor and Ford Driver are impressed:

PROPRIETOR: That's a tight little slice of pig-meat! Damned if I don't believe I'll go to Georgia!

FORD DRIVER: She ain't no pig-meat! That's a married 'oman.

PROPRIETOR: You know her?

FORD DRIVER: Nope, never seen her before.

PROPRIETOR: Well, how can you tell she's married?

FORD DRIVER: Didn't you see that kick? A woman that can kick like that done had some man to practice on.

Soon after this exchange, a new, elegant Chevrolet arrives and the rest of the skit involves a bragging contest between the Ford driver and the Chevrolet driver about which has the greater car.

Hurston would later rewrite and publish *Cock Robin*, the next skit, as "Cock Robin, Beale Street" in the *Southern Literary Messenger* for July 1941 (Hemenway 290). The major difference between the skit and the short story is that in the skit Hurston eliminates Uncle July, the narrator, who has witnessed Cock Robin's death. Unlike the story, the skit begins with Cock Robin staggering into the "shimmy shack" with three arrows sticking in him as he falls dead.8 The birds inquire about the identity of the murderer and why he would kill Cock Robin. The sparrow admits that he did the dirty deed because he caught Cock Robin "shacking up" with his wife.

SPARROW: Well, I'll tell you. When me and my wife first started to nestin, she never laid nothin' but plain white eggs. But since Cock Robin been hangin' round our place--every time I go out on a worm hunt, when I come back, she's done laid another blue egg.

As in the story, the skit has the birds discuss the arrangements for Cock Robin's funeral. In the story, the birds decide "to leave de white folks bury him! Dey always loves to take charge." In the skit, however, the Owl says, "Well, whoever pays de bill can have de body. Who gointer pay de bills?" Since no one wants to pay for Cock Robin's funeral, the birds exit to attend Sister Speckled Hen's "grand barbecue and fish fry." With the orchestra playing, the birds strut off the stage. This is the first mention of an orchestra, but it is prominent in *Heaven*, the third skit.

As the curtain rises on *Heaven*, the audience sees a flight of golden stairs ascending from the orchestra pit at mid-stage. The sound of a mouth organ being played in a blues mood way is heard. Jim, a survivor of the Johnstown flood, appears before St. Peter and attempts to impress him with the power of the flood. Jim begins to describe the horrors of the flood to an old man.

JIM: Hello, old folks, how long you been here?
OLD MAN: Oh, a long time.
JIM: Just got here from de Johnstown flood. Man, dat waz some water! Chickens floatin, folks floatin, horses floatin, houses floatin. Man, dat wuz water. *(Starting away in disgust)* Aw, shucks, you ain't seen no water.

> *(He exits right. Jim looks hurt and puzzled for a moment, then calls out to St. Peter.)*

JIM: Say Peter, thought you said everybody here was nice and sociable. See how dat ole man treated me when I tryin to show him manners and politeness by tellin him bout de flood?
PETER: You can't tell that man bout no flood – that's noah.

At the end of the skit Jim has received his wings and against the angel's wishes, decides to fly, but crashes. However, Jim seems happy enough playing his harp, and the curtain quickly descends as he "plays and sings." Hurston does not provide any instruction as to what Jim is singing.

In the skit, *Mr. Frog*, Hurston emphasizes movement and rhythm. The time is "when animals talked," and the place is "a Florida swamp." Hurston's stage directions call for a "girl dancer" to impersonate a "pine tree":

> *As the curtain rises, the sun is setting. The tree is motionless. With the music it begins to sway slightly, but increases its motion all the time. Enter down stage left, the South Wind dances with the tree for about a minute. Enter West Wind upstage right and both dance with tree. ... The tempo increases with the entrance of each wind. ... When all four winds are on, there is a violent wind dance for a minute till the sun finally sets and the winds take their places at their entrances and sink to the ground and remain there.*

Actors costumed as frogs, an alligator, birds, bettles, flies, and a snake "all enter from different points and take places among the trees and bushes." As the frogs' chorus croaks, "a big frog" enters from "upstage center," hops on a toadstool and sings the old child's ballad, "Mister Frog Went Courtin'." At the climax of the skit Mr. Frog marries "Miss Mousie," and Mrs. Snake passes "all around dat wedding cake decorated with fireflies." The skit concludes when "the groom loads his wife on a tortoise and they start off. The bride and groom exit to a slow curtain, and as they leave the chorus dances and sings 'unhunh, unhunh, unhunh, unhunh.'"

Although Hurston portrays the scene with a child's whimsical imagination, *Mr. Frog* could not possibly be staged in a practical way. The animal characters might be at home in a Walt Disney film, but a director would have a difficult challenge staging the skit. However, the skit does work as a child's story and might be adapted to that genre.

Following the naiveté of *Mr. Frog*, *Lenox Avenue* comes as a shock, an example of what Hurston means by "cold keener," an abrupt change of setting, mood, and language. The stage is set to resemble a busy New York street corner by having a "backdrop showing intersections and houses."

The autos keep whirling past on a scenic band. The action begins when "a very effeminate young man enters with a large cretonne sewing bag on his wrist." The young man is approached by a police officer who inquires what is in the bag; his knitting, he replies, and he is taking it to the army because "the boys must have their sock, you know." As he waves "a fluffy goodbye," he says, "Toodle-oo, old cabbage, I must try to get the boys out of the trenches before Christmas."

The young man exits, and a married couple, who are loudly arguing over the husband's philandering, enter. The woman holds her own, and when the husband says, "Bye, bye, Mamma, you can't snore in my ear no more," the wife answers, "You might as well stop dat wringing and twisting, cause I know you want me some again, cause I'm a damn sweet woman and you know it." They exit and a newly married couple enter who are also arguing over the husband's promiscuity. When the husband threatens to beat his wife, she answers:

WIFE: You better not hit me, nigger.
MAN: I'll hit you just as sure as Jesus rode a jackass.
WIFE: Turn go of me, fool. I dare you to hit me! If you stick your rusty foot in my face, you going to jail.
MAN: How come I'm going to jail?
WIFE: Cause there a cop right there on the corner and I'm going to holler like a pretty white woman.

The skit seems to be an early version of Hurston's short story, "Story in Harlem Slang," which appeared in the *American Mercury* in 1942 (Hemenway 290). In the story two pimps accost a young woman and attempt to hustle her for money and sex, but she verbally outwits them. At the end of the story, the young woman's final retort is the same as that in the skit.

The House that Jack Built is similar to *Mr. Frog* in that

Hurston again structures a skit on a familiar child's story. The setting is an "old-fashioned schoolhouse" in the "deep south," but the children "are large" and the "girls are pretty." The main character, De Otis Blunt, is poorly dressed and the dunce of the class whom the teacher constantly picks on. Because it is Friday, recitation day, the teacher warns the students that "anybody don't know a speech today will get a good whipping and be kept after school." Many of the students fail to perform and provide the usual excuses of "I didn't learn none or I forgot mine."

When it is De Otis's turn everyone expects him to excuse himself, but he surprises the class by providing a ten-minute recitation of *The House That Jack Built*. As De Otis recites he begins to dance, and the teacher and students dance in chorus with him. "De Otis dances till he shudders down to the floor and lies there shivering in rhythm." In the chants and dances De Otis approximates the present day musical form of rap.9

In both *Mr. Frog* and *The House That Jack Built* Hurston uses two well-known English children's stories instead of African American folktales. She is, perhaps, attempting to show that certain stories have become part of the literary lore of both white and black cultures and that African American children interpret the stories in their own way and bring the uniqueness of their interpretation to the stories.

Hurston's script of *Bahamas*, the seventh skit, has several penciled slash marks across it as though she were uncertain as to whether to retain certain parts. The skit opens in Harlem with the arrival of Joe Wiley, a character also of *Mules and Men*, who has been invited to the Bahamas and then to Africa by the Emperor Jones--the main character in Eugene O'Neill's play. With the sound of the "ship's sirens and the sounds of anchors and chains," the setting quickly changes to Prince George's Wharf in the Bahamas, with the singing of "Caesar Riley" as background. The Emperor Jones enters and welcomes Joe Wiley with the statement:

> *To Africa! When I get there with my conquering black*
> *legions I am not going to ask Great Britain what they*
> *are doing there. I'm just going to say get out! ... Board*
> *the fleet, let us sail for Africa and freedom. ... And*
> *ninety days from now, I shall have a Black House, side*
> *by side with the White House in Washington!*

Apparently, Hurston is using the character of the
Emperor Jones to satirize Marcus Garvey and his back-to-
Africa movement.

In the main part of the skit Hurston employs the songs
and dances she had observed while researching folk material
in the Bahamas. This is obviously a rough draft of *Bahamas*,
however. Hurston would later eliminate the character of the
Emperor Jones, but retain the Bahamian dances and songs
which she uses in the conclusion of *The Great Day*. For
example, at the conclusion of *Bahamas*, Hurston includes
a ring dance with drummers playing and actors singing. As
"drums flourish" the actors sing:

> Bimini gal is a hell of a trouble
> Never get licking till you go down to Bimini.

In the last two skits, *Railroad Camp* and *Jook*, Hurston
returns to the Florida setting. These two would also later
appear in a version of *The Great Day*. As the curtain rises
on *Railroad Camp,* there is "a length of railroad track on an
embankment" and "ten men are spiking rails with sledge
hammers." The water boy leads the singing:

Dat ol' (wham) black gal (wham)!
> She keep on grumblin' (wham)!
> New pair shoes (wham), new pair shoes (wham)!

During the entire skit the men sing lining songs and
conclude with "Shove it over! Hey, hey can't you line it, can't
you move it."

In *Jook*, which concludes *Cold Keener*, Hurston returns

to her original dramatic premise that the real Negro theater originated in the "jooks" of the South. As Hurston includes Joe Wiley, a real person, in *Bahamas*, she now introduces Big Sweet who befriended her in the Loughman Turpentine Camp, and who would later play an important role in *Mules and Men*, as well as in *Polk County*. In *Jook* Hurston's folks act out the classic blues motif of drinking, gambling, fighting, and singing about the fickleness of love.

> *The setting is a sawmill jook house with a dilapidated piano in one corner. When the curtain goes up, Nunkie is at the piano playing and singing as three couples "slow-drag" and sing "John Barton." Black-Boy, Stack of Dollars, Blue-Front, and Muttsy stroll into the jook and start to play cards. Big Sweet enters and interrupts the game by asking Stack "to read de deck for me." Stack refuses and accuses Big Sweet of "shackin up" with another man. Sexual tension increases with the arrival of Ella Ward, Hurston's actual rival at the Loughman Turpentine Camp. Ella enters and tries to pick a fight with Big Sweet. Instead of fighting, however, Ella grabs a guitar from beside the piano, walks to the center of the stage, puts one foot up on the chair, and sings "John Henry."*

Hurston's main purpose in *Jook* appears to be to include as many jook songs and dances as possible in a short period of time. The typescript shows that she probably hurried the composition for there are some grammatical errors and names of characters are spelled differently; for example, the final spelling of Ella Ward is Willa Ward.10

After rewriting *De Turkey and De Law*, writing *Cold Keener*, and copyrighting the two plays, Hurston, during the fall of 1931, continued to actively pursue a theatrical production. However, she was still supported by Mason who believed that a theatrical presentation would corrupt the material that would be published as *Mules and Men*. Still, Hurston persisted and wrote three sketches for *Fast and Furious*, a colored revue in thirty-seven scenes (Hemenway 175). After *Fast and Furious* failed at the box office, she wrote several sketches for *Jungle Scandals*, which was also a commercial failure. Hurston admitted that the writing for the two revues was stereotyped and she was not pleased with her work (177). The four skits Hurston copyrighted in July 1931 may well be some of the material that she wrote for the two revues. *Forty Yards*, one of the skits, is about a football game between Howard and Lincoln and may be the skit in which Hurston, playing a cheerleader, made her first dramatic appearance (Hemenway 175).

In September 1932, Hurston completed the manuscript of *Mules and Me*n, thus formally ending her contract with Mason. However, she still needed Mason's financial support so that she could adapt the folk materials in *Mules and Men* into a dramatic script. On 10 January 1932, Hurston finally achieved her dream of producing "real Negro theater." *The Great Day, a Negro Folk Concert*, opened at the John Golden Theater in New York.

> I saw the Negro music and musicians were getting lost in the betting ring. I just wanted people to know what real Negro music sounded like. Not only did I want the singing very natural, I wanted to display West Indian folk dancing. I had witnessed the dynamic fire Dance ... I had to admit to myself that we had nothing in America to equal it. (Appendix 804)

Hurston's production of *The Great Day* changed the course of American musical theater because for the first time the "real voice," "the rich black juice" of the songs she had heard at turpentine camps, prison camps, railroad camps, and jooks were presented as she had conceived them (Appendix 807). Ironically, however, because Mason had provided funds for only the one night's presentation, Hurston was once again frustrated in her attempts to become a successful playwright. With no money to pay the actors and the loss of Mason's patronage, Hurston decided to "go home to Florida, and try to write the book I had in mind" (Appendix 808). Nevertheless, she continued to believe that dramatic presentation was the primary form through which to present African American folklife, songs, and tales.

No completed manuscript of *The Great Day* exists and apparently Hurston did not copyright it. In addition to working on *The Great Day*, Hurston wrote *Spunk*, a musical revue in which she believed she had at last accomplished her goal of realistically presenting African American tales, songs, and dances. She wrote about her hopes for *Spunk* to Mason. In the writing of *Spunk*, she believed "the public will see growth rather than decline" (Hemenway 177). Hurston copyrighted *Spunk*, but a typescript has not been found.11 But, even without the completed manuscript of *The Great Day* or even a portion of *Spunk*, Hurston scholars and admirers may be able to more fully comprehend Hurston's theatrical vision now that some newly located materials are available for study.

Though Hurston was something of a rebel while a student of Montgomery Gregory at Howard University, she still wrote her plays in the conventional forms. Returning to the South during the years 1927 to 1930 as a trained anthropologist, she came to understand the uniqueness of the folk material she had gathered and its fragility. With revolutionary zeal, she determined not only to preserve the folklore, tales, songs, and dances, but to recreate them in a structure that would best bring them to life--and that was drama. Most of her attempts at playwriting, however, were thwarted, whether through disagreements about theme and structure when she coauthored plays with Langston Hughes or Dorothy Waring, or through lack of financial backing.

Perhaps if Mason had provided her more freedom in the

use of her material, Hurston might have had greater success. But by the time *Mules and Men* was finally published, and Mason no longer part of her life and work, the Depression had ended and white America's interest in African American theatrical themes had waned.

For most of her creative life, Hurston continued to rewrite and produce versions of The Great Day. According to RoseMary Barnes,12 who knew Hurston in Eau Gallie during the fifties when Hurston was her babysitter, Hurston arranged a production of *The Great Day*, acted by African American students, for the local Women's Club. Barnes attended the performance and recalls that the mainly white audience was thoroughly entertained. She and her parents, however, were Hurston's employers and knew the physical effort that Hurston had expended in attempts to produce her play. Working as a maid, broke, sick, with her books out of print, Hurston still believed that drama and music represented the soul of her people. She was still determined that while there was life in her body she would continue to see that white and black Americans heard not only her voice, but the voice of the "people farthest down."

NOTES

1. Most of the new Hurston manuscripts are located in the Manuscript Division of the Library of Congress. *Meet the Mamma* is in custody of the Music Division and *Polk County* in the Rare Book and Manuscript Division.

2. Sarah Mack is listed in the 1916 *Baltimore City Directory for Colored Americans* as having an eating establishment at 1507 Laurens Street which was adjacent to Pennsylvania Avenue. At the time this was one of the most segregated areas in the country.

3. Not only was O'Neill a speaker at Howard, but he also helped to bring his play *The Emperor Jones* to campus

with the renowned Charles Gilpin in the lead role. Cleon Throckmorton, technical director of the Provincetown Players, made weekly trips to Howard to teach a class in scenic design. Information about Eugene O'Neill's Howard connection may be found in the Montgomery Gregory papers at Howard University.

4. Information about Hurston's early interest in the theater may be found in correspondence between Hurston and Annie Nathan Meyer during the years 1925 to 1926 when Hurston was a student at Barnard and under Meyer's sponsorship. Meyer was also a playwright, and so the two had much in common. Myrna Goldenberg has researched the letters, and information used in this paper is taken from her essay, "The Barnard Connection: Zora Neale Hurston and Annie Nathan Meyer," which was presented at the First Zora Neale Hurston Conference held in Eatonville, Florida, in January 1990.

5. For more information about the importance of primitivism during this period, see Ann Douglas's *Terrible Honesty, Mongrel Manhattan in the 1920s.*

6. For information about the history of African American popular music from 1895 to 1930, see *From Cakewalks to Concert Halls* (Washington: Elliott and Clark, 1992) by Thomas L. Morgan and William Barlow.

7. Editors' note: Both *Meet the Mamma* (copyrighted before *De Turkey and de Law*) and *Spunk* (copyrighted after) employ a three-act format as well as *Polk County.*

8. Editors' note: As a perusal of the play shows, Cock Robin actually emerges *from* Shimmy Shack, where he has ostensibly been engaging in a dalliance with Mrs. Sparrow.

9. "A History of the Blues." Lecture by Robert B. Jones on 3 October 1997 at Myth, Memory, and Migration in the Black South Conference, University of Alabama, Tuscaloosa. In his lecture Jones demonstrated the close relationship of the blues form to that of present day rap.

10. Editors' note: The typescript contains two sepllings of the character's name, "Ella Ward" and "Wlla Ward" (*not* "Willa"). We have attributed the spelling of "Wlla" to a typographical error and made the character's name "Ella" throughout.

11. Editors' note: Since the publication of Speisman's article, of course, a typescript has been found and is a part of the Library of Congress' collection of Hurston's plays and this edition of it.

12. Interview with RoseMary Barnes held in Macon, Georgia, 16 July 1996.

WORKS CITED

Abrahams, Roger, and Susan Kalcik. "Folklore and Cultural Pluralism." *Frontiers of Folklore in the Modern World.* Ed. Richard M. Dorson. The Hague: Mouton P, 1978. 46.

Day, Wyatt Houston. "Some Newly Discovered Works by Zora Neale Hurston." Eighth Annual Program for the Zora Neale Hurston Festival of the Arts and Humanities. Eatonville, FL: Assoc. to Preserve the Eatonville Community, 1997.

Douglas, Ann. *Terrible Honesty, Mongrel Manhattan in the 1920s.* (New York: Farrar, 1995).

Goldenberg, Myrna. "The Barnard Connection: Zora Neale Hurston and Annie Nathan Myers." *All About Zora.* Winter Park, FL: Four-G P, 1991.

Hemenway, Robert E. *Zora Neale Hurston: A Literary Biography.* Urbana: U of Illinois P, 1977.

Hill, Lynda Marion. *Social Rituals and the Verbal Art of Zora Neale Hurston.* Washington: Howard UP, 1996.

Hughes, Langston. *The Big Sea.* New York: Hill and Wang, 1940.

Hughes, Langston, and Zora Neale Hurston. *Mule Bone, A Comedy of Negro Life.* Ed. George Houston Bass and

Henry Louis Gates, Jr. New York: Harper/Perennial, 1991.

Hurston, Zora Neale. "Characteristics of Negro Expression." *Social Rituals and the Verbal Art of Zora Neale Hurston.* Ed. Lynda Marion Hill. Washington D.C.: Howard UP, 1996. 201, 243-57.

Hurston, Zora Neale. *Appendix. 1942. Dust Tracks On a Road.* Library of America, 1995.

------. *Spears.* Zeta Phi Beta *X Ray*, 1925.

Perkins, Kathy A. *Black Female Playwrights.* Bloomington: Indiana UP, 1989.

From Luababa to Polk County

Zora Neale Hurston Plays
from the Library of Congress

Meet the Mamma *(1925)*

A Musical Play in Three Acts

CAST:

PETER THORPE	FEMALE DINER
hotel proprietor	WOMAN
CARRIE, his wife	BUM 1
EDNA FRASIER, her	BUM 2
mother	WIDOW
BILL BROWN,	CAPTAIN AND SEAMEN'S
Pete's friend, a lawyer	CHORUS
CLIFFORD HUNT,	BREWERY CHORUS
Pete's uncle and	GUIDE
King of Luababa	ZIDO, an African
ESSIE, Bill's fiancée,	princess
cashier at the hotel	WALLA WALLA, a warrior
BELLHOP 1	WARRIORS
BELLHOP 2	VILLAGE DRUMMERS
WAITRESS 1	(male)
WAITRESS 2	VILLAGE DANCERS
MALE DINER	(female)

TIME: Present.
PLACE: New York, U.S.A.; the high seas; Africa.

ACT ONE

SCENE 1.

PLACE: Hotel Booker Washington, N.Y.C.

SETTING: *One half of stage (left) is dining room, the other is a lobby (right), with desk, elevator, etc. The dining room is set with white cloths, etc. Elevator is upstage exit (center). There is a swinging door exit right and left.*

ACTION: *As the curtain goes up, singing and dancing can be heard, and as it ascends the chorus of waitresses and bellhops are discovered singing and dancing about the lobby and dining room. (7-9 minutes)*

ESSIE: *(Looking offstage right)* Psst! Here comes the boss!

> *(Everyone scurries to his or her position and pretends to be occupied. Enter Pete, right, in evening clothes and cane. Walks wearily through lobby and dining room and back again, speaking to everyone in a hoarse whisper)*

PETE: Have you seen my mother-in-law?

> *(Everyone answers "No.")*

PETE: It won't be long now before she comes sniffing and whiffing around. I ain't been home since yesterday, and I got to have an alibi. What can I tell 'em? *(He indicates mental anguish and strolls over to bellhops' bench.)*

BELLHOP 1: Tell 'em you sat up with a sick brother Mason.

PETE: Oh no, - can't say that. I'm supposed to have been at the bedside and funeral of every Mason in New York City. There ain't supposed to be no more left.

BELLHOP 2: Tell her you went to a bone yard to meditate
and see if you could make 'em get up and gallop like
Man O' War.

PETE: Nope, that won't do. Every time I mention bones I get
the shinny in my wrist. I'm trying to fool her, boy, not
tell where I was. I have been out having a yellow time.

BELLHOP 1: What kind of a time is that?

PETE: Well, I been riding in a yellow taxi with yellow girls
and spending yellow money and drinking yellow
whiskey. Can't none of you men *(to the audience)* help
out a fellow? You fellows are the poorest bunch of liars
I ever seen? I could kill that smart aleck Peter.

BELLHOP 2: What Peter?

PETE: The one that killed Ananias.

> I just got back from the church house
> And hear what the preacher said.
> It seems that a dirty look from Peter
> Laid the poor old scout out dead.
> They say he was killed for lying –
> I can't see why that should be
> That they should croak a good old scout like him
> And not do a thing to me.
>
> Now this Pete was a busy body,
> Like a prohibition hound
> When regular guys are having fun
> He's sniffing and whiffing 'round
> He ought to've been brought to justice
> And given life in jail
> With only his wife for company
> And never a chance for bail.
>
> Cause Ananias was a liar
> Much needed in every club
> To fix up things to tell your wife
> And alibi in any rub

> He could fix up a tale for the landlord
> And do just lie a collection to death
> And explain to the wife about the sick friend
> And even explain your breath.
>
> Now why did they kill Ananias?
> I need him beside me right now
> With an income tax blank before him
> That baby would be a wow!
> Oh, why did they kill the best liar –
> That one inspired cub!
> If he were alive, I'll be you five
> He'd be a member of my club.

(As the song ends, Edna enters (right). Pete sees her.)

PETE: Ambush! *(He steps backward into the open door of the elevator and is flashed upward.)*

EDNA: *(Advancing to center downstage)* Where is your boss? *(She glares about and puts ear trumpet to ear.)*

CHORUS: I don't know.

EDNA: Just you let me lay my eyes on him! *(She exits left.)*

> *(Giggling by the chorus. Reenter Edna, left, who proceeds quickly to the elevator which is coming down.)*

EDNA: I'll go upstairs and wait for him.

> *(She pauses beside the elevator, but not where she can be seen by the persons on the elevator. As it reaches the floor, the door flies open and the boss dashes out toward exit, left, as she hurries toward the elevator. They collide and both sit flat on the floor with feet and legs entangled. They sit there facing and glaring at each other for two full minutes. He speaks.)*

PETE: Well, Madam, if you'll pick out what belongs to you, I'll be satisfied with what's left.

> *(They both arise.)*

EDNA: Where have you been? *(Puts trumpet to ear.)*

PETE: *(Pretending to be drunken)* Thass chuss what I been trying to find out.

EDNA: You poor stretched out chocolate éclair – you! Just you wait till I put my mouth on you to my daughter, you ground hog!

PETE: Listen! *(He strides angrily toward her and prepares to speak into the ear trumpet. She removes it before he can say another word and stalks majestically out, right, leaving him gesticulating wildly.)* Five hundred dollars for a new cuss word! If she could hear without that trumpet, I'd set her ears on fire!

(Enter lawyer friend, Bill, left.)

BILL: Why hello, Pete, how's tricks?

PETE: *(Sadly)* Pretty low, pal – suffering from an attack of mother-in-law.

BILL: *(Laughs)* Brace up. It's the first hundred years that worries a fellow.

PETE: What can I tell my wife? I'm simply crazy about her, but her mother! Gee, I wish I'd gone home last night!

BILL: I know, old man, how you feel.

PETE: Say, how do you know? You're not married.

BILL: Oh, I had a wife once, but her husband came and took her back. I'm going to breeze over and talk to my sweet stuff. Here comes your wife.

(He crosses to the desk and converses with the cashier. Pete exits left, hurriedly. Enter wife right, beautifully dressed but sad.)

CARRIE: *(To cashier)* Is my husband here?

ESSIE: No, Mrs. Pete.

CARRIE: Well, when will he be in?

ESSIE: He didn't say.

CARRIE: He hasn't been home all night and I am terribly upset. He's so mean to me.

I'm blue, I'm blue, so blue,
I don't know what to do
Because my man don't stay home;
Every night he has to roam
Because I'm his, he this me slow
But other men don't find me so.

Everybody's man is better to me than my own
Here me cry, hear me sigh
Oh listen to me moan
He cheats me, he cheats me and stays out all night
    long.
When he's out. they're hanging 'round
All those long, tall teasing browns.
Oh, I could get loving, if I'd take a chance
They'll pay the fiddler, if I'll only dance,
But my mean pappa won't bring it home
Oh – everybody's man is better to me than my
    own.

Oh where is my wandering boy tonight
Go search for him where you will
Go bring him to me with all his blight
And tell him I love him still.

(Exit Carrie right.)

BILL: *(Crosses to center)* Say Pete, why do you put those
    boots on the girls?
PETE: To keep the cake-eaters from gazing at their-er
    – limbs.
MALE DINER: Say! *(Bangs fist on table. Everybody
    starts.)* Can't I get any service here?

(Two waitresses hurry to him. Both speak at once.)

WAITRESS 1 AND 2: What can we do for you?
MALE DINER: You can take my order for one thing.

(They take order books and prepare to write.)

MALE DINER: Crab meat cocktail.

WAITRESS 1 AND 2: *(Writing)* Yes.

MALE DINER: Hors d'oeuvres.

WAITRESS 1 AND 2: Yes.

MALE DINER: Russian caviar.

WAITRESS 1 AND 2: Yes.

MALE DINER: Broiled guinea fowl.

WAITRESS 1 AND 2: Yes.

MALE DINER: Endive salad.

WAITRESS 1 AND 2: Yes.

MALE DINER: Hot apple pie, fromage de Brie – black coffee.

WAITRESS 1 AND 2: Yes, anything else?

MALE DINER: No, do you think you can fill that order?

WAITRESS 1 AND 2: We can fill *anything*.

MALE DINER: *(Drawing a pair of stockings from his coat pocket)* All right, then. Have these filled and serve with the dinner.

FEMALE DINER: Waitress, tell your boss I want to talk to him.

PETE: Yes, madam, what can I do for you?

FEMALE DINER: What can you *do*? You can have these teeth replaced that I broke out on those dum dum bullets you served me for biscuits. I'll sue you good and proper!

PETE: Now Madam –

MALE DINER: *(Rising)* Say, do the cooks have to go into a trance to find out from the spirit world whether they ought to cook an order or not? Now, you just go back there and tell 'em not to break up a séance on my account. I've only been waiting an hour.

ANOTHER WOMAN: *(Limps out of elevator)* Fifty thousand dollars' damages you got to pay me for ruining my shape on that bum killinator, of yours. Oh, oh! Such pains.

(They surround Pete, who tears his hair.)

PETE: Great gobs of gun powder! The old jinx is after *me* all right. I'll *kill* myself ! Gimme a gun!

FEMALE DINER: One of those biscuits would do just as well.

BILL: *(Aside to cashier)* I've got to do something to save my pal. He'll go crazy.

(He exits right hurriedly. Enter Carrie.)

CARRIE: Oh, here you are, sweetheart. *(She weeps.)* Oh, you'll break my heart yet, the way you do. Where were you last night?

(Pete puts his arm about her, but does not speak.)

CARRIE: *(Angrily)* You've got to answer me! *(She thrusts his arm away.)*

ALL: And us too! Yes, answer us too!

BELLHOP: *(Pushes through the crowd)* Telegram for the boss.

PETE: Here. Get out of here before I do a murder. Take it away! It's more trouble, I'll bet.

(Exit customers running.)

CARRIE: *(Snatches it)* It's from some woman and you're afraid to open it before me. *(He throws up his hands helplessly. She opens it and reads.)*

"Lualaba, West Africa.

Mr. Peter Thorpe, New York City.

My dear Nephew, Have discovered rich diamond mine. Come at once. Millions for you. Your uncle, Clifford Hunt"

(She dances around and flings her arms about Pete's neck.)

Just think, millions! Let's start at once.

PETE: I don't care half as much about a million as I do for one of your kisses — a really warm, affectionate kiss.

CARRIE: *(Kissing him)* Well, why do you stay away from
    home?
PETE: Somehow a man just loves to roam.
CARRIE: You often leave me all alone.
PETE:

>With contrite heart I do atone,
>But men are creatures strong to do
>The things that they will shortly rue
>But such are we

(He hugs her closely.)

CARRIE:

>I see, I see.
>I love you true.

PETE:

>And I love you.

(He kisses her more – even her hands.)

>If life should hold no other bliss
>Than having you, I would not miss
>The rest, dear sweetheart mine.

(They remain embracing for a moment.)

EDNA: *(Enters left)* Carrie! Are you kissing that reprobate!

(They spring apart.)

CARRIE: Mamma, he's explained everything all right.
EDNA: Oh, yes. He can make you believe the East River is
    not under Brooklyn Bridge!
CARRIE Oh, look, Mamma, he's got a telegram from
    his uncle in Africa. He's got diamond mines
    worth millions and he wants Petey dear to
    come. Here. *(Hands her the telegram.)* Read it!
EDNA: Ha, ha! I know it's the truth!
CARRIE: But, Mamma, he wouldn't want us to come if he

didn't have it!

ENDA: Well, if he's got millions, he's got wives by the hundred. Do you want to take your husband to a place like that?

PETE: *(Angrily)* Now I'll be damned. *(Edna removes the ear-trumpet. He swears silently.)* By heck, I'll go get one of those trumpets and hold to her head until I give her an earful!

CARRIE: *(Holding to Pete's arm)* Honey, don't you think we'd better stay here and run the hotel? I've heard that Africa is very unhealthy for Americans.

PETE: No. I'm going and you're going to leave that walking bunch of trouble and go with me.

EDNA: If you let that piece of tripe talk to me that way, you're no daughter of mine.

PETE: Oh, how I wish she wasn't.

EDNA: Take my advice, Carrie, and stay here. He treats you bad enough right where the law allows only one wife to a customer – don't go one step with him. *(She draws Carrie to her.)*

PETE: *(Snatches Carrie to him)* This is my wife.

EDNA: *(Snatches her back)* She is my child.

PETE: She'll go with me. *(He jerks her back.)*

EDNA: She'll stay with me. *(Snatches her again)*

PETE: Let Carrie speak for herself.

CARRIE: *(Looks sadly from one to the other)* I cannot say. Give me an hour to decide.

> *(She kisses first Pete then Edna then Pete again and exits by the elevator.2 Pete starts to follow, but she rushes away. Pete and Edna stand glaring at each other for a full minute. Enter Bill.)*

BILL: Well, Pete, I heard of your good luck. *(Edna exits glaring.)* Can't you work me into the scheme somehow?

PETE: Sure. You know, I wouldn't want all that wealth without you to help me spend it. You and Essie get married and come along.

BILL: Sure. We've been engaged long enough now. How about it Essie?

ESSIE: *(She comes out from behind the counter.)* No indeed. Bill3 hasn't got but one case, so I can't marry a man who can't support me in the style to which I want to get accustomed. Here, take your ring. I wouldn't go to Africa with anybody at all. I'll be in the same fix with Brownskin Cora.

BILL: Well, all I can do is grin and bear it, Essie. But what about this Cora?

ESSIE:

    Brown Skin Cora, from way down Dixie way,
    Came up North, bud did not want to stay –
    Old man Trouble – that's how she felt
    Was hitting her below the belt
    So she rubbed her tummy, looked at her shoes –
    And wailed them low-down belly-rub Blues.

    I want my good old chicken and stuff
    Um - um - um (Hummed, while rubbing belly)
    I know I never got enough

    (Hum and belly rub)

    Want my chicken good and brown
    With lots of gravy flowing 'round and 'round

    (Hum and belly rub)

    Oh, I wish my daddy would send for me
    Buy me a ticket on the F.E.C.
    Oh Gravy, um – (Hum and belly rub)
    And the sunshine of his kiss
    Is another thing I miss
    That's my way down south in Dixie.

                    Brown skin Cora
                    From my way down Dixie way,
                    Came up North
                    But did not want to stay
                    Old man Trouble –
                    That's how she felt
                    Was landing blows
                    Below the belt
                    So she sighed and shook her head
                    And this is what she said:

                    I want my good old chicken and stuff
                    Um - um - um
                    I know I never got enough
                    Um - um - um
                    I want my chicken good and brown
                    With lots of gravy flowing 'round and 'round
                    Um- um - um
                    Oh, wish my daddy would send for me
                    Buy me a ticket on the I.C.
                    For the sunshine of his kiss
                    Is another thing I miss.

                    *(Essie returns to desk. Enter two men, one carelessly
                    dressed; one rather soiled. Best dressed of the two
                    advances to Pete. He speaks.)*

BUM 1: How do, Mister Thorpe. Will you gimme a
        dollar? *(He reels drunkenly.)*
PETE: I know you Jim, you want to buy gin. No, I wouldn't
        give you a cent! I don't give my money to liquor heads.
BUM 1: *(Offended)* You refuse me a drink?
PETE: Yes, I do!
BUM 1: *(To Bum 2)* Clarence, come here. This man won't
        give us no money – throw a louse on him.

            (Pete makes a rush for him. Bum 1 and 2 run to exit

left). Here the man turns, bows politely but shakily.)

BUM 1: Iss a nice day.

(Exeunt. Enter dowdy lady right.)

WIDOW: Mr. Thorpe, will you assist a poor widow? *(She uses her handkerchief to her eyes)* I know you will, you're so kind.

PETE: Anything I can do except work or lend you money.

WIDOW: Oh, it's nothing as bad as that. *(She produces a piece of paper)* Here's a song my dear husband wrote before he died, and I want you to sing it so I can sell it and make some money. You see, all the life insurance money is spent now –

PETE: And if you can't sell this – *(She hands him the paper)* You'll have to go to work.

WIDOW: Yes. *(Sniffs)* It's such a beautiful thing - so touching! It was the last thing he did before he was killed. *(She begins to weep.)*

PETE: *(Patting her on the shoulder)* There, don't cry. I'll sing it for you, or die in the attempt. *(He unfolds it and reads title aloud.)* "Oh, Fireman, Save my Bustle!" *(To woman)* Say, what was your husband thinking about? All right, I'll try to sing it for you. Come on boys. *(To the orchestra)*

Let's help the lady out.
Oh, why must love and duty call
Such distances apart
Any why should such a burden fall
Upon a human heart?

(Carrie turns toward Pete.)

My lover calls with outflung hands
The one true man who understands
My heart and has its keeping

(She turns to her mother.)

But duty says 'go not away.
Tarry with me, oh stay and play
With heart and mind asleeping.

(Both rush downstage to her sides and take her hands.)

BOTH: You must decide.

(She draws her right hand away from Pete and clasps her mother's neck. Her mother holds her. They hold the picture for a moment. Pete starts away. Re-enter Bill.)

PETE: *(To Bill, bitterly)* Let's be off then to darkest Africa – the darker the better.

BILL: *(Produces papers)* We can leave in an hour – we two heartbroken men.

CARRIE: *(Flies to Pete and catches his arm. He shakes her off; she flings herself about his neck.)* I'll go with you. *(Sings)*

I wish to spread my wings and try
The sea of love and romance
I do not fear a cloudy sky
For danger does but enhance.

(They embrace.)

I steer my prow to the rising sun
And sail with you till the day is done.

(They kiss again.)

I'll say goodbye to Mother.

PETE: We two must have each other. *(Quick curtain, but up again)*

BILL: To the ship, to the ship! Away!

CHORUS: To Africa to stay.

(Curtain)

ACT TWO

SCENE 1.

SETTING: *Deck of ocean liner. Captain and crew on deck.*

CAPTAIN: *(Sings)*
> O, I am the captain of this swift greyhound
> A city of floating steel
> It trips and slips through the bounding waves
> So strong in prow and keel
> Oh the mists may wrap
> And the waves may slap
> But they do not worry me
> For I stand by heck, on the upper deck
> Of the queen of the rolling sea.

CREW:
> Yes, we stand by heck, on the strong steel deck
> Of the mistress of the seas
> We fling our sail to the howling gale
> In the very teeth of the breeze
> Oh we dance and sing and do the highland fling
> And let the ocean rave
> Someday we'll dock her
> In Davey Jones' locker
> And go to a sailor's grave.

> *(Captain walks to rail and gazes out to sea with glasses. Crew exits whistling refrain "Yes we stand" etc. Enter Pete, Carrie, and Bill in becoming traveling costume. They lean on the rail.)*

PETE: Bill, take it from me, you certainly are missing something by not getting a swell wife like mine. Why, we've been alone for two days and I haven't had a dull moment. Here I've been married six months and this is the first time I've had a chance to love her like I want to.

BILL: Oh, don't rub it in.

PETE: Sorry old man, that was the verse you heard, I've got to sing the chorus.

> Oh, what a sweet wife I've got
> Oh ain't she some good looking peach
> Oh, ain't I glad I saw her before you did
> And got her away from her mamma.

BILL: *(Gets down on hands and knees)* Ow-O-oo-oo *(Howling like a dog)* I just hope the S.P.C.A. comes along while you are abusing me like this.

PETE: *(Laughs)* Bear with me, Bill. But remember, we are two days out from New York and my troubles and going farther every minute. Hot damn! Just think of owning diamond mines. Are you happy sweetheart?

CARRIE: I'd be happy anywhere with *you*, but I do hate to leave Mamma. I'm all she's got, you know. It will be such a long time before we'll see her again.

PETE: Yes, I know, dear, but we'll try to bear up under that. Just think of our vast diamond mines –

> *(One of crew enters and places a steamer chair on stage. Exit left. In a moment he re-enters leading someone all wrapped in a steamer rug.)*

BILL: There's someone who ain't got their sea legs on yet.

> *(They all look. Pete and Carrie start.)*

CARRIE: Why – why, it's Mamma! *(She runs to embrace Edna, who drops her rug and glares at Pete)* Mamma, how did you get on board?

EDNA: Come on early and stayed in my stateroom. Just
    had to come to see how you made out. This is a public
    boat, ain't it?

PETE: Yes, but I wish I owned it for a few minutes.

CARRIE: Now, don't you two start again. Let's do something
    to amuse ourselves on this long voyage.

PETE: All right. But what would be fun for me would ruin
    your Ma.

BILL: Let's get up a poker game. Nope, I guess you ladies
    couldn't understand that – let's make it craps.

EDNA: *(Sneering)* This is your husband's company.

CARRIE: I have it! Let's give shows. We can all take parts.

PETE: *(Proudly)* There's brains for you! Yes, let's give shows.

EDNA: I'd just love it! Let's go in the main saloon and start
    right away.

ALL: Yes, let's.

    *(Curtain falls on deck scene; arises immediately on
    grand salon.)*

SCENE 2.

CARRIE: Let's give grand opera first.

BILL: Do you think we can do all that high singing?

CARRIE: Sure we can. We are on the high C's.

PETE: All right, let's give opera and make it up as we go along.

CARRIE: I'll be Galli Cursey.

BILL: I'll be John Phillip Souse.

EDNA: And I'll be Rosa Raza.

PETE: Gee, this is gonnter be a *very* rough party. Here,
    Mother, you got to sing contralto, and Bill, you get gin
    off your mind and sing bass. That's close enough to the
    cellar. I'll be Caruso. That's safe. Let's all go out and
    come back in our new characters.

    (All exit. Quick curtain.)

SCENE 3.

> *(Curtain goes up again on a sea-side scene, ocean background. At left is a great promontory; at right a tall tree. The rock opens a door and Edna's face appears. She sings)*

EDNA:

> I am rock of the earth.
> Who gives the mountains birth
> And trundle sloping hills
> And send forth rippling rills
> It is my fate to watch and wait
> Till time flies back to heaven's gate.

> *(Bill's face appears in the foliage.)*

BILL:

> A tree, I am a tree
> That stands close by the sea
> I hold the strong winds in my arms
> And shout and laugh in the raging storm
> I murmur love songs sweet and low
> As through my leaves the breezes blow.

> *(Carrie sits upright and is seen for the first time to be a part of the sea.)*

CARRIE:

> I spent a long time by the sea
> Telling my woes, it answered me
> For I was feeling blue
> And the sea was lovely too,
> For I love you, and you're not true,
> And the moon breaks the heart of the ocean too
> I wept and cried
> The sad sea sighed
> And turned a deep, deep blue.

CHORUS:
>I know what the wild waves are saying
>I know what the wild waves do.
>I know wht the seashells are whispering
>And that's why I am blue
>For the moon is an errant lover
>That flirts with every breeze
>And kisses the chill, grey mountains
>And caresses the tremling trees
>I call through the night for his kissing light
>I am the sad blue seas.

(Enter Pete at right, riding in a new moon boat, low over the sea. He stops and kisses Carrie prolonged as she sings chorus, and exits behind rock at left, but returns at end of chorus and sings it as a duet with her. He is stationary while he sings, then exits right. Curtain.)

SCENE 4.

(Curtain opens on a romantic melodrama brewery pain'ted on backdrop. Action takes place in brewery yard. All characters in fantastic dress; the men with razors in scabbards like swords.)

(Enter Pete as Count Shake N. Roll, the hero)

COUNT:
>I am the hero, full of prunes.
>I'll win in spite of all.

(He crosses and stands downstage left, arms folded. Enter Edna as Princess Heebie Jeebie)

PRINCESS:
>I am the bloody villainess
>Who's always dark and tall.
>
>*(She crosses also and stands a little upstage. Enter Carrie as Lady Sweet Patootie)*

LADY SWEET:
>And I'm the little heroine
>As good as gold, by heck
>*(Enter Bill as Lord Suds)*

LORD SUDS:
>And I'm the skulking villiyun
>Who gets it in the neck.
>On with the opry!
>
>*(All exit; dim lights. Enter chorus, all laughing, singing, drinking.)*

CHORUS MAN 1: Bring on more beer.

CHORUS MAN 2: It'll cost too much, I fear.

CHORUS MAN 1: Whaddye you keer, the boss will pay. He's wed today.

CHORUS MAN 2: *(Dropping his mug)* Will wed? I thought he was gointer get married. *(Shades his eyes with his hand)* Here comes my Lord of Suds.

>*(There is a blare of trumpets. Lord of Suds enters. He laughs loudly and harshly. All the people flee.)*

LORD SUDS: *(To the tune of "Downward Road is Crowded")*
>Oh, today I'm gointer get married.
>Married, Married
>Oh, today I'm gointer get married
>To Lady Sweet Patootie toot.
>
>*(Enter Princess Heebie Jeebie.)*

PRINCESS: Psst, my Lord Suds. She walks this way with the man I love. I would see her dead. They must not see my face. I must haste away.

> *(She exits right. Lord Suds taps his razor significantly and drawls into a beer barrel. He speaks.)*

LORD SUDS: Ha! Here she comes now with that cake-eater Count Shake N. Roll. I shall polish him off before her very eyes.

> *(Enter Lady Sweet on the arm of Count Shake. They advance to center stage.)*

COUNT: *(Sings)*
> I love but thee, no fooling, kid.

LADY SWEET:
> I'll go where e'er that thou shalt hid.

COUNT: *(Sits on barrel near the one in which Lord Suds hides. Sings)*
> Sit on my knee.

LADY SWEET:
> No, let us flee. I mean, let's go.

COUNT:
> I tell thee no.

LORD SUDS: *(Rises out of the barrel)* Ha! I have you in my power, and you shall die this hour.

COUNT: *(Strapping his razor on his boots)* I fling thy false words back among thy false eeth. Prepare to fight.

> *(He tests the edge of his razor. Lord Suds does likewise. They fight a duel. Lady Sweet runs back and forth wringing her hands. Enter Princess right.)*

PRINCESS: Ha, revenge.

LADY SWEET: *(Sings)*
> Oh, courage love!

PRINCESS: *(Sings)*
> Sweet revenge.

> *(Lord Suds receives a fatal shall and falls. Princess takes the razor from his hand and cuts a few strands of hair from her head and falls dying across his form.)*

LORD SUDS: *(Rises to sitting position and sings weakly)* I think I'm through.

PRINCESS: *(Does same)* I think so too.

LORD SUDS: *(Repeats business)* My blood leaks out.

PRINCESS: *(Repeats business)* I've got the gout.

LORD SUDS: *(Repeats business)* I am dying.

PRINCESS: *(Repeats business)* So am I.

COUNT: *(Sings)*
> I wish they'd die.

LADY SWEET: *(Sings)*
> And so do I.

> *(Lord Suds and Princess sit up for the last time and gaze into each other's eyes soulfully.)*

LORD SUDS & PRINCESS: *(Sing)*
> Dy-y-ing – Oh – ah –

> *(Ends in dying shriek. They both fall back dead. Count plants his foot on Lord's body and strikes a pose. Curtain.)*

> *(Curtain rises on a drama. Setting: A living room. Father (Bill) reads the paper; mother (Edna)*

knits; husband (Pete) gnaws his fingernails and watches the clock.)

TOM: Mother, Sadie left no message for me?

MOTHER: No.

TOM: Then?

MOTHER: Yes.

TOM: I feared.

(Enter Sadie [Carrie] with several parcels. She removes hat and coat.)

SADIE: Well, I am here, Tom.

TOM: Yes, you are here.

SADIE: Yes, here, *here (she flings wide her arms)* here! Shut in with this thing between us.

TOM: Then you have kept something from me.

SADIE: Yes, but how can I blame you, or even me.

TOM: Terrible.

SADIE: Terrible? You clod! *(She rages up and down, tearing her hair.)* How calm you sit with the universe falling in shards about us.

TOM: Clod? I? *(He leaps up and bites a piece of paper from a magazine.)* The fire that has raged within me all these months! God! You call me a clod! It bites into my very flesh. *(He rushes at her to strike her. She recoils)* That you should bring this thing upon us –

(Sadie rushes to the table and tears open a parcel and returns triumphantly with a baby dress. She shows it to him and sinks in a faint to the floor. He revives her.)

SADIE: I – I – didn't know, Tom. Mother never told me. *(She rises and rushes at her mother.)* You! You – to keep me in ignorance that smothers out all our happiness. You! Shirking your duty to the offspring God gave you. Oh Tom. *(She reels towards him.)*

TOM: *(Standing and holding the tiny garment in a dazed manner)* It too must suffer.

MOTHER: *(Half weeping)* I never dreamed. I never knew, dear. *(She puts her arms about Sadie.)* But your father is the real culprit, not I. *(She faces her husband.)* Now, will you speak for the happiness of our daughter and her unborn child.

> *(Father reads the paper for a moment; lays it down, buries his face in his hand, but remains silent. The others draw near and wait breathlessly for a sign from him. At last he motions to speak.)*

FATHER: It has come at last!

> *(Sadie weeps, mother sinks to her knees, Tom grasps a handful of hair on either side of his head and stands glaring.)*

FATHER: Before I married your mother, Sadie I was rather wild.

> *(Sadie becomes hysterical; mother is crawling about on hands and knees and Tom is catching up a newspaper.)*

FATHER: Yes, I was wild and, and rather fond of the girls.

> *(Tom is attacked by St. Vitus' dance; Sadie is having convulsions and Mother weeping softly.)*

FATHER: So I wore tight shoes so often that I have an ingrown toenail! There, my secret is told at last. Do you despise me utterly, my children?

> *(He looks from one to the other of the three. No one answers him. He walks bare-headed to the door slowly. The others do not move until the door closes softly. Mother rushes out after him. They re-enter. Sadie puts on hat and coat and looks questioning at Tom. He appears not to see her. She picks up the garment and steals softly out by another door. Curtain.)*

(Curtain rises on a musical comedy. Setting: Cyclerama, Atlantic City Boardwalk. Enter Pete [Pluto Water] and Carrie [Carbona Kleaner] in appropriate costumes, hand in hand)

PLUTO: *(Sings)*

> I met a little girl down by the sea.
> I looked at her, she looked at me.

CARBONA:

> And soon we'll be married.

PLUTO:

> Now we first met just yesterday
> Love at sight, sure right away.

CARBONA:

> No neither of us tarried.

BATHING BEAUTY CHORUS: *(Dancing across, singing)*

> Married, they'll soon be married

PLUTO: Now what next?

CARBONA: Dance of course. That's always next in a musical comedy.

> *(They do a dance and end with "Black Bottom."5 Re-enter Chorus dancing.)*

PLUTO: Looka here, Chorus, what are you doing back here again?

FIRST CHORUS LADY: Well, that's all a musical comedy is – Chorus.

> *(They dance off left. Enter Mr. and Mrs. Kleaner [Bill and Edna], arm in arm.)*

MRS. KLEANER: *(Looking roguishly at Carbona and Pluto, she sways her feet.)* Remember we was young once. *(She slaps her hand to her stomach – seasick gesture.)*

MR. KLEANER: *(Clutching his stomach also)* I'm seasick too; let 'em gwan marry if they want to – I mean God bless you, my children. Say! Stop this ship from shaking! *(He starts for his stateroom, but collapses on the floor upstage.)*

PLUTO: Carbona!

(He stretches out his arms; she falls in them weakly. She is also seasick.)

CARBONA: Oh Pluto Water! You're so strong and clean.

(She clutches her stomach and attempts to run off right. When she reaches Mr. Kleaner's form she tries to step over it several times but the mtion of the boat carries her backward each time with one foot lifted. At last she sinks down parallel to Kleaner. Mrs. Kleaner tries to approach Pluto as the chorus stagger in holding their stomachs. They open their mouths as if singing, but no sounds come out. They collapse all over the stage. Mrs. Kleaner turns to exit right, but collapses, parallel to Carbona. A look of triumph leaps to Pluto's face. He rushes over to the glass case on the wall that contains the axe and saw and tries to open it. He finds it locked. He rushes over to the prostrate form of his mother-in-law and does a wild savage dance of triumph about her. He looks about for a weapon, but sees none. At last on the table he sees a siphon of water and gets it, sending a stream into her face. He continues to dance and soak her with the carbonated water.)

PLUTO: Not enough water for the old girl. I ought to sink the ship while she's all spread out! *(He is still prancing.)*

(Curtain)

ACT THREE

SCENE 1.

SCENE: *African jungle. Curtain goes up on a dim lit stage. It is night. The southern cross is seen in the sky. The dense mass of the jungle comes halfway downstage toward the footlights.*

ACTION: *As curtain goes up, the dim figures of the party can be seen downstage right, huddled together. There is a native guide.*

VOICE OF PETE: O-o-o wee! I'm scared. Bill, every time I think about you getting me into this, I could kill you before these lions and tigers get to us. *(There is the trumpet of elephants and the head of a big bull with huge tusks appears through the foliage.)* D-d-don't be scared, Carrie. I'm here.

> *(More elephants appear thrusting their heads through the trees. They withdraw shortly and the roar of a lion is heard. They all huddle closer. The lion appears left but exits upstage center.)*

VOICE OF BILL: Whew! That was a close call! This is the *longest* night I ever lived through.

VOICE OF PETE: You ain't lived through it yet. We ought to've took a taxi through this jungle.

VOICE OF BILL: Look Pete, the sky is getting lighter. Day is breaking.

> *(Lights grow brighter. Birds twitter. There is the distant sound of tom toms.)*

VOICE OF PETE: *(To guide)* Let's start right now. The sooner we get there, the better. How much farther have we to go?

GUIDE: We will arrive within an hour.

> *(It is now light, but the sun has not appeared. The party hurries across stage and exits downstage left. The sky is cobalt. The jungle is a riot of color. Curtain.)*

SCENE 2.

SETTING: *Village of Luababa. There is a rhythmic beating of tom toms, the playing of some deep stringed instrument and a chant before the curtain goes up. Curtain discloses totem pole, whose grotesque head breathes fire and smoke. Elaborate religious setting. Upstage to the right is an arch decorated with masks and symbols. It is the "Door of the Sun" (eastern gate). Village is painted on the backdrop. Jungle entire left.*

ACTION: *Zido, young girls, and men are doing tribal ceremonial dance about the pole and arch – Men with gorgeously painted shields and assegais – girls carry a single red flower. All wear ceremonial masks. A number of youths play the drums. One crouched over a large flat stringed instrument that sounds cello-like. All chant as Zido does a solo dance before the pole, then all arise and join in. Enter party, left, and stand behind shrubbery until ceremony is over. Bill starts to applaud, but is stopped by Pete)*

PETE: Cut that out. This ain't no show! This is church to them.

BILL: Is it? I got religion right away. I'm gointer join and I'll bet nobody ever catches me back-sliding.

CARRIE: *(Impatiently)* Tell the guide to take us on to the chief. I'm dead on my feet from this jungle tramping stunt.

BILL: *(Gazing at the native girls who are going upstage toward the village.)* Looka heah, I'll bet that girl *(indicating Zido who lingers behind)* is the preacher. I ought to go over and confer with the pastor.

EDNA: No, you won't either. I'm tired. Let's go on to that village. *(She points upstage.)*

BILL: Pete, I think I'll stay around here and do a little missionary work. I feel that I've been living too selfishly and these poor heathens are dying for the light. Fact is, I could give my whole life to showing them things. *(Zido departs toward village.)*

PETE: Yea be, I feel like the missionary urge myself. Now I see why so many men dedicate themselves to the mission field. *(He motions to follow girls.)*

CARRIE: *(Angrily)* Pete! *(Pulls him back)* Never mind those hunks of chocolate gelatine. I'll do all the dancing in this family.

PETE: *(Comes back and hugs her gently)* Now darling, didn't your Sunday school lessons teach you not to be selfish? While you're trying to keep a whole husband to yourself, think of all the poor unfortunate girls with no husbands at all. Don't be selfish.

EDNA: *(Pointing toward village)* Look at all those vicious-looking heathens coming! Suppose they try to eat us!

PETE: Well, *you* don't need to worry. Go on out Friday night and find out what's the idea.

> *(The guide meets the warriors; they talk and gesticulate for a moment)*

BILL: Pete, I'm getting all crazy about these Africans. They're so darned cheerful.

PETE: How can you tell?

BILL: Lookit all that dark brown skin! Pure baked-in sunshine, that's all!

(Guide returns and salutes.)

PETE: Well, what are they going to do with us?

GUIDE: The chief says, welcome to Luababa. Advance at once. The ladies to the left to rest and bathe, the men come directly to him.

PETE: What's his name?

GUIDE: Mwa Bibo Bike! The master of many spears.

PETE: *(Turning on Bill)* Thought you told me he was my uncle? Instead of getting something to eat, we'll get butchered up plain and fancy. But if he spares us for one hour, I'll fix you! You splay-footed chocolate éclair! *(To guide)* Ain't there no way we can get back to the coast before he gets us?

GUIDE: No. He has known of your coming since you left the ship. His jungle eye has watched you. His spears reach for a whole day's march of the sun. He sent me to guide you.

PETE: *(Feeling Bill's head)* This is the first time I know that hair could grow on a rock. *(To Bill)* To think I left a hotel in Harlem to get et up in Africa.

BILL: Aw shut up! I was trying to be a friend to you and get you out of trouble in New York.

PETE: Trouble? There ain't nothing in New York to hurt me. 'Course there's a few thugs and bandits and gunmen and taxi drivers and gunwomen, but outside of that –

EDNA: Stop that jaw grinding and come on. I'm not going back in that jungle to be killed by varmints. If I must die, let me be killed decently by folks.

(They proceed toward the village. Curtain falls for a minute to indicate lapse of time till they reach the village. Drums and beating all the time.)

SCENE 3.

SETTING: *A very ornate straw hut, center stage; other houses of village on backdrop. Bright silk hangings on walls. Leopard and lion skins on walls and floor, also bright patterned mats. There is a chair of ivory elaborately carved with symbols standing within the door of the palace. A small stream runs diagonally across the stage and off left, with a rude bridge. A large drum stands near the door (right) and the stringed instrument (left).*

ACTION: *Arising curtain reveals six of the girls standing in the stream in the September Morn pose.6 The warriors are grouped at left. They are in striking war pantomime poses. Uncle Cliff seated in the chair with Zido seated on a pile of grass cushions beside him. A man beats upon the drum; the other instrument wails and the guide enters with Pete and Bill, who are visibly frightened. They are led directly before Uncle Cliff and the guide signals them to kneel. They do so. The girls stand erect and make a gesture of welcome.*

UNCLE CLIFF: Where do you come from?

PETE: New York City, U.S.A.

UNCLE CLIFF: Get up quick and have cushions. Did you ever hear of the city of HushPuckanny, Virginia? *(He signs to the girls and boys to retire.)*

PETE: *(Pleasantly surprised)* That's my home. Pete Thorpe is my name.

UNCLE CLIFF: Not my sister Sarah's boy.

PETE: *(Boastfully)* Put it here, Uncle Cliff. I heard you was in Africa. I come hunting you.

(He kicks Bill. Bill grimaces.)

UNCLE CLIFF: Well, well, I'm glad to see anybody from the U.S., let alone my own nephew. What are you doing in Africa?

PETE: *(Very haughtily)* I thought I'd sell my hotel in Harlem and look around a bit. I was sorter overburdened with a business and a mother-in-law. We sold the hotel before we sailed, but we still got the mother-in-law on hand.

UNCLE CLIFF: Well, boys, you've come to the right place. There ain't a mother-in-law in my kingdom.

PETE: How come?

UNCLE CLIFF: As soon as a girl gets married here, we take her mother off and feed her to the lions.

PETE: You're *some* king. Put it here. *(They shake hands.)* But how did you come to get such a *good* system?

KING: Well, you see, back in Virginia I used to love a girl and her mother just kept us apart and married her to a New York guy. Well, there wasn't anything left for me in America, so I set out wandering and finally landed in Africa with a few cents in my pocket, a gun and a dozen cartridges. I didn't know where I was going and didn't care. I beat on through the jungle for days. Just as day was breaking one morning, I arrived at this village. I heard a great shouting and wailing and came rushing up through the door of the sun, gun in hand. You see, I didn't know that no mortal ever steps on that holy ground. A lion had gotten into the village and killed the chief and his wife. He was in easy range so I raised my rifle and fired. He fell dead. The natives thought I was a god, coming at sunrise through the door of the sun, and killing the lion with the "stick with the voice." I won't let them make a god of me. I merely told them I had been sent to be their king. They gladly crowned me and neither the people nor I have had cause to complain. This girl is the daughter of the chief the lion killed. But I have raised her as my own. She was only a few months old when the lion got her parents. She is the Princess Zido.

BILL: Gee, I'm glad she's not Pete's aunt. I think I ought to kiss her to er – sort of make her feel at home.

(Uncle Cliff pushes him back into his seat.)

PETE: But, King – coming back to this mother-in-law business. Have you got a real hungry lion all ready?

UNCLE CLIFF: Sure, we got one expert lion – been getting 'em for years.

PETE: Naw siree! You don't want no old tired lion in this case. You ain't seen *my* mother-in-law. What you wants is a *young*, snappy one – wild and rearing to go, and extry full of appetite.

UNCLE CLIFF: Where is your mother-in-law?

PETE: She's with my wife whereever it is you sent them to bathe and rest.

UNCLE CLIFF: *(Clapping his hands)* We'll soon fix her up. *(A huge warrior appears)* Walla, Walla, take your bunch of lion catchers and go catch me a young, vicious, hungry lion and have him here in half an hour.

> *(Walla salaams and departs right; drums are heard off stage. A big warrior rushes up to Walla the King and gesticulates wildly, jibbering in his native tongue. King listens until he has finished.)*

UNCLE CLIFF: Well, bring them all in. *(Warrior exits.)*

BILL: What did he say?

UNCLE CLIFF: There has been a killing, so I must hold the inquest at once.

> *(Enter two warriors carrying a limp body of another. They deposit it before the king. Two others bring in a man between them. All begin to gesticulate. They jabber away and shimmy in excitement.)*

BILL: What are they saying?

UNCLE CLIFF: They tell me that Mtesa here *(he points to the prisoner)* had caught a string of fish and the other man came up and took them. Mtesa threw a spear at him – you see, Mtesa is the best spearman in Africa – bar none – and so the other fellow is dead.

BILL: Well, what's your verdict?

UNCLE CLIFF: Death from natural causes. As good a spearman as Mtesa is, it's natural for a man to die if he aims at him. Case dismissed.

PETE: Say, uncle king, do you mind us looking over your harem while we're waiting for the lion?

UNCLE CLIFF: I have none. Never have I married. If I can't have what I want, I won't have what I can get. But I'll have Zido and the girls to dance the "Birth of Love" for you.

(He claps his hands and the girls enter, followed by the male musicians. They take their places. Enter Carrie and her mother.)

PETE: *(Whispers to Uncle Cliff)* Here comes my mother-in-law.

UNCLE CLIFF: She won't be your mother-in-law much longer.

(There is a lion's roar offstage. Uncle Cliff rises and places seats for the ladies. Bill and Carrie are on the left of the king; as Edna approaches to sit she stares at Uncle Cliff and he at her.)

UNCLE CLIFF: Edna! My old sweetheart.

EDNA: Cliff!

UNCLE CLIFF: How did you find me?

EDNA: Following my daughter and her husband. I didn't know you were here, but, er I'm mighty glad.

PETE: *(Aside)* That poor lion won't get no dinner right away. I can see that.

(Edna moves to sit on the cushions.)

UNCLE CLIFF: Wait, sit in this chair, Edna. I'm sorry it's no better.

EDNA: But that's your throne. You are a king.

UNCLE CLIFF: And you are a queen, if I got anything to say.

BILL: King, you ain't forgetting about the dance you promised us.

UNCLE CLIFF: *(To Princess Zido)* "The Birth of Love," Zido.

> *(The music begins and the chorus dances first, then Zido takes center stage. Bill and Pete indicate they are captivated by the dancers. Bill seems carried away by Zido.)*

BILL: *(Reaching into his vest pocket and producing a wedding ring)* I'm gointer lasso that shimmy and domesticate it. She's *mine*!

UNCLE CLIFF: Hey, wait awhile! You don't make love to a jungle girl like that. What you need to win her is a "love stick."

BILL: What is a love stick?

KING: I'll show you. *(He speaks to one of his warriors.)* He'll bring one in a minute. You'll have to learn to make "Jungle Love." *(The warrior returns with two or three clubs about the size of a baseball bat.)* This is the *great* love maker. *(He hands one to Bill.)*

BILL: *(Puzzled)* Say, King, what's the idea?

UNCLE CLIFF: *(With a wise wink)* My man tell me one love stick is worth a hundred compliments.

BILL: *(Enlightened)* I get you, King. Just leave me alone with the princess for a few minutes.

> *(Uncle Cliff rises to go. He offers his arm to Edna and Carrie.)*

UNCLE CLIFF: Come Edna, I want you to see our diamond mines and select some stones for yourself and friends.

PETE: *(Abolished)* Real diamonds, Uncle Cliff?

KING: Sure. Come on and make your own selections.

PETE: *(Hurrying after party)* Lead on, not soon, but now if not quicker.

> *(The party exits left; only Bill and Zido are left on stage. Bill practices several swings with the club, flexes the muscles of his arms, limbers up generally. Then with club in hand he approaches Zido who is picking flowers all the while. A warrior enters left with a club in his right hand. He is carrying a limp girl under the left arm. He exits right. Zido's back is still turned. Bill lifts his club to strike. Zido turns smiling sweetly and offers him a flower. He drops the club. He seizes her hand with the flower, kisses it. He leads her over to the throne. She sits on it. He kneels at her feet and pantomimes a proposal. She accepts. They kiss fervently. She breaks away and attempts to run off stage across the bridge.)*

BILL: *(Striking a commanding pose)* Zido! Come back here and finish kissing me! A half kissed man is a mad man. *(He overtakes her. She yields coquettishly. He catches both of her hands in one of his and holds them behind her. Pulls her backward halfway to the ground, giving her a prolonged kiss.)* Boys, this is love!

> The fly's ankles, the eel's hips
> Ain't got nothing on my baby's lips.

> *(There is the sound of men's voices laughing off stage left and Pete and Uncle Cliff enter left. Pete is carrying a large bag which he drops on the floor as soon as he enters, and mops his head with handkerchief.)*

PETE: *(To Bill)* Man, we're rich! *(Points to the bag)* All that's diamonds.

BILL: *(To Pete)* I found one too while you were gone. *(He and Zido look coyly at each other.)*

UNCLE CLIFF: I could see it coming, so I brought you this. *(He hands Bill a large stone.)* That's for her engagement ring. I know you want to do things in United States style.

BILL: Thanks, King. I'm gointer marry her up so bad she'll never get over it long as she lives. *(He looks off stage left)* But where are the women?

KING: They selected some little trinkets from my treasure room and went to try them on. *(Looks off stage left)* Here they are now.

> *(Enter Carrie and Edna. They have taken off their American clothes and Edna wears a bandeau, a breechcloth, anklets, and headdress, all of diamonds. The wristlets are of ostrich. A high ostrich headdress rises from the diamond circlet about her head. Carrie wears no headdress of ostrich but she has a similar outfit entirely of topaz. She advances to center stage.)*

PETE: *(In admiration)* Hot damn! I sure married my cupful when I roped this baby. *(He advances and hugs her.)* When I get back to Harlem, I'm gointer buy that old hotel for her to keep her shoes and stockings in.

BILL: *(In amazement)* Looka here, man, what's coming! *(All look to left at Edna.)*

PETE: Meet the mamma! My mother-in-law sure has been hiding something all these years. *(He rushes up to her.)* Mamma, give your boy a kiss! *(He snatches a kiss quickly and looks down at her legs)* I always knew there was something swell about you, but I couldn't find out what it was.

CARRIE: *(Pulls him away)* Don't be foolish!

PETE: Foolish? I'm sensible now.

BILL: *(To Zido)* Why—er—don't *you* wear diamond pants too, Honey?

(Edna laughs and pinches his cheek.)

ZIDO: *(Making grimace)* Hurt too bad. Can't sit down.

PETE: Now let's set out for the coast and America.

BILL AND EDNA: The good old United States.

UNCLE CLIFF: You all speak so happily of America.
You're going back. You'll leave me twice as sad and
lonely when you leave as when you came. *(He looks
significantly at Edna.)*

PETE: *(Pulling Carrie)* Come on, folks. Let's get packed.

(All exit except Edna and Uncle Cliff.)

EDNA: *(To Uncle Cliff)* Aren't you coming too?

UNCLE CLIFF: Why should I leave?

EDNA: *(Coyly)* I thought maybe you had not forgotten me
entirely.

UNCLE CLIFF: *(Warmly)* I haven't. I have thought of you
every day for all these years. See that little bridge? I
built it with my own hands. And while I was doing it,
I thought a lot about you – and me.

EDNA: *(Eagerly)* Why?

UNCLE CLIFF:

> Life is but a walk o'er a bridge
> With the river of life beneath
> With years full of trouble
> And moments of bliss
> According to friends we meet.
>
> Bright dreams quickly fading
> Youth's days quickly gone
> Soon fled to the nevermore
> A stumble in shadow
> A step in the dark
> And then, love, the other shore.

CHORUS:
>   If you with me will walk o'er the bridge
>   I'll care not how years may go
>   We'll care not for clouds
>   We'll laugh at the rain
>   Nor mind how the river flows
>   We'll just clasp hands and wander along
>   Singing love's old sweet song
>   When summer's gone
>   And we cross the ridge
>   With akies no longer blue
>   I'll not be and
>   I'll just be glad
>   I've walked o'er the bridge with you.

> *(They do a second chorus as a duet, standing up on the center of the bridge. At the end the others enter, all dressed as they came. Uncle Cliff turns to them happily.)*

UNCLE CLIFF: Well, folks, Edna has consented to be the queen. Being now her boss, I command her to go and cover the royal shape. From now on, that diamond suit can be worn only before the royal eyes.

> *(They laugh. She exits quickly. He comes down from the bridge and joins the others center stage.)*

UNCLE CLIFF: Say folks, who's gointer run my kingdom when I'm back in America?

BILL: So you're going?

UNCLE CLIFF: I ain't gointer stay.

PETE: Say, turn it over to Walla Walla. He's a noble lion-tamer. But say, tell him to let up on the mother-in-laws. They ain't so bad after all. I've got a peachy one since I know her better.

> *(Re-enter Edna dressed for travel. She puts Uncle Cliff's pith hat on his head and takes his arm.)*

UNCLE CLIFF: The bearers will take our baggage to the coast
for us – and back to God's country – the U.S.A.! *(He
takes Edna's hands and gazes lovingly at her.)* I know we
won't be sorry, will we?

> *(Hand in hand they start over the bridge slowly. They
> sing in duet the chorus of "Over the Bridge" and the
> others fall in line. First Pete and Carrie, then Bill
> and Zido. They sing to curtain. It goes up again for
> a minute and natives are dancing farewell to them
> boisterously.)*

CURTAIN

Cold Keener

A Review

SKETCHES:
Filling Station
Cock Robin
Heaven
Mr. Frog
Lenox Avenue
The House That Jack Built
Bahamas
Railroad Camp
Jook

FILLING STATION

CAST:

>PROPRIETOR
>FORD DRIVER
>CHEVROLET DRIVER
>GIRL

TIME: *Present.*

PLACE: *A point on the Alabama-Georgia state line.*

SETTING: *A filling station upstage center. It stretches nearly across the stage. The road passes before and through it. There is a line down the center of the stage from the center of the filling station to the footlights that says on the left side, "Alabama State Line," and on the right, "Georgia State Line." The name of the station is "The State Line Filling Station." There are two gas pumps equal distance from the center of the station, so that the door of the house appears between them.*

ACTION: *When the curtain goes up, a fat Negro is reared back in a chair beside the door of the station asleep and snoring. There is an inner tube lying beside him that has fallen out of his hand as he slept. It is a bright afternoon. There is the sound of a car approaching from the Alabama side and a Model T Ford rattles up to the pump on the upstage side of the pumps and stops at the one nearest to the left entrance. He stops his car with a jerk. The proprietor is still asleep. The Ford driver blows his horn vigorously and wakes him. He picks up the tube beside him and arises with it in his hand, stretching and yawning.*

PROPRIETOR: *(Sleepily)* How many?
FORD DRIVER: Two.
PROPRIETOR: Two what?
FORD DRIVER: Two pints.

> *(The proprietor gets a quart cup out and measures the
> gas and wrings the hose to be sure to get it all, then he
> pours it in the tank.)*

FORD DRIVER: You better look at my water and air, too.

> *(He has a very expensive and ornate cap on the
> radiator, but otherwise the car is most dilapidated.
> As the Proprietor pours the water into the radiator,
> the driver gets out of the car and stands off from it
> looking over)*

FORD DRIVER: Say, Jimpson, they tells me you got a new
mechanic 'round here that's just too tight.
PROPRIETOR: That's right. He kin do more wid 'em than the
man that made 'em.
FORD DRIVER: Well, looka here. My car kinda needs overhauling and maybe a little paint. Look her over and
tell me just what you could make her look like a brand
new car for.

> *(Proprietor lifts the hood and looks. Walks around
> and studies the car from all angles. Then stops at the
> front and examines the radiator cap.)*

PROPRIETOR: Well, I tell you. You see it's like this. This car
needs a whole heap of things done to it. But being as
you'se a friend of mine–tell you what I'll do. I'll just
jack that radiator cap up and run a brand new Ford
under it for four hundred and ninety-five dollars.
FORD DRIVER: *(Indignantly)* Whut de hen-fire you think I'm
gointuh let you rob me outa my car. That's a *good* car.

> *(A car enters from the Alabama side with a good-
> looking girl in it alone. She stops on the downstage*

side of the pumps, but somewhat ahead of the Ford.
The Proprietor rushes over to the left side of her car.)

PROPRIETOR: *(Pleasantly)* Yes, ma'am!

GIRL: I had a flat down the road and I changed it, but it's not fixed. Do you vulcanize?

PROPRIETOR: We do everything but the buzzard lope–and that's gone outa style.

(He takes the tire off the back and goes inside, and comes right out again with it.) Do you want it on the wheel or on the spare?

(Girl alights and goes around to back of car.)

GIRL: On the spare, I guess.

(The Proprietor tries to put it on. The Ford Driver tries to help. They get in each other's way.)

PROPRIETOR: *(Peeved)* Man, let go of this thing.

FORD DRIVER: *(Peeved)* Don't you see I'm helpin' you?

PROPRIETOR: *(Angry)* Leggo! I can't utilize myself for you!

(Ford Driver lets go so suddenly that the tire falls to the ground. The girl grabs it before either of them, lifts it on the rack, gives it a good kick, and the tire goes into place perfectly. She gets into the car, hands the Proprietor a dollar and drives off.)

PROPRIETOR: *(Admiringly)* That's a tight little piece of pig-meat! Damned if I don't believe I'll go to Georgia!

FORD DRIVER: She ain't no pig-meat. That's a married 'oman.

PROPRIETOR: You know her?

FORD DRIVER: Nope, never seen her before.

PROPRIETOR: Well, how can you tell she's married?

FORD DRIVER: Didn't you see that kick? A woman that can kick like that done had some man to practice on.

(Enter from Georgia side a man driving a Chevrolet–

*old and battered. He stops on the downstage side of
the right hand pump.)*

PROPRIETOR: *(Advancing to the car)* What's yours?

CHEVROLET DRIVER: Make it a gallon—goin' 'way over in
Alabama. *(He alights and strolls towards the center of
the stage where the Ford Driver is already standing.)* 'Lo
stranger, how's Alabama?

FORD DRIVER: Just fine—couldn't be no better. How's you
Georgy folks starvin'?

CHEVROLET DRIVER: Starvin'? Who ever heard tell of anybody starvin' in Georgy—people so fat in Georgy till I
speck Gabriel gointuh have to knock us in de head on
Judgment Day so we kin go 'long wid de rest.

FORD DRIVER: He might have to knock some of them
Georgy crackers in de head, but you niggers will be all
ready and waitin' for de trumpet.

CHEVROLET DRIVER: How come?

FORD DRIVER: *(Snickering)* Cause dem cracks y'all got over
there sho is hard on zigaboos.

CHEVROLET DRIVER: *(Peeved)* Lemme tell *you* something,
coon. We got *nice* white folks in Georgy! But them
Alabama rednecks is too mean to give God a honest
prayer without snatchin' back amen!

FORD DRIVER: Who mean? I know you ain't talking 'bout
them white folks in *my* state. Alabama is de best state
in de world. If you can't git along there, you can't get
along nowhere. But in Georgy they hates niggers so
bad till one day they lynched a black mule for kickin'
a white one.

CHEVROLET DRIVER: Well, in Alabama a black horse run
away with a white woman, and they lynched the horse,
burnt the buggy and hung the harness.

FORD DRIVER: Well, in Georgy they don't 'low y'all to call a
white female mule Maud.

CHEVROLET DRIVER: What they call her then?

FORD DRIVER: Miss Maud—and you know it durn well, too.

CHEVROLET DRIVER: Well, they tell me y'all can't go into a store and ask for a can of Prince Albert tobacco—not wid dat white man on it - you got to ask for Cap'n Albert.

FORD DRIVER: Well, they tell me they don't 'low y'all niggers to laugh on de streets in Georgy. They got laughin' barrels on certain corners for niggers, and when you gets tickled you got to hold it till you can make it to one of them barrels and stick yo' head in. Then you can cut loose. Laughin' any old place just ain't allowed.

CHEVROLET DRIVER: Well, over in Alabama, if they tell a funny joke in the theatre, y'all ain't allowed to laugh till the white folks git through. Then a white man way down front turns 'round and look way up in the peanut gallery and say, "All right, niggers, y'all kin laugh now." Then y'all just "kah, kah!"

FORD DRIVER: That's all right. They don't 'low y'all to ride no faster than ten miles an hour. If you ride any faster—you liable to get in front of some white folks.

CHEVROLET DRIVER: Well they don't 'low y'all to ride nothin' but Fords so you can't pass nobody.

FORD DRIVER: Now, what's de matter wid a Ford?

CHEVROLET DRIVER: What you askin' me for? I ain't no dictionary.

FORD DRIVER: Naw, you ain't nuthin—do, you wouldn't be drivin' dat ole money rattler you drivin'.

CHEVROLET DRIVER: You can't talk about no Chevvie now. They got everything that a good car need. Speed! Oh, boy!

FORD DRIVER: Yeah, 'bout eight miles a week.

CHEVROLET DRIVER: Still, every time I look back I see a Ford—way behind.

FORD DRIVER: And every time I look in front I see a Chevvie—in my way. On every highway, at every turn, on every hill, on every side road, you see a Ford hitting it up.

CHEVROLET DRIVER: And a Chevvie passing it.

FORD DRIVER: Dat's a lie and otherwise you ain't really seen a Ford run yet. Now I was going down to Miami and I had dat old car doing seventy-eight, man.

CHEVROLET DRIVER: I went dat same road and had mine doing ninety.

FORD DRIVER: I mean I was doin' seventy-eight on the curves, otherwise I was doing a hundred and fifty.

CHEVROLET DRIVER: That was draggin' along. I was doin' two hundred and wasn't pushin' her. Fact is, I was in second.

FORD DRIVER: Man, I was doin' one hundred fifty in first. By the time I got as far south as Jacksonville, I was really running. Man, I come down that Florida Number Four going faster than the word of God! I was doing three hundred in second.

CHEVROLET DRIVER: You ain't lying–you sho was doing dat, 'cause I remember passing you just before we got to Daytona Beach–I knowed I had done seen you somewhere. I'm a Chevvie-shovin' fool.

FORD DRIVER: You'se a Chevvie-shovin liar, 'cause I wasn't on Number Four, I was on Number Two, and I passed everything on de road.

CHEVROLET DRIVER: Aw, yeah you was on Number Four. I seen you. I was goin' four hundred miles an hour when I passed you and I thought you was having tire trouble. I didn't know you was moving.

FORD DRIVER: You'se a seven-sided liar. I passed you before you got to St. Augustine, and I was airing out at eight hundred miles an hour.

CHEVROLET DRIVER: And I come by you so fast till my wind said "wham!"

FORD DRIVER: *(Picking up a wrench)* Halt! Don't you drive dat damn Chevvie another inch–do, I'll comb yo' head wid dis wrench and part it slap in de middle! Put her in neutral!

CHEVROLET DRIVER: Aw, man, don't be so evil! You know I got de best car.

FORD DRIVER: I don't know no such a thing. You'se just a great big old Georgy something ain't so. . . . And look who buys 'em! *(Sings)*

I got a Ford, you got a Ford . . .

CHEVROLET DRIVER: *(Sings)*

Everybody who couldn't get a Chevvie got a Ford . . .

FORD DRIVER: Know what, man? De angels in heben ain't flew a lick since de new Ford come out.

CHEVROLET DRIVER: How come?

FORD DRIVER: Cause de minute God seen them new Fords, he called up Detroit long distance and told Ford, "Send up ten thousand brand new Fords for my angels to get around in." And, man, them angels is giving Jerusalem Street and Amen Avenue an acre of fits . . . Anyhow, nobody can't beat Ford at nothin' he start. Know what he said to John D. Rockefeller?

CHEVROLET DRIVER: Naw, what was it?

FORD DRIVER: Well, they was sittin' around woofing one day 'bout how much money they had. So John D. told Henry, says, "I'm the richest man in the world! I got enough money to build a solid gold highway clear 'round the world." Know what Ford told him? "Go 'head and built it, and if I like it, I'll buy it and put one of my tin lizzies on it."

CHEVROLET DRIVER: Know what they're going to have on the new Chevvies?

FORD DRIVER: A lot of debt.

CHEVROLET DRIVER: Nope. They're going to have a piano attached to the steering wheel and a radio in the ceiling.

FORD DRIVER: Ford is goingter put twin beds on each running board and a bath over the spare tire.

CHEVROLET DRIVER: And General Motors is going to put a horn in the back so you can tell the road hogs what you think of them after you pass.

FORD DRIVER: The Ford is going to be so you won't have to tell 'em. It will know what you're thinking and tell 'em itself . . . Tell you how fast a Ford is—a gang of hants passed my house while I was sittin' on de porch. My car was parked out front. Well, them hants was going at de rate of ten miles a minute. My old man been dead 'bout three years and I seen him wid these other hants and I wanted to ast him something he forgot to tell us before he died, so I jumped in dat Ford and run dem hants down and overtook 'em. Yessuh! Dat Ford is a hant-catcher.

CHEVROLET DRIVER: They's too slow for my line of work. Me, I had done put in a order for a car when I seen dat hant-convention comin' down de road 'bout two thousand miles a hour. So I run to de Chevvie factory and I says, "Got my car ready?" Mr. Sloan tole me no, but he was working on it. I says hurry up, I got to make it to a hant convention before they assemble, and they's on de way right now. Mr. Sloan molded me a motor and put it together and equipped her, and I throwed in some gas and oil and led dat hant parade into Diddy-Wah-Diddy.

CHEVROLET DRIVER: That's right! Stand there with your mouth lookin' like a hole in the ground and lie like the cross ties from New York to Key West.

FORD DRIVER: Dat ain't no lie—dat's de truth, man—and the gearshift and everything is going to be solid silver.

CHEVROLET DRIVER: The new Chevvies will be solid gold with diamond wheels.

FORD DRIVER: And the new Fords will have a lawyer in the tool box—as soon as you have a collision, the lawyer will spring right out and begin to collect damages.

CHEVROLET DRIVER: You mean the garbage man will start to collecting junk–otherwise the new Chevvie's can't have no collision.

FORD DRIVER: How come?

CHEVROLET DRIVER: Because–they're built against it. They got two sets of wheels. One set is put on crossways and they fit up under the housing. On a straight road, when you see somebody about to hit you, you just press a button and the non-collision wheels will hit the ground and run the car right off sideways. And on a curve it's got low compression springs so it can just squat level with the ground and run right under any car that's too far to the left.

FORD DRIVER: *(Menacing)* Git dat damn Chevvie up off dat ground and outa them woods!

CHEVROLET DRIVER: *(Seizing a jack handle)* Come on and make me. I dare you to move! Fool with me and three years from now, you'll be a three year old hant!

PROPRIETOR: *(Coming out of door)* Boys, boys, don't get too tonic, now.

FORD DRIVER: Tell dat crazy guy something. I'll lam him wid lightning! *(Glares a while)* Nohow, no Ford don't have to go squattin' 'round no curve–'cause the new Ford's got wings and they flies 'round all curves and over bad places in the road.

CHEVROLET DRIVER: *(Looks angry for a moment, then laughs)* You way late wid dis flyin' business, big boy. De Chevrolet *been* flyin'–dat's whut Lindburgh flew to Paris in–a Chevvie.

FORD DRIVER: *(Rushes at Chevrolet Driver)* Pull dat damn Chevvie down out de air! Put it on de ground before I send you to hell! *(The Proprietor has a hard time restraining him.)* Stop dat lyin' on Lindbergh and de ocean before I lam you so hard till I'll kill de governor of Georgy.

PROPRIETOR: *(Separating them)* Aw, y'all cut it out! Cut it out before I gets mad, too. *(They back off from one another.)* And gimme my tools, too. *(They lay down their weapons.)*

FORD DRIVER: You low-down Chevvie-shover.

CHEVROLET DRIVER: You dirty Ford-owner!

> *(They feint at each other and both climb hurriedly into their cars.)*

FORD DRIVER: I'm going home and get my 38 Special—and you better not be here when I get back. *(He starts his motor.)*

CHEVROLET DRIVER: *(Starts his motor)* Yes, and I'm going to get my 44 Burner and you better not be gone.

> *(They simultaneously back off, glaring at each other.)*

CURTAIN

COCK ROBIN

CAST:

> COCK ROBIN
> OWL
> SPARROW
> CROW
> JAYBIRD
> BEETLE
> MRS. BLACKBIRD
> SISTER BUZZARD
> FLY
> MRS. FISH
> MRS. BEETLE
> BULL
> OTHER ANIMALS: WRENS, OWLS, FISH, CROWS,
> BLACKBIRDS, BEETLES, JAYBIRDS

PLACE: *Any city.*

TIME: *Present.*

SCENE: *A city street in colored town.*

SETTING: *Straight across the stage, upstage, are (1) a cheap restaurant with a crude sign on which is written "The Grease Spot"; (2) a cheap pool hall called "The Eight Rock"; (3) a dingy rooming house, "The Shimmy Shack." All have practical doors and windows. All are two-story buildings with numerous small-paned windows. There is a generous sidewalk and the rest of the stage is street.*

ACTION: *At the rise there are characteristic noises from each of the places.*

VOICE FROM THE GREASE SPOT: Adam and Eve on a raft—

wreck 'em! Clean up de kitchen for one! Let one come
gruntin', one come switchin', snatch cne from de rear!

VOICE FROM THE POOL ROOM: Now, I'm gong to show you
some of Blue Baby's stuff . . .

ANOTHER VOICE: Aw, shut up! You trying to show yo'
grandma how to milk ducks–shoot!

> (*A crack of balls. In the Shimmy Shack, somebody is
> playing blues on the piano. There is a sudden turmoil
> in the Shack and three shots are heard. The door
> flies open and Cock Robin staggers out with three
> arrows sticking in him and falls dead on his back on
> the sidewalk. All the windows fly up and heads are
> thrust out. Crowds pour out of the doors. Sparrow1 is
> looking out of the second-story window of the Shack.*)

JAYBIRD: (*Standing over Cock Robin*) It's Cock Robin!

BEETLE: (*Gazing down on him*) Dat's him all right, and
murdered in de first degree.

OWL: Who! Who! Who kilt Cock Robin?

MRS. BLACKBIRD: I just knowed something bad was going
to happen–I dreamed last night the air was *full* of
feathers.

BEETLE: I don't know who kilt him–but I do know he was
due for a first class killin'. He give these married men
more aid and assistance than de ice man.

SISTER BUZZARD: (*Belligerently*) I don't keer who kilt him.
But nobody better not cast no slams at my hotel.
(*Points to Shack*) They bet' not say my shack ain't
respectable and they bet' not tell me my eye is black.

OWL: (*Officiously*) Hey, Sister Buzzard, let's squat dat
rabbit and jump another one. What we wants to know
is–who kilt Cock Robin?

SPARROW: (*Has a bow and quiver of arrows, coming out of
Shack to center stage. Very belligerently*) I, the sparrow,
with my bow and arrow, and I kilt Cock Robin–who
wants to know?

OWL: (*Warily*) 'Course we don't keer nothin' 'bout you killin' him, Brother Sparrow, we wants to know how come.

SPARROW: Well, I'll tell you. When me and my wife first started to nestin' she never laid nothin' but plain white eggs. But since Cock Robin been hanging 'round our place—every time I go out on a worm hunt, when I come back, she'll done laid another blue egg.

JAYBIRD: (*Begins to pick feathers violently*) Now, you done got me to scratchin' where I don't itch—come to think of it, I done seen two or three blue eggs in *my* nest.

CROW: (*Glaring at his wife*) You been complaining 'bout my singing ever since this guy (*points at Cock Robin*) has been 'round here. 'Nother thing—I ain't never brought home nothin' but worms, and I been seeing a powerful lot of grasshoppers' bones around lately.

MRS. CROW: (*Crying and trembling*) Oo-oo, you done got me so nervous—I got de haystacks. (*She flutters and an egg falls to the floor.*)

CHORUS OF VOICES: She's lain a egg! And it's blue—robin egg blue.

JAYBIRD: Dere now! De mule done kicked Rucker!

OWL: Let's get dis killin' straight. Brother Sparrow say he kilt him for just causes . . .

CROW: And I don't blame him—when they get so they kin lay mo' eggs in my nest than I kin—they's got to be some changes made.

OWL: Who saw him die?

FLY: I, said the fly, with my little eye. I saw Cock Robin die.

OWL: Tell us 'bout it, Brother Fly.

FLY: I was in de Grease Spot when Mrs. Sparrow and Cock Robin passed, and I heard him say something was on fire—I don't know what—and he says to Mrs. Sparrow, "Come on up in the Shimmy Shack and let's put it out" and she says "All right." So they went on up—and the next thing I know, Bull Sparrow was killin' him.

OWL: Who caught his blood?

MRS. FISH: I did, Brother Owl—in my little dish. (*Wiping a tear*) He had such a lovely voice. (*General skeptical titter runs around.*)

OWL: Since y'all done voted me in as chairman of dis committee—we better make some arrangement 'bout funeralizin' him. Who'll make his shroud?

MRS. BEETLE: I, Mrs. Beetle, with my thread and needle— I'll make Cock Robin's shroud.

OWL: Now, since I got a spade and shovel, I'll dig his grave. Now who'll bear his pall?

WRENS: We, said the wrens, both the cock and the hen— we'll bear Cock Robin's pall.

OWL: Now, who'll mourn his love?

> (*All of the females present come rushing up to the Owl. All the characters come down out of the building and crowd up close.*)

VOICE: Me, Brother Owl, I'll mourn his love! I really can mourn, too. (*They push and jostle each other.*)

OWL: Here! Here! Let's have some order. Don't need but one chief mourner. I'm going to put this thing to a vote and give the job to Sister Dove—she's had more experience in mournin' than anybody else, so she'll mourn Cock Robin's love. Now, who'll toll the bell?

BULL: I'll toll dat bell, Brother Owl.

CROW: How come I can't toll it? I ain't been 'signed to no duty yet.

BULL: I said I was going to toll that bell, and that's all there is to it. I can pull and it takes pull to toll bells. (To Owl) Just put my name down as bell-toller.

OWL: Now, we got things ready, what hall is we goin' funeralize him from?

CROW: He was a Great Grand Exalted Ruler of the High-Roostin' Crows—we oughter conduct de funeral.

BEETLE: He was a Prime and Supreme Butler of the Noble Muckty Beetle Bugs–turn over de 'rangements to us.

JAYBIRD: I know so well, we're going to have something to say over Cock Robin when he was Superior Subordinate Exalted Contaminator in the Personal Parading Jay Birds.

OWLS: We, Order of Night-Stepping Owls, better take over this whole thing to keep peace. He was a member in good standing.

FISH: We certainly going to put a word in, 'cause he was a Bottom Ruler in the Order of The Never Been Caught Fishes.

BLACKBIRDS: Everybody knows de Ever Blooming Blackbirds really puts 'em away. A heap of you folks that's whooping for dis funeral don't know what to do wid one when you gits it.

OWL: Dat's a good idea! Every one of you lodges parade yo' material and de best one gits de funeral. (*Great cheers and hubbub*) Now, you crows got first chance.

> (*Everyone exits but the Owl and the Bull. The Owl takes a high chair and sits in front of the Eight Rock to review the parade. Enter the Crows with a band.*)

CROW: (*Salutes the Owl*) We're going to put Cock Robin in a bronze casket wid ten carriages and strut like this.

> (*The band strikes up, the Crow is the drum major, and the Crows do a hot strut across the stage. Enter the Beetles. They salute the Owl.*)

BEETLES: We'll put Cock Robin in a copper casket wid fifteen carriages and romp like this.

> (*They do their stuff and take places beside the Crows. Enter the Jaybirds and same business.*)

JAYBIRD: Mr. Chairman, we'll put him in a silver casket wid twenty carriages and spread our junk like so.

(They join the Crows and Beetles. Enter Fish—same business.)

FISH: We'll put him in a crystal casket and have thirty carriages. *(They begin to prance)* We're gointer strut our stuff, we're gointer strut our stuff, Good Lawd! We're gointer spread our mess.

(Enter Blackbirds—same business.)

BLACKBIRDS: We'll put him in a solid gold casket wid fifty carriages, and we'll do the Palmer House and strut like Stavin' Chain.[2]

OWL: I don't know who to 'cide on.

BULL: I don't keer who gits de funeral. I'm going to march in front.

OWL: How come, Brother Bull? You don't belong to none of these lodges.

BULL: I know it, but, Brother Owl, you know very well that Bull goes in front of everything.

OWL: Dat's de truth . . . Now, which one of you lodges think you kin do de best job?

ALL: Us! We! Me! Leave de Crows have him! . . . Give him to de Blackbirds . . . De Beetles is the only ones! . . . Let de Fishes funeralize him! . . . *(Etc., etc.)*

OWL: *(After rapping for order)* Well, whoever pays de bills can have de body. Who gointer pay de bills?

(There is profound silence for a moment, then Crow speaks up.)

CROW: Well, brothers and sisters, since we're all here at one time, you know Sister Speckled Hen is having a grand barbecue and fish fry down on Front Street and Beale—why not let's have one grand consolidated, amalgamated fraternal parade down to her place and enjoy the consequences?

ALL: Yes, yes! Let's go!

> (*They begin to organize. The Bull sets his hat at a reckless angle, seizes an elaborate baton and begins to line up the lodges. Then he places himself at the head. The Owl brings up the rear.*)

BULL: We're all set! (*To orchestra*) Turn it on, professor, and let the bad luck happen! (*They strut off.*)

CURTAIN

HEAVEN

CAST:
> JIM
> ST. PETER
> ST. JOHN
> CHARLES KNOWLES
> OLD MAN
> ANGEL 1
> ANGEL 2
> ANGEL 3
> ANGEL 4
> BLACK ANGEL 1
> BLACK ANGEL 2

SETTING: *Heaven, showing the Tree of Life and the intersection of Hallelujah Avenue and Amen Street. The pearly gates stretch across the stage like a curtain. There is a peep-hole in the door. A flight of golden stairs ascends from the orchestra pit in midstage. Just inside the gates, John has a jeweled pulpit that holds the record books.*

ACTION: *At the rise the gates are closed, but a listless drone of "Holy" can be heard and the sound of crowns being cast and retrieved. There comes a sound of a mouth organ being played in a blues mood way down the golden stair. Enter by the stairs a sour-faced man, neatly dressed, who knocks at the gate. The peep-hole flies open and St. Peter peeps out and looks doubtfully at the candidate.*

ST. PETER: Well, who is it?
KNOWLES: One Charles Knowles.
ST. PETER: What do you want?

KNOWLES: I want to enter.

ST. PETER: You don't look just right to me. What good have you ever done?

KNOWLES: *(Thinks a moment)* Well, one time I met a little girl and she was crying because she had lost her money so I gave her three cents.

ST. PETER: *(Over his shoulder)* Look on the books there, John, and see if it's there.

ST. JOHN: *(After a short pause)* Yes, it's here.

ST. PETER: Well, what else did you ever do?

KNOWLES: One time I met a little boy crying because he had lost his money and I gave him two cents.

ST. PETER: *(Over his shoulder)* See if that's there, John.

ST. JOHN: *(After a pause)* Yes, it's here.

ST. PETER: Is that all you ever gave away?

KNOWLES: Yes.

ST. JOHN: *(After a pause)* Well, Peter, you gointer let him in?

ST. PETER: No. Give him his nickel and let him gwan somewhere else.

> *(He hands the man a nickle and slams shut the peephole. The man turns slowly and descends the stairs. The music of the mouth organ is much nearer now. St. Peter opens the peep-hole and looks out with pleased interest as a Negro with a torn hat and the general appearance of a roustabout ascends the stairs and stops before the gate. A dead silence falls. He wipes off his mouth organ and puts it in his pocket. He takes his hat in his hand and faces St. Peter timidly.)*

ST. PETER: *(Amiably)* What's your name?

JIM: Jim–thass whut they call me–Jim.

ST. PETER: *(Opening the gates)* Well come in, Jim. We're mighty glad to see you. *(Jim steps timidly in.)* Where did you come from, Jim?

JIM: *(Gazing with awe upon the magnificence)* From Johnstown. Didn't you hear 'bout de great flood?[1]

> *(Enter four angels walking two and two. One couple enters left, one couple enters right, and they meet at the tree.)*

ANGELS 1 AND 2: Ooo ooh! Y'all ain't seen no water!
ST. PETER: That's all right about the water. We all seen it. Just go with John and get fixed up. Everybody will be nice to you. *(To John)* Take him and dress him up.

> *(John takes Jim's arm and starts off right.)*

JIM: Man, dat water was ten foot deep! You ain't never seen no water lessen you seen de Johnstown flood!

> *(They exit right. Angels pass and repass, all gorgeously clad. Re-enter John with Jim elaborately gowned. John leads him to a seat, places a golden harp beside him and goes back to his post.)*

JIM: Man, dat was some water! *(Feels his pockets as if hunting for something, looks worried for a moment.)* Oh, John, where's my harp?
JOHN: There it is, right on the seat beside you.
JIM: *(Picks up the golden harp and looks it over)* This here ain't *my* harp. Where's de one I been playin' all de time?
JOHN: Oh, that's in your robe pocket.

> *(Jim feels and pulls it out and wipes it off and blows a chord or two. All the angels look interested.)*

JIM: As I was sayin', I ain't never seen it rain lak it rained in Johnstown.

> *(He commences to blow and all the angels tune in with him and heaven is full of harmony. Two huge black angels fly out from the back of heaven and seat themselves beside Jim. Both of them play guitars. John*

> *keeps time with his foot. Peter jingles his keys. This*
> *keeps up till an old patriarch with a long beard and*
> *crooked staff enters t left and proceeds slowly to the*
> *Tree of Life. There he pauses, looks pensively about.*
> *Jim notices him and stops the music and approaches*
> *him.)*

JIM: Hello, old folks, how long you been here?

OLD MAN: Oh, a long time.

JIM: I just got here from de Johnstown flood. Man, dat was some water! Chickens floatin', folks floatin', horses floatin', houses floatin'! Man, dat wuz water.

OLD MAN: *(Starting away in disgust)* Aw, shucks, you ain't seen no water.

> *(He exits right. Jim looks hurt and puzzled for a*
> *moment then calls out to Peter.)*

JIM: Say, Peter, thought you said everybody here was nice and sociable. Se how dat ole man treated me when I tryin' to show him manners and politeness by tellin' him 'bout de flood?

PETER: You can't tell that man 'bout no flood—that's Noah.

> *(Jim sits down, crushed.)*

BLACK ANGEL 1: That's all right, Jim, you'll know better next time. Come on, let's play some more.

JIM: Never mind, I wants to fly some.

BLACK ANGEL 2: You can't fly till they tell you.

JIM: Oh yes, I kin, too. They *my* wings, ain't they? Y'all just lak colored folks—let 'em be 'round de place awhile and they tries to boss de job. (*He gets up and starts off upstage center*)

BLACK ANGEL 1: Now, where you goin'?

JIM: I'm goin' to climb up on some high tower of elevation and fly all over heben.

BLACK ANGEL 2: You better wait. You gointer break up somethin' and they'll sho take yo' wings off and Lawd knows when you'll git any more.

JIM: Aw, y'all just jealous–done got too old on de job. I'm
going' try *my* wings. *(He exits)*

> *(The other angels shake their heads sadly and turn
> again to music. There is a series of tremendous crashes
> and John and Peter rush off stage upstage center
> and return with Jim very mussed up. They lead him
> solemnly to the same sent and snatch off his wings
> seat him, frowning disapprovingly upon him all the
> while. They return to their posts. Jim sits quiet for a
> moment then picks up the golden harp.)*

BLACK ANGEL 1: Unh-hunh, I told you you was gointer git
yo'self into all kinds of trouble flyin' so fast!

JIM: Aw, I don't keer.

BLACK ANGEL 2: Yeah, and now you ain't got no mo' wings
neither.

JIM: *(Making ready to strike his harp)* I don't keer. I was
a flyin' fool when I had 'em. *(Starts to play and sing.
Quick curtain.)*

MR. FROG

CAST:

FROG ON TOADSTOOL
MR. FROG
MISS MOUSIE
OLD UNCLE RAT
REVEREND BUZZARD
FROG CHORUS
MR. BEE
MRS. SNAKE
MR. BUG
MR. TICK
DR. FLY
OTHER ANIMALS: TORTOISE, BIRDS

TIME: *When animals talked.*

PLACE: *A Florida swamp.*

SETTING: *Water is seen through the cypress and magnolia and pine trees. Spanish moss hangs from the trees. There is a large hollow log at left near the entrance. A long-leaf pine is down stage center. A huge toadstool is near footlights at extreme right. The lake in the back glints through all this. The pine tree is a girl dancer. Several birdnests are seen in the tree tops. One large tree near center downstage has a large hollow.*

At the rise, the sun is setting. The tree is motionless. With the music it begins to sway slightly, but increases its motion all the time. Enter downstage left the South Wind, who dances with the tree for about a minute. Enter West Wind upstage right and both dance with tree. Enter East Wind upstage left, who joins the dance, then the North

Wind downstage right. The tempo increases with the entrance of each wind. The Tree is influenced by each. When all four winds are on, there is a violent wind dance for a minute till the sun finally sets and the winds take their places at their entrances and sink to the ground and remain there.

In the darkness hundreds of fireflies swarm over the scene. The scene is lighted from the ground to indicate marsh gas. There is silence for about thirty seconds, then enter a big frog upstage center who leaps to the toadstool downstage right and sits there for a moment staring about him. The voice of an alligator booms from the water. An owl hoots, a chorus of frogs, birds, beetles, flies, a snake, all enter from different points and take places among the trees and bushes. A huge buzzard takes his seat on the hollow log. There is a working door in the log. The frog chorus is down near the footlights in irregular formation. They croak a few seconds.

FROG ON TOADSTOOL: (*Sings*) Mister Frog went courtin' he did ride.

FROG CHORUS: (*Jumping up and down rhythmically*) Unh hunh, unh hunh.

> (*Enter Mr. Frog down stage right riding a tortoise, dressed in green satin or velvet, white vest, sword, spurs and boots.*)

FROG ON TOADSTOOL: (*Sings*) Mr. Frog went courtin' he did ride, sword and pistol by his side.

FROG CHORUS: Unh hunh, unh hunh.

FROG ON TOADSTOOL: He rode right up to Miss Mousie's door.

FROG CHORUS: Unh hunh, unh hunh.

FROG ON TOADSTOOL: Rode right up to Miss Mousie's door where he'd often been before.

CHORUS: (*All birds and everything join frog chorus*) Unh hunh, unh hunh.

> (*Tortoise reaches hollow log and knocks on the door. It opens shyly and Miss Mousie creeps out, behaving coyly.*)

FROG ON TOADSTOOL: (*Singing*) And he took Miss Mousie on his knee.

CHORUS: Unh hunh, unh hunh.

MR. FROG: Oh, I took Miss Mousie on my knee, said Miss Mousie won't you marry me? (*Suits the action to the song*)

CHORUS: Unh hunh.

MISS MOUSIE: (*Coyly*) Not without my pa's consent.

CHORUS: Unh hunh, unh hunh.

MISS MOUSIE: Not without my pa's consent, would I marry the president.

CHORUS: Unh hunh, unh hunh.

> (*Enter Old Uncle Rat from the log, very jovial. He bursts into a big laugh and everybody joins with him for a half minute. He beams happily on all.*)

FROG ON TOADSTOOL: Old Uncle Rat he laughed and cried.

CHORUS: Unh hunh, unh hunh.

FROG ON TOADSTOOL: Old Uncle Rat he laughed and cried.

CHORUS: Unh hunh, unh hunh.

FROG ON TOADSTOOL: Old Uncle Rat he laughed and cried, to see his daughter be a bride.

CHORUS: Unh hunh, unh hunh.

MR. FROG: Where, oh where will the wedding be?

CHORUS: Unh hunh, unh hunh.

MR. FROG: Where, oh where will the wedding be?

OLD UNCLE RAT: Down in de holler of de ol' oak tree.

CHORUS: Unh hunh, unh hunh.

> (*Bride and groom retire into log. The guests begin to approach the tree slowly.*)

MR. FROG: What, oh what will the supper be?

CHORUS: Unh hunh, unh hunh.

MR. FROG: What, oh what will the supper be?

OLD UNCLE RAT: Good fat meat and de black eye pea.

CHORUS: Unh hunh, unh hunh, unh hunh, unh hunh, unh hunh.

FROG ON TOADSTOOL: And the first come in was Mister Bee.

CHORUS: Unh hunh, unh hunh.

(Enter Mr. Bee with a guitar.)

FROG ON TOADSTOOL: The first come in was Mister Bee, wid his fiddle on his knee.

CHORUS: Unh hunh, unh hunh.

(Enter bridal couple and proceed to the hollow oak and take their places. Reverend Buzzard performs the ceremony.)

REVEREND BUZZARD: (*To groom*) Do you take Miss Mousie to be your wife?

CHORUS: Unh hunh, unh hunh.

(Bride and groom nod assent in time to the music.)

MR. FROG: Yes, I take this woman to be my wife, to love her and kiss her for all my life.

CHORUS: Unh hunh, unh hunh.

(Old Uncle Rat tries to cry. Reverend Buzzard kisses the bride. They step away from the altar and seat themselves. General noise of congratulation in various ways—according to the species.)

FROG ON TOADSTOOL: An the next come in was Mrs. Snake, pass all around dat wedding cake.

CHORUS: Unh hunh, unh hunh.

(She is passing the cake, decorated with fireflies. Everybody takes a piece.)

FROG ON TOADSTOOL: And the next come in was Mr. Bug.

CHORUS: Unh hunh, unh hunh.

FROG ON TOADSTOOL: And de next come in was Mr. Bug,
passed all around dat whiskey jug.

CHORUS: Unh hunh, unh hunh.

FROG ON TOADSTOOL: And the next come in was Mr. Tick.

CHORUS: Unh hunh, unh hunh.

(Enter Mr. Tick who starts gobbling everything in sight.)

FROG ON TOADSTOOL: And de next come in was Mr. Tick,
et so much till it made him sick.

CHORUS: Unh hunh, unh hunh.

*(Mr. Tick is flat on his back in the center of the
wedding party.)*

FROG ON TOADSTOOL: And then they sent for Doctor Fly.

CHORUS: Unh hunh, unh hunh.

(Enter Dr. Fly.)

FROG ON TOADSTOOL: And then they sent for Doctor Fly,
said Mr. Tick, you sho will die.

CHORUS: Unh hunh, unh hunh.

*(Mr. Tick is dragged out by his hind legs into the
bushes out of sight. The groom loads his wife on the
tortoise and they start off right. Everybody throws
rice, etc., behind them.)*

FROG ON TOADSTOOL: And that was the last of the wedding
day.

CHORUS: Unh hunh, unh hunh.

FROG ON TOADSTOOL: And that was the last of the wedding
day, and that is all I have to say.

CHORUS: Unh hunh, unh hunh.

*(The bride and the groom exit to a slow curtain and
leave the chorus dancing and singing, "unh hunh,
unh hunh, unh hunh, unh hunh.")*

CURTAIN

Lennox Avenue

CAST:

> OFFICER
> YOUNG MAN
> MAN 1
> WOMAN 1
> PREACHER
> PREACHER'S FOLLOWERS, a man and two women
> GIRL
> MAN 2
> MAN 3
> MAN 4
> LOIS
> MAN 5, Lois's husband
> VARIOUS STREET PEOPLE

TIME: *Present.*
PLACE: *New York City.*
SCENE: *Lenox Avenue at 135th Street.*
SETTING: *Backdrop showing intersection and houses. The autos are on a scenic band and keep whizzing past.*
ACTION: *When the curtain rises there is a traffic officer at the intersection. A very effeminate young man enters left with a large cretonne sewing bag on his wrist. Officer glares at him a moment, then yells at him.*

OFFICER: Come here.
YOUNG MAN: (*Looks all about himself*) Are you speaking to me?
OFFICER: Who else but you? Make it snappy! (*Young man approaches center of intersection where Officer is*

standing.) What you got in that bag?

YOUNG MAN: My knitting.

OFFICER: (*Scornfully*) Oh yeah? And where are you going with your knitting?

YOUNG MAN: To the army.

OFFICER: (*Surprised*) To the army? Say! What are you going to the army for?

YOUNG MAN: Oh well, the boys must have their socks, you know. (*Waves a fluffy goodbye.*) Toodle-oo, old cabbage, I must try to get the boys out of the trenches before Christmas.

> (*He exits right. Officer glares after him. Enter right, a man and woman nearing middle age. They are angry. He is walking a little ahead of her and pauses to talk back at her.*)

MAN 1: Aw, go bag yo' head, woman! You ain't got nothin' to do wid me. It's none of yo' business where I been.

WOMAN 1: (*Catching up to him*) I'm yo' wife, ain't I? I reckon I got something to say 'bout you bugabooing round town all night.

MAN 1: Aw, naw you ain't. God gives every man a lovable chance, and if he don't take it–that's his hard luck. But I'm telling you straight, the world ain't gointer owe *me* nothin' but a hole in de ground when I die.

> (*She glares at him, arms akimbo. He starts to walk.*)

WOMAN 1: You big old evil mule you! You so evil till one drop of yo' spit would poison all the fish in the ocean. Hold on, I ain't through wid you yet!

MAN 1: You might as well be through. I'm through wid you. I got a brand new costume that you don't fit. I'm playin' a brand new game and you ain't it. Bye-bye, mama, you can't snore in my ear no more.

WOMAN 1: (*Slurringly*) Don't put dat lie out, papa. You ain't near through wid me!

MAN 1: Woman, I'm just too through. You gimme the close up cramps every time I look at you.

WOMAN 1: (*Snapping her fingers*) Brother, don't hang dat nasty wash out in my back yard. You ain't through wid me and I know it.

MAN 1: Aw yeah. I don't keer if I never see you no more. That would be soon aplenty.

WOMAN 1: (*Gets right up in his face*) You might as well stop dat wringing and twisting, cause I know you want me some 'gin [again], 'cause I'm a damn sweet woman and you know it.

MAN 1: (*Looks her in the eye for a moment, then grabs her by the arm and faces her about*) Aw, come on and let's go home, woman. I hates to hear folks fussin' on the streets.

> (*They exit right. Enter a street preacher with two sisters and a brother. The preacher has a pair of cymbals and a bag. The sisters carry tambourines. The brother has a soap box. He places the box on the curb and the quartet sing a song. "Wouldn't Mind Dying if Dying Was All." After this the preacher mounts the box and speaks. A crowd collects.*)

PREACHER: You folks ain't right. You needs to be born agin. Now I see some of y'all askin', "How kin a man enter de second time into his mother's esophagus and be born agin . . . "

VOICE FROM THE EDGE OF THE CROWD: What kind of a woman is that!

PREACHER: And moreover, you don't pray enough. You get down on yo' knees and mumble something and jump in yo' beds. Why can't you pray in de bed? You know some of y'all does everything in de bed but praise de Lawd. (*To the brother*) Let's sing "Brothers Get Yo' Peckers Ready, Let's Peck on de Rock."

(The cymbals and tambourines start. The officer runs over.)

OFFICER: Hey! Get de hell outa here, blocking the street!

(They all exit right followed by the crowd. Only two men remain on the curb. Enter left a very slender girl in a form fitting, long dress. It is quite tight about the buttocks. They eye her till she almost reaches the right exit.)

MAN 2: Man, if these new styles keep on the way they're going, we'll find out that the snake's got hips.

(She keeps right on off right. Enter right two women. One is small and doll-like and the other is tall and masculine. They stroll across, arm in arm. At center they pause and whisper a moment, then stroll on across stage to exit at left. The two men glare behind them, then look at each other.)

MAN 3: Well, Bo, I still got this consolation–ain't nobody but a man and the Holy Ghost been the father of a family yet.

(Enter a man at left with a folded newspaper under his arm. He stands on the corner for a moment, then starts walking rapidly across Lenox Avenue. When he reaches the center, the officer stops him.)

OFFICER: Where you going in such a hurry–trying to get run over?

MAN: No, sir.

OFFICER: Well, then, where you think you going?

MAN: To Brooklyn.

OFFICER: Oh yeah? Have you learned the trade? What do you know about going to Brooklyn?

MAN: Oh, I know a lot about it.

OFFICER: Got your papers on you?

MAN: (*Embarrassed*) I didn't get my diploma. You see,

my father died and I had to leave school at eighteen, but I've been taking evening courses at Columbia University. You know, my father was an ambitious man, but life was hard so he never did find out how to get to Brooklyn, but he had high hopes for me. And on his deathbed he made me promise I'd carry on. So I've attended what lectures I could afford, read everything I could find, talked with taxi drivers and police officers–so today I felt I knew enough to try it, in spite of the fact that I didn't have my papers. (*He wrings his hands and looks exalted and wistful.*)

OFFICER: Spell compresstibility.

MAN: C-o-a . . . uh, er . . . p-e-r . . . er, oh I don't think I can spell that.

OFFICER: So you trying to bootleg to Brocklyn, eh? I ought to run you in! The nerve of some of you guys! And can't even spell compresstibility. That's what's the matter with the subway and the L–a whole lot of you amateurs trying to use 'em. Get on back uptown before I hang a charge on you. Beat it!

> (*The fellow turns to run off left and the cop stands akimbo glaring after him. Enter right a good-looking girl walking briskly with a suitcase, followed by a man.*)

MAN 5: Lois! Wait there a minute, baby.

LOIS: (*Sourly*) From not on, my name's lost so far as you're concerned. And otherwise, I don't want you following me around.

MAN 5: Can't a man follow his wife?

LOIS: He sho kin, but there ought to be a law against it. I done told you I don't want you no more, so give yo' shoe-leather a break.

MAN 5: Don't talk like that, baby. (*Reaches in his pocket and takes out a bill.*) Here, take this money and have us a good supper when I get home from work.

Lois: When you get home tonight, brother, I'll be
    spreading my junk in another town.

Man 5: Who with?

Lois: You wouldn't know, but, baby, I'm going to throw
    him some waves the ocean ain't never seen.

Man 5: (*Angrily*) Yeah, and you stand up here and tell me
    that just one more time and I'm going to beat you if
    they have a lawsuit in West Hell.

Lois: You better not hit me, nigger.

Man 5: I'll hit you just as sure as Jesus rode a jackass.

(She starts to walk off. He catches her arm)

Lois: Turn go of me, fool! I dare you to hit me! If you stick
    your rusty foot in *my* face you going to jail.

Man 5: How come I'm going to jail?

Lois: 'Cause there's a cop right there on the corner and I'm
    going to holler like a pretty white woman!

QUICK CURTAIN

THE HOUSE THAT JACK BUILT

CAST:

DE OTIS BLUNT
TEACHER
NELLIE
WALTER
GIRL 1
BOY 1
BOY 2
GIRL 2
BOY 3
OTHER STUDENTS

TIME: *Present.*

PLACE: *Deep South.*

SETTING: *A platform at left. Two practical windows in backdrop with a wall blackboard in between them. Two rows of benches.*

SCENE: *Old-fashioned schoolhouse.*

ACTION: *At the rise the pupils are all seated and attentive. The teacher is an aging man. They are large children and the girls are pretty. Everyone is neat and tidy but De Otis Blunt. He is seated in the last row next to the blackboard. Walter and Nellie are flirting.*

TEACHER: Remember this is Friday afternoon. As soon as we finish this lesson we'll go into the recitation exercise. (*To Walter and Nellie*) Pay attention to the lesson. (*There is a general buzz over the room. He raps for order.*) Who's doing all this talking? (*Fixes his eye on De Otis.*) Come out here, De Otis. I'll teach you how to keep on talkin' when I say quit.

DE OTIS: Aw, it twant me talkin'.

TEACHER: (*Angrily*) Come out here, sir!

DE OTIS: (*Sulkily rises*) Everybody is talkin' *but* me!

TEACHER: Come on out here, De Otis.

> (*De Otis reaches the platform and gets a couple of licks and starts on back. Several of the pupils make faces at him and he makes faces back. His back is towards the platform, but the teacher can see the faces the others are making.*)

TEACHER: (*To De Otis*) What are you makin' faces at these girls for? Come on back, De Otis.

DE OTIS: Aw, they makin' faces at me!

TEACHER: Come on back, De Otis. (*He goes angrily back to the desk and gets two more licks.*) Now see can't you behave yourself.

> (*De Otis resumes his seat. Nellie holds up her hand.*)

TEACHER: (*Flirtatiously*) What is it, Nellie?

NELLIE: May I be excused please?

TEACHER: Yes, dear, you may go. (*Walter lifts his hand.*) Well, what do *you* want?

WALTER: May I be excused?

TEACHER: No!

> (*Girl 1 sitting on front seat puts her foot on top of the desk. Teacher raises the ruler to reprimand her, but his curiosity gets the better of him and he sits staring up under her clothes. The school titters. He catches himself and frowns. He glares down at De Otis.*)

Come out here, De Otis.

DE OTIS: Aw, you just pickin' on me 'cause I ain't got no clothes. I ain't doin' nothin'.

(He goes up to the desk. While the teacher is thrashing him Walter sneaks out. De Otis returns to his seat and then the teacher misses the boy and looks frantic.)

TEACHER: Where's Walter?

GIRL 1: He excused himself.

TEACHER: (*Slams his ruler down in fury two or three times and knocks his roll book off the desk.*) Come out here, De Otis! Come on and fetch it to me! Don't make me have to come down there after it!

(De Otis pouts on up to the desk and gets a couple of licks in the hand and returns to his seat.)

TEACHER: (*To Boy 1*) Go tell Nellie and Walter to come here and don't come back here telling me you can't find 'em. (*The boy exits.*) Now we'll finish this spelling lesson and go on to the recitations. Anybody don't know a speech today will get a good whipping and be kept after school. (*Enter Walter, Nellie and Boy 1 who take their seats. To Walter*) Go to the board. (*Walter goes.*) Spell "mouse." (*Walter writes it correctly.*) Now spell "cat." (*Walter writes "pussy." Teacher gets very angry.*) I didn't ask you what kind of a cat! Where is your mind anyhow? (*Very wild*) Come out here De Otis!

DE OTIS: Aw, what I got to do wid it?

TEACHER: Come out here, De Otis!

(He comes grumbling and gets a licking.)

TEACHER: Now, we'll have the regular Friday afternoon exercise. Begin at the front seats and go back. (*He glances at Walter to begin.*)

WALTER: (*Comes to the platform and bows stiffly*) When I was a lil boy the girls all call me cousin—now I'm a big man, I love 'em by the dozen. (*He bows and resumes his seat.*)

NELLIE: (*Holds out her skirt and bows.*)

> Raccoon up de 'simmon tree
> Possum on de ground
> Raccoon shake de 'simmons down
> Possum pass 'em 'round

BOY 2: (*Comes up dancing and bows.*)
> Little boy, little boy, who made yo' britches?
> Mama did de cuttin' and papa did de stitches.

(He finishes with a "break" and takes his seat.)

GIRL 2: (*Frightened stiff—she sings-songs it rapid fire.*)
> I come from haunts of coot and hern
>> I make a sudden sally
> And sparkle out among the fern
> To bicker down the valley.
> I slip, I slide, I gloom, I glance
> Among my skinning swallows.
> I make the fretted sunbeams dance
> Above my shimmering shallows.

(She vainly tries to remember more, but after two or three false starts and much head and leg scratching, she retires weeping. All the rest say "I didn't learn none" or "I forgot mine," or "Some done said mine" till one boy in the next to the last seat.)

BOY 3:

> Little fishes in de brook
> Willie ketch 'um wid a hook
> Mama fry 'em in de pan
> Papa eat 'em like a man

TEACHER: It's your time, De Otis. Come on out.

DE OTIS: Somebody done said mine.

TEACHER: Well, you better say somebody else's or get a real good killin' and stay after school.

DE OTIS: (*Scratches his head, legs, back—then stands up.*) I believe I know one, sir.

TEACHER: You better had of found one. Come on up here.

(De Otis ascends the platform but does not bow. He puts one hand on his hip.)

DE OTIS:

Oh, this is the house that Jack built.

Oh, this is the malt that lay in de house that Jack built.

This is the rat that ate the malt that lay in the house that Jack built.

Oh-ah-h—this is the cat that killed the rat that ate the malt that lay in the house that Jack built.

Oh! This is the dog that worried the cat that killed the rat that ate the malt that lay in the house that Jack built.

(By this time he is walking back and forth across the platform and gesturing, and the others are keeping time with their feet. Even the teacher has joined in.)

This is the cow with the crumpled horn that tossed the dog that worried the cat that killed the rat that ate the malt that lay in the house that Jack built.

(All have left their seats and are dancing in chorus.)

A-ah—this is the maiden all forlorn that milked the cow with the crumpled horn that tossed the dog that worried the cat that killed the rat that ate the malt that lay in the house that Jack built.

Oh, this is the man all tattered and torn that kissed the maiden all forlorn that milked the cow with the crumpled horn that tossed the dog that worried the cat that killed the rat that ate the malt that lay in the house that Jack built.

A-a-ah–this is the priest all shaven and shorn that
married the man all tattered and torn that
kissed the maiden all forlorn that milked the
cow with the crumpled horn that tossed the
dog that worried the cat that killed the rat that
ate the malt that lay in the house that Jack
built.

Ah, this is the cock that crowed in the morn that
woke the priest all shaven and shorn that
married the man all tattered and torn that
kissed the maiden all forlorn that milked the
cow with the crumpled horn that tossed the
dog that worried the cat that killed the rat that
ate the malt that lay in the house that Jack
built.

Oh, this is the fox that lived under the thorn that
stole the cock that crowed in the morn that
woke the priest all shaven and shorn that
married the man all tattered and torn that
kissed the maiden all forlorn that milked the
cow with the crumpled horn that tossed the
dog that worried the cat that killed the rat that
ate the malt that lay in the house that Jack
built.

Ah–this is Jack with his hound and horn that
caught the fox that lived under the thorn
that stole the cock that crowed in the morn
that woke the priest all shaven and shorn that
married the man all tattered and torn that
kissed the maiden all forlorn that milked the
cow with the crumpled horn that tossed the
dog that worried the cat that killed the rat that
ate the malt that lay in the house that Jack
built.

Ah–this is the horse of the beautiful form that
carried jack with his hound and horn that

caught the fox that lived under the thorn
that stole the cock that crowed in the morn
that woke the priest all shaven and shorn that
married the men all tattered and torn that
kissed the maiden all forlorn that milked the
cow with the crumpled horn that tossed the
dog that worried the cat that killed the rat that
ate the malt that lay in the house that Jack
built.

Ah–this is the groom that ever morn curried
the horse of the beautiful form that carried
Jack with his hound and horn that caught
the fox that lived under the thorn that stole
the cock that crowed in the morn that woke
the priest all shaven and shorn that married
the man all tattered and torn that kissed the
maiden all forlorn that milked the cow with
the crumpled horn that tossed the dog that
worried the cat that killed the rat that ate the
malt that lay in the house that Jack built.

Ah–this is Sir John Barley Corn that owned the
horse of the beautiful form that carried Jack
with his hound and horn that caught the
fox that lived under the thorn that stole the
cock that crowed in the morn that woke
the priest all shaven and shorn that married
the man all tattered and torn that kissed the
maiden all forlorn that milked the cow with
the crumpled horn that tossed the dog that
worried the cat that killed the rat that ate the
malt that lay in the house that Jack built.

*(De Otis dances till he shudders down to the floor
and lies there shivering in rhythm.)*

BAHAMAS

CAST:
>GOOD BLACK
>JOE WILEY
>EMPEROR JONES
>MAN
>SEAMEN'S CHORUS
>DRUMMERS
>DANCERS

TIME: *Present.*

PLACE: *Harlem.*

SCENE: *Seventh Avenue at 135th street. Just a street scene on backdrop. At the rise, several persons are passing up and down avenue. All action from actors' right and left. Good Black is standing by himself as if waiting for someone. It is broad daylight. A man stops and speaks to him.*

MAN: Hello, Good Black, how you get 'em?

GOOD BLACK: Got the town by the tail, man. How they treating you?

MAN: Man, I got this town so skeered of me till the buildings lean backwards when I go down the streets. (*Looks Good Black over thoughtfully*) But you look kinda pentecostal to me, brother. What's the matter?

GOOD BLACK: (*Looking at his watch*) Joe Wiley told me to meet him here at one o'clock and here it is after two. I hates to wait on anybody–even myself.

MAN: (*Looks off right*) here he comes now. See you later.

>(*He exits right. Enter Joe Wiley with a cablegram in his*

hand. Very jovial)

JOE: I bet you done run a hot! (*Good Black sulks.*) Whew! I can smell the smoke! (*Good Black laughs in spite of himself.*)

GOOD BLACK: Nigger biddy, where you been all dis time? Got me tied out here croppin' grass like a mule.

JOE: (*Extends cablegram to Good Black who takes it and reads it*) I got that just as I started to leave home. Ain't that grand?

GOOD BLACK: (*Reading aloud*) "I am about to sail from the Bahamas for Africa, but I would like to see you again before I go. I am sending my flag-ship, The Bellamina, to bring you and your friends out. Signed: The Emperor Jones." (*Slaps Joe on the back*) Say, that's all to the mustard! Let's go.

JOE: (*Shakes hands and puts the cable in his pocket*) That's copasetty, man, just thirty-eight and two. I'm already packed.

GOOD BLACK: When will the boat be here?

JOE: Arrives tonight, sails for Nassau tomorrow.

GOOD BLACK: (*Making an exaggerated motion of tipping away*) Excuse me while I take a creep! I'm going to shake hands with the Emperor Jones. (*Starts towards right exit.*)

JOE: (*Seizes his arm and joins him*) Come, if you're coming, let's go if you're going.

> (*They tip their hats to the audience and exit joyfully. The curtain descends for a moment. A ship's siren can be heard and the sounds of anchor and chains etc. Shouts of greeting, etc. The curtain arises on the ship warping into Prince George's Wharf. The crew is singing "Caesar Riley." In the Bahamas. Joe and Good Black are standing on the deck as the boat comes in. The Emperor Jones in all his glory is standing on the wharf surrounded by a group of his*

nobles and ladies. He is making a speech.)

EMPEROR JONES: To Africa! When I get there with my
conquering black legions I am not going to ask
Great Britain what they are doing there. I'm just
going to say, "Get out!" (*Applause*) I'm not going to
ask France "What are *you* doing here?" I'm going to
say, "Get out!" I'm not going to ask Belgium "What
are *you* doing here?" I'm going to say "Get out!"
(*Great applause*) Ninety days from now I shall have
an ambassador at the Court of St. James. (*Applause*)
Ninety days from now I shall have an ambassador
at the Court of Paris. (*Applause*) Ninety days from
now I shall have an ambassador at the Court of St.
Petersburg. (*Hurrah!*) Ninety days from now I shall
have an ambassador at the court of Moscow. (*Applause*)
And ninety days from now, I shall have a Black House,
side by side with the White House in Washington.
(*Great storm of applause*) Board the fleet, let us sail for
Africa and freedom!

> *(The seamen on the wharf sing a salute to the ship as
> she comes in.)*

SEAMEN'S CHORUS:
> Bellamina, Bellamina, Bellamina in the harbor,
> Bellamina, Bellamina, Bellamina in the harbor.
> Put Bellamina on de dock
> Paint Bellamina bottom black.
> Oh the Maisie, Oh the Maisie, oh the Maisie set
> me crazy,
> Oh the Maisie, oh the Maisie, oh the Maisie set
> me crazy,
> Put Bellamina on de dock
> Paint Bellamina, black, black, black.

> *(As the song ends, Joe and Good Black descend
> the gangplank and are ceremoniously received by*

Emperor Jones.)

EMPEROR JONES: My old friend–Joe Wiley!

JOE: Your High and Mighty Majesty. (*Turns to Good Black*)
And this is my friend, Mr. Good Black, who wanted to
come along.

EMPEROR: Mighty glad to see you, Mr. Good Black. (*To Joe*)
I thought you might have brought some ladies along.

JOE: Sorry. The ones I could have got to come would have
been in my way (*he looks meaningly at the ladies*) after I
got here.

EMPEROR: I guess it's just as well you didn't. You know the
American girls are the snappiest lot on earth but you
have ruined 'em by giving 'em too much rope. Now
they are a whole woman and half a man. But let me
introduce you to the court. (*He stands between the
two and grows very rigid. The court circles about him in
review, as each passes and bows very low, he bawls out*)
Mr. Joe Wiley, Mr. Good Black, meet the Duke of
Egypt, Lady Carrie Hawkins, Sir Willie, Jenkins, K.
C. O. C.–Knight Commander of the Sublime Order
of the Congo, Sir Lemuel Nixon, General of the Black
Legions and Duke of Guinea, Sir Jasper Blunt, Earl of
Uganda, Lady Mittie Harris, Countess of the Nile.

> (*They all go back to their places singing "Don't You
> Hurry, Worry with Me" and vee vee voo.[2] Music of
> drums and cowbells are heard approaching.*)

JOE: What's that?[3]

> (*Parade passes in review.*)

EMPEROR: The John Canoe parade in your honor.

GOOD BLACK: Gee, that's swell–can I get in it or is it just
private?

EMPEROR: Save it for tonight. This is going to be tight like
so, boy! When night comes, we are holding a fire-
dance. To celebrate your coming and my departure

for Africa with my conquering black legions. (*Drums are heard at a distance as the lights continue to fade. It is dark almost at once.*) Hear those drums! Let's go to the fire-dance.

> (*Drums grow louder to a quick curtain. It goes up on a clearing in a tropic wood. It is lighted by a large bonfire to one side. Drummers near the fire. They are dancing when the curtain goes up. They are singing" "T-i-o, T-i-o, mama say T-i-o, mama say T-i-o." They sing one verse before the Emperor and his party arrive. Enter Emperor followed by party. He is very informal. He is joyfully jailed by the dancers.*)

EMPEROR: (*To drummers*) Heat up dat drum, boy, and knock me something!

DRUMMER: (*Holding drum over fire and tunes it*) That's it right now. (*When he gets it right he plays a flourish, dances a step, plays flourish again and cries.*) Gimbay!

> (*All the dancers begin to get excited. Everybody gets in the circle and begins to clap as the drums begin to play.*)

EMPEROR: (*Gets into the ring to dance, with three others. Sings*)

> Wish I had a nickel
> Wish I had a dime
> Wish I had a pretty girl
> To love me all the time.
> Down de road baby–
> Wish I had a needle
> Fine as I could sew
> I'd sew my baby to my side
> And down the road I'd go.
>
> (Refrain) Down the road, baby–

*(The drums flourish and change to new rhythm. Four
dancers enter ring.)*

Bimini gal is a hell of a trouble
Never get licking till you go down to Bimini
Eh, lemme go down to Bimini
Never get a licking till you go down to Bimini.

*(Drums flourish and change rhythm. Three dancers
enter ring.)*

Mama, I saw a sail boat
A-sailing in the harbor
I saw a yaller boy aboard it
And I took him to be my lover.
It's killing mama, etc.

(Drums flourish and change rhythm)

Went to Key West to buy me a dress
How you going to make it ripple tail
How you going to shake it, shake it, shake it.

(Song changes)

Lime, oh lime juice and all
Lime, oh lime, 'Dessa hold your back
Dessa hold your back,
Odessa, Odessa, Odessa.

*(Drums flourish and change rhythm. One dancer
enters ring.)*

Mother may I go to school?
Yes, my darling, you may go
You may put on a ribbon bow.
Why you wheel Miss Curry so?
Wheel Miss Curry buck her so
Wheel Miss Curry, wheel Miss Curry,
Wheel Miss Curry, etc.
Mama, Mama, the old gray cat, she get so fat

She will not run at the old she-rat
Children lose de fine tooth comb
And head run away wid de lice
Oh, something in de hand more than common
Something in de hand more than common.

(*Drums flourish and change rhythm.*)

Mama lay! de drum bust!
Mama lay! de drum bust!
    Oh, when I do so, do so,
Oh, when I do so, do so,
Oh, when I do so, do so
De drum bust!

(*Quick curtain. When it goes up again the Emperor is in front leading the crowd.*)

EMPEROR: To the ships. Let us sail for Africa!

(*Song: "Hoist Up de John B. Sail." Singing offstage.*)

Bellamina, Bellamina, Bellamina in the harbor,
Bellamina, Bellamina, Bellamina in the harbor,
Put Bellamina on the dock
Paint Bellamina bottom black.

CURTAIN

RAILROAD CAMP

CAST:
> CAP'N
> CREW MAN 1
> CREW MAN 2
> CREW MAN 3
> CREW MAN 4
> CREW MAN 5
> WATER BOY

PLACE: *Railroad track in Florida.*
TIME: *Present.*
SETTING: *Palmettos, oak trees hung with Spanish moss on the backdrop. In the foreground a length of railroad track on an embankment. A hand car stands at right end of track.*
ACTION: *Ten men are spiking rails with sledge hammers. The boss is squatting up the line and signaling corrections. The water boy has a pail and dipper and stands in the middle of the track and leads the singing. At the rise they are singing.*

CREW:
> Dat ol' (*wham*) black gal (*wham*)
> She keep on grumblin' (*wham*)
> New pair shoes (*wham*), new pair shoes (*wham*).
> I'm goin' (*wham*) buy her (*wham*)
> Shoes and stockings (*wham*), slippers too (*wham*)
>> slippers too (*wham*).
> I'm goin' (*wham*) buy her
> Draws and dresses (*wham*) shimmy too (*wham*)
>> shimmy too (*wham*).

CAP'N: Line it!

CREW: *(They drop hammers and grab lining bars and sing:)*
When I go and come agin'
You won't know me from Nappy Chin.
Boys, can't you line it, boys can't you shake it!

(The Cap'n hollers "whoop!" The crew moves to another length.)

CAP'N: Jonah head!

CREW: *(Sings)*
Cap'n keep a hollerin' 'bout Jonah heed
Dis linin' bar 'bout to kill me dead.
Boys, can't you line it, boys, can't you shake it.

CAP'N: Whoop! Center head!

CREW:
Me and my gal goin' 'cross de field
Heard 31 when it left Mobile
Boys, can't you line it, boys, can't you shake it.

CAP'N: Center back!

CREW:
Me and my partner and two, three more
Standin' on de corner seein' de 'gator roar
Boys, can't you line it, boys, can't you shake it.

CAP'N: Whoop!

CREW:
Hear a mighty rumblin' round de river bend
Must be de Southern crossin' de L and N.

Boys, can't you line it, boys can't you shake it.

CAP'N: Whoop!

CREW:

Wake up in de mornin' hear de ding dong ring
Look on de table see de same old thing.
Boys, can't you line it, boys, can't you shake it.

CAP'N: Center head!

CREW:

Tip at de White House, tip at de gate
I got a gal got a Cadillac "8"
Boys, can't you line it, boys, can't you shake it.

CAP'N: Center back!

CREW:

Line it, boys, and don't get lost
Ain't no heben for de section boss.
Boys, can't you line it, boys, can't you shake it.

CAP'N: Hammer gang!

(Men drop lining bars and get hammers)

CREW:

Mr. Bugan (wham) on de L and N (wham)
Got de pay car (wham) on de rear end (wham)

CAP'N: Whip steel!

CREW:

Mr. Davenport (wham) got de new store (wham)
Behind de depot (wham) whyncher pick 'em
Set 'em over (wham)

CAP'N: Whip it hot!

CREW:

> I got a woman she's pretty but she's too bull
>   dozin',
> I got a woman she's pretty but she's too bull
>   dozin',
> She won't live long, Lord, Lord, she won't live
>   long.
>
> I got a woman, she's got money 'cumulated,
> I got a woman, she's got money 'cumulated
> In de bank, Lord, Lord, in de bank.
>
> Big fat woman shakes like jelly all over,
> Big fat woman shakes like jelly all over
> When she walk, Lord, Lord, when she walk.
>
> Every pay day de wimmen all call me daddy,
> Every pay day de wimmen all call me daddy
> I wonder why, Lord, Lord, I wonder why.
>
> Bad Lazarus set on de commissary counter,
> Bad Lazarus set on de commissary counter
> And walked away, Lord, Lord, and walked away.
>
> High-sheriff told de deppity, see can you find Bad
>   Laz'rus
> High-sheriff told de deppity, see can you find Bad
>   Laz'rus
> Dead or live, Lord, Lord, dead or live.
>
> Deppity ast de sheriff where in de world can I find
>   him,
> Deppity ast de sheriff where in de world can I find

him
I don't know, Lord, Lord, I don't know.

And they found him way up in between two
    mountains,
And they found him way up in between two
    mountains
With head hung down, Lord, Lord, with head
    hung down.

And they blowed him, blowed him with a great
    big number,
And they blowed him, blowed him with a great
    big number,
A forty-five, Lord, Lord, a forty-five.

Laz'rus cried out, turn me over on my wounded
Laz'rus cried out, turn me over on my wounded
My wounded side, Lord, Lord, my wounded side.

And they drug him, drug Bad Laz'rus to his
    shanty,
And they drug him, drug Bad Laz'rus to his shanty
On his wounded side, Lord, Lord, his wounded
    side.

Laz'rus cried out, bring me a cool drink of water,
Laz'rus cried out, bring me a cool drink of water
I'm burning down, Lord, Lord, I'm burning
    down.

I got a wife and two or three chillun on de
    mountain,
I got a wife and two or three chillun on de
    mountain
Cryin' for bread, Lord, Lord, cryin' for bread.

> Laz'rus daddy went running to de field and crying,
> Laz'rus daddy went running to de field and crying
> Whoa, har, gee Lord, Lord, whoa, har, gee.
>
> Laz'rus mother come running and crying,
> Laz'rus mother come running and crying
> Done kilt my son, Lord, Lord, done kilt my son.
>
> I can stand right here and look 'way over in
>   Alabama,
> Stand right here and look 'way over in Alabama
> It look so far, Lord, Lord, it look so far.
>
> When I get back to Georgy southern Alabama,
> When I get back to Georgy southern Alabama
> Be long farewell, Lord, Lord, be long farewell.

CREW MAN 1: Water boy!

> *(Boy carries him water, he lifts the dipper and drinks and squirts some from his mouth on the ground.)*

CREW MAN 1: Say, nigger biddy, dis water is hotter'n two boxes of matches–go git some fresh water!

WATER BOY: I'm Mr. Pickhandle Slim, when you get time–lousy wid bucks! Got money's mama and grandma's change.

CREW MAN: Aw, boy, go 'head on get some cool water before I be all over you just like gravy over rice–you must smell yo'self.

REST OF CREW: Aw yeah, he's gettin' too mannish. Go 'head and get us a cool drink.

> *(Boy exits left.)*

CAP'N: Line it!

> *(The crew exchange hammers for bars. Water boy*

returns. The crew take their places and sing.)

CREW:

When I get in Illinois,
I'm going to spread de news about de Florida
    boys.
Shove it over! Hey, hey, can't you line it
(Shaking rail and grunt at the end)
Can't you move it.

Me and my buddy and two, three more
Going to ramshack Georgy everywhere we go.
Shove it over! Hey, hey can't you line it
Can't you move it.

Tell you what de hobo told de bum
Get any cornbread save me some.
Shove it over! Hey, hey can't you line it
Can't you move it.

Cap'n got a burner I'd like to have
A thirty-two twenty wid a shiny barrel.
Shove it over! Hey, hey can't you line it
Can't you move it.

Cap'n got a special he try to play bad
But I'm going to take it if he makes me mad.
Shove it over! Hey, hey can't you line it
Can't you move it.

Here come a woman walkin' 'cross de field
Mouth exhaustin' like an automobile
Shove it over! Hey, hey can't you line it
Can't you move it.

Wake up, Cap'n, and light yo' lamp

Highway robbers is in yo' camp.
Shove it over! Hey, hey can't you move it
Can't you line it.

Come on, honey, let's go to bed
Get a lil baby and name him Red.
Shove it over! Hey, hey can't you move it
Can't you line it.

If lil Sissy was a gal of mine
She shouldn't do nothin' but starch and iron.
Shove it over! Hey, hey can't you move it
Can't you line it.

Whut's de matter wid de Cap'n he must be cross
It's done five-thirty and he won't knock off.
Shove it over! Hey, hey can't you move it
Can't you line it.

(A whistle blows in the distance and the Cap'n signals that work is over. The men hurriedly pile the tools on the hand car and climb on, and four of them get to the handles.)

CREW MAN 2: Come on let's go! I got a belly like Eatin' Flukus today.

CREW MAN 3: Who was dis Eatin' Flukus?

CREW MAN 2: He et up camp meetin', backed off Association and drank Jordan dry.

REST OF CREW: That's me right now, let's go!

(They begin to work the handles and one of the crew sings:)

CREW MAN 4:
Oh Lulu, oh gal, want to see you so bad.

CREW MAN 5:

> Blow it like and elephant and do it like an airdale.

(Breaks out with another song.)

> Gointer see my long-haired babe,
> Gointer see my long-haired babe,
> Lord, I'm going cross de water
> To see my long-haired babe.
> Whut you reckon Mr. Treadwell said to Mr. Goff
> Lord, I b'lieve I'll go South
> And pay they poor boys off.

(Slow curtain as this is sung)

> Lord, I ast dat woman
> To lemme be her kid.
> And she looked at me
> And begin to smile
> Said I b'lieve I'll try you
> For my kid awhile.

(Last two lines ought to be sung after curtain is down.)

JOOK

CAST:
> NUNKIE
> STACK-OF-DOLLARS
> BUNK
> BLACK-BOY
> SACK-DADDY
> BIG-SWEET
> PLANCHITA
> JAMES PRESLEY
> ELLA WARD
> DRAWS-LEG
> BLUE-FRONT
> MUTTSY

PLACE: *A saw-mill jook house.*

TIME: *Present.*

SCENE: *Interior of main room in the jook. There is a dilapidated piano in one corner. A small rough table against the wall in the upstage corner. There are a few chairs scattered around against the wall.*

ACTION: *When the curtain goes up, Nunkie is at the piano playing and singing. There are three couples on the floor slow-dragging and joining in with the singing in spots.*

NUNKIE: (*Singing*)
> Babe, I'm lonesome, I'm the lonesomest man in your town.
> Got experience of women—small town turnt me down.

Aw, I wants to tell you people whut de Florida
    East Coast done for me.
Took my regular—come and got my used-to-be.

Say, look here sweet baby, you sho don't know my
    mind,
When you see me laughing, laughing just to keep
    from crying.

If you ever been down you know just how I feel.
I been down so long, down don't worry me.

Says, storm is rising, wind begin to blow
My house done blowed down, I ain't got no place
    to go.

Roll me wid yo' stomach, feed me wid yo' tongue
Do it a long time baby till de sunshine come.

I'd rather be in Tampa, wid de whippoorwill
Than to be 'round here, baby, with a hundred
    dollar bill.

I'd rather see my coffin rolling in my door,
Than my baby to tell me she don't want me no
    more.

I'm sittin' here lookin' a thousand miles away,
I'm going to pack up my suitcase and make my
    getaway.

Says, my heart struck sorrow, tears come rolling
    down.
Says, it seem like, baby, I'm got to leave this town.

> If anybody ast you, baby, who composed this
>   song,
> Tell 'em Little Johnny Barton, he been here and
>   gone.
>
> *(Enter Draws-leg at left and gets to the center of
> the floor. He joins in the song and turns about half
> dancing.)*

DRAWS-LEG: Here! Gimme a woman. I cant do all this by
myself. (*To one of the men*) Say there Bunk, lend me
Planchita for a hot minute, do I wont git well.

> *(He pulls the girl away from the other man who
> laughs it off. He and Planchita begin to dance fancy.
> Bunk walks towards the right exit and looks offstage.
> Nunkie begins to play very fast and the dancers laugh
> and keep up with the music as long as they can.
> When Draws-leg and Planchita laughingly give up
> like the rest, Nunkie stops playing and turns from the
> piano laughing.)*

BUNK: (*Looking into the room off right*) Hey, Black-Boy,
how you doing it?

BLACK-BOY: (*off stage*) Come on in here and find out.

BUNK: Aw, naw! Y'all ain't goingter hem me up in there!
Come on out here so when I wins yo' money, I got a
running chance.

> *(General laughter and the noise of scraping chairs.
> Enter Black-Boy, Stack-of-Dollars, Blue-Front and
> Muttsy. They stroll straight for the table and begin to
> place chairs.)*

STACK: Now, Bunk, you been bugabooing 'round here;
come here and lemme see if you know anything about
skinning.

> *(All the men but Nunkie gather about the table.
> Nunkie plays softly and sings in a whisper along with*

him. The game begins with Black-Boy dealing.)

BUNK: (Pointing to his card) See dat deuce? It's going to carry de whole deck down.

STACK: I don't b'lieve it.

BLUE-FRONT: I bet you a fat man I'll be here last.

BUNK: A dollar I knows de best one!

STACK: A stack of dollars you don't. Deal!

BLACK BOY: Let de deal go down, boys. (*Sings*)

> When yo' card gets lucky, oh partner,
> You oughter be in a rollin' game.
> Let de deal go down, boys,
> Let de deal go down.
> Lost all my money, oh partner,
> In the rollin' game.
> Let de deal go down, boys,
> Let de deal go down.

BUNK: (*Threatening*) I see you peepin them card, Black-Boy!

BLACK-BOY: (*Laughing*) Aw, I ain't tryin to carry no cub— y'all too wise for dat.

BUNK: I don't mind you winnin my money, but if you try to beat me out of it, if God send me a pistol, I'll send him a man.

STACK: (*To Bunk*) You know he ain't gointer try nothin funny in here. He know us ain't no fools. They kilt Fat Sam shootin at Big Boy so all de fools in de world is done dead. Let de deal go down.

ALL: (*As they play cards*)

> I'm going back to de 'bama, where
> They don't want no change.
> Let de deal go down, boys,
> Let de deal go down.
> No mo' rollin' partner,
> Till de man pay off.

> Let de deal go down, boys,
> Let de deal go down.

STACK: Hey, hey! There you go, Blue-Front. You done fell.

ALL: (*As two more cards are dealt off the deck*)

> Ain't had no trouble, partner,
> Till I stop by here.
> Let de deal go down, boys,
> Let de deal go down.

STACK: Dat's yo' cup Sack-Daddy! Here come Bunk!
(*Laughs triumphantly*) This must be de fall of de year.
Now it me and Black-Boy. So good a man, so good a
man!

ALL: (*As three cards fall*)

> When I get in de 'bama, partner,
> Won't be troubled wid you.
> Let de deal go down, boys,
> Let de deal go down.
> Let de deal go down, boys,
> Let de deal go down.

STACK: I'm de best! (*Rakes in the pot.*) I'm too hard for you
boys. Who wants to skin me? Who wants me, any,
some or none?

SACK-DADDY: I hear you cracklin, I know yo' nest ain't far.
Shuffle 'em, Black-Boy and less go.

BIG-SWEET: (*Crosses to the table and lays her hand9,. on the
cards.*) Don't skin no more, Sack-Daddy. Read de deck
for me.

SACK-DADDY: I ain't goin to read nothing till you tell me
who you shacked up wid. A man is liable to get shot
lessen he know something.

BIG-SWEET: Aw, stop woofin and read dem cards.

SACK-DADDY: All right, Big-Sweet. (*He takes up the cards
and walks to the center of the stage. As he calls off a card*

he lets it fall to the floor.)

> Ace means the first time that I met you
> Deuce means there was nobody there but us two
> Trey means the third party, Charlie was his name
> Four spot means the fourth time you tried that
>   same old game
> Five spot means five years you played me for a
>   clown
> Six spot means six feet of earth when the deal goes
>   down
> Now I'm holding the seven for each day in the
>   week
> Eight spot means eight hours that you sheba'ed
>   with your sheik
> Nine spot means nine hours that I work hard
>   every day
> Ten spot means tenth of every month I brought
>   you home my pay
> The jack is Three-card Charlie who played me for
>   a goat
> The queen, that's you pretty mama, also trying to
>   cut my throat
> The king stands for sweet papa Sack-Daddy and
>   he's going to wear the crown
> So be be careful y'all ain't flat-footed when de deal
>   goes down.

PLANCHITA: Now you done gimme de blues. Play
    something, Nunkie.

NUNKIE: You always holler play, but you don't never put
    out nothin.

PLANCHITA: (*Arms akimbo*) Who, me? I ain't putting out
    nothin but old folks' eyes, and I ain't doin that till they
    dead. I'm like de cemetery, I'm takin in but never no
    put out.

(Nunkie starts to play. All start to dance.)

ALL:

    See you when yo' troubles get like mine.
    See you when yo' troubles get like mine.
    See you when yo' troubles get like mine.

    Wonder will he answer if I write.
    See you when yo' troubles get like mine.
    See you when yo' troubles get like mine.

    All of my Sunday clothes in pawn.
    See you when yo' troubles get like mine.
    See you when yo' troubles get like mine.

    Comin' a time when a woman won't need no man.
    See you when yo' troubles get like mine.
    See you when yo' troubles get like mine.

    Don't you hear that East Coast when she blow?
    See you when yo' troubles get like mine.
    See you when yo' troubles get like mine.

    Blow like she never blowed before.
    See you when yo' troubles get like mine.
    See you when yo' troubles get like mine.

    Make me down a pallet on de floor.
    See you when yo' troubles get like mine.
    See you when yo' troubles get like mine.

    Laid in jail my back turned to de wall.
    See you when yo' troubles get like mine.
    See you when yo' troubles get like mine.

    Going down de long lonesome road.
    See you when yo' troubles get like mine.
    See you when yo' troubles get like mine.

BIG-SWEET: (*Leans up against the piano and all but weeps*)
God I wish I knowed where I could slip up on a

drunk! (*Sound of a guitar is heard offstage left. She jumps up with pleasure.*) God I b'lieve that's James Presley. (*Rushes across to left exit.*) Dat James! Come on in here and play me something.

> (*Enter James Presley with a guitar around his neck. Everybody greets him. They get him a seat and a drink. He tunes up.*)

JAMES: (*To Nunkie*) You fram behind me.

NUNKIE: Allright, less go. Somebody git me another drink. (*It is brought.*)

JAMES AND NUNKIE:

> Cold rainy day, some old cold rainy day
> I'll be back some old cold rainy day.
>
> All I want is my railroad fare [*etc.*]
>
> Old Smoky Joe, Lord, he died on the road
> Saying I'll be home some day.
>
> Cold rainy day, some old cold rainy day
> I'll be back some old cold rainy day.
>
> Oh, de rocks may be my pillow, Lord,
> De sand may be my bed.
> I'll be back some old cold rainy day.
>
> (*While the musicians play the others sing and dance. The men yell out in exuberance as they dance slowly and sensuously.*)

BLACK BOY: Oh, what evil have I done. Roll yo' hips—don't roll yo' eyes.

SACK-DADDY: Turn it on and let de bad luck happen—Shake yo' hips, mama.

STACK: Ten dollars for a whoop, six bits for a squallA If you can't shimmy, shake yo' head.

BUNK: I hear you cacklin, mama, I know yo' nest ain't far. Don't you vip another vop till I get in there.

(As the dance comes to a close, the musicians drift on into "John Henry," and Ella Ward grabs a guitar out of the corner beside the piano and walks to the center of the stage and put one foot up on the chair and begins to sing the verses to a slow curtain.)

ELLA:

John Henry driving on de right-hand side
Steam drill driving on de left,
Says 'fore I loet yo' steam drill beat me down
I'll hammer my fool self to death.
I'll hammer my fool self to death.

Captain ast John Henry
"What is dat storm I hear?"
He said, "Cap'n dat ain't no storm
Nothin' but my hammer in de air,
Nothin' but my hammer in de air."

John Henry had a lil baby
Holdin' him in his right hand,
Says, "Lil baby don't you cry
You'll never be a steel drivin' man,
You'll never be a steel drivin' man."

John Henry told his cap'n,
"Bury me under de sills of de floor
So when they get to playin' good old Georgy skin
Bet 'em fifty to a dollar more,
Bet 'em fifty to a dollar more."

John Henry had a lil woman
De dress she wore was red.
Says, "I'm goin' down de track,"
And she never looked back,
"I'm goin' where John Henry fell dead,
I'm goin' where John Henry fell dead."

Who gointer shoe yo' pretty lil feet?

Who gointer glove yo' hand?
Who gointer kiss yo' rosy cheek?
Who gointer be yo' man?
Who gointer be yo' man?

"My father's goin' to shoe my pretty lil feet,
My brother's goin' to glove my hand,
My sister's goin' to kiss my rosy cheek,
John Henry gointer be my man,
John Henry gointer be my man."

Says, "Where did you get yo' pretty lil dress,
De shoes you wear so fine?"
"I got my shoes from a railroad man,
My dress from a man in de mines,
My dress from a man in de mines."

CURTAIN

De Turkey and De Law (1930)

A Comedy in Three Acts

CAST:

Methodists:

JIM WESTON,
    the town bully
WALTER THOMAS
HOYT THOMAS,
    Walter's wife
LIGE MOSELEY
REVEREND SIMMS

LUCY TAYLOR
IDA JONES
SHANK NIXON
MRS. NIXON
WILLIE
MRS. MCDUFFY
MRS. ANDERSON

Baptists:

DAVE CARTER,
    town's best hunter
    and fisherman
JOE CLARKE,
    Mayor & storekeeper
TOD HAMBO,
    the church deacon

JOE LINDSAY
REVEREND SINGLETARY
DELLA LEWIS
Mary Ella
MRS. LINDSAY, Joe's wife
MRS. HAMBO, Tod's wife

Others:

DAISY BLUNT, town vamp
LUM BAILEY,
    town marshall
ESSIE
HAWK
LULU
JENNY

BOOTSIE
TEETS
BIG 'OMAN
MRS. BLUNT
OTHER CHILDREN,
    METHODISTS, BAPTISTS

ACT ONE

SCENE 1.

SETTING: *A Negro village in Florida in our own time.*
PLACE: *Joe Clarke's store porch in the village. A frame building with a false front. A low porch with two steps up. Door in center of porch. A window on each side of the door. A bench on each side of the porch. Axhandles, hoes, and shovels, etc. are displayed leaning against the wall. Exits right and left. Street is unpaved. Grass and weeds growing all over.*
TIME: *It is late afternoon on a Saturday in summer.*

> *Before the curtain rises the voices of children are heard, boisterous at play. Shouts and laughter.*

BOY'S VOICE: Naw, I don't want to play wringing no dish rag! We gointer play chick mah chick mah craney crow.

ESSIE'S VOICE: Yeah, less play dat, and I'm gointer to be de hen.

BOY'S VOICE: And I'm gointer be de hawk. Lemme git myself a stick to mark wid.

> *(The curtain rises slowly. As it goes up the game is being organized. The boy who is the hawk is squatting center stage in the street before the store with a short twig in his hand. Essie, the largest girl, is lining up the other children behind her.)*

ESSIE: *(Looking back over her flock)* Y'all ketch holt of one

'nother's clothes so de hawk can't git yuh. *(They do.)*
Y'all straight now?

CHORUS: Yeah.

(The march around the hawk commences.)

ESSIE AND CHICKS:

> Chick mah chick mah craney crow
> Went to de well to wash my toe.
> When I come back my chick was gone.
> What time ole witch?

HAWK: *(Making a tally on the ground)* One!

ESSIE AND CHICKS: Chick mah chick, etc.

> *(While this is going on Walter Thomas, eating
> peanuts from a bag, appears from the store door and
> seats himself on the porch beside the steps.)*

HAWK: *(Scoring again)* Two!

> *(Enter a little girl right. She trots up to the big girl.)*

LITTLE SISTER: *(Officiously)* Titter, mama say if you don't
come on wid dat soap she gointer wear you out.

ESSIE AND CHICKS: Chick mah chick, etc.

> *(While this is being sung, enter Joe Lindsay, who seats
> himself on right bench. He lights his pipe. The little
> girl stands by the fence rubbing her leg with her foot.)*

HAWK: *(Scoring)* Three!

LITTLE SISTER: *(Insistent)* Titter, titter! Mama say to tell you
to come on home wid dat soap and rake up dat yard. I
bet she gointer beat you good.

ESSIE: *(Angrily)* Aw naw, mama ain't sent you after me,
nothin' of de kind. Gwan home and leave me alone.

LITTLE SISTER: You better come on! I'm gointer tell mama
how 'omanish you actin' cause you in front of dese
boys.

ESSIE: *(Makes a threatening gesture)* Aw don't be so fast and showin' off in company. Ack lak you ain't got no sense!

LITTLE SISTER: *(Starts to cry)* Dat's all right. I'm going home and tell mama you down here playing wid boys and she sho gointer whup you good, too. I'm gointer tell her you called me a fool too, now. *(She walks off, wiping her eyes and nose with the back of her hand)* Yeah, I'm goin' tell her! Jus' showin' off in front of ole John Wesley Taylor. I'm going to tell her too, now.

ESSIE: *(Flounces her skirt)* Tell her! Tell her! Turn her up and smell her! *(Game resumes.)* Chick mah chick, etc.

HAWK: Four! *(He rises and imitates a hawk flying and trying to catch a chicken. Calling in a high voice.)* Chickie!

ESSIE: *(Flapping her wings to protect her young)* My chickens 'sleep.

HAWK: Chickie!

ESSIE: My chickens 'sleep.

HAWK: I shall have a chick.

ESSIE: You shan't have a chick.

HAWK: I'm going home. *(Flies off.)*

ESSIE: There's de road.

HAWK: I'm comin' back.

> *(During this dialog the hawk is feinting and darting in his efforts to catch a chicken and the chickens are dancing defensively.)*

ESSIE: Don't keer if you do.

HAWK: My pot's a-boiling.

ESSIE: Let it boil.

HAWK: My guts a-growling.

ESSIE: Let 'em growl.

HAWK: I must have a chick.

ESSIE: You shan't have nairn.

HAWK: My mama's sick.

ESSIE: Let her die.

HAWK: Chickie!

ESSIE: My chickens 'sleep.

> *(Hawk darts quickly around the hen and grabs a chicken and leads him off and places the captive on his knees at the store porch. After a brief bit of dancing he catches another, then a third who is a chubby little boy. The little boy begins to cry.)*

LITTLE BOY: I ain't gointer play 'cause you hurt me.

HAWK: Aw, naw, I didn't hurt you.

LITTLE BOY: Yeah you did too. You pecked me right here. *(Points to top of his head)*

HAWK: Well if you so touchous you got to cry every time anybody look at you, you can't play wid us.

LITTLE BOY: *(Smothering sobs)* I ain't cryin'.

> *(He is placed with the other captives. Hawk returns to game.)*

HAWK: Chickie.

ESSIE: My chickens 'sleep!

VOICE FROM A DISTANCE: Titter! You Titter

ESSIE: Yessum.

VOICE: If you don't come here wid dat soap you better!

ESSIE: *(Shakes herself poutingly, half sobs)* Soon's I git grown I'm gointer run away. Everytime a person gits to havin' fun, it's "come here, Titter and rake de yard." She don't never make Bubber do nothing. *(She exits into the store.)*

HAWK: Now we ain't got no hen.

ALL THE GIRLS: *(In a clamor)* I'll be de mama hen! Lemme be it!

> *(Enter Hambo left and stands looking at the children.)*

HAMBO: Can't dese young uns keep up a powerful racket, Joe?

LINDSAY: They sho kin. They kin git round so vig'rous

when they whoopin and hollerin and rompin and
racin, but just put 'em to work now and you kin count
dead lice fallin' off of 'em.

> *(Enter Essie from the store with the soap. Hambo
> pulls out a plug of tobacco from his hip pocket and
> bites a chunk from it.)*

HAMBO: De way dese chillun is dese days is, – Eat? Yes!
Squall and holler? Yes! Kick out shoes? Yes! Work?
No!

LINDSAY: You sho is tellin' de truth. Now look at dese! I'll
bet every one of 'em's mammies sent 'em to de store
an' they out here frollickin'. If one of 'em was mine,
I'd whup 'em till they couldn't set down. *(To the
children)* Shet up dat racket and gwan home!

> *(The children pay no attention and the game gets
> hotter.)*

VOICE: *(offstage)* You Tit-ter! You Tit-ter!

WALTER: Titter, don't you hear yo' ma callin' you?

TITTER: Yassuh, I mean naw suh.

LINDSAY: How come you can't answer then? Lawd knows
de folks just ruins chilluns dese deys. Deys skeered tuh
whup 'em right. Den before they gits twenty de gals
done come up wid somethin' in dey arms an' de boys
on de chain gang. If you don't whip 'em, they'll whip
you.

HAMBO: Dat sho is whut de Lawd loves. When I wuz a
boy they *raised* chillen then. Now they lets 'em do
as they please. There ain't no real chastising no more.
They takes a lil tee-ninchy switch and tickles 'em. No
wonder de world is in sich uh mess.

VOICE OFFSTAGE: You Tit-ter! Aw Titter!

ESSIE: *(Stops to listen)* Yessum!

VOICE OFFSTAGE: If you don't come here, you better!

ESSIE: Yassum! *(To her playmates)* Aw shucks! I got to go

home.

*(She exits right, walking sullenly. The game has
stopped.)*

LINDSAY: *(Pointing at Essie)* You see dat gal shakin' herself at
her mammy? De sassy lil bitch needs her guts stomped
out. *(To Essie)* Run! I'm comin' on down there an'
tell yo' ma how 'omanish you is, shakin' yo'self at
grown folks. *(Essie walks slower and shakes her skirt
contemptuously. Lindsay jumps to his feet as if to pursue
her.)* You must smell yo'self! *(Essie exits.)* Now de rest of
you Haitians scatter 'way from in front dis store. Dis
ain't no place for chillen, nohow. *(Gesture of shooing)*
Gwan! Thin out! Every time a grown person open they
mouf y'all right dere to gaze down they throat. Git!

*(The children exit sullenly right. In the silence that
follows the cracking of Walter's peanut shells can be
heard very plainly.)*

HAMBO: Walter, God a'mighty! You better quit eatin' them
ground peas de way you do. You gointer die wid de
colic.

LINDSAY: Aw, tain't gointer hurt him. I don't b'lieve uh cord
uh wood would lay heavy on Walter's belly. He kin eat
mo' penders than Brazzle's mule.

WALTER: *(Laughing)* Aw naw, don't throw me in wid
dat mule. He could eat up camp-meetin, back off
'sociation and drink Jordan dry.

LINDSAY: And still stay so po' till he wuzn't nothin' atall but
a mule frame. *(Enter Lige Moseley right.)* Tain't never
been no mule in de world lak dat ole yaller mule since
Jonah went to Joppy.

*(Lige seats himself on the floor on the other side of the
steps. Pulls out a bone toothpick and begins to pick
his teeth.)*

LIGE: Y'all still talking bout Brazzle's ole useter-be mule?

HAMBO: Yeah. 'Member dat time Brazzle hitched him to de plow and took him to Eshleman's new ground?

LIGE: And he laid down before he'd plow a lick. Sho I do! But who ever seen him work? All you ever did see was him and Brazzle fightin up and down de furrows. *(All laugh.)* He was so mean he would even try to kick you if you went in his stall to carry him some corn.

WALTER: Nothin but pure concentrated meanness stuffed into uh mule hide. Thass de reason he wouldn't git fat – just too mean.

LIGE: Sho was skinny now. You could use his ribs for a washboard and hang de clothes up on his hips to dry. *(All laugh.)*

HAMBO: Lige, you kin lie lak cross ties from Jacksonville to Key West. But layin all sides to jokes, when they told me dat mule was dead, uh just took and knocked off from work to see him drug out lak all de rest of de folks, and folkses dat mule wuz too contrary to lay down on his side and die. He laid on his raw-boney back wid his foots stickin straight up in de air lak he wuz fightin something.

LINDSAY: He wuz – bet he fought ole death lak a natural man. Ah seen his bones yistiddy, out dere on de edge of de cypress swamp. De buzzards done picked 'em clean and de elements done bleached 'em.

LIGE: Everybody went to dat draggin out. Even Joe Clarke shet up his store dat mornin' and went *(turns his head and calls into the store)* didn't you, Mr. Clarke?

CLARKE: *(offstage)* Didn't I whut? *(Enters and stands in door)*

LIGE: Shet up yo' store and go to de draggin out of Brazzle's ole mule.

CLARKE: God, yeah. It was worth it. *(Sees Hambo)* I didn't know you was out here. Lemme beat you uh game of checkers.

HAMBO: Lissen at de ole tush hawg! Well, go git de board,

and lemme beat you a pair of games befo' de mail gits in.

CLARKE: *(To others)* Beat old me! *(To Hambo)* Come on here, you'se my fish. *Calls into store)* Mattie bring me dat checkerboard and de checkers! *(To men on porch)* You got to talk to wimmen-folks lak dat – tell 'em every lil thing do, she'd come rackin out here wid de board by itself.

> *(Enter Mrs. Clarke with homemade checkerboard and coffee can containing the much-used checkers. Clarke sits on a keg and faces Hambo. They put the board on their knees and pour out the checkers.)*

HAMBO: You want black or red?
CLARKE: Oh, I don't keer which – I'm gointer beat you anyhow. You take de black.

> *(They arrange them. The others get near to look on. Hambo sits looking at the board without moving.)*

HAMBO: Who's first move?
CLARKE: Black folks always go to work first. Move!

> *(Hambo moves and the same proceeds with the spectators very interested. Enter Lum Bailey right and joins the spectators. A woman enters left with a market basket and goes on into the store. The checkers click on the board. A girls about twelve enters right and goes into the store and comes out with a stick of peppermint candy.)*

WALTER: Naw you don't Hambo! – Don't you go in dere! Dat's a trap – *(pointing)* come right here and you got him.

LIGE: *(Pointing)* Back dat man up, Hambo, do, he'll git et up.

> *(There is the moise of the checkers for a half minute then a general shout of triumph.)*

SPECTATORS: You got him now, Hambo! Clarke, he's sho got
you.

CLARKE: *(Chagrined)* Aw, he ain't done nothing! Jes' watch
me.

HAMBO: *(Jeering)* Yeah, gwan move! Ha! Ha! Go 'head and
move.

SPECTATORS: Aw, he got you, Bro' Mayor – might as well
give up. He got you in de Louisville loop.

CLARKE: Give up what? He can't beat me! *(Peeved)* De rest
of y'all git from over me, whoopin and hollerin! I
God, a man can't hear his ears.

(The men fall back revealing the players clearly.)

HAMBO: Aw, neb' 'mind bout them, Joe, go 'head and
move. You ain't got but one move to make nohow – go
'head on and take it.

CLARKE: *(Moving a checker)* Aw, here.

HAMBO: *(Triumphant)* Now! Watch me boys whut ahm
gonna do to him. Ah'm gonna laff in notes, while
ah work on him. *(He lifts a checker high in the air
preparatory to the jump, laughing to the scale and
counting each checker he jumps out loud.)* Do, sol, fa,
me, la! One! *(Jumps a checker)* La, sol, fa, me, do! Two!
(Jumps another) Do, re, fa, me, do! Three! Me, re, la,
so, fa! Four! *(The crowd is roaring with laughter.)* Sol,
fa, me, la, sol, do! Five! Ha! Ha! Boys I got de ole tush
hawg! I got him in de go-long. *(He slaps his leg and
accidentally knocks the board off his knee and spills the
checkers.)*

CLARKE: Too bad you done dat, Hambo, cause ah was
gointer beat you at dat.

*(He rises and starts towards the door of the store as
the crowd roars in laughter.)*

HAMBO: You mean you was gointer beat me to de door, not
a game of checkers. Ah done run de ole coon in his

hole.

LIGE: Well, Hambo, you done got to be so hard at checkers, come on less see whut you can do wid de cards. *(He pulls out a soiled deck from his coat pocket and moves toward the bench at the left of the porch.)* You take Lum and me and Walter will wear you out.

HAMBO: You know I don't play no cards.

LUM: We ain't playin for no money, just a lil Florida flip.

HAMBO: Y'all can't play no Florida flip. 'Fore ah joined de church there wasn't a man in de state could beat me wid de cards. But ahm a deacon now, in Macedonia Baptist – ah don't bother wid de cards no mo'.

(He and Joe Lindsay go inside store.)

LIGE: Well, come on Lum. Walter, git yo'self a partner.

WALTER: *(Looking about)* Tain't nobody to git. *(Looks off right)* Here come Dave Carter.

LIGE: You can't do nothing wid him dese days. He useter choose a game of cards when he wasn't out huntin, but now when he ain't out huntin varmints he's huntin' Daisy Blunt.

(Enter Dave right with a shotgun slung over his shoulder.)

WALTER: Come on, fish, lemme bend a five-up over yo' head. You looks just like my meat.

DAVE: Ah'm on mah way to kill me a turkey gobbler, but if you and Lum thinks y'all's tush hawgs ah'll stop long enough to take you down a buttonhole lower. *(He sets his gun down and finds a seat and draws it up to the card table.)*

WALTER: Naw, Dave, we ain't going to fool wid no buttonholes – we gointer tear off de whole piece dat de buttonholes is in. *(They all get set.)* All right boys, turn it on and let de bad luck happen.

LIGE: *(Probing the deck)* My deal.

WALTER: Watch yo'self Dave, don't get to worryin 'bout
    Daisy and let 'em ketch yo' jack.

LUM: *(Winking)* What you reckon he gointer be worryin'
    'bout Daisy for? Dat's Jim's gal.

DAVE: Air Lawd, a heap sees but a few knows. Deal de
    cards man – you shufflin' an mighty lot.

WALTER: Sho is – must be tryin' to carry de cut to us.

LIGE: Aw, we ain't gonna cheat you, we gonna beat
    you. *(He slams down the cards for Dave to cut.)* Wanna
    cut 'em?

DAVE: Nope. Tain't no use cuttin' a rabbit out when you
    kin twist him out. Deal 'em!

(Lige deals and turns up the jack of spades.)

WALTER: Yee-ee! Did you snatch dat jack?

LIGE: Man, you know I ain't snatched no jack. Whut you
    doin'?

WALTER: I'm beggin!

LIGE: Go ahead and tell 'em I sent you.

WALTER: Play just like ah'm in New York, partner. *(Scratches
    his head)* We oughter try to ketch dat jack.

LIGE: Stick out yo' hand an' you'll draw back a nub.

WALTER: Whut you want me to play for you, partner?

DAVE: Play me a baby diamond.

(Walter plays, then Lum, then Dave.)

LUM: *(Triumphant)* Looka pardner, they doin all dat
    woofin on uh queen – sendin' women to do uh man's
    work. Watch me stomp her wid mah king. *(He slams
    his card down and collects the trick.)* Now come in
    under dis ace! *(They all play and he collects the trick.)*
    Now whut you want me to play for you, pardner?

LIGE: How many times you seen de deck?

LUM: Twice.

LIGE: Pull off wid yo' king. *(Lum plays the king of spades. All
    the others play.)* Look at ole low pardner. Ah knowed ah

wuz gointer ketch him! Come right back at 'em.

LUM: *(Stands up and slams down the ace)* Pack up, pardner. Ah'm playin' mah knots, now all play now. Ho! Ho! Dere goes de queen! De Jack's a gentleman! *(Lige takes the jack and sticks it up on his forehead in braggadocio.)* Here comes de ten spot, pardner, ah'm dumpin to yuh!

LIGE: *(As he plays the jack)* Everybody git up off it and dump. High, low, jack, game and gone from de first four.

WALTER: Gimme dem cards! Y'all carried de cub to us dat time *(Riffles the cards elaborately)* but de deal is in de high, tall house now. Dis is Booker T. Washington spreading his mess. *(Offers cards to Lige)* Cut?

LIGE: Yeah, cut 'em and shoot 'em. I'd cut behind mah ma.

(He cuts and Walter deals.)

WALTER: Well, whut sayin'?

LUM: I'm beggin.

WALTER: Get up off yo' knees. Youse dat one.

LIGE: Walter, you sho stacked dese cards.

WALTER: Aw, stop cryin' and play, man. Youse too old to be hollerin' titty-mama.

LUM: Dis ain't no hand, dis is a foot. What you want me to play for you partner?

LIGE: Play yo' own hand partner – I ain't nobody. Lead yo' bosses.

(He leads the ace of clubs. Play goes round to dealer and Walter takes the card off the deck and slams it down.)

WALTER: Get up ol' deuce of diamonds and gallop off wid yo' load. Pardner, how many times you seen de deck?

DAVE: Two times. *(They make signals.)*

WALTER: Watch dis ol' queen. Less go! *(He begins to sing – Dave joins in.)*

When yo' card gits lucky, oh pardner,
you oughter be in a rollin' game.

(He speaks.) Ha! Ha! Wash day and no soap! *(He sticks the jack upon his forehead. He stands up and sings again.)*

Ah'm goin' to de 'Bama, Lawd.
Pardner don't want no change.

(He collects that trick and plays again. Dave also stands.)

DAVE: Here come de man from de White House – ol' king of diamonds. *(Sings, all join.)*
Ahm goin' back to de Bama, Lawd.
Pardner won't be worried wid you.

(He collects the trick.)

Never had no trouble, Lord pardner,
Till I stopped by here.

(They all stand hilariously and slam down their cards.)

WALTER: Aw, we'se just too hard for you boys – we eats our dinner at de blacksmith shop. Y'all can't bully dis game. *(He solemnly reaches over and takes Dave's hand.)*

DAVE: *(To Walter)* Mr. Hoover, you sho is a noble president. We done stuck des shad-moufs full of cobs. They skeered to play us any mo'.

LIGE: Who skeered? Y'all jus' playin ketch up nohow. Git back down and lemme wrap uh fie-up 'round yo' neck.

DAVE: *(Looking off right)* Squat dat rabbit an' less jump another one. Here come Daisy.

WALTER: Aw Lord, you ain't no mo' good now. But ah don't blame you, Dave, she looks warm.

(Enter Daisy right with a scarlet hibiscus over each

ear and smiling broadly.)

LIGE: *(Jumps down and takes Daisy by the arm)* Come on up here, Daisy and ease Dave's pain. He's so crazy 'bout you his heart 'bout to burn a hole in his shirt.

(She steps up on the porch.)

DAVE: *(Bashfully)* Aw, y'all gwan. Ah kin talk.

DAISY: *(Arma akimbo, impudently)* Oh kin you? *(She gets up close to Dave.)*

DAVE: *(Pleased)* You better git way from me 'fore Jim come long.

DAISY: *(Coquettishly)* Ain't you man enough to cover de ground you stand on?

DAVE: Oh, ah can back my crap! Don't worry 'bout me. Where you headed for?

DAISY: *(Audaciously)* Where *you* goin?

DAVE: Out by de cypress swamp to kill us uh turkey. It's uh great big ole gobbler – been slurrin me fer six months. Ahm gointer git him today for you, and yo' mama gointer cook him.

DAISY: Ah sho would love the ham of a turkey.

DAVE: *(Patting his gun barrel)* Well me an' ole Hannah sho gointer git you one. Look here, Daisy, will you choose uh bag of ground peas?

DAISY: I jus' love goobers.

DAVE: *(Sticking out his right elbow)* You lak chicken?

DAISY: Yeah.

DAVE: Take uh wing.

(She locks arms with him and they strut inside the store.)

LIGE: Ah b'lieve dat fool is got some gumption. Jim Weston better watch out.

WALTER: Oh I ain't never figgered Dave was no fool. He's uh bottom fish. Jim talks all de time but Dave will run him uh hot – here he come now. *(Looks off left. All look the same way.)*

LUM: Lawd, don't he look mean? *(He chuckles)* Ah bet he know Daisy's here wid Dave. Ah wouldn't take nothin' for dis.

> *(Enter Jim Weston left with a guitar looking very glum. He stops beside the step for a moment. Takes off his hat and fans with it.)*

JIM: Howdy do, folks.

ALL: Howdy do, Jim.

JIM: Don't do all they say. *(He sees the gun leaning against the rail.)* Who gun dat? *(Points at the gun.)*

LIGE: You know so well whose gun dat is. Ah jus' heard him say he's goin out to git his gal uh ham of a turkey gobbler out round de cypress swamp. He's inside now treatin her to penders and candy. *(He winks at the others and they wink back.)*

WALTER: *(Turns and calls into the store)* Say, Dave! Don't try to keep Daisy in dere all day. Her feller out here waitin to scorch her home.

DAVE: *(From inside store)* Let him come git her if she want him.

LIGE: Umph! Dere now, de mule done kicked Rucker! *(Calls inside to Dave)* I hear you crowin, rooster. I know yo' nest ain't far.

HAMBO: *(From inside store)* Yeah, dis rooster must know something – he's gittin plenty grit in his craw.

> *(General laughter. There is a gay burst of laughter from inside the store. In a moment Dave enters from the store with Daisy on his left arm. With his right he is stuffing shells into his pocket. The air is tense. Lindsay, Hambo and Joe Clarke all enter behind the couple.)*

DAVE: *(Releases Daisy and steps to the edge of the porch right in front of Jim and looks up at the sky)* Well, sun's getting low – better git on out to de swamp and git dat gobbler. *(He turns and picks up de gun and breaks it.)*

JIM: *(Sullenly)* 'Lo Daisy.

DAISY: *(Brightly)* Hello Jimmy *(She is eating peanuts.)* Ain't Dave smart? He's gonna kill me uh turkey an' ah kin eat all ah wants.

JIM: He ain't de onliest person kin shoot round here.

LIGE: Yeah, but he's best marksman just de same. Tain't no use talkin' Jim. You can't buck Dave in de woods. But you got de world beat wid uh git-fiddle. Yessuh, Dave is uh sworn marksman but you kin really beat de box. Less have uh tune.

JIM: Oh I ain't for pickin no box. I come to git some shells for my rifle. Sorta figgered on uh wild turkey or two. *(He comes up on the porch and starts in the store.)*

DAISY: If Dave go git me dat big ole turkey an' you go git me one too – gee! Won't I have uh turkey fit?

LINDSAY: Lord, Daisy, you gointer have dese boys killin up every turkey in Orange County.

WALTER: You mean *Dave.* Jim couldn't hit de side of uh barn wid uh brass fiddle.

JIM: *(Hitching up his trousers)* Who can't shoot? *(To Clarke)* Come on an' gimme uh box uh shells. I'll show yuh who kin shoot! *(He exits into store with Clarke behind him.)*

DAVE: *(To Daisy)* You wait here till ah git back wid yo' turkey.

DAISY: Ah'm skeered.

DAVE: Whut you skeered of? Jim? He ain't no booger boo, if his ears do flop lak uh mule.

DAISY: Naw. Ah ain't skeered uh no Jim. Ah got tuh git back tuh de white folks an ah'm skeered tuh go round dat lake at night by myself.

(Enter Jim from store and stands in door with box of shells in his hand.)

JIM: No girl look like you don't have to go home by yo'self, if it was midnight.

DAVE: *(Gun in hand and ready to exit)* Naw, 'cause ah'm right here –

JIM: Daisy don't you trust yo'self round dat lake after dark, wid dat *(points at Dave)* breath and – britches. You needs uh real man to perteck you from dem 'gators and moccasins.

DAVE: Let somethin' happen and she'll find out who got rabbit blood and who ain't. Well, ah'm gone. *(He steps down off the steps but looks back at Daisy.)*

JIM: Ah'm goin too – git you uh great big ole turkey-rooster.

> *(Dave takes a step or two towards left exit.)*

DAISY: Jim, ain't you gointer knock off a lil tune fo' you go? Ah'm lonesome for some music.

> *(Dave stops in his tracks and looks wistful. Jim sets down the shells on the bench and picks up his box with a swagger and tunes a bit.)*

WALTER: Georgy Buck!

> *(Jim plays the air through once then starts to sing. Dave leans his gun against the fence and stands there.)*

JIM:

> Georgy Buck is dead, last word he said
> I don't want no shortenin in my bread.
>
> Rabbit on de log – ain't got no dog
> How am I goin git him, God knows.

> *(Dave walks on back near the step, and begins to buck a wing. Daisy comes down the step admiring both the playing and the dancing. All the men join in singing and clapping.)*

Rabbit on de log - ain't got no dog
Shoot him wid my rifle, bam! bam!
Oh Georgey Buck is dead, last word he said
Never let a woman have her way.

(The tempo rises. As Dave does a good break he brings up directly in front of Daisy. He grabs her and swings her into a slow drag. The porch cheers. Jim stops abruptly. Enter Lulu and Jenny right. They hurry up to the porch.)

LULU: Don't stop, Jim! Hit dat box a couple mo' licks so some of dese men kin scorch us in de store and treat us.

JIM: Aw, I don't feel lak no playin.

DAVE: *(Grinning triumphantly)* Ah'm gone dis time to git dat turkey. Daisy run tell yo' ma to put on de hot water kittle. *(He exits left with gun on shoulder.)*

DAISY: Oh lemme see if I got a letter in de post office. *(She exits into store.)*

JIM: He better git for home 'fore ah bust dis box over his head.

JENNY: *(Grabbing Lige)* Aw, don't worry 'bout Dave Carter. Play us some music so I kin make Lige buy me some soda water. *(She is playfully dragging Lige towards the door.)* Jenny you grab Walter.

(Walter makes a break to jump off the porch and run. Jenny catches him and there is a very gay bit of tussling as the men are dragged towards the door.)

LULU: I bet if this was Daisy, they'd uh done halted inside and toted out half de store.

JENNY: Yeah. *(Gets Walter to the door.)* Everything you hear is Daisy, Daisy, Daisy! Just 'cause she got a walk on her like she done gone crazy through de hips! *(Yanks Walter into the door.)* Yeah, y'all goin treat us. Come on!

WALTER: Yeah, but Daisy's uh young pullet and you gittin

gray headed.

JENNY: Thank God I ain' gray elsewhere! Come right on. You gointer buy me some soda water nigger. *(To Jim)* Play us some music, Jim, so we kin grand march up to de counter.

JIM: I can't play nothin' – mad as I is. I'm one minute to boilin and two minutes to steam. I smell blood!

LULU: You don't want to fight, do you?

JIM: Sho do. You ain't never seen a Weston yet dat wouldn't fight, have you?

LIGE: That's whut they all got run outa town for – fightin. *(Calls into store)* Hey, Joe, give Jenny and Lulu some soda water and ground pea on me so they'll turn us loose. *(To Jim)* Yeah, y'all Westons b'lieves in fightin.

JIM: Ah'd ruther get run out for fightin than to be uh coward. *(He slings the guitar 'round his neck and picks up his box of shells.)* Well, ah reckon Ah'll go git Daisy her turkey 'cause she sho wont git none less ah go git it. Here come Elder Simms anyhow no tain't no mo' pickin de box. *(To Daisy)* Don't git lonesome whilst ah'm gone.

> *(Enter Daisy from the store smiling, and walks down to where Jim is standing.)*

DAISY: What's all dis talk about fighin?

JIM: Lige throwin it up to me 'bout all my folks been run outa town for fightin. But I don't keer!

DAISY: Mah mouf done got lonesome already. Buy me some chewing gum to keep mah mouf comp'ny till y'all gits back wid dat turkey.

JIM: Don't hafta buy none. *(Reaches in his pocket and pulls out a stick)* What it takes tuh satisfy de ladies, ah totes it. *(He hands her the gum tenderly)* Bye, Daisy. *(He walks to left exit)*

DAISY: *(Coyly)* Bye, till you come back.

(Enter Elder Simms right.)

SIMMS: Good evenin' everybody.

ALL: Good evenin', Elder Simms.

LUM: *(Getting up from his seat on the porch)* Have mah seat, Elder.

> *(Simms takes it with a sigh of pleasure. Lum steps off the porch and sets his hat over one eye.)*

LUM: Say, Daisy, you ain't goin to sprain yo' lil mouf on dat tough chewin gum, is yuh? Not wid de help *you* got. Better lemme kinda tender dat gum up for yuh so yo' lil mouf won't hafta strain wid it.

> *(He places himself exactly in front of her. She glances up coyly at him.)*

DAISY: Ain't you crazy, now?

> *(Lum tries to snatch the gum but she pops it into her mouth and laughs as he seizes her hands.)*

LUM: You don't need no gum to keep yo' mouf company wid me around. Ah'm all de comp'ny yo' mouf need. Ah'm sweet papa chewin and sweetness change.

DAISY: Tell dat to Bootsie Pitts, you can't fool me. *(Turns right)* Guess ah better go home and see mama. Ah ain't been 'round since ah come from de white folk. You goin walk round there wid me?

LUM: Naw, ah ain't gointer *walk.* When ah'm wid de angels ah puts on mah hosanna wings and flies round heben lak de rest. *(He falls in beside her and catches her elbow.)* Less go! *(To the porch)* See you later and tell you straighter.

LINDSAY: Don't stay round to Daisy's too long, Lum, and get run out from under yo' hat!

LUM: Who run?

HAMBO: Tain't no use in you hollerin "who." Yo' feet don't fit no limb.

(General laughter. Exit Lum and Daisy right.)

WALTER: Lawd! Daisy sho is propaganda. She really
handles a lot of traffic. Ah don't blame de boys. If ah
was uh single man ah'd be 'round there myself.

LIGE: Ah'm willin tuh serve some time on her gang as it
is, but mah wife won't lissen to reason. *(Laughter)* Ah
tries to show here dis deep point where tain't right
for one woman to be harboring uh whole man all
to herself when there's heaps uh po' young girls ain't
got no husband atall. But ah just can't sense her into
it. *(Laughter.)*

HAMBO: Now take Jim and Dave for instant. Here they is,
old friends, done fell out and ready to fight – all over
Daisy.

WALTER: Thass me all over. I don't want no partnership
when it comes to my women. It's whole hawg uh none.
Lawd, what wimmen makes us do!

LINDSAY: What is it dey don't make us do. Now take for
instant Jim Weston. He know he can't hunt wid Dave
– Dave is uh sworn marksman, but jes' so as not to
be outdone here he go trying to shoot turkeys – wild
turkeys mind you – 'ginst Dave.

JOE CLARKE: I God, I hope he finds 'em too. If he get
to killin turkeys maybe he'll stay 'way from my hen
house. I God, I done lost nine uh my best layin' hens
in three weeks. *(General laughter.)*

WALTER: Did Jim git 'em?

CLARKE: I ain't personatin' nobody but I been told dat Jim's
got uh powerful lot uh chicken feathers buried in his
back yard. I know one thing if I ever ketch his toenails
in my chicken yard, I God, he's gointer follow his
pappy and his four brothers. He's got to git from dis
town of mine.

*(Enter a little girl right, very neat and starchy. She
runs up to Rev. Simms.)*

GIRL: Papa, mama say send her dat witch hazely oil she
sent you after right quick.

LINDSAY: Whuss matter wid Sister Simms – po'ly today?

SIMMS: She don't keep so well since we been here, but I
reckon she's on de mend.

HAMBO: Don't look like she never would be sick. She look
so big and portly.

CLARKE: Size don't mean nothin'. My wife is portly and
she be's on de sick list all de time. It's "Jody, pain in de
belly" all day. "Jody, pain in de back all night."

LIGE: Besides, Mrs. Simms ain't very large. She wouldn't
weigh more'n two hundred. You ain't seen no big
woman. I seen one so big she went to whip her lil boy
an' he run up under her belly and stayed up under dere
for six months. *(General laughter.)*

WALTER: You seen de biggest one. But I seen uh woman
so little till she could go out in uh shower uh rain and
run between de drops. She had tuh git up on uh box
tuh look over uh grain uh sand.

SIMMS: Y'all boys better read yo' Bibles 'stead of studyin
foolishness. *(He gets up and starts into the store. Clarke
and the little girl follow him.)* Reckon ah better git dat
medicine.

> *(The three exit into store.)*

HAMBO: Well, y'all done seen so much – bet y'all ain't
never seen uh snake big as de one ah seen down 'round
Kissimmee. He was so big he couldn't hardly move
his self. He laid in one spot so long he growed moss
on him and everyobody thought he was uh log layin'
there. Till one day ah set down on him and went to
sleep. When Ah woke up ah wuz in Middle Georgy.

> *(General laughter. Two women enter left and go in
> store after everybody has spoken to them.)*

LINDSAY: Layin' all sides to jokes now, y'all remember dat

rattlesnake ah kilt on Lake Hope was 'most big as dat one.

WALTER: *(Nudging Lige and winking at the crowd)* How big did you say it was, Joe?

LINDSAY: He mought not uh been quite as big as dat one – buy jes' 'bout fourteen feet.

HAMBO: Gimme dat lyin' snake! He wasn't but fo' foot long when you kilt him and here you done growed him ten feet after he's dead.

(Enter Simms followed by the girl with an all day sucker. Simms has a small package in his hand.)

SIMMS: *(Gives the package to the child and resumes his seat.)* Run 'long home now. Tell yo' ma to put on uh pot uh peas.

(Child exits right trotting and sucking her candy.)

WALTER: They's some powerful big snakes round here. We was choppin' down de weeds in front of our parsonage yistiddy and kilt uh great big ol' cotton mouf moccasin.

SIMMS: Yeah, look like me or some of my fambly 'bout to git snake-bit right at our own front do'.

LIGE: An' bit by uh Baptist snake at dat.

LINDSAY: How you make him out uh Baptist snake?

LIGE: Nobody don't love water lak uh Baptist an' uh Moccasin. *(General laughter.)*

HAMBO: An' nobody don't hate it lak de devil, uh rattlesnake an' uh Meth'dis.

(General laughter. Enter Joe Clarke from store. Stands in door.)

SIMMS: Dis town needs uh cleanin in more ways than one. Now if this town was run right, when folks misbehaves, they oughter be locked up in jail and if they can't pay no fine, they oughter be made to work it out on de streets – chopping weeds.

LINDSAY: How we gointer do all dat when we ain't got no jail?

SIMMS: Well, you orta *have* uh jail. Y'all needs uh whole heap of improvements in dis town. Ah ain't never pastored no town so way back as this one here.

CLARKE: *(Stepping out before Simms)* What improvements you figgers we needs?

SIMMS: A whole heap. Now for one thing, we really does need uh jail, Brother Mayor. Tain't no sense in runnin' people out of town that cuts up. We oughter have jails like other towns. Every town I ever pastored had uh jail.

CLARKE: *(Angrily)* Now hold on uh minute, Simms! Don't you reckon uh man dat knows how to start uh town knows how to run it? You ain't been here long enough to find out who started dis town yet. *(Very emphatic, beating his palm with other fist.)* Do you know who started *dis* town? *(Does not pause for an answer.)* Me! I started *dis* town. I went to de white folks and wid *dis* right hand I laid down two hundred dollars for de land and walked out and started dis town. I ain't like some folks – come here when grapes was ripe. I was here to cut new ground.

SIMMS: Well, tain't no sense in one man stayin' Mayor all de time, nohow.

CLARKE: *(Triumphantly)* So dat de tree you barkin' up? Why, you ain't nothin' but uh trunk man. You can't be no mayor. I got roots here.

SIMMS: You ain't all de voters, though, Brother Mayor.

CLARKE: *(Arrogantly)* I don't hafta be. I God, it's my town and I kin be Mayor jes' as long as I want to. *(Slaps his chest.)* I God, it was *me* dat put dis town on de map.

SIMMS: What map you put it on, Brother Clarke? You musta misplaced it. I ain't seen it on no map.

CLARKE: Tain't on no map, hunh? I God, every time I go

to Maitland de white folks calls me Mayor. Otherwise, Simms, I God, if you so dissatisfied wid de way I run dis town, just take yo' Bible and flat foots and git younder cross de woods.

SIMMS: *(Agrressively)* Naw, ah don't like it. You ack lack tain't nobody in de corporation but you. Now look. *(Points at the street lamp)* Tain't but one street light in town an' you got it in front of yo' place. We pays de taxes an' you got de lamp.

CLARKE: I God, nobody can't tell me how to run dis town. I 'lected myself and I'm gonna run it to suit myself. *(Looks all about)* Where is dat Marshall? He ain't lit de lamp!

WALTER: Scorched Daisy Blunt home and ain't got back.

CLARKE: I God, call him there, some of you boys.

LIGE: *(Steps to edge of porch left and calls)* Lum! Lum!

LUM: *(At a distance)* What!

LIGE: Come on and light de lamp it gittin dark.

SIMMS: Now, when I pastored in Ocala you oughter seen de lovely jail dey had.

HAMBO: Thass all right for white folks. We colored folks don't need no jail.

WALTER: Aw, yes we do too. Elder Simms is right. We ain't a bit better'n white folks. *(Enter LuLu and Jenny.)* You wimmen folks been in dat store uh mighty long time.

LULU: We been makin' our market.

HAMBO: Looks mighty bad for some man's pocket. But y'all ain't had no treat on me. Go back and tell Mrs. Clarke tuh give you some candy.

LINDSAY: Have somethin' on me too. Money ain't no good lessen de women kin help you use it. *(Hollers inside.)* Every lady in there take a treat on me.

JENNY: Ain't y'all comin' in tuh help us eat de treat? Come on, Elder Simms!

(Hambo gets up quickly. Lindsay and Joe Clarke also

get up. They go inside laughing.)

HAMBO: Here, lemme git hold of somebody.

(Grabs one of the women by the arm as they exit into the store.)

LIGE: *(Pointing his thumb after the women.)* Ah wouldn't waylay nothin' lak dat. Too old even tuh chew peanuts if ah was tuh buy it.

WALTER: Preach it, brother. But they's all right for mullet heads like Lindsay and Hambo. *(Sings)*
> When they git old, when they git old
> Old folks turns tuh monkeys
> When they git old.

(Looks off right)

> Lawd! They must be havin' recess in heben! Look at dese lil ground angels!

(Yells off right)

> Hello Big 'Oman, an' Teets an' Bootsie!
> Hurry up!
> My money jumpin' up and down in my pocket lak uh mule in uh tin stable.

(Enter three girls right, dressed in cool cotton dresses. They are all lock-armed and giggling.)

LIGE: Hello, folkses.

BOOTSIE: *(Coquettishly)* Hello yo'self – want uh piece uh corn bread look on de shelf.

(Great burst of laughter from inside the store.)

LIGE: *(Catching Bootsie's arm)* Lemme scorch y'all inside an' treat yuh.

BOOTSIE: *(Looks at the other girls for confirmation)* Not yet, after while.

WALTER: Well, come set on de plaza an' les' have some chat.

TEETS: We ain't got time. We come tuh git our mail out de post office.

LIGE: Youse uh Got-dat-wrong! You come after Dave an' Jim an' Lum. But Daisy done treed de las' one of 'em. She got Jim and Dave out in de swamp where de mule was drugged out huntin' her uh turkey. An' she got Lum at her house. Thass how come de light ain't lit.

BIG 'OMAN: Oh, ah 'ain't worried bout Lum. Ah b'lieve ah kin straighten him out.

WALTER: Some wimmen kin git yo' man so he won't stand uh straightenin'.

LIGE: Don't come rollin' yo' eyes at me an' gittin' all mad cause y'all stuck on de boys and de boys is stuck on Daisy. *(Makes a sly face at Walter.)*

TEETS: Who? Me? Nobody ain't studyin' 'bout ole Daisy. She come before me like a gnat in a whirlwind.

WALTER: *(In mock seriousness)* Better stop dat talkin' 'bout Daisy, do I'll tell her whut you say. I think I better call her anyhow and see whether you gointer talk dat big talk to her face. *(Makes a move as if to call Daisy.)*

LIGE: *(Keeping up the raillery, grabs Walter)* Don't do dat, Walter. We don't want no trouble round here. But sho 'nuff, girls, y'all ain't go no time wid Daisy. Know what Lum say? Says Daisy is a bucket flower – jes' *made* her to set up on de porch an' look pretty. I set him how 'bout de rest an' he says "Oh de rest is yard flowers, jes' plant them any which a way."

BOOTSIE: I don't b'lieve Lum said no sich uh thing.

LIGE: You tellin' dat flat – ah know. *(Looks off left)* Here come Lum, now, in uh big hurry jus' lak he ain't been gone two hours.

BIG 'OMAN: Less we all go git our treat!

(They start up on the porch. At that moment Hambo, Lindsay, Clarke, Simms, Jenny and LuLu enter from

the store.)

CLARKE: *(To Lige)* Looka here, I God! Ain't Lum lit dat
lamp yet?

> *(Enter Lum left hurriedly. Clarke stands akimbo
> glaring at him. Lum fumbles for a match, strikes it
> and drops it. Gets another from his pocket and goes to
> the lamp and strikes it.)*

CLARKE: Somebody reach de numbskull uh box.

> *(Walter hands Lum a box of the porch and he gets up
> on it and opens the lamp to light it.)*

LUM: *(To Clarke)* Reckon ah better put some oil in de
lamp. Tain't much in it.

CLARKE: *(Impatiently)* Oh, that'll do! That'll do. It'll be
time tuh put it out befo' you git it lit, I God.

> *(Lum lights the lamp. The men have resumed their
> seats and the women are on the ground near right
> exit. Walter, Lige, Bootsie, Teets and Big 'Oman are
> at the door about to enter the store. Lum has the box
> in his hand and is still under the lamp. He walks
> slowly towards the step, box in hand. At the step he
> looks off left.)*

LUM: Here come Dave.

> *(All look off left. Walter and Lige and the girls
> abandon the idea of the treat and wait for Dave.)*

HAMBO: But ah ain't seen no turkey yet. Dat ole gobbler's
too smart for Dave.

> *(Enter Dave with gun over his shoulder and holding
> his head. A little blood is on his shoulder. He pauses
> under the lamp a moment, then comes to the step.)*

HAMBO: Whuss de matter, Dave? Dat ole turkey gobbler
done pecked you in de head? Whut kind of a

huntsman is you? *(General laughter.)*

DAVE: Naw, ain't no turkey pecked me. It's Jim. Ah wuz out
in de woods and had done squatted down before he
got dere. Ah know jus' where dat ole gobbler roost at.
Son's he hit de limb an' squatted hisself, ah let 'im have
it. He flopped his wings an' tried to fly off but here
he come tumblin' down right by dem ole mule bones.
Jim, he was jus' comin' up when ah fired. So when he
seen dat turkey fallin', whut do he do? He fires off
his gun an' make out he kilt dat turkey. Ah beat him
tuh de bird and we got tuh tusslin'. He tries tuh make
me give him *mah* turkey so's he kin run tuh Daisy an'
make out he done kilt it. So we got tuh fightin' an' ah
wus beatin' him too till he retched down an' got de
hock bone uh dat mule an' lammed me over de head
an' 'fore ah could git up, he done took mah turkey
an' went wid it. *(To Clarke)* Mist Clarke ah wants tuh
swear out uh warrant 'ginst Jim Weston. Ah'm gointer
law him out dis town, too.

SIMMS: Dat wuz uh low-down caper Jim cut sho 'nuff.

CLARKE: Sho its uh ugly caper tuh cut. Come on inside,
Dave, an' ah'll make out de papers. He ain't goin' to
carry on lak dat in *my* town.

(Exit Dave and Clarke into the store.)

LINDSAY: *(Jokingly to Simms)* See whut capers you Meth' dis'
niggers'll cut – lammin' folks over de head wid mule
bones an' stealin' they turkeys.

SIMMS: Oh you Baptis' ain't uh lot better'n nobody
else. You steals an' fights too.

LINDSAY: *(Still bantering)* Yeah, but we done ketched dis
Meth'dis nigger an' we gointer run him right on outa
town too. Jus' wait an' see. Yeah, boy. Dat Jim'll be uh
gone gator 'fore tomorrow night.

WALTER: Oh, I don't know whether he's gointer be gone or
not. We Meth'dis got jus' as much say-so in dis town as

anybody else.

LIGE: Yeah. You Baptis' run yo' mouf but you don't run
de town. Furthermo' we ain't heard nothin' but Dave's
lie. Better wait till we see Jim an' git de straight of dis
thing.

HAMBO: Will you lissen at dat? Dese half-washed
Christians hates de truth lak uh bed-bug hates de light.
God a'mighty! *(Rising)* Ah'm goin' in an' see to it dat de
Mayor makes dem papers out right.

> *(He exits angrily into the store. Simms and all the
> men rise too.)*

SIMMS: Come on Walter, you an' Lige. Less we go
inside too. Dat po' boy got tuh git jestice. An'
'tween de Mayor an' dese Baptists he ain't got much
chance. *(They exit into the store.)*

LULU: Come on you young gals, whut y'all wants be
hangin' 'round de store an' it's way after black dark. Yo'
mammies oughter take an' frail de las' one of yuh!
Come along!

> *(The girls come down off the porch and join the
> women. Loud angry voices inside the store.)*

JENNY: Lawd, lemme git home an' tell my husban' 'bout all
dis. Umph! Umph!

> *(The women and girls exit as the men all emerge
> from the store. Lum comes first with the warrant in
> his hand. Clarke emerges last.)*

CLARKE: Can't have all dat fuss an' racket in my store. All of
you git outside dat wants tuh fight. *(He begins to close up.)*

SIMMS: But Brother Mayor, I said it, an' I'll say it agin,
tain't right –

CLARKE: *(Turns angrily)* I God, Simms, ah don't keer whut
you say. Tain't worth uh hill uh beans nohow. Jim is
gointer be 'rested for hittin' Dave an' takin' his turkey,

an' if he's found guilty he's goin' 'way from here. Tain't no use uh you swellin' up neither. *(To Lum)* Go get him, Lum, an' lock 'im in my barn an' put dat turkey under arrest too. I God, de law is gointer be law in my town.

(Exit Lum with an important air.)

WALTER: Where de trial gointer be, Brother Clarke, in de hall?

CLARKE: Nope, it's too little. It'll hafta be in de Baptist church. Ah reckon dat's de bigges' place in town. Three o'clock Monday evening. Now, y'all git on off my porch tuh fuss. Lige, outen dat lamp for Lum.

(The stage goes black. The crowd is dispersing slowly. Angry voices are heard. The curtain is descending slowly. Offstage right the voice of Lum is heard calling Daisy.)

LUM: Oh Daisy! Oh Daisy!

DAISY: *(At a distance)* What you want, Lum?

LUM: Tell yo' mama to put on de hot water kittle. I'll be round there before long.

CURTAIN

ACT TWO

SCENE 1.

SETTING: *Village street scene. Huge oak tree upstage center. A house or two on backdrop. When curtain goes up Sister Lucy Taylor is seen standing under the tree trying to read a notice posted on the tree. She is painfully spelling it out. Enter Mrs. Thomas, a younger woman in her thirties, at left.*

MRS. THOMAS: Evenin', Sis Taylor.

MRS. TAYLOR: Evenin'. *(Returns to the notice.)*

MRS. THOMAS: Whut you doin'? Readin' dat notice Joe Clarke put up 'bout de meetin'? *(Approaches tree.)*

MRS. TAYLOR: Is dat whut it says? I ain't much on readin' since I had my teeth pulled out. You know if you pull out dem eye teeth you ruins yo' eye sight. *(Turns back to notice.)* Whut it say?

MRS. THOMAS: *(Reading notice)* "The trial of Jim Weston for assault and battery on Dave Carter wid a dangerous weapon will be held at Macedonia Baptist Church on Monday November 10, at three o'clock. All are welcome – by order of J. Clarke, Mayor of Eatonville, Florida." *(Turning to Mrs. Taylor)* Hit's makin' on to three now.

MRS. TAYLOR: You mean it's right *now. (Looks up at sun to tell time.)* Lemme go git ready to be at de trial – 'cause I'm sho going to be there and I ain't goin' to bite my tongue neither.

MRS. THOMAS: I done went and crapped a mess of collard greens for supper – I better go put 'em on – 'cause

Lawd knows when we goin' to git outa there – and
my husband is one of them dat's gointer eat don't keer
whut happen. I bet if Judgement Day was to happen
tomorrow, he'd speck I orter fix him a bucket to carry
long. *(She moves to exit right.)*

MRS. TAYLOR: All men favors they guts, chile. But whut
you think of all dis mess they got going on round here?

MRS. THOMAS: I just think it's a sin and a shame before
de livin justice de way dese Baptis' niggers is runnin'
round here carryin' on.

MRS. TAYLOR: Oh they been puttin out they brags ever
since Sat'day night 'bout whut they gointer do to Jim.
hey thinks they runs this town. They tell me Rev.
Singleton preached a seromon on it yesterday.

MRS. THOMAS: Lawd help us! He can't preach and he look
like ten cents' worth of have-mercy, let 'lone gittin' up
dere tryin' to throw slams at us. Now all Elder Simms
done was to explain to us our rights – whut you think
'bout Joe Clarke running round here takin' up for
these ole Baptist niggers?

MRS. TAYLOR: De puzzle-gut rascal – we oughter have
him up in conference and put him out de Meth'dis'
faith. He don't b'long in there – wanta run dat boy
outa town for nothin'.

MRS. THOMAS: But we all know how come he so hot to law
Jim outa town – hits to dig de foundation out from
under Elder Simms –

MRS. TAYLOR: What we wanta do dat for?

MRS. THOMAS: 'Cause he wants to be a God-knows-it-all
an' a God-do-it-all and Simms is de onliest one in this
town whut will buck up to him.

(Enter Mrs. Jones, walking leisurely)

MRS. JONES: Hello Hoyt, hello Lucy.

MRS. TAYLOR: Goin' to de meetin'?

MRS. JONES: Done got my clothes on de line and I'm

bound to be dere.

MRS. THOMAS: Gointer testify for Jim?

MRS. JONES: Naw, I reckon – Don't make much difference to me which way de drop fall – tain't neither one of 'em much good.

MRS. TAYLOR: I know it. I know it, Ida. But dat ain't de point. De crow we wants to pick is, is we gointer set still and let dese Baptist tell us when to plant and when to pluck up?

MRS. JONES: Dat *is* something to think about when you come to think about it. *(Starts to move on)* Guess I better go ahead – see y'all later and tell you straighter.

> *(Enter Elder Simms right, walking fast, Bible under his arm, almost collides with Mrs. Jones. She nods and smiles and exits.)*

SIMMS: How you do, Mrs. Taylor, Mrs. Thomas.

BOTH: Good evenin', Elder.

SIMMS: Sho is a hot day.

MRS. TAYLOR: Yeah, de bear is walkin' de earth lak a natural man.

MRS. THOMAS: Reverend, look like you headed de wrong way. It's almost time for de trial and youse all de dependence we got.

SIMMS: I know it. I'm trying to find de Marshall so we kin go after Jim. I wants a chance to talk wid him a minute before court sets.

MRS. TAYLOR: Y'think he'll come clear?

SIMMS: *(Proudly)* I *know* it! *(Shakes the Bible)* I'm going to law 'em from Genesis to Revelation.

MRS. THOMAS: Give it to 'em, Elder. Wear 'em out!

SIMMS: We'se liable to have a new Mayor when all dis dust settle. Well, I better scuffle on down de road. *(Exit Simms left.)*

MRS. THOMAS: Lord, lemme gwan home and put dese greens on. *(Looks off stage left)* Here come Mayor

Clarke now, wid his belly settin' out in front of him
like a cow-catcher. His name oughter be Mayor Belly.

MRS. TAYLOR: *(Akimbo)* Jus' look at him! Trying to look
like a jigadier Breneral.

> *(Enter Clarke hot and perspiring. They look at him
> coldly.)*

CLARKE: I God, de bear got me! *(Silence for a moment)* How
y'all feelin' ladies?

MRS. TAYLOR: Brother Mayor, I ain't one of these folks dat
bite my tongue and bust my gall – whut's inside got to
come out! I can't see to my rest why you cloackin' in
wid dese Baptist buzzards 'ginst yo' own Church.

CLARKE: I ain't cloakin' in wid *none*. I'm de mayor of
dis whole town. I stands for de right and against de
wrong. I don't keer who it kill or cure.

MRS. THOMAS: You think it's right to be runnin' dat boy off
for nothing?

CLARKE: I God! You call knockin' a man in de head wid
a mule bone nothin'? 'Nother thing – I done missed
nine of my best-layin' hens. I ain't sayin' Jim got 'em
– but different people has told me he buries a powerful
lot of feathers in his back yard. I God, I'm a ruint man!
*(He starts towards the right exit, but Lum Rogers enters
right.)* I God, Lum, I been lookin' for you all day. It's
almost three o'clock. *(Hands him a key from his ring)*
Take dis key and go fetch Jim Weston on to de church.

LUM: Have you got yo' gavel from de lodge room?

CLARKE: I God, that's right, Lum. I'll go get it from de
lodge room whilst you go git de bone an' de prisoner.
Hurry up! You walk like dead lice droppin' off you!

> *(He exits right while Lum crosses stage towards left.)*

MRS. TAYLOR: Lum, Elder Simms been huntin' you – he's
gone on down 'bout de barn. *(She gestures.)*

LUM: I reckon I'll overtake him. *(Exit left.)*

MRS. THOMAS: I better go put dese greens on – my husband will kill me if he don't find no supper ready. Here come Mrs. Blunt. She oughter feel like a penny's worth of have-mercy wid all dis stink behind her daughter.

MRS. TAYLOR: Chile, some folks don't keer. They don't raise they chillen, they drags 'em up. God knows if dat Daisy was mine, I'd throw her down and put a hundred lashes on her back wid a plow-lane. Here she come in de store Sat'day night *(acts coy and coquettish, burlesques Daisy's walk)* a-wringing and a-twisting!

(Enter Mrs. Blunt left.)

MRS. BLUNT: How y'all Mrs.s?

MRS. THOMAS: Very well, Miz Blunt, how you?

MRS. BLUNT: Oh, so-so.

MRS. TAYLOR: I'm kickin' but not high.

MRS. BLUNT: Well, thank God you still on prayin' ground and in a Bible Country – me, I ain't many today. De niggers got my Daisy's name all mixed up in dis mess.

MRS. TAYLOR: You musn't mind dat, Mrs. Blunt. People just *will* talk. They's talkin' in New York and they's talkin' in Georgy and they's talkin' in Italy.

MRS. THOMAS: Chile, if you talk after niggers they'll have you in de graveyard or in Chattahoochee one. You can't pay no 'tention to talk.

MRS. BLUNT: Well, I know one thing – de man or woman, chick or child, grizzly or gray that tells me to my face anything wrong 'bout my chile – I'm going to take my fist *(rolls up right sleeve and gestures with right fist)* and knock they teeth down they throat. *(She looks ferocious.)* 'Cause y'all know I raised my Daisy right round my feet till I let her go up north last year wid them white folks. I'd ruther her to be in de white folks' kitchen than walkin' de streets like some of dese girls round here. If I do say so, I done raised a lady. She can't help it if all dese men get stuck on her.

MRS. TAYLOR: You'se telling de truth, Sister Blunt. That's what I always say – don't confidence dese niggers, do, they'll sho put you in de street.

MRS. THOMAS: Naw indeed. Never syndicate wid niggers – do, they will distriminate you. They'll be an *anybody*. You goin to de trial, ain't you?

MRS. BLUNT: Just as sho as you snore, and they better leave Daisy's name outer dis too. I done told her and told her to come straight home from her work. Naw, she had to stop by dat store and skin her gums back wid dem trashy niggers. She better not leave them white folks today to come praipsin over here scorn in her name all up wid dis nigger mess – do, I'll kill her. No daughter of mine ain't going to do as she please long as she live under de sound of my voice. *(She crosses to right.)*

MRS. THOMAS: That's right, Mrs. Blunt – I glory in yo' spunk. Lord, I better go put on my supper.

> *(As Mrs. Blunt exits right, Rev. Singletary enters left with Dave and Lindsay and Sister Lewis. Very hostile glances from Mrs.s Thomas and Taylor towards the others.)*

SINGLETARY: Good evening, folks.

> *(Mrs. Thomas and Mrs. Taylor just grunt. Mrs. Thomas moves a step or two towards exit. Flirts her skirts and exits.)*

LINDSAY: *(Angrily)* Whuts de matter, y'all? Cat got yo' tongue?

MRS. TAYLOR: More matter than you kin scatter all over Cincinnati.

LINDSAY: Go 'head on, Lucy Taylor, go 'head on. You know a very little of yo' sugar sweetens my coffee. Go 'head on. Everytime you lift yo' arm you smell like a nest of yellow hammers.

MRS. TAYLOR: Go 'head on yo'self. Yo' head look like it done wore out three bodies. Talking bout me smelling – you smell lak a nest of grand daddies yo'self.

LINDSAY: Aw, rack on down de road, 'oman. Ah don't wantuh change words wid yuh. You'se too ugly.

MRS. TAYLOR: You ain't nobody's pretty baby yo'self. You so ugly I betcha yo' wife have to spread uh sheet over yo' head tuh let sleep slip up on yuh.

LINDSAY: *(Threatening)* You better git 'way from me while you able. I done tole you I don't wanta break a mouth wid you. It's a whole heap better tuh walk off on yo own legs than it is to be toted off. I'm tired of yo' achin round here. You fool wid me now an' I'll knock you into doll rags, Tony or no Tony.

MRS. TAYLOR: *(Jumping up in his face)* Hit me! Hit me! I dare you tuh hit me. If you take dat dare you'll steal a hawg an' eat his hair.

LINDSAY: Lemme gwan down to dat church befo' you make me stomp you. *(He exits right.)*

MRS. TAYLOR: You mean you'll *git* stomped. Ah'm going to de trial too. De nex' trial gointer be *me* for kickin some uh you Baptis' niggers around.

> *(A great noise is heard offstage left. The angry and jeering voices of children. Mrs. Taylor looks off left and takes a step or two towards left exit as the noise comes nearer.)*

CHILD: *(Offstage)* Tell her! Tell her! Turn her up and smell her. Yo' mama ain't got nothing to do wid me.

MRS. TAYLOR: *(Hollering off left)* You lil Baptis' Haitians, leave them chillun alone. If you don't, you better!

> *(Enter about ten children struggling and wrestling in a bunch. Mrs. Taylor looks about on the ground for a stick to strike the children with.)*

CHILD IN CROWD: Hey! Hey! He's skeered tuh knock it off. Coward!

MRS. TAYLOR: If y'all don't git on home!

MARY ELLA.: *(Standing akimbo)* I know you better not touch me, do, my mama will tend to you.

MRS. TAYLOR: *(Making as if to strike her)* Shet up, you nast lil heifer, sassing me! You ain't half raised.

> *(Mary Ella shakes herself at Mrs. Taylor and is joined by two or three others.)*

MRS. TAYLOR: *(Walking towards right exit)* I'm going on down to de church an' tell yo' mammy. But she ain't been half raised herself. *(She exits right with several children making faces behind her.)*

WILLIE: *(To Mary Ella)* Aw haw! Y'all ol' Baptis' ain't got no book case in yo' church. We went there one day an' I saw uh soda cracker box settin' up in de corner so I set down on it. *(Pointing at Mary Ella)* Know whut ole Mary Ella say? *(Jeering laughter)* Willie, you git up off our library! Haw! Haw!

MARY ELLA: Y'all ole Meth'dis' ain't got no window panes in yo' ole church.

METHODIST GIRL: *(Takes center of stage and hands akimbo shakes her hips)* I don't keer whut y'all say. I'm a Methdis' bred an' uh Methdis' born an' when I'm dead there'll be uh Methdis' gone.

> *(Mary Ella snaps fingers under other girl's nose and starts singing. Several join her.)*

MARY ELLA:

> Oh Baptis', Baptis' is my name
> My name's written on high
> I got my lick in de Baptis' church
> Gointer eat up de Meth'dis pie

> *(The Methodist children jeer and make faces. The Baptist camp make faces back for a full minute there*

> *in silence while each camp tries to outdo the other in*
> *face making. A Baptist makes the last face.)*

WILLIE: Come on, less us don't notice 'em. Less gwan down
    to de church an' hear de trial.

MARY ELLA: Y'all ain't the onliest ones kin go. We goin' too.

WILLIE: Aw haw! Copy cats! *(Makes face)* Dat's right,
    follow on behind us lak uh puppy dog tail.

> *(Methodist children start walking toward right exit*
> *switching their clothes behind. Baptist children stage*
> *a rush and struggle to get in front of the Methodists.*
> *They finally succeed in flinging some of the Methodist*
> *children to the ground and some behind them and*
> *walk towards right exit haughtily switching their*
> *clothes.)*

WILLIE: *(Whispers to his crowd)* Less go round by Mosely's
    lot and beat 'em there!

OTHERS: All right!

WILLIE: *(Yelling to Baptists)* We wouldn't walk behind no
    ole Baptists!

> *(The Methodists turn and walk off towards left exit*
> *switching their clothes as the Baptists are doing. Slow*
> *curtain.)*

SCENE 2.

SETTING: *Interior of Macedonia Baptist Church, a rectangular*
    room, windows on each side, two "Amen Corners,"2
    pulpit with a plush cover with heavy fringe, practical
    door in pulpit, practical door in front of church, two oil
    brackets with reflectors on each side wall with all lamps
    missing but one, one big oil lamp in center.

ACTION: *At the rise, church is about full. A buzz and hum fills the church. Voices of children, angry and jeering, heard from the street. The church bell begins to toll for death. Everybody looks shocked.*

MRS. LEWIS: Lawd! Is Dave done died from dat lick?
MRS. THOMAS: *(To her husband)* Walter, go see.

> *(He gets up and starts down the aisle to front door. Enter Deacon Hambo by front door.)*

WALTER: Who dead?
HAMBO: *(Laughing)* Nobody – jus' tollin' de bell for dat Meth'dis' gopher dat's gointer be long long gone after dis trial. *(Laughter from Baptist side.)*
WALTER: Y'all sho thinks you runs dis town, dontcher? But Elder Simms'll show you somethin' t'day. If he don't, God's uh gopher.
HAMBO: He can't show us nothin' 'cause he don't know nothin' hisself.
WALTER: He got mo' book-learnin' than Rev. Singletary got.
HAMBO: He mought be unletter-learnt, but he kin drive over Simms like a road plow.
METHODISTS: Aw, naw! Dat's a lie!

> *(Enter Reverend Simms by front door with open Bible in hand. A murmur of applause arises on the Methodist side, grunts on the Baptist side. Immediately behind him comes Lum Bailey leading Jim Weston. They parade up to the right Amen Corner and seat themselves on the same bench, Jim between Lum and the preacher. A great rooster crowing and hen cackling arises on the Baptist side. Jim Weston jumps angrily to his feet. Enter by front door Reverand Singletary and Dave. Dave's head is bandaged, but he walks firmly and seems not ill at*

all. They sit in the left Amen Corner. Jeering grunts from the Methodist side.)

MRS. THOMAS: Look at ol' Dave trying to make out he's hurt.

LIGE: Everybody know uh Baptis' head is harder'n uh rock. Look like they'd be skeered tuh go in swimmin', do, they heads would drown 'em.

> *(General laughter on Methodist side. Enter Brother Nixon, with his jumper jacket on his arm, who climbs over the knees of a bench full of people and finds seat against the wall directly beneath empty lamp bracket. He looks around for some place to dispose of his coat. Sees the lamp bracket and hangs up the coat, hitches up his pants and sits down.)*

MRS. LEWIS: *(Rising and glaring at Nixon)* Shank Nixon, you take yo' lousy coat down off these sacred walls. Ain't you Meth'dis' niggers got no gumption in de house of Wash-up!

> *(Nixon mocks her by standing akimbo and shaking himself like a woman. General laughter. He prepares to resume his seat but looks over and sees Deacon Hambo on his feet, and glaring angrily at him. He quickly reaches up and takes the coat down and folds it across his knees. Mrs. Taylor looks very pointedly at Mrs. Lewis then takes a dip of snuff and looks sneering at Lewis again.)*

MRS. TAYLOR: Some folks is a whole lot more keerful 'bout a louse in de church than they is in they house. *(Looks pointedly at Mrs. Lewis.)*

MRS. LEWIS: *(Bustling)* Whut you gazin' at me for? Wid your pop-eyes looking like skirt ginny-nuts.

MRS. TAYLOR: I hate to tell you whut yo' mouf looks like. I sho do you and soap and soap and water musta had some words.

MRS. LEWIS: Talkin' bout other folks being dirty – yo' young 'uns must be sleep in they draws 'cause you kin smell 'em a mile down de road.

MRS. TAYLOR: Tain't no lice on 'em though.

MRS. LEWIS: You got just as many bedbugs and chinches marchin' out yo' house in de mornin', keepin' step just like soldiers drillin'. An' you got so many lice I seen 'em on de dishrag. One day you tried to pick up de dishrag and put it in de dishwater and them lice pulled back and tole you "Aw naw, dammed if I'm going to let you drown me." *(Loud laughter from the Methodist side.)*

MRS. LEWIS: *(Furious, rises with arms akimbo)* Well, my house might not be exactly clean, but there's no fly-specks on my character! They didn't have to sit de sheriff to make Willie marry *me* like they did to make Tony marry *you*.

> *(Mrs. Taylor jumps up and starts across the aisle. She is pulled back out of the aisle by friends.)*

MRS. TAYLOR: Yeah, they got de sheriff to make Tony marry me, but he married me and made a me a good husband, too. I sits in my rocking cheer on my porch every Sat'day evening and say "here come Tony and them" –

MRS. LEWIS: Them what?

MRS. TAYLOR: Them dollars. Now you sho orter go git de sheriff and a shotgun and make some of dese men marry yo' daughter Ada.

> *(Mrs. Lewis jumps up and starts across the aisle. She is restrained but struggles hard.)*

MRS. LEWIS: Lemme go, Jim Merchant! Turn me go! I'm going to stomp de black heifer till she can't sit down.

MRS. TAYLOR: *(Also struggling)* Let her come on! If I get my hands on her I'll turn her every way but loose.

MRS. LEWIS: Just come on out dis church, Lucy Taylor. I'll beat you on everything you got but yo' tongue and I'll hit dat a lick if you stick it out. *(To the man holding her)* Turn me go! I'm going to fix her so her own mammy won't know her. She ain't going to slip *me* into de dozens and laugh about it.

MRS. TAYLOR: *(Trying to free herself)* Why don't y'all turn dat ole twist mouth 'oman loose. All I wants to do is hit her one lick. I betcha I'll take her 'way from here faster than de word of God.

MRS. LEWIS: *(To man holding Mrs. Taylor)* I don't see how come y'all want let ole flat-behind Lucy Taylor aloose – make out she so bad, now. She may be red hot but I kin cool her. I'll ride her just like Jesus rode a jackass.

> *(They have subsided into their seats again, but are glaring at each other. Enter Mayor Clarke through the pulpit door. He is annoyed at the clamor going on. He tries to quell the noise with a frown.)*

MRS. TAYLOR: Dat ain't nothin' but talk – you looks lak de devil before day, but you ain't so bad – not half as bad as you smell.

CLARKE: Order, please. Court is set.

MRS. LEWIS: You looks like all hell and de devil's doll baby, but all I want *you* to do is to hit de ground and I'll crawl you. Put it where I kin git it and I'll sho use it.

CLARKE: *(Feeling everywhere for the gavel)* Lum Bailey! Where's dat gavel I told you to put here?

LUM: *(From beside prisoner)* You said *you* was going to git it yo'self.

CLARKE: I God, Lum, you gointer stand there like a bump on a log and see I ain't got nothin' to open court wid? Go 'head – fetch me dat gavel. Make haste quick before dese wimmen folks tote off dis church house.

> *(Lum exits by front door.)*

MRS. TAYLOR: *(To Lewis)* Aw, shet up, you big ole he-looking rascal you! Nobody don't know whether you'se a man or a woman.

CLARKE: You wimmen, shut up!

MRS. LEWIS: *(To Taylor)* Air Lawd! Dat ain't *yo'* trouble. They all *knows* whut *you* is – eg – zackly!

LINDSAY: Aw, why don't you wimmen cut dat out in de church-house! Jus' jawin' and chewin' de rag!

MRS. TAYLOR: Joe Lindsay, if you'd go home and feed dat raw-boned horse of yourn you wouldn't have so much time to stick yo' bill in business that ain't yourn.

LINDSAY: You ain't got nairn to feed – you better go hunt another dead dog and git some mo' teeth. Great big old empty mouf, and no cheers in de parler.

MRS. TAYLOR: I kin git all de teeth I wants – I'd ruther not have no cheers in my parlor than to have them ole snags you got in yo' mouf. I'd ruther gum it out.

LINDSAY: You don't *ruther* gum it out, you *hafta* gum it out. You ain't got no teeth. Dey better send out to dat ole mule and git you some teeth.

MRS. LEWIS: Joe Lindsay, don't you know me better than to strain wid folks ain't got sense enough to tote guts to a bean? If they ain't born wid no sense you can't learn 'em none.

LINDSAY: You sho done tole whut God love now. *(Glaring across the aisle)* Ain't got enough gumption to kill a buzzard.

> *(Enter Lum by front door with gavel in one hand and mule bone in the other. He walks importantly up the aisle and hands Clarke the gavel and lays the bone atop the pulpit.)*

CLARKE: *(Rapping sharply with gavel)* Here! You moufy wimmen shut up. *(To Lum)* Lum, go on back there and shut dem wimmen up or put 'em outa here.

(Lum starts walking importantly down the aisle towards Mrs. Taylor. She almost rises to meet him.)

MRS. TAYLOR: Lum Bailey, you fresh little snot you! Don't you dast to come here trying to put me out – many dispers as I done pinned on *you*! Git 'way from me befo' I knock every nap off of yo' head, one by one.

(Lum hurries away from her apologetically. He turns towards Mrs. Lewis.)

MRS. LEWIS: 'Deed God knows you better not lay de weight of yo' hand on *me*, Lum. Here you ain't dry behind de ears yet and come telling me what to do. Gwan 'way from here before I kick yo' clothes up round yo' neck like a horse collar.

(Lum goes on back and takes his seat beside the prisoner.)

CLARKE: *(Glaring ferociously)* This court is set and I'm bound to have some order or else. *(The talking ceases. Absolute quiet)*

CLARKE: Now less git down to business. We got folks in dis town dat's just like a snake in de grass.

MRS. BAILEY: Brother Mayor! We ain't got no business going into no trial nor nothin' else 'thout a word of prayer – to be sure de right spirit is wid us.

VOICE ON METHODIST SIDE: Thass right, Elder Simms, give us a word of prayer.

(He rises hurriedly.)

VOICE ON BAPTIST SIDE: This is a Baptist church and de pastor is settin' right here – how come he can't pray in his own church?

VOICE ON METHODIST SIDE: Y'all done started all dis mess - how you going to git de right spirit here? Go 'head, Rev. Simms.

VOICE ON BAPTIST SIDE: He can't pray over me. Dis church

says one Lord, one faith, one baptism – and a man
that ain't never been baptized atall ain't got no business
praying over nobody.

CLARKE: *(Rapping with gavel)* Less sing! Somebody raise a
tune.

> *(Voice on Baptist side begins "Onward Christian
> Soldiers" and the others join in. Voice on Methodist
> side begins "All Hail the Power of Jesus' name" and
> the Methodists join in. Both shout as loud as they can
> to the end of the verse. Mayor Clarke raps loudly for
> order at the end of the verse and lifts his hands as if to
> bless a table.)*

CLARKE: *(Praying)* Lord be with us and bless these few
remarks we are about to receive, Amen. Now this
court is open for business. All of use know we came
here on serious business. This town is 'bout to be tore
up by back-biting and malice. Now everybody that's a
witness in this case stand up. I wants the witnesses to
take the front seats.

> *(Nearly everybody in the room rises. Hambo frowns
> across the aisle at Mrs. McDuffy, who is standing.)*

HAMBO: Whut *you* doing standin' up for a witness? I know
you wasn't there. You don't know one thing about it.

MRS. MCDUFFY: I got just as much right to testify as you is.
I don't keer if I wasn't there. Any man that treats they
wife bad as *you* can't tell nobody else they eye is black.
You clean round yo' *own* door before you go sweeping
round other folks.

MRS. LINDSAY: *(To Nixon)* What you doin' up there
testifiying? When you done let yo' hawg root up all my
p'tater patch.

NIXON: Aw shut up woman – you ain't had no taters for no
pig to root up.

MRS. LINDSAY: Who ain't had no taters? *(To Lige)* Look

here, Lige, didn't I git a whole crocus sack full of tater slips from yo' brother Sam?

LIGE: *(Reluctantly)* Yeah.

MRS. LINDSAY: 'Course I had sweet p'taters! And if you stand up there and tell *me* I ain't had no p'taters I'll be all over you just like gravy over rice.

NIXON: Aw shut up – we ain't come here to talk about yo' tater vines, we come –

MRS. LINDSAY: *(To her husband)* Joe! What kind of a husband is you? Set here and let Nixon 'buse me out lak dat!

WALTER: How is he going to give anybody a straightening when he needs straightening hisself. I bought a load of compost from him and *paid for it in advance* and he come there when I wasn't home and dumped a half-a-load in there and drove on off wid my money.

MRS. HAMBO: Aw, you ain't got no right to talk, Walter, not lowdown as you is – if somebody stump their toe in dis town you won't let yo' shirttail touch you till you bolt over to Maitland and puke yo' guts to de white folks – an God knows I 'bominates a white folks nigger.

WALTER: Aw you just mad 'cause I wouldn't let your old starved-out cow eat up my cow-peas.

MRS. HAMBO: *(Triumphantly)* Un hunh! I knowed you was the one knocked my cow's horn off! And you lied like a doodle-bug going backwards in his hole and made out you didn't do it.

WALTER: I didn't do no such a thing.

MRS. HAMBO: I say you did and I belong to Macedonia Baptist Church and I can't lie.

WALTER: Yo' mouf is cut crossways, ain't it? Well then, yo' mouf ain't no prayer-book even if yo' lips do flap like a Bible. You kin lie and then re-lie.

HAMBO: Walter Thomas, talk dat biggity talk to me, not to my wife. Maybe you kin whip her, but if you can't whip me too, don't bring de mess up.

CLARKE: *(Rapping)* Y'all men folks shut up before I put you
both under arrest. Come to order everybody.

LINDSAY: I just wanta say this before we go any
further. Nobody bet' not slur my wife in here – do, I'll
strow 'em all over de county.

MRS. NIXON: Aw, youse de nastiest threatener in three
states but I ain't seen you do nothin'. De seat of yo'
pants is too close to de ground for you to be crowin' so
loud. You so short you smell right earthy.

MRS. LINDSAY: De seat of yo' husband's britches been
draggin' de ground ever since I knowed him. Don't
like it dontcher take it, here's my collar come and
shake it. *(She puts the palms of her hands together
and holding the heels together, flaps the fore part of her
hands like a 'gator opening and shutting its mouth. This
infuriates Mrs. Nixon.)*

CLARKE: Shut up! We didn't come here to wash and iron
niggers. We come here for a trial. *(Raps.)*

MRS. NIXON: *(To Clarke)* I ain't going to shut up nothin' of
de kind. Think I'm going to let her low-rate me and
I take it all? Naw indeed. I'm going to sack dis female
out before we any further go.

MRS. LINDSAY: Aw, I done dished you out too many times.
Go 'head on and try to keep yo' lil squatty husband
away from down on de lake wid wimmens and you'll
have *all* you can do. How does old heavy-hipped3
mama talk? *(Snaps her fingers.)*

MRS. NIXON: Nobody wouldn't have you if he could get
anybody else. *(She makes a circle with her thumb and
first finger and holds it up for Mrs. Lindsay to see.)* Come
thru – don't you feel cheap?

CLARKE: Mrs. Nixon, shut up!

MRS. NIXON: You can't shut me up, not the way you
live. When you quit beatin Mrs. Mattie and
dominizing her all de time then you kin tell other folks
what to do. You ain't none of my boss. Don't let yo'

wooden God and cornstalk Jesus fool you now. Not de way you sells rancid bacon for fresh.

NIXON: Aw, honey, hush a while, please and less git started.

(A momentary quiet falls on the place. Mayor glowers all over the place. Turns to Lum.)

CLARKE: Lum, git a piece of paper and a pencil and take de names of all de witnesses *who was dere while de fight was going on.*

LUM: *(Pulling a small tablet and pencil out of his coat pocket)* I brought it with me.

CLARKE: Now everybody who was at de fight hold up yo' hands so Lum can know who you are.

(Several hands go up. Mrs. Anderson puts up her hand.)

CLARKE: You wasn't there, Mrs. Anderson, not at that time.

MRS. ANDERSON: I hadn't been gone more'n ten minutes 'fore Dave come in from de woods.

CLARKE: But you didn't see it.

MRS. ANDERSON: It don't make no difference – my husband heered every word was spoke and told me jes' lak it happen. Don't tell *me* I can't testify.

HAMBO: Nobody can't testify but de two boys 'cause nobody wuz at de fight but dem.

MRS. ANDERSON: Dat's all right too, Brother, but I know whut they wus fightin' about an' it wudn't no turkey neither. It wuz Daisy Blunt.

MRS. BLUNT: Just you take my chile's name right out yo' mouf, Becky Anderson. She wuzn't out in dat cypress swamp. Leave her out dis mess.

SIMMS: You ain't got no call to be so touchous 'bout yo' girl, but you sho said a mouthful, Mrs. Blunt. Dis sho is a mess. Can't help from being uh mess. *(Glares at Mayor)* Holdin' a trial in de Baptist Church! Some folks ain't got sense enough to do 'em till four o'clock and it's way after half past three right now.

MAYOR: Shet up, dere, Simms! Set down! Who ast yo'
pot to boil, nohow? Court is de best church they is,
anyhow, 'cause you come in court. You better have a
good experience and a strong determination. *(Raps
vigorously)* Now lemme tell *y'all* something. When
de Mayor sets Court – don't keer when I sets it nor
where I sets it, you got to git quiet and stay quiet till
I ast you tuh talk. I God, you sound lak a tree full
uh blackbirds! Dis ain't no barbecue, nor neither no
camp meetin'. We 'sembled here tuh law uh boy on a
serious charge. *(A great buzz rises from the congregation.
Mayor raps hard for order and glares all about him.)*
Hear! Hear! All of us kin sing at de same time, but
can't but one of us talk at a time. I'm doin' de talkin'
now, so de rest of you dry up till I git through. I God,
you sound lak uh passel uh dog fights! We ain't here
for no form and no fashion and no outside show to de
world. We's here to law. *(To Lum)* You done got all de
witnesses straight – Got they names down?

LUM: Yessuh, I got it all straightened out.

CLARKE: Well, read de names out and let de witnesses take
de front seats.

LUM: Mr. Clarke, I done found out nobody wasn't at dat
fight but Jim and Dave and de mule bones. Dere's de
bone Dave got hit wid up on de rostrum and dere's
Jim and Dave in de Amen Corners.

DAVE: *(Rising excitedly)* Mist' Clarke! Brother Mayor,
I wants to ast uh question right now to git some
information.

CLARKE: All right, Dave, go 'head and ast it.

DAVE: Brother Mayor, I wanted to know whut become of
my turkey gobbler?

CLARKE: I God, Dave, youse in order. Lum! I God, I
been layin' off to ast you whut you done wid dat
turkey. Where is it? *(A burst of knowing laughter from*

the house.)

LUM: *(Very embarrassed)* Well, when you tole me to go
'rrest Jim and de turkey, I took and went on round to
his ma's house and he wudn't dere so I took and turnt
round and made it t'wards Daisy's house an' I caught
up wid him under dat Chinaberry tree jest befo' you
gits tuh Daisy's house. He was makin' it on t'wards her
house wid de turkey in one hand – his gun crost his
shoulder when I hailed 'im. I hollered "Jim, hold on
dere uh minute!" He dropped de turkey and wheeled
and throwed de gun on me.

CLARKE: I God, he drawed uh gun on de City Marshall?

LUM: Yessir! He sho did. Thought I was Dave. Tole me:
"Don't you come another step unless you want to see
yuh Jesus." I hollered back "It's me, I ain't no Dave
Carter." So he took de gun offa me and I went up to
him and put him under arrest, and locked him up in
yo' barn and brought *you* de key, didn't I?

CLARKE: You sho did, but I God, I ast you whut become of
de turkey?

LUM: De turkey wasn't picked or nothin', so I put him
under 'rrest too, jus' lak you tole me. *(General
laughter.)*

CLARKE: I God, Lum, whut did you *do* wid de turkey after
you put him under 'rrest?

LUM: Jim, he didn't want to come wid me till he could
make it to Daisy's house to give her dat turkey but,
bein so close up on him till he couldn't draw his rifle,
I throwed my .32-204 in his face an' tole him I said
"Don't you move! Don't you move uh pig – do, I'll
burn you down! I got my burner cocked dead in yo'
face and I'll keer you down jus' lak good gas went up.
Come on wid me!" So I took his rifle and picked up
de turkey and marched him off to yo' cow-lot. Ast him
didn't I do it. I tole him, I said "I know you Westons
goes for bad but I'm yo' match." I said "you may be

slick but you kin stand another greasing." Now sir! I ain't skeered uh nobody. I'll put de whole town under 'rrest.

CLARKE: I God, Lum, if you don't tell me whut you done wid dat turkey, you better! *(Draws back the gavel as if to hurl it at Lum.)* I'll lam you over de head wid dis mallet! Whut did you do wid dat gobbler turkey?

LUM: Being as he wasn't picked or nothin', I know you didn't want to be bothered wid it, so I took and carried it over to Mrs. Blunt's house and she put on some hot water and we set up way Sat'day night pickin de turkey and fixin him so nex' day she cooked him off – just sorta baked him wid a lil stuffin an' such, so he'd keep.

CLARKE: Didn't you know my wife knowed how to cook? Go fetch dat turkey here, and don't let no dead lice fall off of you on de way.

LUM: *(Extremely embarrassed)* I don't speck he's dere now, Mist' Clarke.

CLARKE: *(Ferociously)* How come?

LUM: I passed by dere on Sunday and et a lil piece of shoulder offa him, an' being everybody else was eatin' turkey too, I et some breast meat an' uh mouf'ful or two of stuffin' an' uh drumstick wid de hum part of de leg hung on to it wid a lil gravy. *(General laughter.)* I thought I was doin' right 'cause de turkey was kilt for Daisy anyhow. So I jus' took it on to her. Dave was all hurt up and Jim was locked up so –

CLARKE: Dat'll do! Dat'll do! Dry up, suh! *(Turns to Dave)* Stand up, Dave. Since youse de one got hurted, you be de first witness and tell me just whut went on out dere.

(Dave rises slowly.)

MRS. TAYLOR: Dat's right, Dave. Git up dere and lie lak de cross ties from New York to Texas. You greasy rascal you! You better go wash yo'self before you go testifying on people.

DAVE: I'm just as clean as you.

SINGLETARY: *(Jumping to his feet)* Wait a minute! Tain't none of y'all got no call to be throwin' off on dis boy. He come here to git justice, not to be slurred and low-rated. He ain't 'ssaulted nobody. He ain't stole no turkeys *nor* chickens. He's a clean boy. He set at my feet in Sunday school since he was so high, *(measure knee height)* and he come through religion under de sound of my voice an' I baptized him and I know he's clean.

MRS. TAYLOR: It'll take more'n uh baptizin' to clean dat nigger.

DAVE: I goes in swimmin' nearly every day. I'm just as clean as anybody else.

(Mayor begins rapping for order.)

MRS. TAYLOR: *(Shouts out)* Swimmin! Dat ain't gointer clean de crust offa *you.* You ain't had a good bath since de devil was a hatchet. If you ain't been parboiled in de wash pot and scoured wid Red Seal lye, don't bring de mess up.

CLARKE: I'm goin' to have order here or else! Gwan, Dave.

DAVE: It's just lak I tole you Sat'day night.

CLARKE: Yeah, but dat wuz at de store. Dis is in court and it's got to be tole agin.

SIMMS: Just uh minute, Brother Clarke, before we any further go I wants to ast de witness uh question dat oughter be answered before he open his mouf.

CLARKE: Whut *kind* of a question is dat?

SIMMS: Dave, tell de truth. Ain't yo' heart full of envy and malice 'gainst dis chile? *(Gestures towards Jim. Dave shakes his head and starts to deny the charge but Simms hurries on.)* Wait a minute now! Wait till I git through. Didn't y'all used to run around everywhere playin' and singing and everything till you got so full of envy and malice and devilment till y'all broke up? Now, Brother

Mayor, make him tell de truth.

DAVE: Yeah, I useter be crazy 'bout Jim, and we was buddies till he tried to back bite me wid, wid my girl.

JIM: Never *was* yo girl. Nohow I ain't none of yo' buddy. I ain't got no buddy. They kilt my buddy tryin' to raise me. But I did useter lak you till you seted so lowdown tryin' to undermine me and root me out wid my girl.

CLARKE: Aw, table dat business an' less open up new business. We ain't here to find out whose girl it is. We wants to know 'bout dis fight and who hit de first lick and how come. Go 'head on Dave and talk.

DAVE: Well, jus' lak I tole yuh, Sat'day night, I been watchin' dat flock uh wild turkeys ever since way last summer roostin' in de ledge of dat cypress swamp out by Howell Creek, where Brazzle's ole mule was dragged out. It was a great big ole gobbler leadin' de flock. So last time I seen him I said I was gointer git him for my girl if it taken me uh year. So Sat'day, kinda late, I grabs Ole Hannah, my gun, I calls her Ole Hannah, and come to de store to buy some shells. Y'all know whut went on at de store. Well, it made me feel lak I wuz gointer git dat ole gobbler if I had to follow him clean to Diddy-Wah-Diddy or slap into Ginny-Gall.5 But I didn't have to do nothin'. When I got out by de ole mule bones, I seen 'em flyin' 'round lak buzzards. So I loaded both barrels, squatted down on uh log where I had dead aim on dat big ole cypress pine where they roosts at. Sho 'nuff, soon's de sun had done set, here dey came followin' de leader. He lit way out on de end of de limb kinda off from de rest and I caved Ole Hannah up on him. Man! I got so skeered I wuz gointer miss him till I got de all overs. He gobbled two three times to see if all his fambly was safed den he settled down and bam! I let him have it! He spread his wings lak he wuz gointer fly on off an' I *cried* lak a chile! But I got him all right and down

he came floppin, and me grabbin him before he quit
kickin. Gee, I was proud. He felt lak he weighed forty
pounds. Whilst I was kinda heftin him in my hands
I heard uh rifle fire and I looked and dere was Jim
firin into de turkey flock dat was flyin round skeered.
He didn't hit a God's thing, but he seen me wid my
gobbler and come runnin up talking 'bout give him
his turkey. I ast him "Who turkey you talking bout?"
He says dat one of his I had done grabbed. I tole him
he must gone crazy in de head. He says, I better give
him his turkey before he beat my head off. I tole
him I wasn't gointer give nobody but Daisy Blunt
dat turkey. Otherwise, if he wanted to try my head, I
wasn't, runnin uh damn step. Come on. So he jumped
on me and tried to snatch de turkey. We fit all over
de place. First we was just tussling for de bird, but
when he found out he couldn't take it he hit me wid
his fist. Den I ups wid my African soup bone and I
bet I plowed up uh acre uh bushes wid his head. He
hit ker-bam! right in dat pack uh mule bones and I
turnt and started off, when lo and behold, he gits up
wid dat hock bone and lams me in de head and when
I come to, him and my turkey was gone. So I come
swore out uh warrant aginst him 'cause didn't fight fair.
I ain't mad. I always lakted Jim, but he sho done dirty
– lammin me wid uh mule bone and takin' my turkey.

> *(Dave resumes his seat and Jim drops his head for a
> moment, then snatches it up arrogantly and glares
> at the Baptists. The whole place is very silent for a
> moment. Then Mayor Clarke clears his throat, raps
> with his gavel and looks sternly at Jim.)*

CLARKE: Jim Weston, stand up suh! *(Jim rises sullenly.)*
You'se charged wid 'saulting Dave Carter wid uh
dangerous weapon and then stealin his lawful turkey
gobbler. You heard de charge – guilty or not guilty?

JIM: *(Arrogantly)* Yeah, I hit him and I'll hit him agin if he crowd me. But I ain't guilty uh no crime. *(He hitches up his pants and sits down arrogantly.)*

CLARKE: *(Surprised)* Whut's dat you say, Jim? *(Raps sharply)* Git up from there sir! Whut's dat you say?

JIM: *(Rising)* I say, yeah, I lammed ole Dave wid de mule bone, but I ain't guilty uh nothin.

> *(Jim sits down amid jubilant smiles of Methodists. There is a stark silence for a few seconds. Then Clarke raps nervously.)*

CLARKE: How come you ain't guilty?

> *(Simms chuckles out loud and wipes his face with his handkerchief. He gets to his feet still gloating.)*

SIMMS: *(To Jim)* Lemme show dese people dat walks in de darkness wid sinners an' Republicans de light.

SINGLETARY: You just as well tuh hush up befo' you start, then, Simms. You can't show nobody uh light when you ain't got none tuh show.

HAMBO: Ain't dat de gospel?

NIXON: Aw, let de man talk. Y'all sound lak uh tree full uh blackbirds. Go 'head on, Elder Simms.

WALTER: Yeah, you can't teach 'em nothin' but talk on. We know whut you talkin' about.

CLARKE: *(Raps once or twice)* I God, tell it. Whutever 'tis you got tuh tell.

MRS. LEWIS: Aw yeah, hurry up and tell it. I know it ain't goin' tuh be nothin' after you git it told but hurry up and say it so yo' egg-bag kin rest easy.

WALTER: Aw shet up an' give de man uh chance.

MRS. LEWIS: My shetters ain't workin' good. Sposin' you come shet me up, Walter. Den you'll know it's done right.

LIGE: Aw, whyn't y'all ack lak folks an' leave de man talk.

CLARKE: *(Rapping repeatedly)* Order in dis court, I God, jus' like you was in Orlando! *(Silence falls.)* Now, Simms, talk yo' chat.

SIMMS: *(Glances down into his open Bible, then looks all around the room with great deliberation. It is evident he enjoys being the center of attraction. He smiles smugly as he turns his face towards the pulpit. He speacks slowly and accents his words so that none will be lost on his audience.)* De Bible says, be sho you're right, then go ahead. *(He looks all around to collect the admiration he feels he has earned.)* Now, we all done gathered and assembled here tuh law dis young lad of uh boy on uh mighty serious charge. Uh whole passel of us is rarin tuh drive him 'way from home lak you done done off his daddy an' his brothers.

HAMBO: We never drove off his pappy. De white folks took an' hung him for killin' dat man in Kissimmee for nothin'.

SIMMS: Dat ain't de point, brother Hambo.

HAMBO: It's jes' as good uh point as any. If you gointer talk – tell de truth. An if you can't tell de truth, set down an' leave Rev. Singletary talk.

SIMMS: Brother Mayor, how come you let dese people run they mouf lak uh passle uh cow-bells? Ain't I got de floor? I ain't no breath-and-britches. I was *people* in Middle Georgy befo' I ever come to Floridy. Whut kind of Chaimran is you, nohow?

CLARKE: *(Angrily)* Heah! Heah! Don't you come tryin' show yo'self round me! I God, I don't keer whut you wuz in Georgy. I God, I kin eat fried chicken when you can't git rain water tuh drink. Hurry up an' say dat mess you got in yo' craw an' set down. We needs yo' space more than we needs yo' comp'ny.

NIXON: Don't let him skeer you, Elder Simms. You got plenty shoulders tuh back yo' fallin.

HAMBO: Well, each an' every shoulder kin hit de ground an' I'll git wid 'em. Don't like it dontcher take, here my collar come an' shake it.

WALTER: Hambo, everybody in Orange County knows you love tuh fights. But dis is uh law hearin' – not no wrassle.

HAMBO: Oh you Meth'dis' niggers wants tuh fight bad enough, but youse skeered. Youse jus' as hot as Tucker when de mule kicked his mammy. But you know you got plenty coolers.

MRS. TAYLOR: Aw, tain't nobody skeered uh you half-pint Baptists. God knows ah'm ready an' willin'.

> *(She glares at Mrs. Lewis. Mrs. Lewis jumps to her feet but is pulled back into her seat. Mayor Clarke raps for order and the room gets quiet.)*

CLARKE: Aw right now, Simms. I God, git through.

SIMMS: *(Pompously)* Now, y'all done up an' took dis po' boy an' had him locked up in uh barn ever since Sat'day night an' done got him 'ccused uh assault an' stealing uh turkey an' I don't know whut all an' you ain't got no business wid yo' hands on him atall. He ain't done no crime, an' if y'all knowed anything 'bout law, I wouldn't have tuh tell you so.

CLARKE: I God, he is done uh crime and he's gointer ketch it, too.

SIMMS: But not by law, Brother Mayor. You tryin' tuh lay uh hearin' on dis boy an' you can't do it 'cause he ain't broke no law – I don't keer whut he done, so long as he don't break no law you can't tetch him.

SINGLETARY: He committed assault, didn't he? Dat sho is breakin' de law.

SIMMS: Naw, he ain't committed no 'ssault. He jus' lammed Dave over de herd an' took his own turkey an' come on home, dat's all. *(Triumphantly)* Yuh see y'all don't knows whut you talkin' 'bout. Now, I done set in de court house an' heard de white folks law from mornin' till night. *(He flips his bible shut.)* I done read

dis book from lid tuh lid an' I knows de law. You got
tuh have uh weapon tuh commit uh 'ssault. An' tain't
in no white folks law and tain't in dis Bible dat no
mule bone is no weapon.

CLARKE: *(After a moment of dead silence)* I God, whut's dat
you say?

SIMMS: *(Sitting down and crossing his legs and folding his
hands upon his Bible)* You heard me. I say you ain't got
no case 'ginst dis boy an' you got tuh turn him go.

SINGLETARY: *(Jumping up)* Brother Chairman –

CLARKE: *(Raps once and nods recognition)* You got de floor.

SINGLETARY: I ain't book-learnt an' I ain't rubbed de hair
offen my head agin' no college wall, but I know when
uh 'ssault been committed. I says Jim Westion did
'ssault Davie. *(He points at Dave's head.)* An' steal his
turkey. Everybody knows Jim can't hunt wid Dave. An'
he 'ssaulted Dave too.

SIMMS: *(Arrogantly)* Prove it!

> *(Singletary stands there silent and puzzled. The
> Methodist side breaks into a triumphant shout
> of "Oh Mary, Don't You Weep, Don't You Moan,
> Pharoah's Army got Drownded." Singletary sinks into
> his seat. When they have shouted out three choruses,
> Simms arises to speak.)*

SIMMS: I move dat we sing doxology and bring dis
meetin' to uh close. We's all workin' people, Brother
Mayor. Dismiss us so we kin gwan back to our
work. De sun is two hours high yet. *(Looks towards the
Methodist side)* I move dat we adjourn.

WALTER: I second de motion.

SINGLETARY: *(Arising slowly)* Hold on there uh minute wid
dat motion. Dis ain't no lodge meetin'. Dis is uh court
an' bofe sides got uh right tuh talk. *(Motions towards
Simms' Bible)* Youse uh letter-learnt man but I kin read
dat Bible some too. Lemme take it uh minute.

SIMMS: I ain't uh gointer do it. Any preacher dat amounts to uh hill uh beans would have his own Bible.

CLARKE: I God, Singletary, you right here in yo' own church. Come on up here an' read out yo' pulpit Bible. I God, don't mind me being up here. Come on up.

> *(A great buzzing breaks out all over the church as Singletary mounts the pulpit. Clarke raps for order. Simms begins to turn the leaves of the Bible.)*

SIMMS: Brother Mayor. you oughter let us outa here. You ain't got no case 'ginst dis boy. Don't waste our time for nothin'. Leave us go home.

CLARKE: Aw, dry up, Simms. You done talked yo' talk. I God, leave Singletary talk his. *(To Singletary)* Step on out when you ready, Rev.

SINGELARY: *(Reading)* It says here in Judges 18:18 dat Samson slewed three thousand Philistines wid de jawbone of an ass.

SIMMS: *(On his feet)* Yeah, but dis wasn't no ass. Dis was uh mule, Brother Mayor. Dismiss dis meetin' and less all go home.

SINGELTARY: Yeah, but he was half-ass. A ass is uh mule's daddy and he's bigger'n uh ass, too. *(Emphatic gestures)* Everybody knows dat – even duh little chillun.

SIMMS: *(Standing)* Yeah, but we didn't come here to talk about no asses, neither no half-asses, nor no mule-daddies. *(Laughter from the Methodists)* We come to law uh boy for 'ssault an' larceny.

SINGLETARY: *(Very patiently)* We's comin' to dat pint now. Dat's de second claw uh de sentence we's expoundin'. I say Jim Weston did have uh weapon in his hand when he 'ssaulted Dave. 'Cause y'all knows dat de further back you gits on uh mule de more dangerous he gits an' if de jawbone slewed three thousand people, by de time you gits back tuh his hocks, its pizen enough to kill ten thousand. Tain' no gun in de world ever kilt dat many mens. Tain' no knives nor no razors ever kilt no three thousand people. Now, folkes. I ast y'all whut kin be mo' dangerous dan uh mule bone? *(To Clarke)* Brother Mayor, Jim didn't jes' lam Dave an' walk off. *(Very emphatic)* He 'ssaulted him wid de deadliest weapon there is in de wrold an' while he was layin unconscious, he stole his turkey an' went. Brother Mayor, he's uh criminal an' oughter be run outa dis peaceful town.

> *(Great chorus of approval from Baptists. Clarke begins to rap for order.)*

SIMMS: *(Standing)* Brother Mayor, I object. I have studied jury law[7] and I know what I'm talkin' about.

CLARKE: Aw dry up, Simms. Youse entirely out of order. You may be slick, but you kin stand antoher greasing. Rev. Singletary is right. I God, I knows de law when I hear it. Stand up dere, Jim.

> *(Jim rises very slowly. Simms rises also.)*

CLARKE: Set down, Simms. I God, I know where to find you when I want you. *(Simms sits.)* Jim, I find you guilty as charged an' I wants you to git outa my town and stay gone for two years. *(To Lum)* Brother Marshall, you see dat he gits outa town befo' dark. An' you folks befo' you start. And don't use no knives and no guns and no mule bones. Court's dismissed.

> *(Curtain)*

ACT THREE

___

SCENE 1.

SETTING: *Curtain goes up, on a stretch of railroad track with a luxurious Florida forest on the backdrop. Entrance left and right. It is near sundown.*

ACTION: *When the curtain goes up there is no one on the stage, but there is a tremendous noise and hub-bub offstage right. There are yells of derision, shouts of anger. Part of the mob is trying to keep Jim in town and a part is driving him off. After a full minute of this, Jim enters with his guitar hanging around his neck and his coat over his shoulder. The sun is dropping low and red through the forest. He is looking back angrily and shouting back at the mob. A small missile is thrown after him. Jim drops his coat and guitar and grabs up a piece of brick and threatens to throw it.*

JIM: *(Running back the way he came, he hurls the brick with all his might.)* I'll kill some of youle box-ankled niggers – *(grabs up another piece of brick)* I'm out yo' ole town – now jus' some of you ole half-pint Baptists let yo' wooden God and Cornstalk Jesus fool you to hit me! *(Threatens to throw. There are some frightened screams and the mob is heard running back.)* I'm glad I'm out yo' ole town, anyhow. I ain't never comin' back no more, neither. You ole ugly-rump niggers done ruint de town anyhow. *(There is complete silence offstage. Jim walks a few steps then sits down on the railroad embank-*

*ment facing the audience. Jim pulls off one shoe and pours
the sand out. He holds the shoe in his hand a moment and
looks wistfully back down the railroad track.)* Lawd, folks
sho is deceitful. *(He puts on the shoe and looks back
down the track again.)* I never woulda thought people
woulda acted lak dat. *(Laces up the shoe)* 'Specially
Dave Carter, much as me an' him done proaged round
together goin' in swimmin' and playin' ball an' serena-
din' de girls an' de white folks. *(He sits there gloomily
silent for a while, then looks behind him and picks up his
guitar and begins to pick a tune. It is very sad. He trails
off into "You May Leave an' Go to Halimuhfack." When
he finishes he looks back at the sun and picks up his coat
also. He looks back again towards the village.)* Reckon
I better git on down de road an' git somewhere, Lawd
knows where. *(Stops suddenly in his tracks and turns
back towards the village and takes a step or two.)* All dat
mess and stink for nothin'. Dave knows good an' well
I didn't mean to hurt him much.

> *(He takes off his cap and scratches his head
> thoroughly, then turns again and starts on down the
> road towards left. Enter Daisy left walking briskly.)*

DAISY: Hello, Jim.

JIM: Hello, Daisy. *(Embarrassed silence)*

DAISY: I was just coming over to town to see how you come
out.

JIM: You don't have to go way over there to find dat out –
you and Dave done got me run outa town for nothin'.

DAISY: *(Putting her hand on his arm)* Dey didn't run you
outa town, did dey?

JIM: *(Shaking her hand off)* Whut you reckon I'm countin'
Mr. Railroad's ties for – just to find out how many ties
between here and Orlando?

DAISY: *(Hand on his arm again)* Dey cain't run you off like
dat!

JIM: Take yo' hand off me, Daisy! How come they can't run me off wid you and Dave an' – *everybody* 'gainst me?

DAISY: I ain't opened my mouf 'gainst you, Jim. I ain't said one word – I wasn't even at de old trial. My Madam wouldn't let me git off. I wuz just comin' to see 'bout you now.

JIM: Aw, go 'head on. You figgered I was gone too long to talk about. You was bawlin' it over to town to see Dave – dat's whut was doin' – after gittin me all messed up.

DAISY: *(Making as if to cry)* I wasn't studying 'bout no Dave.

JIM: *(Hopefully)* Aw, don't tell me. *(Sings)*
    Ashes to ashes, dust to dust,
    Show me a woman that a man can trust.

(Daisy is crying now.) Whut you crying for? You know you love Dave. I'm yo' monkey-man. He always could do more wid you than I could.

DAISY: Naw, you ain't no monkey-man neither. I don't want you to leave town. I didn't want y'all to be fightin' over me, nohow.

JIM: Aw, rock on down de road wid dat stuff. A two-tim-ing cloaker like you don't keer whut come off. Me and Dave been good friends ever since we was born till you had to go flouncing yourself around.

DAISY: What did I do? All I did was to come over town to see you and git a mouf'ful of gum. Next thing I know y'all is fighting and carrying on.

JIM: *(Stands silent for a while)* Did you come over there Sat'day to see me sho 'nuff, sugar babe?

DAISY: Everybody could see dat but you.

JIM: Just like I told you, Daisy. I'll say it before yo' face and behind yo' back. I could kiss you every day – just as regular as pig-tracks.

DAISY: And I tole you I could stand it too – just as regular as you could.

JIM: *(Catching her by the arm and pulling her down with him onto the rail)* Set down here, Daisy. Less talk some chat. You want me sho nuff – honest to God?

DAISY: *(Coyly)* 'Member whut I told you out on de lake last summer?

JIM: Sho 'nuff, Daisy?

(Daisy nods smilingly.)

JIM: *(Sadly)* But I got to go 'way. Whut we gointer do 'bout dat?

DAISY: Where you goin', Jim?

JIM: *(Looking sadly down the track)* God knows. *(Offstage from the same direction from which Jim entered comes the sound of whistling and tramping of feet on the ties. Brightening)* Dat's Dave! *(Frowning suspiciously)* Wonder whut he doin' walking dis track? *(Looks accusingly at Daisy)* I bet he's goin' to yo' workplace.

DAISY: Whut for?

JIM: He ain't goin' to see de Madame – must be goin' to see you.

(He starts to rise petulantly as Dave comes upon the scene. Daisy rises also.)

DAVE: *(Looks accusingly from one to the other)* Whut y'all jumpin' up for? I –

JIM: Whut you got to do wid us business? Tain't none of yo' business if we stand up, set down or fly like a skeeter hawk.

DAVE: Who said I keered? Dis railroad belongs to de *man* – I kin walk it good as you, can't I?

JIM: *(Laughing exultantly)* Oh yeah, Mr. Do-Dirty! You figgered you had done run me on off so you could git Daisy all by yo'self. You was headin' right for her workplace.

DAVE: I wasn't no such a thing.

JIM: You was. Didn't I hear you coming down de track all

whistling and everything?

DAVE: Youse a big ole Georgy-something-ain't-so! I done got my belly full of Daisy Sat'day night. She can't snore in my ear no more.

DAISY: *(Indignantly)* Whut you come here low-rating me for, Dave Carter? I ain't done nothin' to you but treat you white. Who come rubbed yo' ole head for you yestiddy if it wasn't me?

DAVE: Yeah, you rubbed my head all right, and I lakted dat. But everybody say you done toted a pan to Joe Clarke's barn for Jim before I seen you.

DAISY: Think I was going to let Jim there 'thout nothing fittin for a dog to eat?

DAVE: That's all right, Daisy. If you want to pay Jim for knockin' me in de head, all right. But I'm a man in a class – in a class to myself and nobody knows my name.

JIM: *(Snatching Daisy around to face him)* Was you over to Dave's house yestiddy rubbing his ole head and cloaking wid him to run me outa town – and me looked up in dat barn wid de cows and mules?

DAISY: *(Sobbing)* All both of y'all hollerin' at me an' fussin' me just 'cause I tries to be nice – and neither one of y'all don't keer nothin' 'bout me. *(Both boys glare at each other over Daisy's head and both try to hug her at the same time. She violently wrenches herself away from both and makes as if to move on.)* Leave me go! Take yo' rusty paws offen me. I'm going on back to my workplace. I just got off to see 'bout y'all and look how y'all treat me.

JIM: Wait a minute, Daisy. I love you likes God loves Gabriel – and dat's His best angel.

DAVE: Daisy, I love you harder than de thunder can bump a stump – if I don't – God's a gopher.

DAISY: *(Brightening)* Dat's de first time you ever said so.

DAVE AND JIM: Who?

JIM: Whut you hollering "who" for? Yo' foot don't fit no limb.

DAVE: Speak when you spoken to – come when you called, next fall you'll be my coon houn' dog.

JIM: Table dat discussion. *(Turning to Daisy)* You ain't never give me no chance to talk wid you right.

DAVE: You made *me* feel like you was trying to put de Ned book on me all de time. Do you love me sho 'nuff, Daisy?

DAISY: *(Blooming again into coquetry)* Aw, y'all better stop dat. You know you don't mean it.

DAVE: Who don't mean it? Lemme tell you something, mama, if you was mine I wouldn't have you counting no ties wid yo' pretty lil toes. Know whut I'd do?

DAISY: *(Coyly)* Naw, whut would you do?

DAVE: I'd buy a whole passenger train and hire some mens to run it for you.

DIASY: *(Happily)* Oo-ooh, Dave.

JIM: *(To Dave)* De wind may blow, de door may slam. Dat whut you shootin' ain't worth a damn. *(To Daisy)* I'd buy you a great big ole ship – and then baby, I'd buy you a ocean to sail yo' ship on.

DAISY: *(Happily)* Oo-ooh, Jim.

DAVE: *(To Jim)* A long train, a short caboose – Dat lie whut you shootin', ain't no use. *(To Daisy)* Miss Daisy, know what I'd do for you?

DAISY: Naw, whut?

DAVE: I'd like uh job cleanin out de Atlantic Ocean jus' for you.

DAISY: Don't fool me now, papa.

DAVE: I couldn't fool YOU, Daisy, 'cause anything I say 'bout lovin' you, I don't keer how big it is, it wouldn't be half de truth. I'd come down de river riding a mud cat and leading a minnow.

DAISY: Lawd, Dave, you sho is propaganda.

JIM: *(Peevishly)* Naw he ain't – he's just lying – he's a noble liar. Know whut I'd do if you was mine?

DAISY: Naw, Jim.

JIM: I'd make a panther wash yo' dishes and a 'gator chop yo' wood for you.

DAVE: Daisy, how come you let Jim lie lak dat? He's as big a liar as he is a man. But sho 'nuff now, laying all sides to jokes, Jim, there don't even know how to answer you. If you don't b'lieve it, ast him something.

DAISY: *(To Jim)* You like me much, Jim?

JIM: *(Enthusiastically)* Yeah, Daisy, I sho do.

DAVE: *(Triumphant)* See dat! I tole you he didn't know how to answer nobody like you. If he was talking to some of them ol' funny looking gals over town he'd be answering 'em just right. But he got to learn how to answer *you.* Now you ast *me* something and see how I answer you.

DAISY: Do you like me, Dave?

DAVE: *(Very peoperly in a falsetto voice)* Yes ma'am! Dat's de way to answer swell folks like you. Furthermore, less we prove which one of us love you de best right now. *(To Jim)* Jim, how much time would you do on de chain gang for dis 'oman?

JIM: Twenty years and like it.

DAVE: See dat, Daisy? Dat nigger ain't willing to do no time for you. I'd *beg* de judge to gimme life. *(Both Jim and Dave laugh.)*

DAISY: Y'all doin' all dis boo-kooing out here on de railroad track but I bet y'all crazy 'bout Bootsie and Teets and a whole heap of others.

JIM: Cross my feet and hope to die! I'd ruther see all de other wimmen folks in de world dead than for you to have de toothache.

DAVE: If I was dead any any other woman come near my coffin de undertaker would have to do his job all over – cause I'd git right up and walk off. Furthermore, Miss Daisy, ma'am, also, ma'am, which would you ruther be, a lark a flying or a dove a-settin' – ma'am, also ma'am?

DAISY: 'Course I'd ruther be a dove.

JIM: Miss Daisy, ma'am, also ma'am – if you marry dis nigger over my head, I'm going to git me a green hickory club and season it over yo' head.

DAVE: Don't you be skeered, baby – papa kin take keer a *you*. *(To Jim)* Counting from de finger *(Suiting the action to the word)* back to de thumb – start anything I got you some.

JIM: Aw, I don't want no more fight wid you, Dave.

DAVE: Who said anything about fighting? We just provin' who love Daisy de best. *(To Daisy)* Now, which one of us you think love you de best?

DAISY: 'Deed I don't know, Dave.

DAVE: Baby, I'd walk de water for you – and tote a mountain on my head while I'm walkin'.

JIM: Know whut I'd do, honey babe? If you was a thousand miles from home and you didn't have no ready-made money and you had to walk all de way, walkin' till yo' feet start to rolling, just like a wheel, and I was riding way up in de sky, I'd step backwards offa dat airyplane just to walk home wid you.

DAISY: *(Falling on Jim's neck)* Jim, when you talk to me like dat I just can't stand it. Less us git married right now.

JIM: Now you talkin' like a blue-back speller. Less go!

DAVE: *(Sadly)* You gointer leave me lak dis, Daisy?

DAISY: *(Sadly)* I likes you, too, Dave, I sho do. But I can't marry both of y'all at de same time.

JIM: Aw, come on, Daisy – sun's gettin' low. *(He starts off pulling Daisy.)*

DAVE: *(Walking after them)* Whut's I'm gointer do?

JIM: Gwan back and hunt turkeys – you make out you so touchous nobody can't tell you yo' eye is black 'thout you got to run git de law.

DAVE: *(Almost tearfully)* Aw Jim, shucks! Where y'all going?

> *(Daisy comes to an abrupt halt and stops Jim)*

DAISY: That's right, honey. Where *is* we goin' sho 'nuff?

JIM: *(Sadly)* Deed I don't know, baby. They just sentenced me to go – they didn't say where and I don't know.

DAISY: How we goin' know how to go when we don't know where we goin'?

> *(Jim looks at Dave as if he expects some help but Dave stands sadly silent. Jim takes a few steps forward as if to go on. Daisy makes a step or two, unwillingly, then looks behind her and stops. Dave looks as if he will follow them.)*

DAISY: Jim! *(He stops and turns)* Wait a minute! Whut we gointer do when we git there?

JIM: Where?

DAISY: Where we goin'?

JIM: I done tole you I don't know where it is.

DAISY: But how we gointer git something to eat and a place to stay?

JIM: Play my box for de white folks and dance just like I been doing.

DAISY: You can't take keer of me on dat, not where we hafta pay rent.

JIM: *(Looks appealingly at Dave, then away quickly)* Well, I can't help *dat*, can I?

DAISY: *(Brightly)* I tell you whut, Jim! Less us don't go nowhere. They sentenced you to leave Eatonville and youse almost a mile from de city limits already. Youse in Maitland now. Supposin' you come live on de white folks' place wid me after we git married. Eatonville ain't got nothin' to do wid you livin' in Maitland.

JIM: Dat's a good idea, Daisy.

DAISY: *(Jumping into his arms)* And lissen, honey, you don't have to be beholden to nobody. You can throw dat ole box away if you want to. I know where you can get a *swell* job.

JIM: *(Sheepishly)* Doin' whut? *(Looks lovingly at his guitar.)*

DAISY: *(Almost dancing)* Yard man. All you have to do is wash windows, and sweep de sidewalk, and scrub off de steps and porch and hoe up de weeds and rake up de leaves and dig a few holes now and then with a spade – to plant some trees and things like that. It's a good steady job.

JIM: *(After a long deliberation)* You see, Daisy, de Mayor and de Corporation told me to go on off and I oughter go.

DAISY: Well, I'm not going tippin' down no railroad track like a Maltese cat. I wasn't brought up knockin' round from here to yonder.

JIM: Well, I wasn't brought up wid no spade in my hand – and ain't going to start it now.

DAISY: But sweetheart, we got to live, ain't we? We got to git hold of money before we kin do anything. I don't mean to stay in de white folks' kitchen all my days.

JIM: Yeah, all dat's true, but you couldn't buy a flea a waltzing jacket wid de money *I'm* going to make wid a hoe and spade.

DAISY: *(Getting tearful)* You don't want me. You don't love me.

JIM: Yes, I do, darling, I love you. Youse de one letting a spade come between us. *(He caresses her.)* I loves you and you only. You don't see *me* dragging a whole gang of farming tools into us business, do you?

DAISY: *(Stiffly)* Well, I ain't going to marry no man that ain't going to work and take care of me.

JIM: I don't mind working if de job ain't too heavy for me. I ain't going to bother wid nothin' in my hands heavier than dis box – and I totes it round my neck 'most of de time. I kin go out and hunt you some game when times gits tight.

DAISY: Don't strain yo'self huntin' nothin' for me. I ain't goin' to eat nobody's settin' hen. *(She turns to Dave finally.)*

JIM: Whut ole sittin hen? Ain't you and Lum done et up de turkey I – I – bought8?

DAISY: You might of brought it, but Dave sho kilt it. You couldn't hit de side of uh barn wid uh bass fiddle.

DAVE: 'Course I kilt it, and I kilt it for you, but I didn't kill none for Lum Bailey. De clean head hound!

DAISY: *(Turning to Dave)* Well, I reckon you loves me the best anyhow. You wouldn't talk to me like Jim did, would you, Dave?

DAVE: Naw, I wouldn't say whut he said atall.

DAISY: *(Cuddling up to him)* Whut would *you* say, honey?

DAVE: I'd say dat box was too heavy for me to fool wid. I wouldn't tote nothing but my gun and my hat and I feel like I'm 'busing myself sometime totin' dat.

DAISY: *(Outraged)* Don't you mean to work none?

DAVE: Wouldn't hit a lick at a snake.

DAISY: I don't blame *you*, Dave *(looks down at his feet)* 'cause toting dem feet of yourn is enough to break down your constitution.

DAVE: They carries me wherever I wants to go. Daisy, you marry Jim cause I don't want to come between y'all. He's my buddy.

JIM: Come to think of it, Dave, she was yourn first. You take and handle dat spade for her.

DAVE: You heard her say it is all I can do to lift up dese feets and put 'em down. Where I'm going to git any time to wrassle wid any hoes and shovels? You kin git round better'n me. You done won Daisy – I give in. I ain't going to bite no friend of mine in de back.

DAISY: Both of you niggers can git yo' hats an' yo' heads an' git on down de road. Neither one of y'all don't have to have me. I got a good job and plenty men begging for yo' shame.

JIM: Dat's right, Daisy, you go git you one them mens whut don't mind smelling mules – and beating de white folks to de barn every morning. I don't wanta be bothered wid nothin' but dis box.

DAVE: And I can't strain wid nothin' but my feets and my gun. I kin git mo' turkey gobblers, but never no job.

(Daisy walks slowly away in the direction from which she came. Both watch her a little wistfully for a minute. The sun is setting.)

DAVE: Guess I better be gittin' on back – it's 'most dark. Where you goin, Jim?

JIM: I don't know, Dave. Down de road, I reckon.

DAVE: Whyncher come on back to town? Tain't no use you proagin' up and down de railroad track when you got a home.

JIM: They done lawed me 'way from it for hittin' you wid dat bone.

DAVE: Dat ain't nothin'. It was my head you hit. An' if I don't keer, whut dem ole ugly-rump niggers got to do wid it?

JIM: They might not let me come in town.

DAVE: *(Seizing Jim's arm and facing him back toward the town)* They better! Look here, Jim, if they try to keep you out dat town we'll go out to dat swamp and git us a mule bone apiece and come back and boil dat stew down to a low gravy.

JIM: You mean dat Dave? *(Dave nods his head eagerly.)*

DAVE: Us wasn't mad wid one 'nother nohow. Come on less go back to town. Dem mullet heads better leave me be, too. *(Picks up a heavy stick)* I wish Lum would come tellin' me bout de law when I got all dis law in *my* hands. An' de rest of dem 'gator-face jigs – if they ain't got a whole set of mule bones and a good determination they better not bring de mess up.

CURTAIN

Poker! (1931)

CAST:
>NUNKIE
>AUNT DILSEY
>TOO-SWEET
>TUSH HAWG
>BLACK BABY
>BECKERWOOD
>SACK DADDY

TIME: *Present.*

PLACE: *New York.*

SCENE: *A shabby front room in a shotgun house. A door covered by dingy portieres upstage center. Small panel window in side wall left. Plain center table with chairs drawn up about it. Gaudy calendars on wall. Battered piano against wall right. Kerosene lamp with reflector against wall on either side of room.*

> *At rise of curtain Nunkie is at piano playing. Others at table with small stacks of chips before each man. Tush Hawg is seated at table so that he faces audience. He is expertly riffing the cards. He looks over his shoulder and speaks to Nunkie.*

TUSH HAWG: Come on here, Nunkie – and take a hand! You're holding up the game. You been woofin' round here about the poker you can play – now do it!

NUNKIE: Yeah, I plays poker. I plays the piano and Gawd knows I plays the devil.

BLACK BABY: Aw, you can be had! Come on and get in the game! My britches is cryin' for your money!

NUNKIE: Soon as I play the deck I'm comin' and take you alls money! Don't rush me.

> Ace means the first time that I met you
>
> Deuce means there was nobody there but us two
>
> Trey means the third party - Charlie was his name
>
> Four spot means the fourth time you tried that same old game –
>
> Five spot means five years you played me for a clown
>
> Six spot means six feet of earth when the deal goes down
>
> Now I'm holding the seven spot for each day of the week
>
> Eight means eight hours that she Shebaed with

your Sheik –
Nine spot means nine hours that I work hard
every day –
Ten spot means tenth of every month I brought
you home my pay –
The Jack is Three-card Charlie who played me for
a goat
The Queen, that's my pretty Mama, also trying to
cut my throat –
The Kin stands for Sweet Papa Nunkie and he's
goin' to wear the crown,
So be careful you all ain't broke when the deal
goes down!

*(He laughs and crosses to the table, bringing piano
stool for a seat.)*

TUSH HAWG: Aw now, brother, two dollars for your seat
before you try to sit in this game.

*(Nunkie laughs sheepishly and puts money down.
Tush Hawg pushes stack of chips toward him.)*

NUNKIE: I didn't put it down because I knew you all goin'
to be puttin' it right back in my pocket.
BECKERWOOD: Aw, y'all go ahead and play. *(To Tush Hawg)*
Deal!

*(Tush Hawg begins to deal for draw poker. The game
gets tense. Sack Daddy is the first man at Tush's left
– he throws back three cards and is dealt three more.)*

SACK DADDY: My luck I sure is rotten! My gal must be
cheatin' on me. I ain't had a pair since John Henry had
a hammer!
BLACK BABY: *(Drawing three new cards)* You might be
fooling the rest with the cryin' you're doin' but I'm
squattin' for you! You're cryin' worse thatn Cryin'
Emma!

TOO-SWEET: *(Studying his three new cards. Sings)*
> When yo cards gets lucky, oh Partner,
> you oughter be in a rollin' game.

AUNT DILSEY: *(Enters through portieres, stands and looks disapproving)* You all oughter be ashamed of yourself, gamblin' and carryin' on like this!

BLACK BABY: Aw, this ain't no harm, Aunt Dilsey! You go on back to bed and git your night's rest.

AUNT DILSEY: No harm! I know all about these no-harm sins! If you don't stop this card playin', all of you all goin' to die and go to Hell.

> *(Shakes warning finger and exits through portieres. While she is talking the men have been hiding cards out of their hands and pulling aces out of sleeves and vest pockets and shoes - it is done quickly, one does not see the other do it.)*

NUNKIE: *(Shoving a chip forward)* A dollar!

SACK DADDY: Raise you two!

BLACK BABY: I don't like to strain with nobody but it's goin' to cost you five. Come on, you shag-nags!

TOO-SWEET: You all act like you're spuddin'! Bet some money! Put your money where your mouth is!

TUSH HAWG: Twenty-five dollars to keep my company! Dog-gone, I'm spreadin' my knots!

SACK DADDY: And I bet you a fat man I'll take your money – I call you. *(Turns up his cards. He has four aces and king.)*

TUSH HAWG: *(Showing his cards)* Youse a liar! I ain't dealt you no aces. Don't try to carry the Pam-Pam to me 'cause I'll gently chain-gang for you!

SACK DADDY: Oh yeah! I ain't goin' to fit no jail for you and nobody else. I'm to get me a green club and season it over your head. Then I'll give my case to Miss Bush and let Mother Green stand my bond! I got deal them aces!

NUNKIE: That's a lie! Both of you is lyin'! Lyin' like the cross-ties from New York to Key West! How can you all hold aces when I got *four*? Somebody is goin' to West Hell before midnight!

BECKERWOOD: Don't you woof at Tush Hawg. If you do, I'm goin' to bust hell wide open with a man!

BLACK BABY: *(Pulls out razor)* My chop-axe tells me I got the only clean aces they is on this table! Before I'll leave you all rob me outa my money, I'm goin' to die it off!

TOO-SWEET: I promised the devil one man and I'm goin' to give him five! *(Draws gun.)*

TUSH HAWG: Don't draw your bosom on me! God sent me a pistol and I'm goin' to send him a man! *(Fires. Business for all.)*

AUNT DILSEY: (*Enters after shooting business. Stands. Drops to chair*) They wouldn't lissen. *(Looks men over)* It sure is goin' to be a whole lot tougher in hell now!

CURTAIN

Lawing & Jawing (1931)

CAST:
- JUDGE DUNFUMY
- CLERK
- GIRL
- BOY
- OFFICER SIMPSON
- SECOND OFFICER
- JEMIMA FLAPCAKES
- CLIFF MULLINS
- CLIFF'S WIFE
- DE OTIS BLUNT
- LAWYER 1
- LAWYER 2

TIME: *Present.*

PLACE: *Way 'cross Georgia.*

SCENE: *Judge Dunfumy's court.*

SETTING: *Usual courtroom arrangement, except that there is a large red arrow pointing offstage left, marked "To Jail."*

ACTION: *At rise everybody is in place except the Judge. Suddenly the Clerk looks offstage right and motions for everybody to rise. Enter the Judge. He wears a black cap and gown and has his gavel in his hand. The two policemen walk behind him holding up his gown. He mounts the bench and glares all about him before he seats himself. There is a pretty girl in the front row left, and he takes a good look at her, smiles, frowns at her escort. He motions the police to leave him and take their places with the spectators and he then raps vigorously with his gavel for order.*

JUDGE: Hear! Hear! Court is set! My honor is on de bench. You moufy folks set up! *(He glares at the boy with the pretty girl)* All right, Mr. Whistle-britches, just keep dat jawing now and see how much time I'll give you!

BOY: I wasn't talking, your honor.

JUDGE: Well, quit looking so moufy. *(To Clerk)* Call de first case. And I warn each and all dat my honor is in bad humor dis mawnin'. I'd give a canary bird twenty years for peckin' at a elephant. *(To Clerk)* Bring 'em on.

CLERK: *(Reading)* Cliff Mullins, charged with assault upon his wife with a weapon and disturbing the peace.

(As Cliff is led to the bar by the officer, the Judge glares ferociously at him. His wife, all bandages, limps up to the bar at the same time.)

CLIFF: Judge, I didn't go to hurt her. Saturday night I was down on Dearborn Street in a buffet flat.

JUDGE: A buffet flat?

CLIFF: Aw, at Emma Hayles' house.

JUDGE: Oh, yes. Go on.

CLIFF: Well, (*points thumb at wife*) she comes down dere and claim I took her money and she claimed I wuz spending it on Emma.

CLIFF'S WIFE: And dat's just whut he was doing, too, Judge.

CLIFF: Aw, she's tellin' a great big ole Georgia lie, Judge. I wasn't spendin' no money of her'n.

CLIFF'S WIFE: Yes he was, Judge. There wasn't no money for him to git *but* mine. He ain't hit a lick of work since God been to Macon. Know whut he 'lowed when I worry him 'bout workin'? Says he wouldn't take a job wid de Careless Love Lumber Company, puttin' out whut make you do me lak you do, do, do.

JUDGE: So, you goes for a sweet-back, do you?

CLIFF: Naw suh, Judge. I'd be glad to work if I could find a job.

JUDGE: How long you been outa work?

CLIFF: Seventeen years –

JUDGE: Seventeen years? (*To Cliff's Wife*) You been takin' keer of dis man for seventeen years?

CLIFF'S WIFE: Naw, but he been so mean to me, it seems lak seventeen years.

JUDGE: Now you tell me just where he hurt you.

CLIFF'S WIFE: Judge, tell you de truth, I'm hurt all over. (*Rubs her buttocks*) Fact is I'm cut.

JUDGE: Did you git cut in de fracas?

CLIFF'S WIFE: (*Feeling the back of her left thigh below her buttocks*) Not in de fracas, Judge – just below it.

> (*She starts to show the Judge where she has been cut. He motions to stop her.*)

JUDGE: Stop! (*To Officer Simpson*) Grab him. Put him in de shade.

CLIFF: Judge, I'm unguilty! I ain't laid de weight of my hand on her in malice. You got me 'cused of murder and I ain't harmed a child.

JUDGE: Lemme ast *you* something. Didn't you know dat all de women in dis town belongs to me? Beat my women and I'll stuff you in jail. Ninety years. Take 'im away. (Cliff is led off to jail. Judge looks angrily at the boy who is holding hands with the pretty girl) You runs me hot and I'm just dyin' to sit on *yo'* case. Whut you in here for?

BOY: Nothin'.

JUDGE: Well, whut you doin' in my court, you gater-faced rascal?

BOY: My girl wanted to see whut was goin' on, so I brought her in.

JUDGE: Oh yeah! *(Smiles at Girl)* She was usin' good sense to come see whut I'm doin', but how come *you* come in here? You gointer have a hard time gittin' out.

BOY: I ain't done a thing. I ain't never done nothin'. I'm just as clean as a fish, and he been in bathin' all his life.

JUDGE: You ain't done nothin', hunh? Well den youse guilty of vacancy. Grab 'im, Simpson, and search 'im –and if he got any concealed weapons, I'm gointer give 'im life-time and eight years mo'. (*The Officer seizes the boy and frisks him. All he finds is a new deck of cards. The Judge looks at them in triumph.*) Uhn hunh! I knowed it, one of dese skin game jelly-beans. Robbin' hard workin' men out they money.

BOY: Judge, I ain't used 'em at all. See, dey's brand new.

JUDGE: Well, den youse charged wid totin' concealed cards and attempt to gamble. Ten years at hard labor. Put him in de dark, Simpson, and throw de key away. *(He looks at the girl and beams.)* Don't you worry 'bout how you gointer git home. You gointer be took home right, 'cause I'm gointer take you myself. Bring on de next one, Clerk.

CLERK: Jemima Flapcakes, charged with illegal possession and sale of alcoholic liquors.

(She is a fat, black, belligerent looking woman. Judge looks coldly at her)

JUDGE: Well, you heard whut he said. Is you guilty or unguilty? And I'm tellin' you right now dat when you come up befo' *me* it's just like youse in church. You better have a strong determination, and you better tell a good experience.

JEMIMA: *(Arms akimbo)* Yes, I sold it and I'll sell it again. *(Snaps fingers and shakes hips)* How does ole booze-selling mama talk?

JUDGE: Yes, five thousand dollars and ten years in jail. *(Snaps fingers and shakes hips)* How does ole heavy-fining papa talk?

(She is led away, shouting and weeping.)

CLERK: De Otis Blunt, charged wid stealin' a mule.

(Lawyer 1 arises and comes forward with the prisoner.)

LAWYER 1: You can't convict this man. I'm here to represent him.

JUDGE: Yo' mouf might spout lak a coffee pot but I got a lawyer *(looks at other lawyer)* dat kin beat yours segastuatin'. *(Looks admiring at girl)* How am I chewin' my dictionary and minglin' my alphabets?

LAWYER 1: Well, I kin try, can't I?

JUDGE: Oh yeah, you kin try, but I kin see right now where he's gointer git all de time dat God ever made dat ain't been used already. From now on. *(To Lawyer)* Go 'head, and spread yo' lungs all over Georgy, but he's goin' to jail! Mules must be respected.

LAWYER 1: *(Striking a pose at the bar)* Your Honor, *(looks at the pretty girl)* Ladies and Gentlemen –

JUDGE: Never mind 'bout dat lady. You talk yo' chat to *me*.

LAWYER 1: This is a clear case of syllogism! Again I say syllogism. My client is innocent because it was a dark night when they say he stole the mule and that's against all laws of syllogism.

JUDGE: *(Looks impressed and laughs.)* Dat ole fool do know somethin' 'bout law.

LAWYER: When George Washington was pleading de case of Marbury vs. Madison, what did *he* say? What *did* he say? Scintillate, scintillate, Globule orific. Fain would I fathom thy nature's specific. Loftily posed in either capacious, strongly resembling a gem carbonaceous. What did Abraham Lincoln say about mule –stealing? When torrid Phoebus refuses his presence and ceases to lamp with fierce incandescence, then you illume the regions supernal, scintillate, scintillate, semper nocturnal. Syllogism, again I say syllogism.

(He takes his seat amid applause.)

JUDGE: Man, youse a pleadin' fool. You knows yo' rules and by-laws.

LAWYER 2: Let me show my glory. Let me spread my habeas corpus.

JUDGE: Tain't no use. Dis lawyer done convinced me.

LAWYER 2: But, lemme parade my material –

JUDGE: Parade yo' material anywhere you want to exceptin' befo' me. Dis lil girl wants to go home and I'm goin' with her and enjoy de consequences. Court's adjourned.

CURTAIN

Woofing (1931)

TIME: *Present.*

PLACE: *Negro Street in Waycross, Georgia.*

SETTING: *Porch and sidewalk, etc.*

ACTION: *Through the open window of one of the shacks a woman is discovered ironing. Good Black is sitting on the floor of the porch asleep. The woman hums a bar or two, then comes to the window and calls to the man.*

BERTHA: Good Black, why don't you git up from dere and carry dese white folks' clothes home? You always want money but you wouldn't hit a lick at a snake!

GOOD BLACK: Aw, shut up woman. I'm tired of hearin' bout dem white folks clothes. I don't keer if dey never git 'em.

BERTHA: You better keer! Dese very clothes took and brought *you* out de crack. 'Cause de first time I saw you, you was so hungry till you was walkin' lap-legged. Man, you had de white-mouf, you was so hungry.

> *(She exits. Enter Cliffert leisurely. Good Black sees him and calls)*

GOOD BLACK: Hey, Cliffert, where you headed for?

CLIFFERT: Oh, nowhere in particular.

GOOD BLACK: Come here then, fish, and lemme bend a checker game over yo' head. Come on, youse my fish.

CLIFFERT: *(Comes to the porch and sits)* Git de checkers and I'll have you any, some or none. I push a mean chuck-a-luck myself.

BERTHA: *(From inside)* Dress up and strut around? Yes! Play checkers? Yes! Eat? Yes! Work? No!

> *(The game starts. A period of silence in which they indicate their concentration with frowns, cautious moves, and head scratching. Good Black is pointing his index finger over the board indicating*

moves. *He wig-wags, starting to move, scratches his
head thoroughly, changes his mind and fools around
without moving.)*

CLIFFERT: Police! Police! Come here and make dis man
move!

GOOD BLACK: Aw, I got plenty moves. *(Scratches his
head)* Jus' tryin' to see which one I want to make. But
when I *do* move, it's gointer be just too bad for you.

*(A guitar is heard offstage and Cliffert brightens. He
cups his hand and calls.)*

CLIFFERT: Hey Lonnie! Come here! Ha, ha, ha! I got me a
fish.

*(Enter Lonnie picking "East Coast" on his box and
stands watching the game. He ceases to play as he
stops walking.)*

CLIFFERT: Ha, ha! You see ol' Good Black goes for a hard
guy. He tries to know more than a mule and a mule's
head longer'n his'n. Ha, ha! I set a trap for him and he
fell right into it. Trying to ride de britches! *Now* look
at him.

GOOD BLACK: Aw, shut up! You tryin' to show yo' grandma
how to milk ducks. You can't beat me playin' no
checkers. *(Scratches his head again)* Just watch me
show my glory.

BERTHA: *(Leans out of window)* Good Black! When you
gointer come git dese clothes!

(He does not answer. He is trying to concentrate.)

LONNIE: You got him Cliffert. You got him in Louisville
Loop. He's yo' fish all right.

CLIFFERT: *(Boastfully)* Man, didn't I push a mean chuck-
a-luck dat time! I'm good, better, and best. *(To Good
Black)* Move, man! I told you not to do it.

GOOD BLACK: All dat noise ain't playin' checkers. You just

wait till I make my move.

BERTHA: All right, now, Mr. Nappy-Chin! I don't want to
have to call you no mo' to come keer dese white folks'
clothes! I'm tired of takin' and takin' affa you! My
belly's full clear up to de neck. I don't need no lazy
coon lak you nohow. I'm a good woman, and I needs
somebody dats gointer give aid and assistance.

GOOD BLACK: Aw, go 'head on, woman, and leave me
be! Every Saturday it's de same thing! Yo' mouth
exhausting like a automobile. You worse than "Cryin'
Emma." You kin whoop like de Seaboard and squall
lak da Coast Line. *(Taps his head)* You ain't got all
dat b'long to *you*, and nothin' dat b'long to nobody's
else. You better leave me 'lone before you make a
bad man out of me. Fool wid me and I'll go git me
somebody else. I'm a much-right man.

BERTHA: Now you ain't no much-right man neither. You
didn't *git me* wid no sawmill license – You went to de
court house and paid a dollar and a half for me. Tain't
no other woman got as much right to you as I got. De
man got to tell you youse divorced befo' yo' kin play
dat much-right on me!

GOOD BLACK: De man don't have to tell me nothin'! I got
divorce in my heels.

BERTHA: You ain't de only one dat knows where de railroad
track is, I done made up my mind, and I done
promised Gabriel and a couple of other men dat if
yo' don't do no better than yo' been doin,' I'm gointer
pack me a suitcase and grab de first smoky thing I
see. I'll be long gone.

GOOD BLACK: Aw, yo' ain't no trouble. Yo' can be had. Yo'
ain't never gointer leave me.

BERTHA: How come I won't? Just 'cause I been takin' keer
of yo', don't make me a park ape out yo'self. I'll leave
yo', just as sure as yo' snore!

GOOD BLACK: *(Rises and hitches up his trousers)* Aw, yo'ain't

gointer leave me, and if yo' go, yo' wouldn't stay, 'cause
I'm a damn sweet man, and yo' know it!

LONNIE: Hey, hey!

> *(Lonnie begins to pick and Good Black sings. Lonnie*
> *sings a line now and then.)*

GOOD BLACK:
> Yo' may leave and go to Hali-muk-fack
> But my slow drag will – uh bring yo' back
> Well yo' may go, but this will bring yo' back
>
> I been in de country but I moved to town
> I'm a tolo-shaker from my head on down
> Well, yo' may go, but this will bring yo' back
>
> Some folks call me a tolo-shaker
> It's a doggone lie I'm a back-bone breaker
> Well, yo' may go, but this will bring yo' back
>
> Oh, ship on de sea, boat on de ocean
> I raise hell when I take a notion
> Well, yo' may go, but this will bring yo' back
>
> Oh, who do, who do, who do wackin'
> Wid my hells a'poppin' and my toenails crackin'
> Well, yo' may go, but this will bring yo' back.

BERTHA: Dat's all right too, pap but if yo' can't make me
tote dese clothes home, don't bring de mess up. Yo'se
abstifically a humbug.

CLIFFERT: Man, come on back here and move, or else own
up to de folks yo' can't push no checkers wid me.

> *(He sits and begins to lay out moves with his fingers*
> *and scratch his head. Enter Skanko who stands arms*
> *akimbo looking over Cliffert's shoulder.)*

CLIFFERT: *(Looking up)* Don't stand over me lak dat, ugly as yo' is.

SKANKO: You ain't nobody's pretty baby yo'self!

CLIFFERT: Dat's all right, I ain't as ugly as yo' – youse ugly enough to git behind a Simpoon weed and hatch monky.

SKANKO: And youse ugly enough to git behind a tombstone and hatch hants.

CLIFFERT: Youse so ugly dey have to cover yo' face up at night so sleep can slip up on yo'.

SKANKO: You look like ten cents worth of Have-Mercy. Yo' face look lak ole Uncle Jump-off. Yo' mouth look lak a bunch of ruffles.

CLIFFERT: Yeah, but yo' done passed me. Yo' so ugly till they could throw yo' in de Mississippi River and skim ugly for six months.

SKANKO: Look here, Cliff, don't yo' personate me! Counting from de little finger back to de thumb – yo' start anythin', I got yo' some.

CLIFFERT: Go head and grab me buddie, but if yo' don't know how to turn me loose too, don't bring de mess up! If yo' hit me, I may not beat you, but yo'll be so dirty when St. Peter git yo' dat he can't use yo'.

SKANKO: Don't call *me* buddy. Yo' buddy is huntin' coconuts. Don't yo' try to throw me for a nap. Do, I'll kill yo' so stiff dead they'll have to push yo' down. Yo' gointer make me do some double cussin' on you. *(He picks up a heavy stick and walks back towards Cliffert.)* Now I got dis farmer's choice in my hands, yo' better git outa my face.

CLIFFERT: Yo' wanta fight?

SKANKO: Yeah, I wanta fight. Put it where I kin use it and I'll sho' use it. I'll fight anybody. I git so hot sometimes I fights de corner of de house. I'm so hot I totes a pistol to keep from getting' in a fight wid myself. I prints dangerous every time I sit down in, in a chair.

CLIFFERT: Man, this ain't no fighting weather. Ha, ha, ha!
Did yo' think I was mad sho' nuff? Yo can't fight me.
They's got to be runnin' before fightin' and they's got
to be plenty *good* runnin' before dis fight comes off.

MAN: All right now. Yo' leave me alone and I'm a good
man. I'm just like an old shoe. If yo' rain on me and
cool me off I'm soft. If yo' shine on me and git me hot,
I'm hard.

*(He drops the stick and exits. Cliffert is shaking all
over. He looks after to be sure he is gone.)*

GOOD BLACK: *(Laughing)* Kah, kah, kah. Whut yo' so
scared about? De way yo' was talkin' I thought yo' was
mad enough to fight.

CLIFFERT: I was. I gits hot real quick! But I'm very easy
cooled when de man I'm mad wid is bigger'n me. *(He
drops into his seat, wiping his face.)* Man did yo' see how
he grabbed up dat check? He done skeered me into a
three-week's spasm!

BERTHA: Good Black, dese clothes is still waiting.

GOOD BLACK: Well, let 'em wait on, I done tole yo' once.
Yo' kin run yo' mouf but yo' can't run my business.

*(Enter Bea Ethel, a pretty girl. She strolls happily across
without stopping. Good Black pretends to cough.)*

BEA: Who is dat? *(Turns and glares at him)* My old man got
something for dat cough yo' got.

CLIFFERT: Dat's right, tell dese old mullet head married
men to mind they own business. Now, take *me*
for instance. I'm a much-right man. *(Gets up and
approaches her flirtatiously)* I didn't quite git yo' name
straight. Yo' better tell it to me again.

BEA ETHEL: My name is Bea Ethel, turned round to Jones.

CLIFFERT: *(Flirtatiously)* Yo' pretty lil ole ground angel go'?
Where did yo' come from?

BEA ETHEL: Detroit. Yo' like me?

CLIFFERT: Do I lak yo'? I love yo' just lak God loves
Gabriel, and dat's his best angel. Go 'head and say
somethin'. I jus' love to hear yo' talk.

BEA ETHEL: Gimme five dollars. I need some stockings.

CLIFFERT: *Now* Mama, dis ain't Gimme, Georgia. Dis is
Waycross. I'm just lak de cemetery. I takes in but never
no put out. I ain't puttin' out nothin' but old folks'
eyes – and I don't do that till they's dead. Run long,
mama. *(Bea Ethel exits and he resumes his seat.)* Come
on, Good Black, lemme wrap dis checker round yo'
neck.

GOOD BLACK: Gimme time, gimme time! Don't try to rush
me.

> *(He begins same business of figuring out moves and
> scratching his head. Enter three girls and fellows.
> The girls are dressed in cool summer dresses, but
> nothing elaborate.)*

LONNIE: I know I'm gointer play something now.

> *(He tunes and plays "Cold Rainy Day."1 He begins
> to sing and the others join in. All start dancing. They
> couple off as far as possible and Lindy. The men
> unpaired men do hot solo steps.)*

MEN: *(Crying out in ecstasy.)*
Shimmy! If you can't shimmy, shake your head.
Look, baby, look! Throw it in de alley.
Look, if you can't look, stick out, and if you can't
stick out, git out.

> *(At the end of the song and dance, one of the girls
> exclaims.)*

GIRL: *(At the end of the dance)* Aw, we got to go. Mama's
looking for me.

> *(The three girls exit, walking happily. The men watch
> them go.)*

CLIFFERT: Oh, boy, look at 'em! Switching it and looking back at it. *(He imitates the girl's walk.)*

GOOD BLACK: Yeah Lawd, ain't they specifyin'! They handles a lot of traffic.

CLIFFERT: *(Seating himself again)* Yeah, but dat don't play no checkers. Come on here, Good Black and lemme finish wearing your ant.

BERTHA: Good Black, yo' better come git dese clothes.

LONNIE: Good Black, yo' wife kin cold whoop for what she want.

GOOD BLACK: Yeah and if she don't git, she keep right on whoopin'. B'lieve I wants a drink of water. Wisht I knowed where I could slip up on me a drink.

CLIFFERT: Aw man, come on back here and move. Yo' doin' everythin' but playin' checkers. You'd ruther move a mountain wid a bar than to move *(Points)* dat man.

GOOD BLACK: *(Seats himself)* Lemme hurry up and beat dis game befo' yo' bust yo' britches.

> *(He wags his finger to indicate moves, scratches his head, but doesn't move. Several men enter and group around the players. All offer suggestions.)*

MAN 1: You got him, Cliffert. He's locked up just as tight as a keyhole.

MAN 2: Aw, man he kin break out!

MAN 3: Yeah, but it'll cost him plenty to git out of dat trap.

CLIFFERT: Police! Police! He won't move!

MAN 4: Aw, leave go de checkers and less shoot some crap.

> *(Enter a woman in a house dress, head rag on, run down house shoes. She goes to the edge of the porch and calls inside.)*

WOMAN: Hi there Bertha, what yo' doin'?

BERTHA: Still bumpin' de white folks clothes – hittin' for de sundown man. Come on in and have some sit down.

WOMAN: Ain't got time. Got a house full of company. I

took a minute to see if yo' could let me have a little
skeeting garret.

BERTHA: How come yo' didn't git yo'self some snuff whilst
yo' was at de store? De man ast yo' what else. I ain't no
Piggly Wiggly. Reckon I kin spare yo' a dip, though.

*(She hands out the box and the woman fills her lip
and hands it back.)*

WOMAN: Much obliged, I thank yo'. Reckon I better heel
and toe it on back, to see how de comp'ny is makin' out.

BERTHA: Step inside a minute – I want to put a bug in yo'
ear.

*(She makes an urgent gesture and the other woman
goes inside. Lonnie is sitting off to himself and
picking "Rabbit on de Log" softly. A small boy dashes
on with a lolli pop in his hand. He is pursued by
a little girl yelling "You gimme my all day sucker!
Johnny! You gimme my candy, now!" They run all
over the stage. The men take notice of them and
one of them seizes the boy and restores the candy to
the girl. She pokes out her tongue at the boy and
says "goody, goody, goody, goody, goody!" She notes
the guitar playing and begins to dance. The boy
makes faces back at her and dances back at her. The
music gets louder, dancing faster, the checkerboard
gets upset. General laughter at that. When dance is
over, boy snatches the lolli pop again and races away
and the girl runs behind him yelling "Johnny! You
gimme my candy! Johnny!" The music stops and the
crap game gets under way. Furious side bets for five
and ten cents each. Loud calls on Miss "Daisy Dice,"
snake eyes, "Ada from Decatur." Somebody suggests a
soft roll, others object on the ground that it's too easy
for the experts to cheat.)*

GOOD BLACK: Gimme de dice! I'm gointer play 'em like

John Henry.2

LONNIE: John Henry didn't bother wid da bones. He used to play Georgy Skin.

GOOD BLACK: He shot crap too. He played everythin' and everythin' he played, he played it good. Just like he uster drive steel. If I could whip steel like John Henry, I wouldn't stay here and nowhere else.

CLIFFERT: Whut would yo' do?

GOOD BLACK: I'd go somewhere and keep books for somebody.

LONNIE: I know how to play "John Henry."

GOOD BLACK: Well, turn it on and let de bad luck happen.

(As Lonnie plays thru a verse warming up, all the men get interested and start to hum. Cliffert shouts out.)

CLIFFERT: Lawd, Lawd, what evil have I done?

(They sing "John Henry." At the close, the woman who came to borrow snuff emerges from the house still talking back at Bertha.)

WOMAN: He ain't no trouble. I tole him, I says, "yo' must think youse de man dat made side meat taste lak ham." See yo' later.

(She exits hurriedly. The crap game goes on until a band is heard approaching.)

LONNIE: Who dead?

CLIFFERT: Nobody. Don't you know de Imperial Elks is goin' to New York to de Elks Grand Lodge? Yeah, bo, and they's takin' they band. Dat's supposed to be de finest band in de United States.

(The band approaches followed by a great crowd. The craps game is instantly deserted and all follow the band.)

CURTAIN

Forty Yards (1931)

CAST:
    HOWARD CROWD
    LINCOLN CROWD
    HOWARD BAND
    CHEERLEADERS
    HOWARD TEAM
    LINCOLN TEAM

TIME: *Present.*
PLACE: *Washington, D.C.*
SCENE: *The ball park*
SETTING: *The park with grandstands on either sides and upstage.*
ACTION: *At rise, the grandstands are full, the cheer leaders are violently gyrating to whip up the mob. The Lincoln colors fly from the right. Howard's fly from the left. Both have cheerleaders. First is heard the Lincoln mob singing "Didn't He Ramble, Ramble."*

LINCOLN MOB:

> And didn't he ramble, ramble, ramble all around, in and out of town
> He rambled, he rambled, rambled til Ol' Lincoln cut him down

HOWARD MOB:

> There'll be nothing but sweetmeats for our football teams
> There'll be nothing but sweetmeats for our football teams
> Baked Hampton, boiled Shaw, fried Union, Lincoln slaw,
> There'll be nothing but sweetmeats for our football team.

(Enter the Howard band, led by a hot-strutting drum major. They parade the field and the men students pile down and fall in behind the team. They sing and shout the Team Song.)

This is the T-E-A-M team
On which the hopes of Howard lean
Beat Ol' Hampton, beat Ol' Union
Sweep Ol' Lincoln clean

We are the B-E-S-T best
Of the R-E-S-T rest
Come and watch us put Ol' Howard
On top of Lincoln's chest.
We'll hit the L-I-N-E line
For a hundred ninety-nine
For we love Ol' Howard, yes we love her
All the T-I-M-E time.

(At the conclusion the teams take the field. The ball is put into play and Lincoln kicks off to Howard. As the ball is caught and when the player who is carrying the ball plunges, followed by his team, the Lincoln players fall on their knees and begin to sing "I Couldn't Hear Nobody Pray." The Howard team charges down shouting "Joshua fight the Battle of Jericho." Whenever there is a player tackled there is a duet of dancing. Every step there is a dance. Finally the grandstand catches fire and the dancing and shouting runs riot up there. When the ball is on Lincoln's ten-yard line, they hold Howard there by rounding up both teams into a huddle and the bunch shout and sing to a quick curtain.)

Spunk (1931)

Cast:

    Spunk
    Evalina
    Jim Bishop, Evalina's Husband
    Hodge Bishop, Jim's Father
    Ruby Jones
    Nunkie
    Oral
    Willie Joe
    Blue Trout
    Admiral
    Georgia Watson
    Teazie
    Daisy
    Maggie Mae
    Railroad Gang Leader
    Boss
    Captain Hammer
    Convict
    Railroad Gang
    Chain Gang
    Cat-men (6)

ACT ONE

SCENE 1.

SETTING: *All action from spectators viewpoint.*
A railroad track through the Florida woods. Luxuriant foliage on the backdrop. A hand car with tools is standing on the track at extreme left.

ACTION: *The white boss of the extra gang is leaning on the car. The gang is "lining" a rail downtage, center. The gang leader is moving about downstage, right. He dramatizes every utterance. Half dances every step. He chants and the men grunt rhythmically as they pull on the lining bars.*

RAILROAD GANG LEADER: Ah Mobile!
MEN: Hanh!
RGL: Ah, in Alabama!
MEN: Hanh!
RGL: Ah Fort Myers!
MEN: Hanh!
RGL: Ah, in Florida!
MEN: Hanh!
RGL: Ah, let's shake it!
MEN: Hanh!
RGL: Ah, let's break it!
MEN: Hanh!
RGL: Ah, let's shake it!
MEN: Hanh!
RGL: Ah, just a hair! *(Men straighten up from their strain, mop their faces and start for the hand car)*

Boss: Line another one before you spike. Come on, bullies!

RGL: All right. Nine hundred pounds of steel in place! Let's go. *(Men grab bars and jump into place)* Come on if you're coming, let's go if you're going! *(He struts to center and begins to sing)*

> When I get in Illinois
> I'm going to spread the news about the Florida boys
> Shove it over! Hey! Hey! Can't you line it?
> Ah, shack-a-lack, a-lack, a-lack, a-lack, a-hunh!
> Can't you move it?
> Hey! Hey! Can't you try?
>
> *(The men grin and work furiously. He sings five verses1 and men join in chorus.)*

Boss: *(Peering down the rail to see if it is lined correctly)* All right, boys, the gets it. Hammers!

> *(The men all start towards the car with the bars to exchange them for snub-nosed hammers. RGL is humming "This Old Hammer"2 and two or three others are harmonizing the hum. Offstage right can be heard the picking of a guitar and a baritone voice singing sketchily. All stop and look that way.)*

NUNKIE: Who you reckon that is giving that box that nasty fit? If he can't play that guitar there ain't a hound dog in Georgia, and you know that's de puppy's range.

RGL: Wished I know myself. He sure is propaganda.

> *(Enter Spunk walking energetically down the track. His hat is far back on his head, his shirt collar thrown wide open. He stops playing as he reaches the gang.)*

ORAL: *(In admiration)* Hey, box-picking fool, where you

come from?

SPUNK: *(Pleased with the compliment)* From Polk County, where the water taste like cherry wine. *(He plays a few bars of "Polk County." The men are in high glee. The Boss frowns.)*

BOSS: All right, boys, get to work. You killing up the company's time.

BLUE TROUT: *(Cajoling)* Us going to work, Cap'n. Leave him play just a little bit, please. We could work twice as good then. *(To Spunk)* Hit dat box, Big Boy.

> *(Spunk starts to smile, then frowns. Advances threateningly on Blue Trout.)*

SPUNK: Who you calling Big Boy? You must be want to see your Jesus. Elephant is bigger than me, and they call him Elephant. I got a name.

ORAL: Tell a dumb man something! He know better than to be calling folks Big Boy. When these white folks say it you can excuse they ignorance 'cause they don't know no better. Blue just trying to be cute.

BLUE TROUT: Aw, y'all blowin' a mole hill into a rocky mountain! I didn't mean no harm. I beg your pardon, mister.

SPUNK: *(Mollified)* It's granted. Ain't nobody mad no more. *(Crosses to Boss)* Say, Cap'n, don't you need another man on this job?

BOSS: Yeah, I sure do. But I can't take you because I got all this breath-and-britches on the payroll. If some of them don't do better you can start to work Monday morning.

NUNKIE: Cap'n, you're getting good service. Look what we done done since morning.

SPUNK: Anybody know where I can get a job of work 'round here? I ain't used to doing nothing. I got to work.

BOSS: *(Thoughtfully)* It's hard to tell exactly. Times is

hard. You just follow the track into town – 'bout three
miles, I reckon. It's a sawmill there and they 'most
always taking on men.

ORAL: They got a job right there now, but they can't get
nobody to take it.

SPUNK: How come? They make payday, don't they?

ORAL: Yeah, good pay, too. But folks 'round here done got
scared of that job.

SPUNK: What's the matter with it?

ORAL: Well, looks like everybody that takes it gets killed
sooner or later.

SPUNK: What's it doing?

ORAL: Running the big circle saw at the sawmill. Somehow
or 'nother they gets killed.

SPUNK: I'll ride that saw till it's bow-legged. All I want
them to do is to pay me. I'll ride it till it wear clean
out. Boys, I'm gone like a turkey through the corn.

BOSS: *(Impatiently)* All right, boys! What you all trying to
do – make me mad? Fool with me, I'll have a brand
new crew out here after payday.

RGL: Yassuh!

> *(Spunk hurries to the exit left. Gang Leader
> pretending to sing for the boys chants after him)*
>
> Hey, you guitar picker, play it some more
> Big toe party over town tonight, and I know you
> want to go!
> Let's spike it, boys!

SPUNK: *(Calls back over his shoulder)* I heard you
buddy! *(His guitar and voice come back)*

> Oh I don't want no cold corn bread and molasses
> Oh I don't want no cold corn bread and molasses
> Gimme beans, lawd, lawd, gimme beans
> I got a woman, she shake like jelly all over

I got a woman, she shake like jelly all over
Her hips so broad, Lawd, Lawd, her hips so broad.

(Curtain)

SCENE 2

ACTION: Group singing "All Ye Sins." At the rise Mrs.
    Georgia Watson is presiding behind the refreshment
    stand. Admiral is beating out a rhythm on a soda crate
    and Blue Trout is trying to "buck and wing." People
    stand around in easy poses, eating, and talking or just
    looking on.

MRS. WATSON: Hey there, Blue! Did anybody hit you to
    start you? 'Cause if they did I'm going to hit you to
    stop you.

BLUE TROUT: *(Attempting a fancy break and botching
    it)* What's the matter with my dancing, Mrs. Watson?

MRS. WATSON: Don't ask me. I ain't never seen none
    of it. That what you doing ain't *nothing.* If you
    was dancing for peanuts you wouldn't even get the
    hulls. You ain't no trouble. Git out there Oral and do
    some sure enough dancing.

ORAL: *(Sitting on the ground)* Wait! I don't want to spread
    my *[blank space in MS]* till Maggie Mae git here. Then
    I'll dance up camp meeting, dust off associations and
    strut Jordan dry. Hello!

MRS. WATSON: She's liable not to pay *you* no mind when
    she come. All I can hear is the girls screaming over that
    new fellow that's working at the sawmill. I can't hear
    nothing but Spunk.

TEAZIE: From what I heard he got some stuff for all you
    fellows round here. I wish he would come on so we
    could see if he's like they say.

ORAL: Oh, he's sort of over average built with oakobolic

hair.

ADMIRAL: Let's squat that rabbit and jump another one. I'm a business man. Who want to for a boat-ride? I got my boat there. Only ten cents a ride.

MRS. WATSON: *(Laughs)* Now Admiral, you know ain't nobody here going to go out on the lake in that boat of yours. It's got so many cracks it looks like somebody worked it full of buttonholes. We's assembled for a toe party tonight. Not no swimming match. *(General laughter)*

ADMIRAL: It don't leak so much. Come one, come all! Ten cents a ride!

WILLIE JOE: Aw, shut up, Admiral, about your old beat up boat! Lemme tell you all what else that Spunk done today. Men, you ought to seen him! Soon as he got the hang of that saw he begin to talk to it just like a man would to his dice.

ORAL: *(Gleefully)* What he say to it?

WILLIE JOE: First he didn't say nothing. You know how a saw sound when it's cutting a log. A high moaning *(imitates sound)*. Well, Spunk leaned his head down and listen to the saw till it got through. Then he answered the saw back in a kind of singing way. Man, everybody stopped to listen, even the boss. And all the time he was really milling the lumber.

BLUE TROUT: Hurry up and tell us what he *say*.

WILLIE JOE: Oh, I can't remember exactly. Something about how that old saw had done chewed up a thousand million trees and spit out the dust, and had done chopped down men just like they was trees but it wouldn't never get him.

ORAL: Do it. Go 'head on, Willie Joe, and show us how he done it.

WILLIE JOE: Oh, I can't do it like him. Wait till he get here. He'll do it for you.

DAISY: Come on, Teazie! Let's me and you go find him and

bring him on to the party.

BLUE TROUT: You all don't need to bother. Ruby Jones done grabbed him. He was eating supper at her house just now. She done got him all sewed up.

DAISY: Aw, she ain't no trouble. That old beat-looking gal! All she can do is sing.

BLUE TROUT: Now here! Ruby ain't got nobody so it's all right for her to pull after the new man. But the rest of you girls belong to us. Better leave him alone. Eh, boys?

ORAL: Them girls know better. They just trying us out. Don't pay 'em no mind. Come on, Willie Joe. *You* go on and show us. Spunk and Ruby might not come atall.

WILLIE JOE: All right, you all help me out some with the saw. You got to moan high like the saw while I'll talk like Spunk. *(He places Oral, Blue Trout, and Admiral together in a line and close together.)* Now you all is the saw. Go 'head on and sound like one.

(They get pitch and hum. He begins to chant.)

Oh, you done cut trees into lumber and –

(There is the sound of a group talking off left and they all look that way.)

WILLIE JOE: Here come Spunk and them now. Hey, Ruby, rush your frog to the frolic!

(Ruby enters proudly on Spunk's arm. Two other couples are with them. Spunk has his guitar slung across his back. Everyone looks at him with interest.)

SPUNK: I heard you before I got here, but that ain't what I said.

WILLIE JOE: That's what I told 'em. I knowed I couldn't say what you said. They all wants to hear it.

SPUNK: Tain't nothing much to tell, but if you all so desire,

I'll tell you and show you the best I can.

ORAL: We's already the saw for you.

SPUNK: All right, let's go. Wait a minute. Do you know what the saw says?

ORAL: Now, do it say anything besides noise?

SPUNK: Yeah man. Before the log gets there the saw is grumbling to itself and saying "I done cut a tree into a board, done cut a board into a box." By that time the log is there. And the saw is glad so it can go to cutting. That's what it loves. Cutting. Filling up its jaws with trees. Spitting out sawdust and lumber. So when it hits the log it laughs like the horse in the valley of Jehoshophat. It says

(Boys begin hum of saw)

"I'm going to make me a graveyard of my own
I'm going to make me a graveyard of my own
I carry 'em down a smoky road
Bring 'em back on a cooling board
I'm going to make me a graveyard of my own."

So I listened good and answered it back:

"You done gaped your jaws
You done rolled your eyes
You done cut a coffin
But it ain't my size
You can growl and thunder
You can howl and sigh
But I'll wear you out, Lawd, before I die.
Cut your timber, cut your ties
Cut your timber, cut your ties
Show your teeth, Lawd, roll your eyes."

ORAL: Gee, youse powerful! Wish I could be there to hear you talking to that old saw. It's done killed several round here.

>*(They crowd around Spunk for a moment. Ruby*
>*seizes his arm and stands there in ecstasy. Enter Blue*
>*Trout, Maggie Mae and two or three others.)*

WILLIE JOE: Blue, I know you ain't been by Maggie Mae's house and brought her. Oral say he ain't going to hear that.

BLUE TROUT: Naw, I ain't no trouble 'round there. We met up on the road. *(To Spunk)* Hello, buddy! I see you got here.

SPUNK: Oh yeah, I always likes to be where the ladies and the music and the fun is. You ain't sold out all the toes is you? 'Cause I got some money to buy some toes too.

BLUE TROUT: Nope, you know our people never hold nothing on time. They just coming now.

MRS. WATSON: *(Beating on a skillet)* All you young pullets and all you all hens go behind the curtain. We're going to sell off the toes. Everybody come on. Hurry up!

>*(There is a lot of bashful giggling as the girls haltingly*
>*make their way to the quilts. Ruby stands by Spunk*
>*without moving.)*

Hey, Ruby, ain't you taking no part in the party? What you come here for?

RUBY: *(Coyly)* I don't know whether my gentlemen friend want me to play that or not. He might choose for me to just stay with him. *(She looks coyly into his face.)*

SPUNK: Oh, that's all right with me, baby. Don't let me stop your fun. The boys might think hard of me if they didn't get a chance at your toe.

>*(Ruby is chagrined and goes slowly to join the others*
>*behind the quilts. Spunk pulls his guitar from behind*
>*him and plays a chord or two in an absentminded*
>*way.)*

MRS. WATSON: Whilst the girls is getting their toes ready to show, maybe our new friend will favor us with a guitar selection.

> *(Everyone begins to clap hands and Spunk plays "Polk County." His hearers are delighted.)*

MRS. WATSON: *(In admiration)* That's a box-picking fool! Gwan, play us some march music for the boys to march up and choose by.

SPUNK: I wants to march, too. I aims to buy a toe myself.

MRS. WATSON: *(Arranging line)* Get on the tail end of the line and play and march at the same time, like a nice boy. Don't make nobody beg you to play.

> *(Spunk goes to the end of the line and begins to pick softly. The sale of toes begins. There is much laughter and shouting as the girls come from behind the curtain and the men see whom they have bought. Some are proud and strut up to the table, others hang back. Willie Joe pretends that he will jump in the lake to get away from his. Spunk buys the last toe and find he has Ruby.)*

DAISY: *(Sneering)* I see how come she never put her toe out till the last!

RUBY: *(Seizing Spunk's arm triumphantly)* Young coon for running, old coon for cunning! Ha! Ha! Come on y'all let's play a ring play.

DAISY: *(Gladly)* I'm in the ring!

> *(They begin to organize around Daisy. Enter at left Jim Bishop and Evalina, who stand a moment looking about.)*

ORAL: The very person we need to make this play go good. *(Calls out)* Come on, Evalina! We fixing to play Baby Child!

> *(Evalina brightens and takes a step. Jim catches her*

elbow.)

JIM: *(Turning towards refreshment stand)* You better come on here and get this little treat while I'm in the notion of buying it!

EVALINA: *(Pulling away slightly)* I don't choose no treat yet a while. I just got here. *(She advances towards the game a step or two.)*

JIM: Don't think you going to keep me up here half the night. I'm a working man. By the time we walk 'round the place and see it all we going on back home. Come on here and get some sweeten water.

EVALINA: *(Coldly)* I ain't in no hurry atall and I done told you I don't want no lemonade yet awhile. *(She turns again towards the circle, and finds herself looking straight into Spunk's eyes.)*

JIM: *(At the stand)* Two glasses of that sweeten water y'all call lemonade and make it good and cold.

> *(Evalina hesitates a moment, undecided whether to follow her husband or to join the ring.)*

ORAL: Come on here, Eva! You can get a treat any old time. Quit acting scared.

> *(She turns smiling towards the game. Jim drinks his lemonade and follows Evalina with a glass for her.)*

JIM: Here your treat, Lina. Here, take it before I spill it.

EVAINA: Spill it, then! Nobody don't care. I don't aim to drink nothing unless I want it. *(He catches her arm and tries to hold it to her lips. She pulls away.)* Don't you spill that mess on me and ruin up my good clothes.

JIM: *(Tries to thrust it into her hands)* Aw, here take this lemonade and drink it, Lina. You ain't going to make me waste up my money for nothing.

EVALINA: Nobody didn't ask you to buy it, did they? You always trying to put your mind in my head.

JIM: Fool with me I'll leave you here. Get home the best

way you can.

EVALINA: *(Over her shoulder)* Go on then. Nobody don't care. *(Exit Jim, left, furiously)*

WILLIE JOE: You better go on with him, Evalina. He going to tell his papa what you done done. He'll be working some more of his roots on you.

ORAL: Yeah, that's where he gone. He figger his old man can hit a straight lick with a crooked stick. Watch out. It won't be long before Old Hodge Bishop will be here.

EVALINA: Let him go and get his pappy! I don't care. Come on, let's dance!

> *(She hurries to break into the circle. Ruby sees the look on Spunk's face as he watches Evalina.)*

RUBY: Aw naw, this game is for young folks. This ain't for no old married women. They ought to go class off to theirselves.

> *(Evalina draws back quickly with a hurt "oh" on her lips.)*

ORAL: Who you calling old? Evalina is a whole heap younger than you, Ruby.

RUBY: That's all right. She's married, ain't she? We's all courting couples. She ain't got no business in with us. *(She looks up at Spunk in triumph.)*

SPUNK: *(Gazing after Evalina)* I don't believe I choose no ring play. B'lieve I'll just stroll around and look things over. *(He starts to break his hand clasp.)*

RUBY: *(In panic)* Aw, come on and play, Lina. Can't you take a joke? Meet my gentleman friend, Mrs. Lina Bishop, Mr. Spunk. *(Rolls her eyes in admiration)* Papa tree-top, tall.

EVALINA: Pleased to meet you, Mr. Spunk.

SPUNK: My compliments, Mrs. Lina. Hope to be better acquain'ted.

ORAL: *(Jumping and clapping)* Come on, let's go, people. *(Clapping gets hot. He begins to sing)*
    Eh, yeh, Lollie Lou, Eh, yeh, Lollie Lou.

> *(Daisy chooses Oral and he chooses a girl and she chooses Blue Trout and he chooses anothe girl and she chooses Admiral and he chooses Evalina. They rhythm has grown terrific and Oral begins to chant "Baby Chile." Evalina dances it to a high pitch and chooses Spunk and they end the dance in a frenzy of rhythm. Everyone is overheated and tired. Some drop laughing on the grass. Others rush over for a cooling drink. Spunk raises Evalina from their final dance position and stands holding her hands. Oral hands him his guitar.)*

SPUNK: Miss Lina, would you do me the favor to step over to the refreshment stand and choose your ruthers on me?

EVALINA: *(Coyly)* Much obliged, Mr. Spunk, and my mouth is a little parched from all this dancing. I'll choose some lemonade.

> *(They stroll towards the table with Ruby and several others staring hard. While Evalina drinks the lemonade he quietly buys her a huge stick of peppermint candy and places it in her hand. She accepts it gladly and they cross near the water.)*

SPUNK: Whilst we's so hot from dancing, we ought to try one of them boat rides. I loves to pull a boat.

EVALINA: Them boats is full of leaks. Admiral ain't fooling nobody on his boat rides. *(They laugh lightly.)*

SPUNK: *(Earnestly)* Well, anyhow we can git in one of them and sit down, can't us?

EVALINA: *(Nodding yes)* Uh, huh, I reckon.

> *(He helps her to a seat in the prow and seats himself in the rower's bench and picks up an oar. Everybody begins to stare silently.)*

SPUNK: Must I shove off, Miss Evalina?

EVALINA: *(Nervously)* We better not get out into deep water, Mister Spunk. It's dangerous, in the dark too.

> *(Enter Hodge Bishop, left. An ominous silence falls as he looks all about him. He walks slowly to center and stands glaring at EvaEvalina and Spunk. Then he lifts his hat, fumbles in the band and puts it on again, but backwards this time and exits again, left, insolently.)*

SPUNK: Nothing can't be dangerous when you with me. I can swim real good. I could take the Mississippi River for a dusty road if I had to. I'd love to be out on that lake.

EVALINA: *(Looks about nervously)* We better not, though. Not out on the water. Let's just set in the boat.

SPUNK: *(Seating her facing the audience and he facing her)* Whatever you say, Miss Evalina. But I done found out it ain't no use being scared of things. If you feel to do a thing, do it. You can't die but one time nohow. *(She looks at him softly. He gets back into position.)* I got a song made up in me for you.

EVALINA: For me? You must have made it up awful quick. This the first time you ever seen me.

SPUNK: It don't seem that way. Seem like I always been knowing you. When I seen you come walking in just now it seem like you had been off somewhere and just got back home.

EVALINA: You don't seem strange to me neither. Look like I been knowing you, too. And that's a nice feeling. I don't like to feel strange 'round people. And that's the way I been.

SPUNK: I know how that is by my own self. That's how come I already got your song made up. But anyhow it ain't hard for me to make up songs. If I get to feeling real strong inside a song makes itself up and all I have to do is sing it. Like this one I'm going to sing right now.

EVALINA: I'll be glad. Your compliments is nice.

(He begins to sing "Halimuhfack" and people listen amazed and then burst into a thudding monotone and pantomime of gossip as a comment on the situation. He sings two verses.)

EVALINA: Let's see! I can make up some to go with that.

(She sings a verse to him. The rumble and the gestures keep up. They sing the fourth verse together. While it is being sung Hodge Bishop re-enters with Jim and glares ominously in the direction of Spunk and Evalina. As the song ends Jim struts over and stands glaring at her.)

JIM: Get yourself out that boat, Evalina! Anybody would think you was some courting girl, sitting up there! We going home.

(She alights with deliberation as the rumble rises to a thudding tempo. She haughtily strides across the stage behind Jim to left. Spunk rises too and walks slowly after her to center stage. As Evalina reaches the left exit she stops and gives Spunk a long dragging look. He returns it in kind. Then she is gone. He continues to stare after her. Ruby creeps to him and hugs his left arm. He is impatient.)

RUBY: What's the matter, daddy? Look like you thunder-struck by lightning.

SPUNK: *(Staring and straining like a dog on a leash to keep from following Evalina)* Aw, naw! I done got a letter from love and so help me I'll go to hell but what I answer it.

(Curtain)

ACT TWO

SCENE 1

ACTION: *At the rise there is the crack of mallet against ball and Nunkie rushes across the court from upstage left to downstage right. His ball rests very near another. He stoops to arrange the balls.*

DAISY: *(Approaching him)* What you doing, Nunkie? You never hit my ball.

NUNKIE: *(Indignantly)* Who never hit it? I almost sent it to Georgia.

ORAL: Aw, you never hit it. Stop cheating.

NUNKIE: I don't have to cheat you when I'm beating you. Talking about I didn't hit it! *(He goes on preparing to roquet the balls)* I bet you I'll send it to Diddy-Wah-Diddy.

ORAL: That's all right, Daisy, let him roquet you. It's my next shot. I'm going to hit him and send him back to Ginny-gall, where they eat cowhead, skin and all.

NUNKIE: I ain't from no Ginny-gall. Tain't no such place nohow.

ORAL: Well, where is you from, then?

NUNKIE: I'm from Bandandy, Georgia. *(All laugh)*

ORAL: You can gum, Nunkie, but don't bite. You know there ain't no such place. Bandandy! Where is that?

NUNKIE: I don't recollect. I was too small when we left there for me to remember, but I done heard mama speak of it many a time.

ORAL: That's a name your mama made up so she could

claim you was born in a town. Tain't no Bandandy *nowhere*. Stop your cheating and let's play.

TEAZIE: Who cheating? You all the one trying to cheat us. I was looking right at you, Oral, shoving your ball into position at that last wicket.

ORAL: Teazie, youse a – er, er, Got-that-wrong! Girl, you can mold 'em. I ain't pushed my ball. Nothing of the kind. We going to beat you and have our correct amount of fun while we doing it. I mean to die bold.

MRS. WATSON: Aw, you-all hurry up and get through so somebody else can play. Me and Willie Joe going to take the winners.

RUBY: Naw, let all of 'em come off when they finish that game. Let four brand new ones get on there. I'm tired of waiting.

JIM: *(Pulls coin from his pocket)* Here, Admiral, run get me a cold Coca-Cola.

ADMIRAL: Yessir. Don't you want me to bring you some cigarettes, too? I need a smoke.

JIM: Well, all right. But I wasn't figgering on none right now.

(Admiral darts off left running.)

DAISY: *(To Nunkie, gloating)* Now, you dead on the game and ain't even made your center wicket. You ain't no trouble.

NUNKIE: Aw, shoot and shut up! You have to play this game. Your talk don't help none. I done belled the buzzard, crowned the crow; got the key to the bushes and I'm bound to go.

MRS. WATSON: *(Slams card down on the table)* High, low, jack and the bendwood tosser. Roasting ears ripe and the corn's et offa. Gone from two! Out and gone!

WILLIE JOE: Gone out your head! Where you all get any two from?

(Re-enter Admiral who hands Jim Coca-Cola and change. He begins to open the cigarettes as Jim wipes the mouth of the bottle with his hand and places it to his lips.)

RUBY: Aw, let it go. Nobody don't care, nowhow. We ain't bet money. Let 'em have it. *(She looks about her absently and begins to hum.)*

> Oh Lord, Oh Lord, let the words of my mouth, O Lord

(The others begin to pick up.)

Let the words of my mouth, meditations of my heart
Be accepted in thy sight, O Lord.

(They sing it the second time in full harmony.)

MRS. WATSON: Ain't y'all *never* going to get through with that game?

> *(There is the sound of full guitar chords offstage. Jim starts violently, almost strangles himself and removes the bottle from his lips and listens painfully.)*

WILLIE JOE: Spunk and Evalina all set for their afternoon stroll. Listen! He's coming down the steps when he play like that.

(Ruby drops her head upon the table.)

NUNKIE: Yep. Every day, him and EvaEvalina and the music going for a walk after work. Wonder how come they go walking every day.

ORAL: Why don't you ask him when he get here! Then you'll know. Betcha Spunk got a magnolia bloom in his hat!

ADMIRAL: Betcha he ain't!

ORAL: He is too! You ain't never seen them out walking

'less Evalina had a magnolia stuck in his hat band.

ADMIRAL: I have.

ORAL: When was that?

ADMIRAL: Yesterday. They was out walking and he didn't
have no magnolia in his hat band. ORAL: I don't believe
it.

ADMIRAL: He done been out a lot of times without a
magnolia bloom in his hat. *(Laughs)* Man, you don't
you know magnolias ain't in bloom this time of the
year? Ha! Ha! Evalina's going to put some kind of
a flower all over him every day. Magnolias is her
preference, but she can't get 'em if they ain't on the
tree.

(They laugh. Guitar heard approaching.)

WILLIE JOE: *(Winking broadly)* Jim, how you and Evalina
making out these days?

JIM: *(Starts painfully)* We'd be all right, I reckon, if we – if
– if somebody didn't come between us.

NUNKIE: You ain't no kind of a man or nobody couldn't
come between you. Some things ain't decent for a man
to take. You low-rates yourself if you do. So what you
going to do?

WILLIE JOE: What's he going to do? Mildew! Do like the
folks the oher side of the creek – do without!

RUBY: *(Jumping up suddenly with wet eyes)* Why don't
you-all leave him alone? You ain't got no gumption
– teasing him 'bout a thing like that. If a person can't
get the one they love, it's pitiful! It ain't nothing to be
cracking over. Leave Jim be!

WILLIE JOE: How come he's got to be different from
everybody else 'round here? Y'all laughed and made all
manner of jokes when Pearl left me and went down
the East Coast. Jim and all the rest of y'all cracked me
hard. How come he can't take what he give?

ORAL: That ain't the first time a man's wife been took away

from him. Jim is just a fool to keep hanging after Evalina when she's done told him she don't want him and gone to living with Spunk.

NUNKIE: Yeah, I had a good woman. *(Shrugs resignedly)* The fool laid down and died.

JIM: *(Stands with hands in pockets)* Just like you say, Nunkie, I reckon it is my fault for being so easy. *(Strikes a belligerent pose)* But Spunk done gone too far. I stopped by here today just in order to tackle 'em when they pass. I'm going to know from him today what he means by coming between me and Evalina. I love that girl! I love her! If I don't love her, God's a gopher! *(All but sobs)*

WILLIE JOE: That's right, Jim. Make him tell you something. Man ain't nothing but a man.

> *(There is a tinkle of music and EvaEvalina enters, left, clinging to Spunk's arm. He touches the guitar now and then. His broad-brimmed Stetson is full of honeysuckle. A bit hangs from his shirt pocket.)*

SPUNK: Hello, Oral! Hello Nunkie and Willie Joe! How you making it, Teazie?

ALL: Hi, there Spunk and Evalina. Y'all sho' looks good to this world. Red hot!

MRS. WATSON: Say, Spunk, they all wants to know how come you and Evalina go for a walk to the woods every day the Lord sends. How come that?

SPUNK: *(Laughing)* Evalina, you know, is wild about her flowers, and she done made me make her a flower garden. So she always want to hear whatever new song I done made up setting out in the flower yard under the tree. But just as soon as I get to playing my song she begin to point out more work for me to be doing in the yard. So I just take her off into the woods where God done planted all the flowers she want and I don't have to work 'em. *(Everybody laughs.)*

WILLIE JOE: Women folks don't love to see a man sitting down. If you stay 'round the house they'll find plenty for you to do.

SPUNK: And ain't you noticed you can't never chop more stone wood than a woman needs? If you chop six pieces she'll get the meal. If you chop a hundred pieces she'll burn every last stick of it just the same. *(Laughter)*

EVALINA: *(Scolding tenderly)* Now, honey, you know I don't burn wood like that.

SPUNK: Yes you do, cuteness. But if I didn't let you burn it the way you want to I'd be so mad with myself till I'd have to tote a pistol to bed to keep me from getting up and beating myself to death for worrying you. So I done made arrangements 'bout the whole thing. The boss is sending me a load of slabs every week from the sawmill and I done got Admiral to keep plenty chopped up. Burn *all* the wood you want, baby. Youse all I'm working for.

JIM: *(Swallowing convulsively)* Spunk, I want to speak to you.

SPUNK: *(Cool)* Well, I'm standing in front of you.

JIM: Spunk, I done told Evalina, and I done told her mama and now I'm telling you. I want you to leave my wife alone.

SPUNK: Who do you call your wife?

JIM: Evalina, there. That's my wife.

SPUNK: That's a big old Georgia lie! You multiplied roach, you! She's mine!

JIM: How come she's yourn? I know you-all is living together like man and wife, but I got *papers* for her. I went to the big court house and got the papers and stood up in her mama's house and married her. Tell *me* that ain't my wife.

SPUNK: *(Laughs shortly)* Court house! Papers! Standing up on the floor! Humph! That don't make a woman yours. That don't mean nothing. Evalina is *mine*. God took and made her special for me. When I was a lad of a boy I seen her in a vision standing 'round the throne waiting for me and I been hunting for her ever since. You the one shoved yourself out of place when you went and got them papers. She's mine!

JIM: *(Doggedly)* Naw she ain't neither. She is so my wife.

SPUNK: She is not! All right, you say she's yours. A woman know who her boss is and she'll go when he call. There Evalina is. You call her and see if she'll come to your command.

JIM: *(Nervously)* Evalina, Evalina, why don't you come on back home and quit this living like you is? Got everybody in town talking about you like you was a dog. Come on home!

EVALINA: *(Impatiently)* I'm living home now. All the I home I ever expect to have. Spunk ain't took me away from you. I went to him. And furthermore ain't nobody talking about me like a dog excepting you and your meddlesome old root-working papa! *(Draws away scornfully)* Leave me be! I loose you.

SPUNK: *(Involuntarily puts his arm about her)* All right now, Jim. That's the word with the bark on it. Now as long as a mule go bareheaded don't you stop my wife on the streets no more and be nam-namming at her and trying to crumple her feathers. You talk your big talk to me. If you was a man my size I would have been done stopped you. I ignores men your size. If there's anything I hate worse'n no fight it is a poor fight. I hates to look imposing and bull-dozing. But you leave her be. I'm telling you. Let's go, doll-baby. Bye, everybody. See you later. *(They exit with admiring glances of all following.)*

ADMIRAL: *(Looking after Spunk)* I hear you crowing, rooster! *(To others)* You have to give the man credit. He got grit in his craw.

> *(Jim stumbles back to his seat and sits with his head in his hands.)*

RUBY: I don't give him no credit. Many single girls as it is round here he got to take a man's wife away from him. It's low-down!

NUNKIE: *(In mock sympathy)* I know just how you feel, Ruby. Here you was all set to love Spunk yourself and Evalina took and taught him the amendment to love. It's tough! You gets just as hot as jailhouse coffee everytime you see 'em.

RUBY: I ain't got Spunk and his woman to study 'bout.

WILLIE JOE: Oh yes you is, Ruby. We all see you every afternoon all primped up and sitting out on your steps waiting for Spunk to pass by. Oh yeah, you still loves him.

RUBY: I don't neither.

WILLIE JOE: Oh yeah, you do. But why not take *me*, Ruby? I know I ain't nothing but you could use me till a real man come along. Lawd, that would be swell! Me coming home from work and find you singing all over the house with that pretty voice! 'Course you got that oakobolic hair, but I'd make it a habit to listen to you, baby. I wouldn't rest my love on looking at you.

RUBY: Your head looks like a pepper patch itself so you ain't got no cause to talk about nobody else. Looks like policemen on a beat.

WILLIE JOE: All right, let's don't talk about hair, then. Let's talk about something else. How about love?

RUBY: Rock on down the road, Willie Joe. I don't want to talk about no love with you.

WILLIE JOE: What's the matter with me? Nobody didn't tell me but I heard that I'm a mighty sweet man to have around a house.

RUBY: Umph! I hope you ain't trying to call yourself a pimp! That face of yours would handcuff a devil-fish and he got eight arms. *(Laughter)*

WILLIE JOE: Naw, indeed. I make a payday every week. And baby *(exaggerated)* I'm crazy about you. You know it. *(Gesture of pretended affection)* I'll do anything for you except work for you and give you my money. Anything else you just let papa know. I know I ain't no Spunk.

RUBY: *(Shoving him off)* I ain't studying about you and Spunk neither. He ain't nothing.

BLUE TROUT: Oh yes, he is some good, too. He's plenty trouble. Most any man I know would be glad to be in his place. I know I don't fault him atall.

ORAL: Yeah, Spunk's all right! Jim, thought your papa was such a good hoodoo man he could make a crooked road straight? That's what folks been saying 'round here. Your papa worked roots and made Evalina marry you. How come he can't work 'em and keep Spunk from biting you in the back? Your papa must be losing his stroke.

MRS. WATSON: I don't believe he ever had none. He just been going 'round here fooling up anybody that would pay him any mind. Making out he know every chinch in China! I don't b'live a thing!

WILLIE JOE: *(Fearfully)* Well, I do. I done seen some might funny things happen. I know things *can* be done. Spunk better watch out.

ORAL: Maybe things can be done, but I don't b'lieve old man Bishop can do none of it. I useter b'lieve, but since he done talked and prophesied all he was going to do to Spunk and ain't none of it come to pass, I don't b'lieve a thing. I don't even b'lieve that lard is greasy. Let's sing off of it according to common meter. I'm going to line it out. Y'all sing! *(To the tune of "Get on Board that Ship of Zion, It Has Landed Many a Thousand.")*

> Oh, Spunk ain't scared of Bishop's conjure
> Oh, Spunk ain't scared of Bishop's conjure
> Oh, Spunk ain't scared of Bishop's conjure
>
> He ain't scared, Lawd, he ain't scared.

(The others join in the spirit of fun. Full harmony.)

> Oh, he done made sweet Evalina love him
> Oh, he done made sweet Evalina love him
> Oh, he done made sweet Evalina love him
> Wish 'twas me, Lawd, wish 'twas me.

NUNKIE: Let me line out a verse, there. One done come to me:

> He told me the boss head a mess, Lawd
> Told that boss's head a mess, Lord (Oh sing it children)
> Oh yes, he told his head a mess, Lawd
> Ain't I glad, Lawd, ain't I glad.

MRS. WATSON: *(Smiling)* Ain't they crazy? *(Laughing)* If you all ain't the biggest fools I ever seen!

WILLIE JOE:

> What made sweet Evalina take and love him
> What made sweet Evalina take and love him
> What made sweet Evalina take and love him
> Wish I knowed, Lawd, wish I knowed.

JIM: *(Jumps up jerkily)* Whilst you all carrying on like a passel of fools, I'm going in them woods and bring my wife back.

WILLIE JOE: *(Rising seriously and catching Jim's arm)* Jim, sit down. I wouldn't go out there if I was you.

JIM: Yes, I'm going and I'm going to bring Evalina back with me, too. *(Draws a razor from his hip pocket and*

tests the edge) And Spunk better not fool with me
neither. I done took and took until I'm sick and tired.

ORAL: Spunk got a gun. He always totes one.

JIM: *(Twisting the blade)* Yes, and I got this razor, too. And
I got a way to get him. And a firm determination.
I'm going out there and he sho God better not gripe
me today *(dashes off right)* I'm out and gone! *(All look
behind him.)*

MRS. WATSON: Why don't some of you men go catch that
gump and bring him back?

NUNKIE: Mrs. Watson, you know that fool ain't going
out there after Spunk sho 'nough! There have to be
some running before that fight come off. *(Laughs)* Yes
ma'am! Some darn good running before any fighting
between them two. Jim's got a willing mind, but too
light behind. He just bluffing us. He'll hide that razor
behind the first palmetto bush he come to and sneak
back here and lie 'bout all he done. He ought to know
that Spunk will kill him if he come drawing any razor
on him or Evalina.

ORAL: Spunk wouldn't hurt him, I don't believe. I done
seen him pass up the chance to fight two or three runts
like Jim. If he push him, Spunk might cut a switch
and whip his can for him, but he wouldn't knock him
around with his fist.

WILLIE JOE: *(Gloomily)* I don't know, now. Remember he
ain't round the sawmill. He's off with Evalina. A man
don't take much when he's round women folks that
he prize. I wouldn't push him, if twas me. *(Pause)* I
wonder what makes him think he can outdo Spunk?

ADMIRAL: Maybe he's peeping through his liquor. His
whiskey told him to go fight and he's gone.

RUBY: Aw naw, he ain't drunk, neither! You all drove him
to that with your cutting capers and carrying on. You
ain't got no sense, none of you.

MRS. WATSON: *(Looking off left)* Ain't that Jim's papa

coming yonder?

RUBY: Yes, ma'am. It sure is. I'm glad, too.

(Enter Hodge Bishop.)

BISHOP: Good evening everybody.

MRS. WATSON: I'm mighty glad that you come along, Mr. Bishop. Jim is gone behind Spunk and Evalina with a razor. Says he's going to fetch Lins and get Spunk. You ought to stop him. Maybe he will listen to you.

BISHOP: *(Shortly)* Naw, I wouldn't move out of my tracks to stop him from killing that Spunk. Jim's got *my* wisdom teeth in him. That's what he ought to have done six months ago. No jury in the world would convict a man for protecting his home. Let him kill the varmint. Loping up and down the road, taking off folkses wives.

MRS. WATSON: *Your* wisdom teeth! Humph. Some folks is just like a possum – the older they get the less sense they got. If anybody got sense to see you won't pay no attention to that laugh of Spunk's. He's a man that gives 'em hard and stops 'em short. Youse better go call that son of yours.

NUNKIE: Why, you told me long time ago that you was protecting Jim's home with roots. It must not have worked cause Spunk got the girl, the best job 'round here and done gone to housekeeping. Your conjure must be getting all beat up. You ain't no trouble *atall*.

BISHOP: I got him set for still bait. I'm just waiting for a certain thing to come about, then I'll make him gimme a back view. I'm slow walking him down. *(Murmur of disbelief.)*

ORAL: Sing it boys!

> It may be so, but I'm 'bliged to doubt it
> It may be so, but I'm 'bliged to doubt it
> Oh it may be so, but I'm 'bliged to doubt it
> Sounds like a lie, Lord, just like a lie.

(They pretend to shout, talk the unknown tongues and grow boisterous. Shouting "peace," "Thank you, father," and "It's truly wonderful." There is the report of a gun, and everyone stops still and listens for a moment. Ruby shudders and begins to sob quietly.)

WILLIE JOE: Gosh a'mighty! You reckon anything done come off? I feel like I'm running in my skin.

NUNKIE: Come on Oral and Admiral. Less we go see.

ADMIRAL: *(Timidly)* We don't have to run and see do we? We'll get there quick enough walking.

(They start off hesitantly. Before they can get offstage there is the sound of sobbing approaching. In a minute Spunk enters with Evalina sobbing beside him. Everybody stares and he stands there a moment before he speaks.)

SPUNK: Well, that creeping cat come out there and made me kill him. *(He whirls and shows his back.)* See where he cut my clothes? Yeah, instead of coming to my face if he wanted to fight and fight me like man, naw, he got down on his hands and knees and crawled up behind the log where we was setting and tried to cut me in the back. So before I could think, I wheeled and shot him, so he's dead. Somebody better go get him and bury him. I never meant to kill him, though. He made me do it.

(Oral, Nunkie, and Admiral bolt off right. Hodge Bishop crouches and comes close to Spunk from the rear.)

WILLIE JOE: Jim was just naturally death struck. I tried to get him not to go out there. Well, I reckon we better swear ourselves in, kind of deputize ourselves, and form a posse to place Spunk under arrest and turn him over to the high sheriff.

SPUNK: *(Angrily)* If anybody puts their hands on me, just

like God sent me a pistol I'll send him a man! That's
the reason I always tried to stay out of trouble – so
nobody wouldn't be tying me up like I was some
cow! I'll go on over and tell the white folks what I
done and how come I done it and everybody can come
testify. But don't touch me.

*(He puts his arms about Evalina and they
walk downstage center. Hodge creeps after him
threateningly.)*

Lina, don't cry like that. I'm not gone for good. I ain't
done no hanging crime. I'll be back sometime. Maybe
not very long. And no matter what come, I'll be
back. Even if they was to kill me, in twenty minutes
after I was dead my spirit would be in the house with
you. Go home, honey. You know where everything
is. *(Takes his guitar from around his neck and places it on
hers.)* You know next to you I love my box. Take good
care of it and come see me as much as they let you. Oh
God, I wish I didn't have to go! Go on home, now,
before I move out my tracks.

*(He kisses her and watches her exit, left. Then he
glances around and sees Hodge gesturing behind him
and wheels to defend himself. As he does so, Hodge
retreats, snarling. As soon as Spunk turns to walk off
right, he rushes up behind him again.)*

HODGE: Took my son's wife and then kill him like a dog! I
curse you! I put bad mouth on you!

*(Spunk turns and glares and Hodge retreats in fear
to a safe distance. As Spunk turns, left, he rushes up
behind him again.)*

I point my dog-finger at you! *(Spunk turns and he is
so close that Hodge thinks Spunk has seized him. He
almost falls in fright.)* I'm picking up your track! Ah

(gloatingly) now I got you in the go-long. I put bad mouth on you!

(Each movement takes Spunk closer to left exit, until finally he goes off with old Hodge following after with his right arm pointed menacingly. He stoops and takes sand out of Spunk's track and straightens up gloating and full of malice and hate.)

You won't never get out of this! I done put my mark on you! The white folks will hang you! I got you now and I'm going to throw you away! I'm going to nail you up in a tree! You'll *die*! *(Curtain)*

SCENE 2.

ACTION: *At the rise about a dozen convicts are working on the highway in their stripes. The guard with a rifle in his arms walks slowly back and forth. The men are singing.*

CHAIN GANG:
>   Please don't drive me because I'm blind
>   B'lieve I can make it if I take my time
>   Lift up the hammer and let it fall down
>   It's a hard rocky bottom and it must be found.

CAPTAIN HAMMER: Can't you all find nothing to sing besides that damn mournful tune?

>   *(All look from one to the other but say nothing, except Spunk who is working near center. He pauses and rests on his shovel.)*

SPUNK: I could sing plenty more if I have my guitar here with me. But I ain't. Left it with my wife. Didn't know what was liable to happen and I want it taken good care of.

CAPTAIN HAMMER: You reckon she'll do it?

SPUNK: Why certainly! She'll do just what I say, no matter what it is. I'm sure glad I ain't got to be away from her but thirty more days. *(Pauses a moment and thinks.)* Cap'n, is you got a cigarette you could gimme? I don't know how come Evalina didn't come bring me some yesterday. It was visiting day. She must be sick or something.

CAPTAIN HAMMER: *(Pulls out a pack and hands it to Spunk. Looks at other convicts and scowls.)* Hey, you bastards, get to work! What the hell you two doing whispering? Get away from one 'nother! *(He fingers his rifle suggestively.)* Here's a match, Spunk. I don't mind obliging you atall. You been a good prisoner. Ain't gimme one mite of trouble the two months you been here.

SPUNK: *(Lighting cigarette and returning pack to guard)* I ain't come here for no trouble. I wants to get through with this the quickest way possible and get back home. I ain't no conzempt! This the first time I ever been on a gang and I wouldn't be here now if that Jim hadn't of tried to kill me with a razor. *(Sadly)* I just don't know how come Evalina never come to see me yesterday. She know she can't see me but once a month and look like she wouldn't miss. *(Begins to work hard and hum. Then sings. Others join.)*

> Got on the train didn't have no fare
> But I rode some, I rode some
> Got on the train, didn't have no fare
> But I rode some, I rode some
>
> Got on the train, didn't have no fare
> Conductor asked me what I'm going there
> But I rode some, I rode some

(Men begin to get in a happier mood.)

Well, he grabbed me by the hand and he led me to
the door
But I rode some, I rode some
He grabbed me by the hand and led me to the
door
Hit me over the head with a forty-four
But I rode some, I rode some

*(Everybody begins to laugh, even the guard. Spunk
stops abruptly and stands brooding.)*

Look like she could have sent me some kind of word if
she didn't come herself. *(Begins to hum and sing again.)*

All day long, you heard me moan, don't tell my
cap'n which way I gone

I'm going to loose this right hand shackle from
'round my leg

(Others join and harmonize.)

Cap'n, Cap'n, can't you see, this work you got is
killing me.

I'm going to loose this right hand shackle from
'round my leg.

(Spunk wipes his brow and laughs.)

Lord, Lord, Lord! Where'll I be thirty days from
now?
Oh sitting up beside Evalina! Lord, Lord!

CONVICT: If some other man ain't done tee-rolled you with
her. Ha! Ha! Maybe it's another mule kicking in your
stall.

> *(Spunk goes cloudy and his chest begins to swell slowly as he glares coldly and fixed until his chest has reached its limit.)*

SPUNK: Now you done got me just as hot as the alligator when the pond went dry. You son of a conbunction! Evalina's name don't come in your conversation. When I call her name out here I'm talking to myself. Now you just crack *one more* time and you're going to make a *bad* nigger out of me. *(He tenses his muscles ominously.)*

CAPTAIN HAMMER: Nixon! You leave Spunk be! Work more and talk less. *(Gently)* Here, take another smoke, Spunk.

> *(Spunk is fumbling a cigarette out while Captain Hammer holds the pack. Suddenly he throughsts the pack into Spunk's hand and starts walking left rapidly. Spunk turns and sees Willie Joe walking through' the gang staring at each prisoner as if he is searching for someone. Captain Hammer gets his rifle ready to fire as he crosses.)*

Halt there! Hey, stray nigger, what you doing 'round here?

WILLIE JOE: *(Lifts both hands in the air trembling. He has a letter in one hand.)* Ah just come here to bring Spunk a letter. Yessuh, somebody done sent me with it.

CAPTAIN HAMMER: Why didn't you take it to camp and leave it? Fetch it here! *(Willie Joe advances.)* Know this nigger, Spunk?

SPUNK: Yessir, Cap'n. I know him well.

> *(His eyes burn with eagerness as he fixes them on the letter. Cap'tain Hammer feels it for any concealed object and reaches it towards Spunk.)*

CAP'N: Now the next time anybody send you with a letter, you take it where it belongs.

WILLIE JOE: Yessir, Cap'n. I sure will. *(To Spunk)* I reckon I won't wait round for no answer. I'll tell 'em you can write later. *(He hurries off left, looking back fearful of being shot.)*

SPUNK: Cap'n, can I glance through it, please sir?

CAPTAIN HAMMER: *(Starts to refuse, but softens a bit. Spits tobacco juice and nods his head yes.)* I reckon so, Spunk, since youse a trusty. *(He glares at the others to main'tain discipline.)*

SPUNK: *(Reads. Others sing a verse of song and work hard.)* Cap'n, I got to go. This letter come to me and it's telling a lie, Cap'n Hammer. I got to go.

CAPTAIN HAMMER: Spunk is you gone crazy? You know you got twenty nine more days to make. You can't leave the camp, and you know damn well you can't.

(Other convicts work in listening pose.)

SPUNK: *(As if he has not heard)* Cap'n, I got to go. *(Looks up at sun)* I'll be there by black dark. She say in the letter she done give me up. I got to go. *(Racks his tools beside the road)* Says she's never to be with me no more. I got a letter and it done told a lie. I got to go.

CAPTAIN HAMMER: Spunk! Grab up them tools and git to work! I'll kill you!

(The others, sensing trouble, work furiously, looking fearfully over their shoulders at the guard.)

SPUNK: *(Hitches up his pants and looks off left)* I'd rather to be dead than to be like this. *(Turns left)* You'll just have to kill me, Cap'n Hammer, 'cause I'm going. It's on the bill and it's got to be filled. I aim to go in the flesh, but if I don't make it I'll be there in the spirit. Bye, Cap'n.

(He starts striding heedless towards the left. The others divide fearfully to let him pass.)

CAP'N: Halt there! I'll shoot you down! *(Softer)* Spunk! You Spunk! I hate to kill you! *(Spunk never looks back. The others fall down fearful of being hit by stray bullets. As he reaches the exit the gun fires three times rapidly but Spunk strides off.)* Missed him, dammit to hell! He's got clean away! *(Turns fiercely upon the others.)* Get up off that ground you damn dog-meat, you! Grab them tools. I'll shoot you just to see you jump.

SPUNK: *(Singing mournfully in the distance)*

> She used to rock me, rock me in the cradle by the window
> Rock me, rock me, Lord, rock me in the cradle by the window
>
> Poor gal, don't do it now, poor gal *(hums mournfully)*
>
>
> She used to put them sweet magnolias in my hat band
> She used to put them sweet magnolias in my hat band
> Hibiscus too, Lord, Lord, hibiscus too.
>
> I got a rainbow, wrapped and tied around my shoulder
> I got a rainbow, wrapped and tied around my shoulder
>
> It ain't going rain, Lord, Lord, it ain't going rain! *(Mournful hum. Curtain)*

SCENE 3.

SETTING: *Nighttime. At extreme left is the front of Ruby's house with practical door and steps. A wooden window stands wide open revealing an oilcloth-covered table, a wood-burning cookstove. Bright little fixings about the place. A china-berry tree at left of house. At extreme right is Evalina's house beneath a magnolia tree at left. A white picket fence. Window beneath the tree with lowhanging limb across the window. The wooden shutter stands open. A light inside. Street is downstage before both houses.*

ACTION: *At the rise, Ruby is puttering around between the stove and table. Evalina sits by her window with Spunk's guitar in her lap. She touches it now and then and sings. Ruby listens and hums an obligato above EvaEvalina's chorus.*

EVALINA:

> Love come my way, stayed but a day
> Went and left me crying like a child
> It left me feeling sad, left me feeling bad
> Maybe things will straighten after while

CHORUS:

> I'm going down the long lonesome road, oh
> I'm going down the long lonesome road
> I'm going down that long, lonesome road

> *(Sobbingly)* Oh weep like a willow, mourn just like a dove

> Weep like a willow, mourn just like a dove
> Oh, fly to the mountain, light on the man I love.

All my dreams is dead, things ain't like he said
I been leaning on a broken reed
He never meant to stay, just stopped by for a day
On his string of life I'm just a bend.

I'll see you when your troubles get like mine, oh
I'll see you when your troubles get like me
I'll see you when your heart is broke like mine.

(She sits there a moment touching the strings absentmindedly. Enter Spunk left crossing rapidly. He steps over the fence and rushes to the window. Evalina starts up.)

EVALINA: Spunk! What you doing here?

SPUNK: *(Reaching through'the window to touch her)* A letter come. It had your writing on it and it said you was never to look for me back no more.

EVALINA: *(Scared)* Spunk, you done broke gang!

SPUNK: It ain't broke. I just left to see 'bout you. You don got religion like you say in the letter and done promised everybody to keep 'way from me?

EVALINA: *(Quietly)* Yeah, Spunk. They done prayed with me and laid me under conviction of my sins. They showed me that my sins done got Jim killed and you on the gang. It's time for me to turn. I want to live clean.

SPUNK: I never felt no dirtiness being with you. I didn't know you felt that way 'bout me. So you done promised, huh?

EVALINA: Yeah, Spunk. They all done made me see. (*There is a long silence. Spunk hangs his head.*) Your guitar is right here, Spunk. I took good care of it like you said. *(She hands it to him and he takes it slowly.)* Hold up your head. You won't miss me long. Ain't that what you say?

SPUNK: You doing the talking, Evalina. I'm struck dumb. Guess I better jolt on down the road.

(He walks slowly out of the gate. She leans out of her window hungrily.)

EVALINA: Better come in and hide yourself from the white folks, Spunk.

SPUNK: Oh, let 'em get me! I'm guilty!

(He walks slowly towards left. Ruby steps out of the door and stands before him.)

RUBY: Hello, Spunk! Where you bound for?

SPUNK: Oh, just trucking on down the road. God knows.

RUBY: *(Seizing his arm)* You can't go 'way from here like that. Mama got shrimp with okra and tomatoes! Dry rice, too. You got to come eat some. Come on now, big doll-baby.

(He lets himself be carried inside and sits by the stove and rears back in a chair gloomily.)

RUBY: *(Standing before him)* Take all them knots out your face. You got friends a-plenty. Where one door is closed, there's a thousand open. *(Calls loudly)* Mama! Come look who's here! *(To Spunk)* You big, old good-looking thing, you! Play me something on that box whilst I put the supper on the table.

SPUNK: I don't feel to play. *(Begins to tune)* But I reckon I will a little. Songs make themselves up in you and then you have to sing 'em. They got to come outside. *(Strums)* Never can tell what's going to come out. *(Strums)* Sometimes they got light with a brightness, but sometimes they sad. You could wring tears out of 'em. *(Laughs bitterly)* Maybe I been sleep-walking and just woke up.

RUBY: Sing, Spunk, but don't sing nothing sad. I hates blues!

SPUNK: How can I tell what I'm going to sing? We got the power to open our mouth, but God gives us our words.

RUBY: Play something you already know. Like that pretty song you played sitting in the boat at the toe-party that night.

SPUNK: *(Shakes his head sadly)* Wisht I could, Ruby. But I ain't the same man. To myself I looked like the king of the world that night. Now I'm round here looking like the figure of fun. I was in my element that night. A fish loves to swim in water, but he's dead when he's swimming in grease.

> *(Begins to improvise. Strikes a definite tune, "Gethsemane." Evalina listens hard.)*

RUBY: Play it, papa, play it! You got the business and you know it!

> *(She cuts a caper or two. He begins to sing. Ruby senses the song is not for her and gets quiet. Evalina closes the window. Opens it again. Goes to the door and comes outdoors and creeps to Ruby's window. Ruby is sitting on the arm of the chair and puts her arm about Spunk's shoulders. He sings. Finally she pats his cheek.)*

EVALINA: *(Yells)* Spunk!

> *(She runs home and take her same seat at the window. Spunk jumps when he hears his name and looks all about him.)*

SPUNK: Look like I heard Evalina call my name.

RUBY: What would she be calling you for? She done stood up in church and told everybody she was through with you. Say she aims to live free from all sin till she die.

SPUNK: *(Crossing to door)* So she figger it's a sin to be with me, huh? I didn't know that. *(A short pause)* Still, she called me.

RUBY: *(Clings to his hand)* Nobody ain't called you, Spunk. Maybe it's a ghost. You better not answer. If you do you'll die soon.

SPUNK: *(Dragging Ruby as he goes)* Evalina called me. And if
she didn't her spirit did. I got to go and see. Loose me.

RUBY: *(Still clinging)* Aw, Spunk, stay here and get treated
right. Somebody done told her you got a wife and
child somewhere 'round Bartow and she b'lieves it. She
don't want you no more. With anybody else I'd say the
same thing myself, but with you I don't care. Don't go,
Spunk. Hear?

SPUNK: *(Standing in the door. Pushes Ruby off.)* I couldn't
have been mistook. She called me. *(He leaps the fence
and rushes to the window.)* What you want with me,
Evalina? You called me.

EVALINA: What make you think I called you, Spunk?

SPUNK: 'Cause I heard you. And if your mouth was too
stuff to say my name, your spirit called me. I heard it.

EVALINA: Maybe it was your wife and children down in
Bartow calling you home.

SPUNK: Who told you that lie, Evalina?

EVALINA: It wasn't told to me, but I heard it.

SPUNK: I swear to God that's a lie, Evalina. A great big old
Georgia lie. What you reckon I come back for if it
wasn't 'cause I love you?

EVALINA: Oh, some comes for a reason and some comes for
a season.

SPUNK: *(Shortly)* The capacity of your vocabulary
ain't nothing but sawdust, Evalina. Stop talking
foolishness. I swear I love you.

EVALINA: Don't swear to a lie, Spunk. That makes
everything even worser than it is already.

SPUNK: I ain't never told you a lie, Evalina. Why you doubt
my word now?

EVALINA: First old man Bishop come told me that he met
somebody from Bartow and they told him you had
a family there you had done walked off and left. So
I told him to get out of my face with his lies. Then

somebody wrote me a letter with no name signed
to it and told me the same thing. Then a man come
hunting you. A strange man. Said he was right from
there and come to take you home to your wife. He was
asking everybody where you was so somebody pointed
me out and he come here asking. Said you had a habit
of going off like that to spend a while but you always
come home whenever your wife sent for you. Said he
had your railroad fare in his pocket. So then I told him
where you was so he thanked me and left to go out
there where you was. Didn't he come?

SPUNK: Je-sus! What a lie! Ain't no man been to see me
'cepting these boys from here. That's some of old Hodge
Bishop's doings. He still trying to hurt me. So that why
you quit me, honey? Lawd, Lawd, it's just like the old
folks say, "You can't make buckling tongues meet."

EVALINA: Yes. You see I worried and fretted a heap. I said
I would just wait and see. Then the waiting go to be
too tiresome for me. Waiting for you to come when
maybe you'd be in Bartow done forgot all about me. It
got to the place where I had done tasted all the food
in the world. So I wasn't hungry no more. I didn't
need no more sleep or nothing. I told myself it would
be easier to quit waiting then it would be to wait for
nothing. So I told 'em all I had done give you up. So
they prayed over me and I joined the church Sunday
and wrote you about it.

SPUNK: So the fight between me and them Bishops ain't
over yet! And they all alike – underhand. He knowed
that parting us would hurt me worse'n anything he
could do, so he went to work and done it. I wished
he had of killed me. Done experienced everything I
hate to make my love come out right and love done
throwed me down.

EVALINA: Hurry up and tell me, Spunk, if you got that wife
or not.

SPUNK: What you want to know that for? You don't want me no more.

EVALINA: *(Bantering)* Maybe I don't, but you see the waves a long time after the ship done passed. Maybe I want to know just for old time's sake.

SPUNK: What you trying to do – put the hot-box to my head? You got me like a stepped-on worm. Half dead but still trying to crawl.

EVALINA: I done throwed up a highway in the wilderness for you to walk on. Answer me what I asked you.

SPUNK: I'll tell you with a parable, Evalina. You know God got a long rail fence in Heaven, made out of gold. And when he makes the people out of clay he stand 'em up against that fence to dry. And when they's good and dry, he blows the breath of life in 'em and turns 'em go. Evalina, soon as God breathed on me I knowed I was lonesome and I knowed you was somewhere looking for me. So I come straight from God's drying fence to you. I might have stumbled 'round examining a few girl babies to find out if it was you. But I am never even breathed marriage to another woman in my life.

(Evalina drops her head and sits silently.)

I hope you did call me, Evalina. I needs calling. Ring the bells of mercy and call the sinner man home.

(Evalina leans out of the window and breaks a bloom from the magnolia tree and sticks it in his hat band. Then draws back shyly.)

Move that chair out the way, Evalina.

(She moves the chair. He steps through the window and closes it behind him. There is the baying of bloodhounds in the distance.)

CURTAIN

ACT THREE

SCENE 1.

SETTING: *Croquet Court.*

ACTION: *A game is in progress. It is late afternoon and all the young folks are out, some playing, some sitting around. Enter Mrs. Watson, left, fanning with a palm leaf fan.*

DAISY: I know you want to play, Mrs. Watson. You can take my hand.

MRS. WATSON: Naw, indeed! All I want to do is get off my feet. *(Pulls off shoes as she sits.)* My feet so sore from so much standing I don't feel like I can wear nothing on 'em but a pillow-slip. The mess you all made at my house last night worked me nearly to death to get cleaned up. But wasn't that a reception, though? Old Spunk and Evalina looked good on that floor! Aand when the preacher pronounced 'em man and wife I thought he would knock her down kissing her. *(Laughs)*

DAISY: I know she was tickled to death to get him. But I can't see what she go and have a big wedding for and everybody know how it come about.

MRS. WATSON: That's their own business. If they want to brag off of they feelings let 'em do it. They ain't trying to hide nothing. At least they know what they getting married for and that's more'n a lot of other folks know.

DAISY: Wonder how come they didn't take him back to the chain gang to finish out his time?

WILLIE JOE: 'Cause his boss talked to the high sheriff
over the 'phone and told the sheriff he need Spunk
in the mill so he could meet his contract to some
lumber. Sheriff come on over to the mill and him
and Wilkins set in the office and drank liquor and
laughed and talked. He wasn't arrested for killing, Jim,
nohow. That was self-defense. They give him them
ninety days for toting a gun.

NUNKIE: He sure got off light. Kill a man, they give him
ninety days and he don't even serve that out. He must
be got roots.

MRS. WATSON: Aw naw! He didn't kill no white man,
did he? The white folks don't care nothing 'bout one
nigger killing another one. And then again Spunk is a
good worker and Jim was lazy. So they figger they don't
even miss him. *(Big laugh)*

NUNKIE: Yeah, they 'bout figger that Spunk saved them the
trouble of killing him theirselves. *(More laughter)*

WILLIE JOE: Yeah man, the boss called Spunk into the
office to talk with the sheriff. Know what he say? Says,
"Well, Spunk, the country is running short of groceries
so you'll have to get off the gang and go working for
yourself." Then he laughed, one of them big blow-out
laughs, and told Spunk not to give the boss no trouble.

ORAL: And to tell you the truth, white folks don't care
nothing 'bout our moral doings. If you work good and
don't give 'em no trouble youse a good nigger and they
like you. Otherwise they don't give a damn. And you
all know that the God's truth. So don't heat up your
gums and lie. *(Laughter)* Naturally his old man feels
bad 'bout Jim.

WILLIE JOE: Naturally. *(Looks at his watch)* Spunk and
Evalina is late today for their stroll.

MRS. WATSON: Late? They don't just have to get here no
special time, do they? What you rushing 'em for? They
looks just the same as ever.

WILLIE JOE: Oh, I just want to see and hear what new
song he made up for today, being he makes a new
one nearly every day. *(To Admiral)* Let's set up a *good*
game of croquet. Me and Nunkie will play you and
Oral. Let's go.

> *(All rise. There is a heavy chord on the box and
> Spunk and Evalina enter. She carries a guitar made
> out of a cigar box. Both are beaming.)*

Hey Spunk! What you say? What you say? What is it
today?

SPUNK: *(Beaming)* It's about the family this time. Me and
Evalina and our baby boy.

MRS. WATSON: Where you all get any baby boy from? I
ain't seen none.

SPUNK: Us got married last night, didn't we? It won't be
long now. I done gone to fixing for him.

ORAL: What that you got in your hand, Lina?

EVALINA: That's the baby's guitar.

ORAL: The *baby's* guitar!

SPUNK: Yeah, man. I made it at the mill today. I'm not
going to let my son sit up in the cradle and ask his
daddy "Papa, how you let me come in this world
without no instrument to play on?" So I done made
it already. Man, by the time he's ten years old I'd be
shame to play in front of him. And what make it so
cool, he's going to look just like me.

MRS. WATSON: How you know that, Spunk? It's liable
to take after Evalina or some of her folks or some of
yours. You never can tell.

SPUNK: Oh no! My first baby got to favor *me*. She can mold
some of the others to favor our kinfolks, but that first
one got to be the very spit of me.

> *(Plays and sings "Evalina." All join in chorus.)*

Yeah man, that boy of mine is going to be a whip!

EVALINA: *(Seriously)* If nobody don't do nothing to him.

SPUNK: Nobody better not do nothing to our son and stay on this earth. I'll run 'em as slick as a meat-skin.

EVALINA: They might not come out bold. Some folks takes undercurrents. Throw at you and hide they hand.

SPUNK: You talking about old man Bishop? I done told you ain't nothing to him.

EVALINA: *(Generally)* You know Spunk don't believe in nothing. He don't b'lieve folks can hurt you.

SPUNK: I b'lieve they can hurt me if they get something in my stomach and cut me or shoot me. But burying things for me to step over and things like that, naw! You cooks for me so he can't put no spider in my dumpling. I keep my eye on him 'round the mill so he can't steal with a knife or a gun. And I watch them logs he loads on the carriage so he can't trick none to throw me on that saw. So what is it to worry about?

EVALINA: Still and all things can be done, can't they? *(Makes a general appeal.)*

WILLIE JOE: I know they can. I done seen things happen. Plenty things. I seen a hoodoo doctor up in Georgia put a man to barking like a dog.

SPUNK: Well, if these hoodoo doctors can do so much why don't they conjure these white folks and get hold of some money and some power? Why don't they hoodoo the bank? How come they don't put a spell on the jail house and keep colored folks out of it? These white folks is rawhide to their backs and they 'round here throwing hoodoo at each other! Ain't nothing to 'em. Let me catch old Bishop 'round my house and I'll let him hoodoo all he wants to while I run a railroad 'round he neck. He's abstifically a humbug! But I just got married so I feel like treating. *Every*body have something on me. Talk fast. *(There is general clamor for various soft drinks, gum and cigarettes.)* Come on, Oral, and help me tote it. *(He exits right with Oral.)*

EVALINA: Spunk would get hurt if I listened to him. But I done sent down to Lakeland to that doctor down there. He's supposed to be better than Dr. Buzzard. He say anything old Bishop try to do to Spunk, he'll throw it back on him.

MRS. WATSON: And, honey, he can do it, too. I know him. He has worked for me. He's good. He works with rattlesnakes. And you know the spirit they represent lives under God's footrest. Tain't nothing more powerful than that. Did he give you anything to keep in the house?

EVALINA: Yes. Some special dressed mustard seed. I told him about something like a cat coming in our bedroom every night. He give me some mustard seed to sprinkle by the door. If anybody get out of their skins to come through our keyhole he'll salt their hides. They'll never get back in it no more. They'll die.

(She halts in fright. Enter Bishop, left. Stares about him and approaches Mrs. Watson.)

MRS. WATSON: Howd'do, Brother Bishop?

BISHOP: I ain't none of your brother. Your brother is out hunting coconuts. I'm going to have you up in church and see can't they handle you.

MRS. WATSON: What for?

BISHOP: You know what for. Letting murdering infidels marry in your parlor and then you holding a reception for 'em! The church ought to handle you. I'm going to have you up.

MRS. WATSON: You grassgut goat, you! I begged you to stop your son from tackling Spunk with that razor. You said leave him alone. Now don't come blaming me.

(Enter Spunk and Oral, loaded down but running)

SPUNK: Hey, folks! My lumber done come! Going to

build us a new house under the magnolia tree. Made arrangements to get it yesterday and now the boss done sent it. Y'all drink! Come on, Evalina! Less me and you walk this off!

(He drops the packages and crosses to Evalina in high spirits. All but bumps into Bishop. Looks grim as their eyes meet. Starts right with Evalina.)

NUNKIE: *(Clapping)* Hey Spunk, you and Evalina do the short walk.

(Others clap. Spunk squats down, takes Evalina's hand and she leads him off in a rhythmic waddle that makes the others laugh.)

MRS. WATSON: Bishop, Spunk ought to pay you good for working for him. Heh! Heh! You *say* you working against him, but look like you gives him the best of luck. Heh! Heh!

BISHOP: I ain't worked against him yet. I just been letting nature take its course but before long I mean to raise hell and put a chunk under it.

ORAL: That ain't what you said. You told us the *very* night that Spunk met Evalina at the toe-party that you had done put travel-dust down for him and he couldn't stay here more'n three days. It's nearly a year now.

BISHOP: Oh, that's all right, it will get him to go. You just watch.

NUNKIE: Yeah, and you said you had done dressed that saw to kill him and that ain't happened, neither. He's making *good* money at it.

BISHOP: Oh tain't too late. Ten years ain't too long for a condor to wear a stiff bosom shirt.

(Razzing noise)

MRS. WATSON: And you put out your brags that he was going to be hung 'bout that shooting and look what happened! Sixty days. And come home, got his old job back and done married Evalina and now building a brand new house. You have put him on the ladder. *(Laughter)* If you keep on working at him like you is we'll soon have a jig governor of Florida. *(Laughter)* You make out youse Old Man Jump-off. Make out you can peep through muddy water and see dry land.

ORAL: Thought you said that Spunk was going to die on the chain gang? Thought you said you had done parted him to Evalina. You ain't no trouble! Just heating up your gums for nothing. Done made a big mess then fell in it. *(Laughter)* Hope it doesn't give you the protolapsis of the cutinary lining.

BISHOP: *(Angrily awesome)* That's right! Laugh, fools and show your ignorance! I ain't done nothing yet 'cause I ain't tried nothing yet. Not nothing serious. And how come I didn't? 'Cause the right elements ain't come together. I works with cats, the most powerful thing in God's world. So the cat-bone told me to wait. It's been hard, but I done waited. Now the cat-bone says next Friday night is my time. Then the seventeen quarters of the spirit will meet in the upper air. I'll meet 'em! *(They begin to be awed)* The black cat-bone will take the throne in power! I'm going to show you that ugly laugh. *(He exits in trembling anger. The others watch him go in awe. Curtain.)*

SCENE 2.

Conjure Scene.
TIME: *One a.m. Friday.*
PLACE: *Hodge Bishop's altar room.*
PERSONS: *Hodge Bishop and six others .*

SETTING: *It is a small room with rafters and joists showing. There is a big altar upstage right. A small one in the corner, upstage left. The entrance, a rude door, downstage left, fastened with a bar. Altar set for a death ceremony. Ceremonial objects about the room.*

ACTION: *At the rise, the six men, dressed in cat robes, stand around the peavine emblem on the floor. They stand silent and tense, hands to the sides. Bishop is before the altar lighting the candle "earth" and the incense. He takes six blue candles from the altar and gives one to each of the men. They hold the candles in the left hand. Bishop returns to the altar and takes up a doll on it that is bound hand and foot and places it in the power spot. Takes a large black candle and lights it from the earth candle and begins to dance towards the first man. They join right hands and dance a step around each other. Bishop lights the man's candle from his and dances on to the next one and so on until all are burning. Then he dances back to the altar via the pea-vine and assaults the doll and cries out.*

BISHOP: Death! Follow this man! Follow this Spunk. Take his body and his footsteps off the earth.

> *(The men cry out like great angry cats. Bishop pours whiskey out before Death.)*

I'm paying you to follow that man!

> *(They all cry out again. Bishop deposits a nickel and cries again and the others answer. He dances down the pea-vine with the others growling and snarling and dances back to the altar, more excited this time.)*

The great cat! Born of the cat! I ask you to follow this man.

> *(Same business as before. He dances down the peavine*

once again. This time the tempo is increased. When
he returns to the altar he beats and stabs the doll
violently with the cat-men crying and snarling.)

He is not to the north for we have been there
He is not to the south for we have searched there
He is not to the east for we have looked well.
So we hurry to the west for we shall find him.

(There is a wild burst of gloating, crying, dancing.)

Bring in the Winds!

(They make the gesture of sweeping the four winds
in to the altar. They drop the cat robes and stand
nude and shining black. They dance fiercely. Hodge
takes the black cat-bone from the altar and places
it in his mouth. The dance continues. They all rub
him violently for a moment with their hands until he
trembles violently, then leaps away in terror as far as
possible. Bishop begins to writhe and his black skin
begins to split at the top of his head.)

CAT-MEN: Slip 'em and slip 'em again!
BISHOP: *(The skin peels down to the neck.)* Cat men! Guard
my skin! Cat men! Guard my skin from evil.
CAT-MEN: It shall be protected from pepper and salt!

(The black skin peels on down slowly and Bishop
stands dripping blood as he steps out of his skin and
picks it up and stretches it before the altar. That done,
he creeps downstage center and glares all about him.)

BISHOP: *(In a thundering voice)* Where is my saddle cat?

(There is a great cat-call and the shadow of a huge
bristling cat is seen on the back wall. Bishop makes
to mount it. There is a great wall of cars. Darkness.)

SCENE 3.

SETTING: *Street scene from Act 2, Scene 3. Late afternoon. Many homey flowers around both houses. A pile of new lumber beneath the magnolia tree. Evalina sits at her window humming and braiding her hair. She dresses it attractively and looks at herself well in the mirror. Ruby in a clean wash dress enters and sits on her steps but turns her back to Evalina pointedly. Evalina laughs and humming, comes outside to cut a red hibiscus bloom which she fixes in her hair. She walks to the gate and leans over. Enter Mrs. Watson, right, who stops at Evalina's gate.*

EVALINA: How do you do, Mrs. Watson? You looking fine.

MRS. WATSON: Oh, so-so. Waiting for that husband, eh?

EVALINA: Oh, I just come out this minute. You know I got to have a flower to wear. Where you headed for?

MRS. WATSON: Right here. I want some flowers for my sitting room. I'm expecting company from way off. Presiding Elder.

EVALINA: *(Opens gate)* Come in. Get all you want of what you see. *(She enters and begins to pick flowers leisurely)* I'd pick 'em for you but I'm too busy looking up the road for my husband. *(Laughs)* That first glimpse is always so nice. Sort of like daybreak. You know it's coming but it gives you a glad surprise every time. It's funny, ain't it?

MRS. WATSON: Oh, I reckon so. I done got past all that. Sometimes my husband come home and get in the bed with me and I don't know it till I wake up next morning.

EVALINA: You know, I'm worried 'bout Spunk. He makes good money and the boss is good to him, but I wish he'd quit that job. Old Bishop is working against him and he ain't never going to stop till Spunk is dead. I woke up screaming last night. Look like a great big tiger cat was springing on us in the bed.

MRS. WATSON: Do, Jesus! Umph! Umph! Umph!

EVALINA: Yes, honey, there was the howling and the growling of cats 'round this house last night form midnight till nearly daybreak when that big cat something jumped at us in the bed. But somehow it halted right in the air over us and vanished. *(Tearfully)* I want to leave here! That's why I haven't let Spunk start on the new house. I want us to go.

MRS. WATSON: Why don't you tell him, honey?

EVALINA: I done told him but he won't listen. He says he'll he a well-off man in five years if he keep on like he's going. But I'm afraid he won't be alive by then. He ain't got it to study about. It's me. *(They sit on the front steps)* And today I can't sit nowhere in peace. Not after that dream I had. It still seem too plain for a dream.

MRS. WATSON: Oh, they say Friday night, dark of the moon, is the time for dreams and visions. Some say that whatever you see then is true. I don't know. *(More cheerfully)* What you got good for supper?

EVALINA: Spare-ribs and Hopping John. It's seasoned down, too. Don't you want some of it?

MRS. WATSON: *(Laughs)* Lord, naw! I got the same thing. My husband buys five pounds of black-eyed peas every Saturday. Only I got bacon instead of spare-ribs. *(Look of listening)*

EVALINA: *(Half rising in alarm)* Sounds like I hear some singing at a distance. *(She listens intensely)* Songs and crying mixed.

> *(Waits listening. Ruby rises and moves about restlessly like an animal sensing danger.)*

MRS. WATSON: *(Wide-eyed in apprehension)* Reckon I better get along home. Go inside, Evalina, and set down.

(She coaxes Evalina to her gate tenderly, then moves to left exit.) I better go see. *(Exits)*

> *(Ruby moves to left exit and back to her own door with nervous, jerky movements. Evalina stands, violently a-tremble, near her gate. So far not a sound has been heard. Then the sound of chanting, mournful and high comes faintly to them. They answer, Ruby in a high, keen wailing,6 Evalina a throaty, sustained moan.)*

RUBY: Oh, Lord, to never know! To never know!

> *(The wailing comes nearer. A voice can be heard "lining out" "Hark from the Tomb A Doleful Sound Mine Ears Attend a Cry." This is sung by a chorus, mostly male. Muted, doleful. Evalina staggers to her step and sits down heavily and begins moaning to herself.)*

EVALINA: *(Raises her head bravely)* I ain't to cry. That wouldn't be right. It would look like I was sorry 'bout something when I ain't. *(Strangles a sob.)* He done filled every little corner in my heart. Ain't nothing been left out. He done showed his love in every way a man could do. *(Moans sadly, triumphantly)* I done had love from on high. *(Rises)* I got to pick some flowers for him to rest under because he was that kind of a man – big, and sweet-smelling and clean, like magnolias.

> *(She enters gate and pulls down a limb and begins to break blooms hurriedly. Ruby sees her and begins to pick roses frantically. Both keep looking offstage left. The weird chant breaks out again right at hand. The group are about to enter, left. Evalina comes out of the gate with a large bunch of flowers and stands trying to be brave.)*

These flowers in my hand don't keep the water out of

my eyes, though. *(Sings)*

> Stand by me, Lord, stand by me
> Stand by me, Lord, stand by me
> Standing in the world, Lord, the world don't like
>   me
> Stand by me, Lord, stand by me.

(The cortege enters. Six men bear a crumpled body on an improvised stretcher, a wide, new board with three short lengths of timber beneath it as handles. Ruby stops picking roses and starts downstage. Evalina walks resolutely to meet the group and wipes her eyes and looks lovingly down. hen she starts violently, puzzled for a moment. Then joyfully drops the flowers from her hand. A flower or two rolls off onto the ground.)

EVALINA: Tain't Spunk! It's old man Bishop!
WILLIE JOE: Yeah, death took the old man kind of sudden-
    like.

(They move on. Evalina nearly bursts with joy. Ruby also expands. The sounds of a guitar is heard off left. Joyful. Evalina's feet fly that way as Spunk comes walking fast and joyfully.)

SPUNK: Hello, sugar! How's papa's lil ground angel!

(Evalina does not answer. Catches hold of him and searches his face. Picks up a fallen flower and signals him to bow his head. He does so and she throughsts it in his hat band.)

SPUNK: What's the matter, honey? Look like you 'bout
    to cry. You really ought to be laughing. Old Hodge
    Bishop was so busy trying to get *me* onto that saw that
    he let a log fall on him. And when they moved it,
    there was the old conjure man pressed just as pretty as

a flower. *(They both laugh.)*

EVALINA: *(Sniffing and tearing off into the house)* Come on in. I smell my supper burning! *(She dashes inside.)*

RUBY: *(Sidling up)* I'm so glad you ain't hurt, Spunk, I had to go pick some flowers. Bet mama going to kill me 'bout her flowers. *(Smells roses and gets ready to offer them)* Yes, indeed, I'm real glad you ain't hurt.

SPUNK: *(Laughs) Me*, get hurt! Who going to hurt me? So long, Ruby. *(He dashes in after Evalina.)*

> *(The guitar begins to sound gaily inside and Ruby tiptoes to the window and peers in. They begin to sing. After the first verse Ruby sings.)*

RUBY:

> Me with flowers in my hand and love and me
>   apart
> Flowers withered like the house stretching on to
>   break of heart
> Roses scorned and drooping low to die
> Empty hours weeping, creeping as they pass me
>   by.

SPUNK AND EVALINA:

> I squat beside the way of life where highways meet
>   and aprt
> With wilted flowers in my hand and trouble in my
>   heart
> The flowers ungiven in my hands to die
> And life unmingled on my heart to lie.

> *(Ruby walks slowly towards her step, the flowers dropping one by one from her hand. She hums sadly an obligato over Spunk and Evalina's song.)*

CURTAIN

Polk County (1941)

An Authentic Negro Musical in Three Acts
Co-authored with Dorothy Waring

CAST:
   NOTHING LISTED???
   NOTHING LISTED???
   NOTHING LISTED???
   NOTHING LISTED???

ACT ONE

SCENE AND SETTING: *The Lofton Lumber Company has its big mill and quarters deep in the primeval woods of South Central Florida. Huge live oaks, pines, magnolia cypress, "sweet gum" (maple) and the like grow lush. Spanish moss drapes the trees. Tall cabbage palms tilt their crowns in clusters above the surrounding trees. Scrubby palmettos make dense undergrowth.*

The woods surround everything. Bull alligators can be heard booming like huge bass drums from the lake at night. Variegated chorus of frogs, big owls, and now and then the cry of a panther.

There are a hundred or more houses in the quarters. They are laid out in straight rows like streets. There is a main street, wider than the others called "The Square". On it are the public places like the Jook, or pleasure houses furnished by the management. There is a piano in it (sometimes a Victrola also), tables for card games made of unpainted lumber, and a big table with a trip-string for dice. This is the life of the camp after work hours. There is a sort of cafe where soft drinks, tobacco, dried fish, chitterlings, etc. are sold. It is the second place in popularity.

The streets of the quarters are unpaved, sandy places. There are trees that have been left standing here and there.

The houses are of raw, second grade lumber, unpainted, each with a porch and two or three rooms. Each man with a "family" is allotted a house for which he is docked about fifty cents a week. The single men live with others or room at the rooming house next door to the cafe. No fenced in yards, few flowers, and those poorly tended. Few attempts at any kind of decoration or relief of ugliness. Everyone lives temporary. They go from job to job, or from job to jail and from jail to job. Working, loving temporarily and often without thought of permanence in anything, wearing their switch-blade knives and guns as a habit like the men of the Old West, fighting, cutting and being cut, such a camp where there is little law, and the peace officers of state and county barred by the management, those refugees from life see nothing unlovely in the sordid camp. They love it and when they leave there, will seek another place like it.

Such a place is the cradle of the blues and work songs. There they are made and go from mouth to mouth of itinerant workers from one camp to the other.

They are ephemeral in every way. The murderous fight of today is forgotten tomorrow and the opponents work together in utmost friendship inside of twenty-four hours. The woman of today may be forgotten tomorrow. Certainly it is remarkable for a love affair to survive a change of scene. There will be more women where they are going, and they say, "Let every town furnish its own. It's a damn poor town that can't furnish its own. Take no woman anywhere." Here and there an attachment becomes permanent, and they settle down together, or travel together from camp to camp.

The women are misfits from the outside. Seldom good looking, intelligent, or adjustable. They have drifted down to their level, unable to meet the competition outside. Many have made time in prisons also. Usually for fighting over men. They too pack knives. No stigma attaches to them for prison terms. In fact, their prestige is increased if they have made time for a serious cutting. It passes for bravery – something to give themselves a rating in their small world, where no intellectual activities exist. Hence the boastful song: "I'm going to make me a graveyard of my own, etc. "

Rough, fighting drinking, loving, reckless, but at
times a flash of religion comes to the top when they
are very troubled or scared. Then for a short while, a
Spiritual will well up out of them and be much-felt for
the moment. Small churches have a hit-and-miss existence
on the camps. They feel the need of a preacher for funerals.
He is more often a man of the same stripe who reformed.

But these people have given the world the blues, work
songs, guitar picking in the Negro manner, and the type
of piano playing which made Fats Waller famous, and is
now being taken up by the world. Because it is typical,
they call that type of piano playing "jooking".

SCENE 1.

SCENE: *It is dawn. Birds twitter from the woods. A rooster
crows lustily from offstage, and is answered by another.
The Square is silent and deserted. Snores can be heard
from the houses nearest the footlights.*

LONNIE: *(Enters upstage left. He has a heavy stick and raps
on the porch of the house closest to where he enters and
chants)* Wake up, Jacob! Get on the rock! Tain't quite
day, but it's five o'clock! *(Raps again and crosses the stage
and raps on the porch opposite)* Wake up bullies! Day's
a-breaking. Get your hoe-cake a-baking and your shirt-
tail shaking! *(Crosses back, raps again)* Hey, you rowdy
mule-skinners! You better learn how to skin. Cap'n got
a new job and needs a hundred men!

> *(A drowsy hum of noise begins to rise inside the
> houses. Lights begin to appear, and there is movement
> behind the drawn shades. Lonnie crosses and keeps*

rapping and chanting.)

Wake up, bullies! I know you feel blue! I don't want you, but the Bossman do!

(The communal noises mount. More movement and lights and other signs of waking.)

What did the rooster say to the hen? Ain't had no loving in the Lord knows when. *(In a bantering tone)* Git out from under them covers, Sop-The-Bottom! You could have been in the bed when you was skinning last night. Fall out! *(He turns away grinning)* Wake up, bullies! Pull for the shore! Big crap game on the other side, and I know you want to go! *(Mounts a porch and listens at the window a minute)* Git up from there, Stew Beef! If you ain't made it by now, you better wait till night again. Git on up!

(Leaps off porch grinning. A hum in harmony follows his chants now. The camp is stirring. Lonnie is down at the footlights. He makes a last general call.)

All up, bullies! Unlessen you want some trouble with the bossman! *(Turns to exit, right)* I done called you once! I done called you twice!

(He holds the hum of his last syllable until he disappears off right. The lights have come up gradually, but not very much. Rooster crows, flaps wings, begins to strut as his flock of hens follow him on.)[2]

HEN 1: Ground cold to my feet this morning. I wish I had some shoes.

ROOSTER: *(Doing a love dance around her)* What did the rooster say to the hen? Ain't had no loving in the Lord knows when.

HEN 1: *(Uninterested)* These Polk County roosters! They want plenty loving, but they don't buy you no shoes.

ROOSTER: *(Love dance around another hen)* How about a lil kiss?

HEN 2: *(Evading him)* I want some shoes!

ROOSTER: *(Dances around another)* Oh, gimme a lil kiss.

ALL HENS: *(Complaining in rhythm)* Well, I lay all the eggs, and I go barefooted! *(Rhythmic imitation of cackle)*

ROOSTER: *(Trying to evade the issue)* Tain't a man in Tennessee can make a shoe to fit your foot!

(It is a well established chant-dance by this time.)

ALL HENS: *(Chanting in imitation of cackle and dancing)* Well, I lay all the eggs and I go barefooted!

ROOSTER: *(Trying his luck with first one hen then another)* Tain't a man in Tennessee can make a shoe to fit your foot!

(Same chants and business for duration of dance)

ROOSTER: *(At end of dance)* Aw, cutta-cut cut! You Polk County hens always hollering for shoes! Why I have to buy you shoes to love you? You get just as much out of it as I do. Aw, cutta-cut cut! *(He leads them off between the houses clucking disgustedly.)*

> *(Lights are up in kitchens. The wooden shutters are open. Shades are up. There is a clatter of pots and pans. Breakfasts are being hurriedly eaten, and buckets being packed with dinners. Men begin to drift out into the Square, collecting in a bunch to go to work.)*

SOP-THE-BOTTOM: *(Comes out playing his mouth organ and men begin singing)*

> I'm going to make me a graveyard of my own
> I'm going to make me a graveyard of my own
> Oh, carried me down on the smoky road
> Brought me back on the cooling board.

> I'm going to make me a graveyard of my own
> I'm going to live anyhow until I die
> I'm going to live anyhow until I die
> Sticks and stones may break my bones
> Talk all about me when I'm dead and gone
> But I'm going to live anyhow until I die.

DO-DIRTY: And that sure is the truth, man. I'm liable to make me a graveyard all by myself. I'm so mean till I'll kill a baby just born this morning.

FEW CLOTHES: Me too. Man, I'm mean! I have to tote a pistol with me when I go to the well, to keep from gitting in a fight with my own self. I got Indian blood in me. Reckon that's come I'm so mean.

(They all admit to Indian blood and meanness.)

DO-DIRTY: *(Yawning)* I sure ain't like Lonnie. I swear I wouldn't let nobody beat me out my money like Nunkie done him last night. Stacking the deck, and carrying the cub and everything.3 I would have kilt Nunkie so dead that he couldn't fall over. They would have to shove him over.

SOP-THE-BOTTOM: Lonnie didn't even know Nunkie was carrying the cub to him. Lonnie can't skin worth a cent. He ought to quit trying to gamble.

FEW CLOTHES: I seen Nunkie what he was doing, but I ain't no bet-straightener. It's more folks in the graveyard right now from straightening bets than anything else. Blind man ain't got no business at the show.

DO-DIRTY: You done right. It wasn't none of your business. Blind man ain't got no business at the show. But it is a good thing Big Sweet didn't come along about then. She would have cut Nunkie a brand new one.

SOP-THE-BOTTOM: I told Nunkie he better leave Lonnie's change alone, and then after he got it, I told him he better make it clean off this place before Big Sweet find out he got it.

FEW CLOTHES: Oh, she bound to find it out. My woman done found it out and she wouldn't let her shirt-tail touch her till she run tell Big Sweet all she know. If Nunkie ain't gone, he better be on his way.

SOP-THE-BOTTOM: He claim that his knife going to back Big Sweet off him. Claim he ain't scared, but I know better. He's talking at the big gate.

DO-DIRTY: *(Laughs aloud)* Did the fool talk like that? You just wait till Big Sweet get a hold of him. Before she turn him loose she'll make him tell her that she is Lord Jesus, and besides her there is no other.

STEW BEEF: I wouldn't exactly say Lonnie is blind. He ain't really dumb to the fact. He just ain't got his mind on no gambling. Let's folks talk him into the game. You know how he is---half the time his mind is way off on something else.

FEW CLOTHES: Yeah, them sort of visions he have. But I likes to hear him tell about 'em.

STEW BEEF: Me too!

LONNIE: *(Singing offstage)*
> I ride the rainbow, Amen.
> I ride the rainbow, Amen.
> I ride the rainbow, when I see Jesus
> Trouble will be over, Amen.

STEW BEEF: Here he come now. Sound like he been off on one of his trips.

> *(There is an eagerness as Lonnie enters. They all want to hear*

ALL: *(Very eager like children to hear a story)* Hi there, Lonnie!

LONNIE: *(Brings himself back to the present with a visible effort)* 'Lo, folks. *(They draw around him.)*

STEW BEEF: Sound like you been off this morning.

LONNIE: Fact of the matter is, I is been off.

STEW BEEF: Where was you at? Tell us so we can know.

LONNIE: *(Casually)* Oh, sort of knocking around heaven a while.

SOP-THE-BOTTOM: *(Intensely interested)* Tell us how you managed to git there. I ever wanted to see the place.

LONNIE: *(Illuminated)* On a great bird. A crow, diamond-shining black. One wing rests on the morning and the other one brushes off the sundown. He lights down out the sky, and I rides on his back.

FEW CLOTHES: How do you manages to git where he is, Lonnie?

LONNIE: He comes right here. You all just don't see him when he come.

STEW BEEF: How you know when he come?

LONNIE: A drum. A way off drum begins to throB It gits closer and closer, and afterwhile, here come the Great Crow circling round to light down on the ground. I jumps on. Never do know where he going take me, but I don't care. I just goes.

STEW BEEF: Umph! Umph! Umph! Ain't that wonderful?

LONNIE: Sure is. This time, he took me 'crost a ocean, all made out of melted down pearls. And the shore was this coarse grainy gold. Wasn't no sand, no dirt-sand there at all. It was wonderful!

SOP-THE-BOTTOM: How come we don't miss you when you go?

LONNIE: *(Laughs in a superior way)* Oh, that's easy! I just leaves my hull around here making motions, and you all thinks that I am here.

SOP-THE-BOTTOM: That's a good thing, too, 'cause if the Boss ever figured you even got far enough off the ground to crack your heels, he sure would dock you for the time you was up in the air. *(They all agree to this and laugh)*

STEW BEEF: Aw, let the man tell us what Heaven was like.

That's what I wants to hear about. *(General clamor)*

LONNIE: Tell you when we get to work.

SOP-THE-BOTTOM: What you trying to do – make out youse High John de Conquer?4

LONNIE: I knows him well. Awe – *can it be possible?* – in their faces. Nothing can't git too bad when Ole John de Conquer is around. *(Laughs)* Yeah, John de Conquer can find a way to beat out everything.

(This makes a deep impression in their faces.)

Awe, and can it be possible?

SOP-THE-BOTTOM: I know that High John was around in slavery days, but I thought he was gone back to Africa for good.

LONNIE: Supposing he was in Africa? What he care about distance? He could be right here in Lofton the next minute. He gits around right smart. Takes me off with him every occasionally.

SOP-THE-BOTTOM: No wonder you gits along so good. If you got the inside tracks on John de Conquer, youse something on a stick. Gimme some luck in a skin game.

LONNIE: It's too big to be brought down to that. It's for something big, like in your bosom.

SOP-THE-BOTTOM: Oh, to hell with it then. If it can't make me hold the last card I'm through with John de Conquer right now. You can have him. He got a willing mind, but too light behind.

DO-DIRTY: It's a fact. Why he don't distribute out whole hams?

LONNIE: Oh, he comes in handy. They got hams at the commissary if that's all in the world you wants.

FEW CLOTHES: That put me in the mind of something. *(Opens his dinner pail and looks in)* Looka here! Bunch done gimme the wrong thing in my dinner bucket. I done told her, I don't want no cold cornbread and molasses. I told her to fix to me some black-eyed peas with fat-back. She going to fix this bucket all over again, else hell is going to break loose in Georgy! *(Exits left in a hurry)*

DO-DIRTY: I don't blame Few a bit. Don't give me no half-handed dinner bucket. I don't want no stingy woman over my cook-stove.

SOP-THE-BOTTOM: Some women folks ain't exactly stingy, they's just contrary to that. I shacked up with a woman once that was so contrary she used to sleep humped up in the bed so you couldn't find no way to stretch out comfortable to sleep.

DO-DIRTY: Yeah, and I done been with some that pulls bed-covers. Won't let you stay covered up. Them kind of women don't look like they know what you bought a bed for. They think it's some place to lay up and study evil. *(All laugh)*

LONNIE: You telling the truth, I done seen 'em dreaming. They don't never dream about roses and scenery and sunshine like a sweet woman do. Naw, they dreams about hatchets and knives and pistols, and ice-picks and splitting open people's heads. I done seen 'em dreaming it! *(There is a wild burst of laughter at this.)*

SOP-THE-BOTTOM: Lonnie ain't lying. I had one like that down round Tampa one time. I tried hard to be good to that woman, but she wouldn't let me. Bought her shoes for her feet, and a brand new wig for her head. But she used to hump up in the bed and pull bed-covers right on. Lay up there and dream about killing folks *every night*. Go to bed evil and get up evil. Know what I done? One Day I just told her say, "Mary, gimme back the wig I bought you." She hollered and cried and asked me, "What is I'm going to do for hair?" "Let your head go bald." Man, I grabbed it, and I was out and gone. Left her without a dust of meal or flour. *(They all laugh in approval.)* Dicey put me in the mind of Mary more than anybody I ever seen. Just won't agree with nobody or nothing. Why, I seen Mary get into a fuss with a signboard one day. We was coming long the road and a signboard said Sweetheart Soap. Mary stopped and called the signboard a liar! Said it was Octagon Soap.5 *(They all laugh loudly.)*

LONNIE: I better go see where My Honey is. I woke him up, but I don't hear that guitar of his, so he might have dozed off again.

DO-DIRTY: Let's all go wake up the rascal. I know he ain't woke because he tunes that box before he pulls on his pants. Let's go git him.

LONNIE: The Bossman is getting mighty tight about losing time. I don't want us men that been together for a long time to get parted. That's why I most in general wakes the camp ahead of time – to get everybody up and on the job.

SOP-THE-BOTTOM: Yeah, look like the more money he make, the more he feel like firing folks. But what can we do? He got us in the go-long.

LONNIE: *(Dreamily)* Old John de Conquer could always find a way. He could make a way out of no-way. I'm gone to see about My Honey.

SOP-THE-BOTTOM: Come on, let's we all go long with Lonnie to My Honey's house, and come on back with the music.

> *(This meets with general favor, and there is a stir of them all heading off left.)*

My Honey always got something good to be picking on his box.

> *(There is a general, happy exodus. The lights have come up further. Calls and answers can be heard from different directions. Male and female voices, and general stir. Big Sweet enters left, crosses quickly*

*and stealthily to right and wedges herself against
the wall of a house. She has on a man's felt hat set
rakishly on the back of her head. She is smoking a
cigarette, but she douses it, pushes the hat far back,
and listens carefully. She peeps around the corner of
the house on the alert in her ambush She tenses as
she hears stealthy footsteps, and gets ready to spring.
Nunkie enters from between two houses, very close
to Big Sweet but does not see her as he steals along
looking fearfully over his shoulder.)*

BIG SWEET: *(Pounces on Nunkie, seizes him by the lapels of his
coat and buttons him up.)* Where you think you going?

NUNKIE: *(Scared, startled, but recovers and tries to appear
defiant)* Take your hands off of me!

BIG SWEET: Gimme that money back!

NUNKIE: *(Struggles to free himself, but vainly)* Take your
hands out of my collar, woman! I don't allow no
woman to button me up.

BIG SWEET: *(Tightens her grip firmly)* Well, I done done it,
Mr. Nunkie, and look like there ain't no help for it.
Gimme my Lonnie's money! You know I don't allow
none of you low-life-ted gamblers to hook Lonnie out
of his money. Give it here!

NUNKIE: *(Starts his hand to his pocket nervously, but looking
into Big Sweet's angry face, thinks better of it)* I ain't
supposed to teach Lonnie how to skin, is I? *(Tries to
wrench free)* Naw, I ain't going to give you nothing! I
ain't putting out nothing but old folks' eyes, and I ain't
doing that till they dead. *(Struggles)* Let go!

BIG SWEET: *(Tightens his clothes around his neck until he is
being choked. Shakes him violently)* Gimme!

NUNKIE: *(Desperate)* Take your hand out my collar! *(It is
half appeal.)*

BIG SWEET: I'll beat you till you slack like lime! Gimme
that six dollars you beat Lonnie out of. *(Another twist)*

Gimme!

NUNKIE: *(In desperate straits, tries to get to his pocket knife)*
I'll cut your throat –

BIG SWEET: *(Lands a terrific blow to his stomach)* You going
to cut me, eh? *(Another blow to his face, and Nunkie
goes down. She kicks him hard.)* I'll kill you. Gimme!

NUNKIE: *(Trying to cover up)* Murder! Help!

BIG SWEET: *(Trying for another good place to kick)* You didn't
die! You multiplied cockroach. *(Aims another kick)* I'll
teach you to die next time I hit you! Die!

NUNKIE: Murder! Murder! Somebody come git this woman
off of me!!

BIG SWEET: Shut up that racket! I mean to kill you. Beating
my Lonnie out of his money. Gimme! If you don't,
and that quick, they going to tote you through three
yards – this yard, the churchyard, and the graveyard.
Gimme!

> *(Sop-The-Bottom, Do-Dirty, Laura B, Few Clothes
> and Bunch rush in and take in the scene.)*

LAURA B: Oooooh, Big Sweet done caught Nunkie!

SOP-THE-BOTTOM: *(With admiration)* Look at that lump
on his jaw! Big Sweet, you sure hit him a lick.

BUNCH: You told that right.

LAURA B: *(To Big Sweet)* Did you all have some words
before you fell out?

BIG SWEET: *(Hovering over Nunkie so that he cannot escape)*
He better gimme Lonnie's money before I finish him.
I asked him nice and kind to gimme Lonnie's money,
but naw, he had to get up in my face with some of his
big talk. I'm going to kill him!

DO-DIRTY: *(To Nunkie)* Give it to her, man, if you got
good sense. Tain't nothing in the drugstore will kill you
quicker than Big Sweet will about Lonnie Price. Give
it to her.

SOP-THE-BOTTOM: You might as well give it to her. You

can't whip her. She got them loaded muscles. Come
on, hand it to her. Give her that little spending change.

*(Nunkie, sullen and silent, rolls his eyes hatefully at
Big Sweet.)*

BIG SWEET: *(Looks from the spectators back to Nunkie on the
ground all curled up like a worm. This sends her into a
fresh frenzy)* Don't you lay there all curled up like that!
*(Puts her foot on top of him and presses down to make
him straighten up)* Straighten up and die right! *(She
glares at him, then turns full of self-pity to the crowd)*
See? That's how so many lies gets out on me. They
twist theyselves all up and dies ugly, and then folks
swears I kilt 'em like that. *(Kicks Nunkie)* You ain't
going to die a lie on me like that. Straighten up!
LAURA B: *(Pleadingly)* Give him one more chance, Big
Sweet. Maybe he's fixing to give you Lonnie's money
right now.

*(They all look expectantly at Nunkie, but he is sullen
and slyly looking for a chance to run.)*

DO-DIRTY: Why you want to die so young, Nunkie? Give
her Lonnie's money and live to get old.
SOP-THE-BOTTOM: I know I don't aim to get hurt trying
to hold Big Sweet off you when she start to finish you.
Big Sweet is two whole women and a gang of men.
BUNCH: *(Disgusted, takes Few Clothes' arm)* Oh, leave her
kill him! If he ruther to die than to part with Lonnie's
money, let him have his ruthers. Come on Few, let's
go. Hard head make sore behind, you know.
FEW CLOTHES: *(Disgusted)* Yeah, come on everybody, so we
won't know nothing about it. Big Sweet can kill him
dead for all I care. He ain't no kin to me.
BIG SWEET: And I am going to kill him too. Old trashy
breath-and britches ain't got no business beating folks
out of money they done worked hard for. Run get me

my gun, Bunch! If God send me a pistol, I'll send him a man!

NUNKIE: *(Terrified)* Here's them few little old dimes is. *(He flings a little roll of bills at Big Sweet's feet and jumps to his knees.)* I got plenty more.

BIG SWEET: *(Knocks him back down)* Pick it up! You didn't get it off the ground did you? You got it out of Lonnie's hands. Pick it up!

(Nunkie grabs up the money.)

You ain't going to discount me like that. Git up from there and place it in my hand.

(Nunkie hurriedly hands Big Sweet the money.)

BIG SWEET: *(Snatches it angrily)* Now, stand back and lemme see if it is all here. *(Counts it)* Yeah, this is it. *(Puts it in her dress pocket)* I ought to beat you till your ears hang down like a Georgy mule for putting me to all this trouble. You ain't no good for what you live, nohow. Just like your no-count brother, Charlie. Git! Sweep clean! Broom!

NUNKIE: *(Dodges the blow Big Sweet aims at him to speed him and dashes off right. At the exit, he pauses)* I'll get you for this. I ain't scared of you. I'll –

QUARTERS BOSS: *(Rushes in right and seizes Nunkie who jumps in fright)* What the hen-fire is coming off here? *(He has his gun in his hand and his eyes on Big Sweet.)*

(Dicey, and several more people, mostly men, enter left on the run attracted by the excitement.)

NUNKIE: Big Sweet jumped me when I wasn't looking, and robbed me out my money.

QUARTERS BOSS: Big Sweet, ain't I done told you about your meanness? You ain't to cripple up everybody on the place. You hear me?

BIG SWEET: Youse a Got-that-wrong. I wasn't bothering

that thing. *(She indicates Nunkie with contempt)* It come here bothering *me.*

QUARTERS BOSS: *(Examining Nunkie's messed up condition)* Big Sweet –

DO-DIRTY: *(Giving Nunkie an unfriendly look)* He don't belong on this job, Mr. Pringle.

QUARTERS BOSS: *(Turning unfriendly eyes on Nunkie)* He don't? Then what is he doing in these quarters?

SOP-THE-BOTTOM: Come in here last night to gamble. Bothering Big Sweet about Lonnie's money.

QUARTERS BOSS: *(A great light)* Oh, he did, did he? She ought to have kilt him dead. Bulldozing the place and stealing, eh? *(Begins to frisk Nunkie roughly. Finds the knife and a greasy deck of cards)* Toting knives and weapons. *(Finds about a dollar's worth of small change and transfers it to his own pocket immediately)* Stealing honest people's money too! *(Examines the deck of cards, then fixes Nunkie with an accusing look)* Up to all kinds of meanness, too. *(Shakes the deck under Nunkie's nose as if it were a set of burglar's tools)*

QUARTERS BOSS: Unhunh! And toting concealed cards, highway shuffling, and attempt to gamble! *(Grabs Nunkie roughly)* You going down to Bartow to the big jail. Let's go!

NUNKIE: Don't take me to jail! Please, Cap'n! Lemme go this one time and I –

QUARTERS BOSS: *(Still glaring to intimidate Nunkie)* Well, I'm going to let you go this time. But you know no outside folks ain't allowed in these quarters. If I ever catch you on these premises again, I'll git you ninety-nine years and a jump-back in jail. Hit the grit!

NUNKIE: *(Pulling his hat down tight on his head)* Yassuh! *(Nunkie starts to walk rapidly towards right, watching nervously out of the corner of his eye for signs of threats to his escape.)*

DICEY: Poor Nunkie! It could be that he ain't harmed a

soul. *(General growl of disagreement)*

SOP-THE-BOTTOM: *(Shortly)* Aw, Dicey, you always got to pull different from everybody else. You know Nunkie is a mink.

NUNKIE: *(Hearing Dicey defend him, thinks that things are improving for him, halts and decided to hit back at Big Sweet)* Nam, I ain't stole nothing. Big Sweet –

QUARTERS BOSS: *(Firing off his gun into the air)* Git! Didn't I tell you to git?

> *(Nunkie departs in a hurry, and all laugh but Dicey.)*

DICEY: *(Not daring to accuse Big Sweet directly, mutters out loud)* Some folks thinks they is a lord-god sitting on a by-god. They just loves to 'buke and boss.

BIG SWEET: Who you personating, Dicey? You must of woke up with the Black-ass this morning.

DO-DIRTY: Just like usual. *(Sings)*

> She got the blues, she got the black-ass too.
> The blues don't hurt her, but the black-ass do.

(Disapprovingly) Always thinking evil.

DICEY: How come you all always get to take a pick-out after me? I can't break a breath without somebody got to hurt my feelings.

QUARTERS BOSS: Here! Here! Squat that rabbit and let's jump another one. *(To Big Sweet)* Big Sweet, not that I fault you for what you done this morning, but I been laying off to caution you for some time.

BIG SWEET: Caution *me*? Caution me about what?

QUARTERS BOSS: *(Placating)* Now, I ain't after no fuss. I gits paid to keep order in these here quarters, and I tries my level best to do it.

BIG SWEET: Well, who told you not to? I know it wasn't me.

QUARTERS BOSS: You been lamming folks a mighty heap round here.

SOP-THE-BOTTOM: Who? Big Sweet? Big Sweet don't

bother nobody. You must be talking about somebody else.

BUNCH: I ain't heard nobody say nothing against Big Sweet. She's even nice.

DO-DIRTY: If folks leave her alone, she'll leave them alone. She just don't like to see nobody bulldozing the place and running the hog over other folks. She'll cold crawl you for that.

LAURA B: And nobody can't coldwater her for that. Some folks is too biggity and imposing.

(Everybody but Dicey joins in the testimonial by noises of approval.)

QUARTERS BOSS: *(Mocking)* Yeah, yeah, I know. That's all I can hear from most of you. Big Sweet ain't never done a thing but praise the Lord. Her mouth is a prayer-book and her lips flap just like a Bible. But where do all these head-lumps come from that the Company Doctor is always greasing? Somebody done told me. Big Sweet lumps your heads, and kicks your behinds for you, and you all lie and make out you don't know who done it. How can I keep order like that?

LAURA B: But we already got order! Lonnie don't like no rough stuff and Big Sweet, she –

QUARTERS BOSS: I'm the one getting paid to look after things. Big Sweet is too heavy with her hands. Now, take Lonnie Price for instance: Lonnie is a *good* man. No better conditioned man ever been on the place. Works hard and regular and don't git into no cutting scrapes. But I can count the paydays on Lonnie's head. Big Sweet's got a lump up there for every pay-day. But will he tell *me* she done it? Naw, indeed! A piece of lumber flew up and hit him, or something like that.

BIG SWEET: *(Aroused)* I don't aim to let *nobody* tell me that I mistreats Lonnie. It's my lifetime pleasure to do what I know he want done. Lonnie, he's different. He don't like all this old rough doings and fighting, so I makes 'em live better cause what Lonnie says is right. *(Tenderly)* Lonnie is just a baby, in a way of speaking. He thinks everybody will just naturally do right, but I knows different. So I gets around to see to it that they do.

QUARTERS BOSS: Well, why you lam Lonnie? He don't act rough.

BIG SWEET: *(A self-conscious laugh)* I don't lam Lonnie. I just sort of taps him once in a while. You see, Lonnie got his mind way up in the air, and I taps him to make him know that the ground is here right on, and that there's minks on it trying to take advantage of him all the time. They can't fool *me*. Lonnie dreams pretty things. That's what make I love him so.

QUARTERS BOSS: *(Touched by Big Sweet's sincerity, looks at her a long time)* I believe you do, Big Sweet. *(Back to his official manner)* No use in talking, I reckon. If the rest of you all don't care how much Big Sweet whips your heads and kicks your behinds, I don't give a damn. *(He turns shortly to leave, right)* But still and all, the Company don't want all the help kilt off. You got to leave somebody to do the work on this joB

SOP-THE-BOTTOM: So far as that is concerned, more men makes time now than they used to do cause Big Sweet keeps a lot of 'em from cutting the fool 'and going to jail. She don't bother nobody.

BIG SWEET: *(Seriously)* No, I don't bother nobody, They bothers *me*. Looks like to me, folks ought to improve up some.

LAURA B: *(Triumphantly)* See that? Big Sweet –

QUARTERS BOSS: *(Exasperated)* All right! All right! Big Sweet is the bellcow, and to hell with it! *(Exits right quickly)*

> *(The minute he is gone, they all break into boisterous laughter. They dance and caper. Few Clothes pulls out*

> *his harp and begins to play "Train." Big Sweet buck*
> *dances a few steps to a "break" then finishes off with a*
> *belly-wobble. They laugh and exclaim some more.)*

BUNCH: Big Sweet, youse a mess!

DICEY: *(Who has taken no part in the jubilation)* Reckon I
better go see about My Honey's bucket. I baked a cake
so he could have some to carry in his dinner bucket.
*(She simpers, and goes off left quickly, walking as if she
had some romantic secret.)*

LAURA: Is Dicey done shacked up with My Honey?

BIG SWEET: Aw, naw! He rooming with us right on.

BUNCH: What she doing fixing him a bucket, then?

BIG SWEET: Lord knows, I fixed My Honey's bucket last
night just like always. He did mess with her for a day
or so when he first come on the job, but that was long
time ago. He don't mean Dicey no good, and she know
it. She call herself fooling folks.

SOP-THE-BOTTOM: I thought My Honey could do better
than that. Me, I wouldn't have her for a Christmas gift.

LAURA B: So contrary. What she got to take up for Nunkie
for? Everybody know he ain't worth doodley-squat. Bet
he will stay out of these quarters now. *(Laughs)* You
sure give his head a straightening.

DO-DIRTY: But I would watch out for him if I was you, Big
Sweet. You heard him say he aimed to get you.

BIG SWEET: I heard him, but I ain't scared of that trash. I'll
finish him next time he mess with me. Specially with
my Lonnie.

DO-DIRTY: But he's the kind wouldn't come up and fight
you a fair fight. He would lay 'way for you and try to
steal you.

SOP-THE-BOTTOM: And he hangs out around that Ella Wall
in Mulberry all the time. She's jealous because you got
such a swing around here. They're liable to try to gang
you. They's dirty!

(From offstage comes the sound of a guitar and men's voices singing "Jesus Going to Make Up My Dying Bed.")

DO-DIRTY: Listen at old My Honey! That fool can cold pick a box!

BIG SWEET: *(Proudly)* You listen at *my* baby singing. Listen! That's Lonnie singing right in there. Listen!

LONNIE: *(Voice offstage)*

> Well, I'm going down to the river.
> Stick my sword up in the sand
> Going to shout my troubles over, Lord
> I'm going to make it to the Promised Land.

MALE CHORUS:

> Well, well, well! I'm going to cross over
> Well, well, well! I'm going to cross over
> Well, well, well! I'm going to cross over
> Jesus going to make up my dying bed.

LONNIE: *(Singing)*

> Oh, meet me, Jesus, meet me
> Meet me up in the middle of the air
> And if my wings should fail me, Lord
> Won't you meet me with another pair!

BIG SWEET: *(In ecstasy)* Do it, Lonnie, do it!

(The men come in singing the chorus. Lonnie and My Honey are walking side by side and the others are grouped close to keep the harmony straight. They are strutting, smiling and feeling anything but religious. They are carried away by melody and rhythm. A loud-laughing cheer goes up from the spectators. They egg the other on. My Honey is conscious of the good finger work he is doing and is grinning about it.)

LONNIE: *(Sings)*

And in my dying hour
I don't want nobody to moan
All I want you to do for me
Is just to fold my dying arms.

(This manner of delivery pleases everyone. They show it by smiles and laughs. Men start on chorus. Dicey enters running hard from left with an open switch-blade knife in her hands, leaps on My Honey and tries to button him up. He flings her off, but she attacks again grabbing hold of the pocket of his jumper and winding her hand in it and feinting at his middle with her knife. Everybody is struck dumb for a moment by the suddenness of the attack.)

DICEY: Oh, Yeah! *(Panting)* I got you! Trying to duck and dodge from me, but I got you!

MY HONEY: *(Recovering his faculties somewhat, struggles to break the hold)* Git away from me, Dicey! Is you gone crazy in the head? *(Flings her off again so hard that she is off balance)* I don't want to hurt you. Why don't you leave me alone?

DICEY: *(Seeking an opening)* I'll fold your dying arms for you!

(Big Sweet is tensing herself to seize Dicey from behind, and waiting for a favorable moment as she makes threatening motions with her knife at My Honey.)

Trying to scorn me! I won't stand a quit. I mean to cut you just as long as I can see you.

(Big Sweet darts in and grabs Dicey's uplifted right hand and wrests the knife away. Dicey gives a short scream of fright as she fears that Big Sweet means to cut her with it. But Big Sweet looks at it good, closes it, and puts it in her pocket.)

DICEY: Gimme back my knife! I mean to stick my knife in him and pull it down. Gimme my knife! My money paid for it.

BIG SWEET: *(Calmly)* Naw, I better keep it. You doing too much talking about cutting folks to death these late days. You keep on flourishing that old free around here, and somebody is going to hurt you.

> *(Dicey rushes back and grabs hold of My Honey. She tries to hit him in his face but he blocks every blow, and keeps shoving her off.)*

DICEY: I mean to kill you and go to jail for you.

MY HONEY: Why don't you leave me be, Dicey? I done told you I don't want no parts of you. Behave yourself!

> *(There is a strong growl among the males.)*

SOP-THE-BOTTOM: It's a good thing it ain't me she's pulling on. God knows I'd get her to go. She better not never draw no knife on *me*.

LONNIE: *(Angrily)* I don't believe in knocking lady people around like I would a man, but if I was God, I sure would turn Dicey into a hog, and then I would cement the world all over, so she wouldn't have a damn place to root.

DICEY: *(Furiously to Lonnie)* You keep your big mouth out of me and My Honey's business. That's what the matter now – me and him was getting along fine till you had to go tole him off and turn him against me. Yeah, I'm going to cut him, and a heap more round here if they mess with me.

LONNIE: Big Sweet, why don't you talk some sense into this crazy fool? You know My Honey ain't got no more use for her than he is for his baby shirt. She's just taking advantage because he won't knock her down like some mens would. *(To Dicey)* Turn My Honey go! Take your hands off of his clothes!

DICEY: Ain't a-going to do it till I get good and ready. He ain't going to quit me like I was some old dog.'

MY HONEY: *(Tartly)* I ain't never said I wanted you yet. You better wait till somebody ask-es you before you go claiming 'em.

LONNIE: *(Distressed)* How come we got to have all this changing words and disturbment? How come everything can't go on nice and friendly?

BIG SWEET: *(Looks at Lonnie's unhappy face, then interferes)* Lonnie is right. Tain't no use in all this who-struck-John. *(Approaches Dicey)* Me, myself, I done learnt better about a lot of things since I been with Lonnie. *(Kindly to Dicey)* Dicey, on the average, I am for the women folks, because the mens take so much undercurrents of us. But, Dicey, My Honey's case done come up in your court. He ain't fooled you and mistreated you. All he ever done was joke with you a time or two. He done told you he don't want you. I wouldn't want no man that didn't want *me*. Pulling after a man that don't want you is just like peeping in a jug with one eye. You can't see a thing but darkness. Take a fool's advice and leave the man alone, like Lonnie say.

MY HONEY: *(Sullenly)* I done tried and tried to tell her that. But look like her head is hard.

STEW BEEF: I sure would soften it up for her, if it was me.

LONNIE: I never did choose no woman that run me down.

DICEY: *(Full of self-pity)* Why you all want to double-team on me? Always faulting me for everything. I can't even talk to my gentleman friend without everybody got to dip in.

MY HONEY: If you talking about me, you ain't got none. You'll never snore in my ear if I can help myself.

DICEY: I know I ain't yellow, and ain't got no long straight hair, but I got feelings just like anybody else. Go on, treat me mean if you want to, but someday, you all going to wish you had of treated me right. *(Exalted)* I'm going to be propaganda! Everybody going to be talking about me. Mens is going to scream over me more'n they ever did over Ella Wall, going to make up songs about me too and they going to talk about me more'n they do about Big Sweet.

LONNIE: How you going to bring all that about, Dicey?

DICEY: I'm going go git me a new, big knife. That kind you touch a button and the blade fly open, and I'm going to make me a graveyard of my own. *(As if visualizing)* I'm going to cut everybody that bother me. I'm going to stick 'em just to see 'em jump. Carry me down to Bartow to jail and folks will come running from way off just to look at me. They'll say, "There she is! That's Dicey, the one that kilt so many folks. Big Sweet? What you talking about, man? Big Sweet can't hold a light to Dicey Long. She'll kill you without a doubt. Slice you too thin to fry. Shoot until her gun jumps the rivets! Don't care who it is and where it is, that Dicey Long will fight. She'll shoot in the hearse, don't care how sad the funeral is. That's Dicey Long!" *(In her reverie, she has released My Honey's coat and made gestures of exaltation. Now she comes out of it)* Then My Honey and a whole heap of mens will be pulling after me. I'm going to scorn him then. Tell him to come 'round another day. All of you all going to be trying to git in with me, but I aim to turn my nose up at you. I'll be Miss Dicey Long, with finger rings and things.

(The whistle blows loud and long and the men respond automatically. Before Dicey realizes it, they are moving off and My Honey is out of her reach.)

LONNIE: Come on boys! Another day! The work is hard, and the boss is mean. Can you make it?

MALE CHORUS: Yeah!

LONNIE: Can you break it?

MALE CHORUS: Yeah!

LONNIE: Can you shake it?

CHORUS: Yeah!

LONNIE: All right, then! Follow me, Bullies! *(Chants)*
Cutting timber! Ha! Cutting ties!

DICEY: *(Plain'tive)* My Honey! *(She moves towards him, but Lonnie blocks her.)*

MY HONEY: Aw, don't bother me woman. I'm going to leave this job just to get rid of you.

DICEY: I'll wait for you. How long you going to be gone?

MY HONEY: From since when till nobody knows!

DICEY: Going to take me with you.

LONNIE: Tell her, "no!" Let every town furnish its own.

DICEY: Where you figger on going?

MY HONEY: Way up in Georgy.

STEW BEEF: Man, is you crazy? Christ walked the waters just to go around Georgy, and you fool enough to go right in it!

DICEY: *(Almost sobbing)* My Honey, tell me sure enough, if you go, when you coming back?

MY HONEY: Not that it is any of your business, but I'll be back some old cold rainy day.

(The second whistle blows short and sharp.)

LONNIE: Let's go!

(They all make motions of leaving.)

STEW BEEF: Let's go! The work is hard and the boss is mean. *(Sings)*
Asked my cap'n what the time of day
He got mad and throwed his watch away.

LONNIE: *(Entering into the spirit of kidding bossmen)*
Cap'n can't read and cap'n can't write.
How the hell do he know when the time is right?

MY HONEY:

> Cap'n got a pistol and he try to play bad
> But I'm going to take it if he makes me mad.

DO-DIRTY: My Honey, you better not take that box. Didn't Cap'n tell you not to bring it on the job no more?

MY HONEY: I ain't got that man to study about. I takes my music and my meanness everywhere I go.

STEW BEEF: Aw, you make the time, don't you? Play that box, man! Give us something to walk on. Git with him Few Clothes.

> *(The men wave and yell back at the women who wave and yell at them and go off singing "Cold Rainy Day."6 The animation in the women dies as the singing fades out. They are drab again, and begin to make slow motions of dispersal to homes. Dicey stands looking forlorn after the men when all other women have turned away. Big Sweet looks at her and grows sympathetic. She approaches Dicey and starts to put her arms around her, but Dicey spurns her.)*

DICEY: You old destruction-maker! Taking My Honey away from me!

BIG SWEET: Nobody ain't took him because he never was yours.

DICEY: You did!, You did! You and that Lonnie, and you more especial. Keeping him laying 'round your house night and day. I'm going to got even with you for it too. I'll put Ella Wall on you!

BIG SWEET: Ella Wall ain't my mama. I ain't a bit more scared of her than I is of you. And than again, what I got to be scared about? Ella Wall ain't no big hen's biddy, if she do lay gobbler's eggs.

DICEY: You'll find out. You done more than Lonnie think you done to git My Honey away from me, and keep him tied up round your house like a yard dog.

BIG SWEET: *(Angry)* That's a lie! *I called you a liar.* You don't like it, don't you take it. Here's my collar, come and shake it!

> *(The atmosphere becomes tense. The others crowd around expecting action. Dicey backs off cringing.)*

DICEY: Your time now, be mine after while.
BIG SWEET: So be it in the grand lodge. *(Curtain)*

SCENE 2.

Scene: *It is late afternoon. The sun is strong in the Square. Housework is done and suppers are cooked and waiting for the men to return. Women have changed into clean cotton housedresses, well starched, and sitting around on porches. Several large boys and frying-size girls are out in the square playing Chickamy Chickamy Craney Crow, as the women sit around and patch, or here and there two or three "visit" on the porch of a neighbor. A boy about fifteen is the Crow. A girl about the same age is the hen.*

MAUDELLA: All right, Alwishus, you be the Crow. I'll be Mama Hen.
ALWISHUS: Okay, now, but don't make out I didn't catch you when I did.
MAUDELLA: Aw, go on and get ready.

> *(Alwishus gets a stick about the size of a large pencil and squats in the center of the play area. The girls form in line behind Maudella, each holding the girl in front around the body, or by her dress in the back, and start the march around the Crow chanting.)*

Chick mah chick mah craney crow
Went to the well to wash my toe

> When I come back my chick was gone.
> What time, Old Witch?

ALWISHUS: *(Making a mark on the ground)* One!

> *(Same business till the count is three. The Crow gets up and assumes a predatory posture. The Hen and all her chicks go on the alert to avoid capture. The whole movement is a rhythmic dance with chanted words.)*

ALWISHUS: Chickie!

MAUDELLA: *(Dancing counter to Crow with all chicks with her)* My chickens sleep!

ALWISHUS: *(Wing and foot movement)* Chickie!

MAUDELLA: *(Foiling him)* My chickens 'sleep.

ALWISHUS: I shall have a chick!

MAUDELLA: You shan't have a chick.

ALWISHUS: My pot's a-boiling!

MAUDELLA: Let it boil!

ALWISHUS: *(Executing banking flight as if he is leaving)* I'm going home.

MAUDELLA: *(Undeceived)* There's the road!

ALWISHUS: I'm coming back! *(Suits action to words)*

MAUDELLA: Don't care if you do!

> *(Leafy Lee enters from right. A slim mulatto girl with a cheap suitcase in her hand. Walking slowly and looking about her as if searching. It is hot, and she wipes her face. She is not discovered immediately because of the excitement of the play-dance. She watches the dance with interest a minute, then advances more rapidly.)*

ALWISHUS: *(Working up to a high pitch)* My mama's sick!

MAUDELLA: Let her die!

ALWISHUS: *(Coming in closer for the kill)* Chickie!

> *(Darts in suddenly and seizes one of the chicks to loud screams of mock terror. It is then that Leafy Lee is*

discovered. They all stop and look.)

LAURA B: *(Under guise of a cough)* Who is that?

NEIGHBOR: Look like she is white. What you reckon she want in here?

LAURA B: Lord knows.

> *(Dicey enters from her house and stands on porch staring at Leafy. Leafy approaches the girls and boys playing.)*

LEAFY: Hello.

MAUDELLA: *(Bashfully)* How de doo.

LAURA B: *(Undertone to others)* Seem like she colored from the sound.

LEAFY: *(Exhibiting a small piece of white paper)* Can you tell me where I can find Miss Bunch?

LAURA B: *(Undertone)* She colored. Hear her put that handle to Bunch's name. *Miss Bunch. (To Leafy)* Who was it you wanted to see?

LEAFY: *(Approaching Laura's porch, setting down her bag and wiping her face.)* Miss Bunch. They told me at the office that she could let me have a room.

LAURA B: Oh, then you expecting to stay here a while? *(Catching herself)* Oh, where is my manners today? Won't you come up on the porch and have some set down? It's sort of hot out there today.

LEAFY: Much obliged to you. It *is* real hot in the sun.

> *(Bunch enters from her house across the street and stands on her porch listening.)*

LAURA B: *(Raising her voice so that Bunch can hear)* You say you looking for Bunch? Is you some kin to her?

LEAFY: Oh, no. I never seen her in my life. The man at the office just give me her name on this piece of paper and said she might let me have a room to stay if she had one to spare.

LAURA B: Bunch ain't around home right now. Seens like I

seen her going to the commissary awhile back. You say
you aim to stay here? You going to teach the school?
You sort of looks like a schoolteacher.

LEAFY: No ma'am. I'm not a schoolteacher at all. I just
come to stay around awhile.

LAURA B: Is you married?

LEAFY: Oh, no Ma'am. I haven't got no husband at all. All
by myself.

LAURA B: Oh, I see. You got a man friend here, and you
come to live with him.

LEAFY: *(Shocked)* Oh, no ma'am. I haven't got nobody likes
that atall. I don't know a soul here so far.

> *(All the women are out where they can listen and give
> each other significan't glances on Leafy's answers.)*

DICEY: *(Calls over)* Er, Laura B, come here. Maybe I can tell
you where Bunch went.

> *(Laura B understands that Dicey wants to talk to her
> and gets up. Two or three other women head towards
> Dicey's porch at the same time, including Bunch.)*

LAURA B: *(To Leafy)* You better step in the house and have
a seat. It may be a little cooler in there. Maudella, pick
up the lady's suit-satchel and take it inside for her.
She can set there until Bunch come home and let her
know.

MAUDELLA: *(With eyes devouring Leafy in admiration)*
Yassum. *(She picks up bag and proceeds Leafy into the
house.)*

LEAFY: *(Up on the porch)* That was a pretty game you all
were playing. I wish you would teach it to me.

MAUDELLA: *(Happily)* Sure will because I likes to play it my
own self. *(They exit into house.)*

LAURA B: *(As she joins the others at Dicey's porch)* You got a
bug to put in my ear?

DICEY: Ain't got nothing different. Don't be pointing out

Bunch to that gal. She ain't nothing! Bunch don't want nothing like that in her house causing disturbment.

BUNCH: Oh, you knowed her before?

DICEY: Not to speak to, but look like I seen her somewhere. But if I never seen her before, you can tell she ain't nothing. Just a old storm-buzzard out for what she can get. I wouldn't have her in *my* house. *(There is a thoughtful silence.)*

LAURA B: She don't seem like no fan-foot to me.7 I figgered her out for sort of nice, didn't you, Bunch?

BUNCH: Sort of kind of. Wants to play ring play with the young'uns. That don't sound so bad.

DICEY: *(Heated)* That ain't nothing but a form and a fashion and a outside show to the world. She done heard about the money our mens makes on this job, and she done come in time to make a payday. Better git her on off from here before sundown and the mens come home from work. She'll be after all us men before you can turn around. Let's git her way from here.

LAURA B: The Quarters Boss must have figgered she was all right, else he wouldn't have let her in here.

DICEY: Aw, that white man don't know what he talking about. I has words with Big Sweet sometimes, but she ain't wrong all the time. She ain't going to like no stomp-down fan-foot round here tearing up peace and agreement. Let's call Big Sweet and tell her. She'll get her gone from here, Quarters Boss or no Quarters Boss. You know Big Sweet. Us ought to halt her right now before the means gits a chance to see her and cut the fool over her. Don't let the 'gator beat you to the pond, do, he'll give you more trouble than the day is long. Send Alwishus after Big Sweet. She home.

(The first lines of "Polk County" are heard off stage left)

BIG SWEET: *(Singing offstage)*
> You don't know Polk County like I do
> Anybody been there, tell you the same thing too.

LAURA B: Here she come now. I sure is glad, because I sure don't know what to do.

BUNCH: Me neither. I was going to tell Laura B to bring her on over to my house, but if she is like Dicey say she is, I don't want no trouble with Few Clothes.

LAURA B: None of us don't want no kind of trouble like that. These mens don't want to half do nohow. Its just like pulling eye-teeth to git a pair of shoes out of 'em. They got a mouth full of gimme, and a hand full of much-obliged.

BIG SWEET: *(Enters left, still humming "Polk County")* Say, what's the matter over there? You all got your head together like crows in a storm.

> *(They all motion her to hurry over. Big Sweet crosses quickly and joins them without another word.)*

The law in here hunting somebody?

DICEY: *(Very friendly)* It's a woman. A fan-foot.

LAURA B: Oh, we ain't so sure about that part yet. But its a young, real high yaller-- I got her in my house till we can find out what to do about her. The Quarters Boss give her a note to Bunch to stay with her.

DICEY: A regular old strumpet making paydays. Just somebody on the road somewhere. Color struck, too. Crazy about that little color she got in her face, and that little old hair on her head. You ain't going to like her a bit. And she'll be after Lonnie and My Honey and everybody else right off.

BIG SWEET: Come on, Laura B.

> *(She turns resolutely towards Laura B's house. Big*

> *Sweet and Laura B lead the way with the others*
> *following slowly so as to appear just to happen up in*
> *time to see the show.)*

LAURA B: *(At her porch, and in a low tone)* She don't look
  bad to me. If Dicey hadn't of said –
BIG SWEET: *(Grimly)* Call her out. *(She rests her left foot on*
  the steps, and her left elbow on her left thigh.)

> *(The voices of Leafy Lee and Maudella can be heard*
> *in gay talk and laughter inside.)*

LEAFY:

> Well, I went up on that meat-skin
> And I come down on that bone
> And I grabbed that piece of cornbread
> And I made that biscuit moan.

> See, I got it right that time, didn't I?

> *(They both laugh)*

LAURA B: *(At door)* That Maudella is too fast and
  womanish. *(Proudly)* She ain't scared of nothing! *(She*
  exits into house while Big Sweet waits grimly.) Miss, er,
  you child, it's somebody out here wants to have a talk
  with you. Just step outside a minute.

> *(The other women are drifting up and around the*
> *porch.)*

LEAFY: Leafy is my name. Leafy Lee. *(Coming to door)* Is it
  Miss Bunch done come?

> *(Sees Big Sweet. Big Sweet looks Leafy over from*
> *head to foot slowly and deliberately, and back again.*
> *There is either hostility or cold indifference in the*
> *faces of every woman about her, as Leafy stands there*
> *on the porch and takes in the circle. Finally she meets*
> *Big Sweet dead in the eye. They eyeball each other*

well, then Leafy breaks into a grin. Big Sweet tries to hold her solemn pose, but she also begins to grin. She purses her lips, but the chuckle gets bigger and bigger as she and Leafy expand their smiles. Finally Big Sweet gives in, takes her foot down, stands akimbo and with an attempt to conceal her admiration under rough good humor.)

BIG SWEET: You crazy thing!

LEAFY: *(Laughing, imitates Big Sweet's stance)* Crazy your own self.

(The women look from one to the other in amazement.)

BIG SWEET: Youse all right, Little Bits. Tain't nothing wrong with you. I been told you was stuck up and color struck, but youse all right. You grins natural. If you was stuck up you would try to smile. *(They both laugh at that.)* Where you come from and where you going? *(All listen intently.)*

LEAFY: Well, I come from New York, but I wasn't born up there. Mama and Papa is both dead, so I had to go for myself. Folks always told me I could sing, and I ever wanted to sing like Ethel Waters. But I haven't had no real good job yet. I got to sort of wandering around, and next thing I know, I was way down here. They told me if I wanted to learn to sing blues right, I ought to come learn how on a sawmill job, so I heard about here, and come on. The Bossman says I can stay here and learn all I want to. So he sent me to Miss Bunch to get myself a room. But she is away from home somewhere. I'm waiting for her to come.

BIG SWEET: *(Dawning happiness, though hard to believe)* You mean you want to sing blues – sure enough blues?

LEAFY: That's right. Maybe I can make something out of myself if I do. Go back to New York and make enough money to take care of myself.

BIG SWEET: Well, you done come to the right place. What
　　name did you say you was going by?

LEAFY: *(Surprised)* What name I'm going by? The one my
　　mama give me when I was born. Leafy, Leafy Lee.

BIG SWEET: That's a pretty name to have. Specially when
　　it's yourn for real. Folks on these kinds of jobs uses
　　different names at different times. I see what you come
　　here for. You come here for a reason, and not for a
　　season, and Leafy, you done come to the right place.
　　Me and my man sings them blues every night at our
　　house. And we got a friend man that cold picks 'em on
　　a guitar. If he can't whip a box, tain't a hound dog in
　　Georgy, and you know that's the puppy's range.

LEAFY: Well you all the very people I want to meet up with.
　　I wants to sing the blues.

BIG SWEET: *(Grabs Leafy by the hand and pulls her down
　　off the porch)* Come on go home with me so we can
　　talk some. You ain't got a bit more sense than me and
　　Lonnie got. I loves to meet up with folks that loves
　　good singing.

> *(The whole atmosphere has changed to warmth.
> Everybody is beaming on Leafy, except Dicey, who is
> tragically disappointed.)*

LAURA B: And Big Sweet sure can sing them blues. When
　　she gits hold of a good one, she turn it every way but
　　loose. She's the one can help you out a lot.

LEAFY: *(Happily, then checks herself)* But if I go off with you,
　　I'll miss Miss Bunch, then I won't have no place to
　　stay.

BUNCH: Did you say Bunch? Here I is. I thought all the
　　time you was asking for Lena Branch. But you said
　　Bunch, didn't you? You can git your suit-satchel and
　　come on 'cross the way right now. I got a good room
　　you can use.

BIG SWEET: *(Picking up the bag)* She going home with

me for awhile. This child ain't after nobody's man.
Anyway, I don't figger on nobody taking Lonnie away
from me. Come on Little Bits. You going home with
me.

LAURA B: *(Calling after them as they start upstage left)* Me
and Stew Beef will be on over there after supper.

BUNCH: And me and Few.

BIG SWEET: That's right, you all come on and make the
poor child feel welcome. You see she's a orphan child.
Everybody come on. Don't look to eat up none of our
groceries, but we going to have plenty music, and cut
Big Jim by the acre.

> *(Big Sweet and Leafy go off chatting happily. The
> others watch them go. Dicey alone looks unhappy and
> stands looking after them grimly. Curtain.)*

SCENE 3.

Scene: *Interior of Big Sweet's house. Raw, unpainted lumber
with rafters and uprights showing. Furniture cheap
and the decor garish. Bright colored calendars and
advertisements nailed on wall. Watermelon pink calico
curtains at the two windows. White iron bedstand in one
corner with starched lace fringed pillowslips and a cheap
spread. Three kitchen chairs and a cheap wooden rocker
with a lace doily.*

*At the rise, Big Sweet and Leafy are discovered in the
front room. Big Sweet is seated on the bed, and Leafy
in the rocker, She has removed her hat and dress, and is
cooling off in her underwear. There is an easy air of old
acquaintance between them.*

BIG SWEET: It's a wonder that your boyfriend let you come off by yourself like this.

LEAFY: I haven't got no fellow.

BIG SWEET: What's the matter? You all had a falling out?

LEAFY: *(Shakes her head slowly)* Never had one – not no real one.

BIG SWEET: *(Astonished)* How you mean? You look round twenty years old to me.

LEAFY: Twenty-two.

BIG SWEET: What's the matter? Is you been sick, or something?

LEAFY: Oh, I had fellows to come take me out to the moving pictures and things like that once in a while. And one fellow, he liked me real well, but I didn't care nothing about him. He even went and asked papa for my hand.

BIG SWEET: Your *hand*? What did he want with that?

LEAFY: Why, why, he wanted to marry me So he asked my papa for my hand.

BIG SWEET: How come he didn't say what he mean, instead of go asking for your *hand*?

LEAFY: That's what you say when you want to marry a girl.

BIG SWEET: *(Loud and embarrassed laughter)* Is that what they say when they want to shack up with a gal? When they feel they love come down?

LEAFY: That's the proper way.

BIG SWEET: *(Dumbfounded)* Umph! Umph! Umph! That just go to show you how bad it is to be ignorant. But, when you don't know, you don't know. Here, all this time these ignorant mens being going round here asking folks for they *can* when they ought to be asking for they hand. The no-manners-ted things! *(Indignant)* I better not hear no more of that kind of talk round here. They better not say can to me no more, even if it's got tomatoes in it. *(Deep respect and awe comes over Big Sweet and a wistfulness.)*

BIG SWEET: Youse wonderfly, Leafy. You knows a heap of good things.

LEAFY: Oh, that ain't nothing much to know.

BIG SWEET: I think it's fine. Wisht I had of knowed that long time ago. *(A minute of deep thought.)* You mean you ain't never knowed nothing about no man?

LEAFY: That's right. *(Apologetically)* Maybe it's because I have never been in love with nobody that was in love with me.

BIG SWEET: *(In awe)* You ain't joking?

LEAFY: *(Embarrassed)* No ma'am. I ain't never given to no man.

BIG SWEET: I never expected to find nothing like that sure enough. *(She leans her head against the bedpost with a far-off bitter look on her face and thinks)* I'm glad for you, Leafy. 'Cause you done won the battle that I lost.

LEAFY: What do you mean by that?

BIG SWEET: I wanted to be a virgin my own self. I always said that I was going to be one till I got married, when I was growing up, and I meant to, too. That was my firm determination. 'Course I didn't know what his name was going to be, but I knowed that I was going to find Lonnie some time or other. And I often wish that I could have come to him like you is now. *(A deep, long sigh)* No use wishing now. Them years is behind the mountains. I think that I would have made it too, but you see, Papa died when I was fifteen, and times got mighty hard. It was too expensive for somebody in the fix I was. I couldn't afford to be a virgin. *(Pause)* Then, after that, I got to knocking around, and found out what folks mean by careless love. You mean good, and think maybe it will lead to something permanent. But he hits you a love-lick and be gone! So when you get through thinking and feeling, you try another one. Pretty soon, you be feeling again like you been drug through hell on a buzzard gut. You find out it's a lot of bulldozing, imposing and biggity folks in the world that loves to take advantage. They looks fine from the top of their heads down, but if you see 'em from the foot up, they's another kind of people. They sings and says that the water in Polk County taste like cherry wine. So I come pulling here like a heap more girls done done. *(A bitter laugh)* Well, after while, I met up with Lonnie, and then things was all right. But by that time, I had done got my craw full of folks doing they bullying and bulldozing and trompling on everything and everybody they could git they foot upon.

LEAFY: *(Rushes across to Big Sweet and flings her arms about her)* You make me feel so little. Just being a virgin ain't a thing besides what you are, honey.

BIG SWEET: *(Wraps Leafy in a tight embrace)* Oh, you going to be a lot of help to me. You got more schooling than I got.

LEAFY: But you knows the most. Mama used to always tell me that study-ration beat education all the time.

BIG SWEET: *(Laughs heartily)* And that's right too in a way. We can sort of swap. You don't know a thing about this world, but I aim to put *my* wisdom tooth in your head. I mean to be your fore-runner like John the Baptist. Fight everything from graybeard to battle height.

LEAFY: You mean you really fights?

BIG SWEET: Yeah, I has to sometimes. Some folks ain't going to do right unlessen you do. I don't mean no harm, but one day about six years ago, me and God got to sort of controversing on the subject of how some folks loves to take advantage of everybody else. He said that sure was the truth, and He never had meant it to be that-a-way. Preaching and teaching didn't do some of 'em no good. Jailing 'em didn't help 'em none, and hanging was too good for 'em. They just needed they behinds kicked.

LEAFY: Did God tell you to kick 'em?

BIG SWEET: *(Laughing)* Well, He didn't exactly tell me to kick 'em, but He looked down at my big feets and smiled.

LEAFY: So you been kicking Æem, eh? *(Laughing)*

BIG SWEET: Sure is, and its done a heap of 'em good. I done made over this place more nearly like Lonnie say it ought to be. No need in all this fighting and carrying on every pay night. Pole cats trying to make out they's lions!

LEAFY: Don't hurt yourself too much for other folks. Just like Mama used to say, "Good nature make nanny goat wear short tail."

BIG SWEET: *(Laughing heartily)* Youse crazy! You must of told God the same thing I did. When He ask-ed me, "Little angel, where do you want to go?" I told Him, "It matters a difference where I go, just so I go laughing."

> *(There is a group noise of loud talk and laughter at a distance, and Big Sweet sits up and listens.)*

That's the men folks done come home from work. Git into your clothes right quick. You got to be ready when my Lonnie and My Honey git here. Everybody will come pulling in here to meet the new stranger. *(She jumps and opens the suitcase on the floor)* I'll help you some.

> *(Leafy goes to bag quickly and selects an attractive, but inexpensive wash dress, and throws it over her head. Big Sweet pulls it down and helps fasten it.)*

BIG SWEET: *(Gives Leafy a playful slap on her behind after the dress is adjusted)* My Lord, Little Bits, you ain't got a bit of meat on your bones! The man marry you, going to have to shake the sheets to find you. *(They both laugh.)*

LEAFY: Maybe nobody won't ever want me enough to marry.

(There is a sound of footsteps at the outer door, and Big Sweet starts out of the room with a big smile on her face.)

LONNIE: *(Outside)* Hey, in there! Housekeepers!
BIG SWEET: That's my baby! *(Calls)* Hey yourself! Want a piece of cornbread, look on the shelf!

(She bolts out of the room, leaving the door wide open. Leafy hurriedly powders her face and puts on lipstick. The sound of a loud smack of a kiss comes to her as she applies the lipstick.)

LEAFY: *(Half wishful)* I wonder if these men do any raping around here? *(Curtain.)*

SCENE 4

SCENE: *Interior of Big Sweet's house.*
TIME: *Two hours later. Big Sweet, Lonnie, Leafy, My Honey, Stew Beef, Laura B, Bunch, Few Clothes, Sop-The-Bottom, and Do-Dirty, are all in the room.*

LONNIE: *(In a clean, starched shirt and overalls, is in the middle of the floor)* We done took Leafy for a little sister. She want to sing blues, so we all got to help her out all we can. Each and every one of you teach her what you know.
BUNCH: I don't know none. I like to hear 'em, but I never did know too many of them old reels and things.
FEW CLOTHES: Youse the boss, Lonnie. We's bound to do the best we can. I'll play one, and My Honey, you help me out with that Guitar. The rest of you can sing the words. Big Sweet, you verse it out.

(He wipes off his harp and begins to play "Nasty Butt," and My Honey falls in playing with him. They

> *play through a verse with flourishes, and vamp for the voices.)*

STEW BEEF: *(Carried away by the swing, starts to sing)*
> Thought I heard somebody say
> You nasty-butt, you stinky butt
> Take it away! Oh, you –

BIG SWEET: *(Jumps up furious)* Stop it! Don't you sing nothing like that in front of Leafy. She's a lady.
STEW BEEF: Oh, excuse me. I didn't mean no harm.

> *(The men all look from one to the other, puzzled.)*

BIG SWEET: Teach her another one. I'm going to pass out the lemonade whilst you all go ahead helping Leafy. *(She exits through door.)*
SOP-THE-BOTTOM: *(Brightly)* Us don't have to sing under the clothes of them Tampa fan- foots. Let's we sing about a man. *(Pats his foot to get the swing and begins)*

> Uncle Bud, Uncle Bud, Uncle Bud, Uncle Bud,
> Uncle Bud
>
> Uncle Bud is a man, a man like this
> Great big man with a great big fist.

LONNIE: *(Catches on fire)*
> Uncle Bud's got gals that's long and tall
> And they rocks their hips from wall to wall.

> *(It is their favorite song at work and they take up the refrain with great gusto.)*

STEW BEEF:
> Oh, little cat, big cat, little bit of kitten!
> Going to whip their backs if they don't stop
> spitting!

*(The enjoyment mounts. The men are putting plenty
pep into it.)*

LONNIE:

Oh, little cat, big cat playing in the sand
Little cat cuss like a natural man.

(Shout of laughter as they tear into refrain)

Oh, who in the hell, the goddamned nation
Put this trash on Pa's plantation?

(Wild yell of approval)

BIG SWEET: *(Bursting through door with tray of glasses full of
lemonade)* Stop it! Don't you vip another vop on that.

LONNIE: *(Injured)* Good Lord, Baby. How we going to
teach the girl if you won't let us sing?

BIG SWEET: You can sing without singing that, can't you?

*(My Honey fools around with his box and drifts
into "Angeline" and begins to sing it softly and
absentminded. The men pick him up and make
harmony.)*

MY HONEY:

Oh, Angeline! Oh, Angeline!
Oh, Angeline, that great, great gal of mine.

BIG SWEET: Now, that's a new one that I don't know, but it
sound nice.

MY HONEY:

And when she walks, and when she walks
And when she walks, she rocks and reels behind.

BIG SWEET: *(The drinks are passed out, but she has the empty
tray in her hand, which she brandishes)* Stop. That one
ain't fitten' neither.

LONNIE: *(Disgusted)* Oh, go ahead and instrument the box,

My Honey. Big Sweet won't let us sing nothing at all.

> *(Great howl for My Honey to play)*

LEAFY: Oh, please do, Mr. My Honey. I ever loved box-picking.

MY HONEY: *(So pleased at her interest that he gets all fussed)* Oh, thank you ma'am, Miss Leafy, er, my compliments, er, excuse me, of what you want me to pick for you?

LEAFY: Just anything you will or may.

LONNIE: Polk County! You know you does that thing.

ALL: Yeah, man! Polk County!

> *(My Honey plays the piece excitedly and with extra flourish, and is acclaimed.)*

LEAFY: *(Deeply moved by his artistry)* That's great!. I never thought to hear nothing as good as that. My Honey, you're an artist.

LONNIE: Don't be calling my buddy out of his name. What is a artist nohow?

LEAFY: It's somebody can do something real fine and high and noble. And My Honey is one from way back. If he was to go to New York and pick his box like that, he would be famous, and make a lot of money besides. I wish I could sing like he can pick.

LONNIE: My Honey, look like you done got to be somebody. You hear what Leafy say?

MY HONEY: *(Over modest)* Oh, she just joking me. I just fools with this box 'cause I loves it better than anything else in the world. Nobody wouldn't be fool enough to pay money to hear nobody pick a box. That's something done for pleasure.

LEAFY: Yes, they would, too.

BIG SWEET: I know you telling the truth, Leafy, 'cause I love to hear good picking so that I would give something to hear some if it wasn't 'round here free.

And them white folks in New York could be even crazier than I is. *(Burst of laughter)* Now, lemme tell you all something. Lemme tell your heads something in front. I don't want no slack talk over Leafy. She's trying to make something out of herself. And I know when mens gits to slack-talking, next thing it's something further. No loose talk and slack mouth around Leafy.

LONNIE: And that's right, too.

BIG SWEET: And, oh, yes. No more mention about "cans." I done learnt the right way, now. You all got to come up to time. You supposed to ask a lady for her *hand*, not her can. You hear me? That's stylish.

LONNIE: That a fact? I'm proud to know it.

BIG SWEET: You done all the asking you ever going to do, Lonnie, so this don't come before you. But tell everybody else on this joB

STEW BEEF: Well, sir! Hand! I done caught on New York style.

BIG SWEET: And don't be telling Leafy nothing about your after-ten-o'clock-at-night feelings, neither.

LONNIE: And my tongue is in Big Sweet's mouth. I say the same thing.

MY HONEY: And I string along with my buddy. I'll fight about her too.

LEAFY: *(Quickly and brightly)* Will you, My Honey?

LONNIE: Will he? That's a true fact. Me and My Honey is buddies. Jack the Rabbit, Jack the Bear, two sworn buddies on the road somewhere. We backs one another up in everything.

(There is a general murmur of confirmation.)

LAURA B: Let's we women teach Leafy a song.

MY HONEY: Go ahead, and I'll pick it off for you.

LAURA B: *(Hesitates a minute)* Oh, we don't know just which one it is just yet. You all liable to laugh at us.

Come on, let's we all go out in the kitchen and practice up. Then we'll come back and show you if we make it.

BIG SWEET: That's a good idea. Come on, you gals!

(They all exit to the kitchen hurriedly and the men are left alone. Few Clothes, warming up on his mouth organ, begins to play "The Fox Hunt," and the men egg him on to the end.)

MY HONEY: That was real good, Few.

FEW CLOTHES: Let's me and you practice on together.

MY HONEY: Just a minute. I want to speak with Lonnie private. Be back in a minute. Come over here Lonnie, where we can be to ourselves.

(They cross over near the kitchen door. Few Clothes fumbles around blowing a chord here and there.)

MY HONEY: You reckon Miss Leafy think I'm any good, sure enough?

LONNIE: *(Indignant)* Think you any good? How can she help it if she got any sense? Youse a good man. Work regular, save your money, don't gamble and don't git drunk, what more can a woman want out of anybody? And then, you got a cool kind disposition, and looks good in clothes.

MY HONEY: But do you reckon she believe it like that? You reckon – Oh, I wants you to talk to her for me. Tell her about me. Git Big Sweet to talk to her for me.

LONNIE: *(In great surprise)* My Honey! I ain't never seen you this way before. You claimed that the woman you wanted for a regular wasn't born yet, and her mama was dead. All you wanted was that box to pick.

(My Honey stands silent while the voices of the female quartet comes from the kitchen singing "Careless Love.")

WOMEN: *(Offstage)*

It was love, O love, O careless love
Love, O love, O careless love
You caused me to weep, you caused me to moan
You caused me to leave my happy home.

When I wore my apron strings low
When I wore my apron strings low
When I wore my apron strings low
You were always standing at my door.

Now I wear my apron to my chin
Now I wear my apron to my chin
Now I wear my apron to my chin
And you pass my door and won't come in.

See what careless love has done
See what careless love has done
You've broken the heart of a many poor gal
But you'll never break this heart of mine.

MY HONEY: Yeah, I know I said all of that, and I meant it too, when I said it. But Big Moose done come down from the mountain. *(Listens to the singing for a space)* I done got a letter from Love, and I'll go to hell, but what I answers it.

LONNIE: You said that like a man. *(Great admiration in his tones)*

> *(The women burst in laughing triumphantly and all in good spirits.)*

BIG SWEET: Leafy is doing all right, I'm telling you.

LAURA B: Yeah, she going to sing good too, when she learn some songs.

LONNIE: Git your box fixed, My Honey, let's hear what she done learnt.

LEAFY: Oh, I don't believe I know it well enough just yet.

Maybe in a day or so. Let Big Sweet sing something.

LONNIE: Big Sweet, why you don't teach her John Henry? That song they sings on the railroad camps?

BIG SWEET: My Honey plays that all the time. He can teach her and tell her.

MY HONEY: Be glad to. *(Begins to tune)* Lemme git it tuned in Vastopol. *(Vastopol tuning. He runs off a few scales and chords.)* But I can't handle the singing and the playing too. You sing it for her, Big Sweet, and I'll bottle-neck it off.

STEW BEEF: Now, you going to hear something, Miss Leafy. Big Sweet and My Honey is a mess on that.

BIG SWEET: Oh, nothing much. A woman ain't even supposed to sing it. But I messes around with it on every occasionally.

LONNIE: *(Proudly)* Aw, go ahead and sing, Big Sweet. You ain't had no complain'ts from nobody yet.

> *(My Honey does a brilliant introduction, and Big Sweet takes the center of the floor and sings.)*

BIG SWEET:

> John Henry driving on the right hand side
> Steam drill driving on the left
> Says 'fore I'll let your steamdrill beat me down
> I'll hammer my fool self to death, Lord!
> I'll hammer my fool self to death.

> *(All join in the chant)*

ALL:

> Anhhanh! Aaaahahah! Anhhanah! Etc.

BIG SWEET:

> John Henry told his captain
> When you go to town
> Please bring me back a nine-pound hammer
> And I'll drive your steel on down, Lord!

I'll drive your steel on down. *(Same business)*

John Henry had a little woman
The dress she wore was red
Says I'm going down the track, and she never
    looked back
Says I'm going down the track, and she never
    looked back.
I'm going where John Henry fell dead, Lord!
I'm going where John Henry fell dead!

The captain asked John Henry
What is that storm I hear?
He says captain that ain't no storm
Tain't nothing but my hammer in the air, Lord!
Nothing but my hammer in the air.

Who's going to shoe your pretty lil feet?
And who's going to glove your hand?
Tell me who's going to kiss your dimpled cheek
And who's going to be your man? Lord!
Who's going to be your man?

My father's going to shoe my pretty lil feet
My brother's going to glove my hand
My sister's going to kiss my dimpled cheek
John Henry's going to be my man, Lord!
John Henry's going to be my man!

Where did you get your pretty lil dress?
The shoes you wear so fine?
Lord, I got my shoes from a railroad man
My dress from a man in the mines, Lord –
My dress from a man in the mines.

(The crowd comes in the hum, pat their feet for

> *drums, and in the last choruses, they clap hands on it as the excitement rises to a high pitch. It ends on a sort of frenzy. They cheer Big Sweet and My Honey and themselves when it is over.)*

STEW BEEF: We did that thing! Man, we whipped that thing to a cold jelly.

BIG SWEET: *(Proudly)* And did you hear Leafy coming in just like a old timer towards the end?

> *(General clamor of praise for Leafy)*

I done got me something fine when I friended with Leafy. I mean to go with her, and stand by her, and prop her up on every leaning side.

LONNIE: I hope you do. It something I'd love to see. Women folks don't stand with one another like men friends do. Not on the average, they don't.

BIG SWEET: I mean this. I'm promising God and a couple of other responsible characters to stand by Leafy through thick and thin. Anybody that picks a fight with her, if they can't whip me too, they better not bring the mess up. You all can strow that around. I'm backing Leafy up. She's green as grass, and then she don't know nothing. But I'm with her in *everything*.

LAURA B: We hear you. And then again, we going to tell it around.

BIG SWEET: Don't miss. Some folks like to take advantage of weak folks. Tell 'em in front, so they can know that Leafy ain't by herself in the world.

> *(There is a sharp knocking on the door, and Big Sweet goes and opens it quickly.)*

Oh, hello, Dicey, You coming in?

DICEY: *(In the door)* Naw. I didn't come here to come in. *(She does come far enough to take in the whole scene and looks around the room with a grim expression. Sees Leafy seated next to My Honey, and the general happy air in the room.)* Big Sweet, I'll thank you to give me back my knife.

> *(Big Sweet studies Dicey's face for a long minute. Sees the challenge there. Comes to a decision, and reaches in her pocket and hands Dicey the knife without a word. Everyone in the room except Leafy realizes that a challenge has been flung, and accepted. Dicey goes quickly, and Big Sweet shuts the door sharply.)*

LONNIE: Poor Dicey, she sure is set on cutting out her own coffin. But me and High John ain't going to let her. Are we, Big Sweet?

> *(Curtain)*

ACT TWO

SCENE 1.

SCENE: *Following Saturday night. The Jook. The interior of the Jook is a large rectangular room. The piano is against the wall upstage center. The long sides of the room are parallel with the footlights. The room is lighted by naked bulbs hanging from cords. There are entrances right and left in the ends of the building, and one at right of the piano. A few streamers of crepe paper hang from the ceiling, fragments of a past celebration that have not been removed. There is a table for dice, green top, string across the center for tripping the dice to the right of center and a rough pine table for cards to the left. There is a third table pulled out untidily from the left wall with unpainted kitchen chairs haphazard around it where the occupants of the night before have left them. There is a deck of cards on it.*

At the rise, Do-Dirty and Sop-The-Bottom are at the dice table practicing throws. The piano player is playing a hot stomp and Stew Beef, Laura B, Bunch, Few Clothes are dancing. The women have on hats of their men. Box Car is dancing alone and cutting steps and cheering himself with every "break."

Dicey enters left and begins to work her way across the room to a seat on one of the benches against the wall at right. When she starts to pass Box Car, he grabs her and tries to dance with her. She snatches away rudely.

BOX CAR: *(Annoyed)* Aw, come on and dance, why don't
you?

DICEY: *(Proceeding)* 'Cause I don't want to.

BOX CAR: Well, what you come here for if you don't want
to be sociable?

DICEY: *(Tartly)* I didn't come here to dance. I come for a
reason and not for a season. *(She switches on across the
room.)*

BOX CAR: *(Looking at her angrily for a moment, then shakes
his head rolls his eyes up and sighs)* My people, my
people! I likes folks that's nice and friendly.

DICEY: *(Tightening her skirts up to sit)* It matters a difference
to me if you likes me or if you don't. None of you old
mullet heads ain't studying about me nohow. I ain't
yellow, and ain't got no long straight hair. Go dance
with some of them you screams over. If Big Sweet and
that Leafy was in here you wouldn't know I was even
in here.

BOX CAR: *(Maliciously)* You told that right.

> *(He goes back into his dancing and laughing at
> himself, and Dicey settles herself into a pose that
> indicates she is there but not of the place. The dance
> music mounts to a climax and ends abruptly. The
> dancers all exclaim cheerfully.)*

LAURA B: Hello there, Dicey. Look like you ain't having
yourself no fun.

DICEY: Maybe not right this minute, but I will be. *(Laughs
unpleasantly)* Oh yeah! Before the night is far spent,
I'll be having my proper amount of fun. *(Mysteriously)*
Some that goes for a great big stew will be simmered
down to a low gravy. *(Laughs again)* Then I'm going to
show 'em my ugly laugh. *(They all look puzzled, one to
the other for a moment but Dicey laughs again.)*

STEW BEEF: Dicey laugh like she done found a mare's nest

and can't count the eggs.

BOX CAR: *(Impatiently)* Oh, squat that rabbit, and let's jump another one. *(To Laura B)* Laura B, you always 'round Big Sweet, tell me something about that pretty little frail eel Big Sweet got at her house. Is she from New York sure enough?

LAURA B: That's what she say, and she sure is got them kind of clothes.

BOX CAR: And she sure do become her clothes too. I really would like to git in there. How come you don't tell her about me? I ain't got nobody.

STEW BEEF: *(Scoffing)* Oh, oh! With nearly every man on the job after her? Boy! You sure going to get a plenty hindrance on that joB

DICEY: *(Mysteriously)* I know one won't be pulling after her. You mean that stray, half dead-looking yeller gal that drug in here a few days back? Shucks! She ain't no trouble.

SOP-THE-BOTTOM: Which one ain't going to pull after her? I know it ain't me. She sure can git every cent I make, just like I make it.

DICEY: *(Coquettishly)* My Honey ain't.

BOX CAR: You better say "Joe" cause you don't know. *(Significan'tly)* He could be worser off than anybody else around here.

SOP-THE-BOTTOM: Yeah, he been buying a mighty lot of ice cream lately, and toting it to Big Sweet's house. He could be guilty.

DICEY: I don't see nothing on her to scream over.

FEW CLOTHES: That's natural. *(General laughter)* Who did you say was the crazy fool that wouldn't have that pretty little doll baby if he could git her?

DICEY: You heard me. I say My Honey wouldn't. He got somebody he like more better.

BOX CAR: *(Scornfully)* Maybe you got some inside information on My Honey that the rest of us don't know about.

DICEY: *(Taking him literally)* I don't have to tell you all me and My Honey's business.

FEW CLOTHES: I ain't never heard nobody say you and My Honey had no business together. You must have dreamt it.

DICEY: *(Stung)* I'll show you if My Honey is mines or not. You just let that yaller consumpted thing, or anybody else get to messing around My Honey now.

FEW CLOTHES: What can you do if they do?

DICEY: I'll take my knife and go 'round the ham-bone looking for meat. That's what I'll do. I'll slice her too thin to fry. *(She crosses quickly over to table, snatches a chair and drags it over to the bench.)*

DO-DIRTY: Don't take that chair off, Dicey. We fixing to git up a game.

DICEY: Git it up then. You won't git this chair. I'm saving it for My Honey when he come. He got to have a chair to sit in when he pick his guitar.

DO-DIRTY: *(Sarcastically)* Oh, excuse me. I didn't know that My Honey had done bought any chairs in here, no more'n anybody else, I thought it was first come, first serve. *(Growing angry)* And then again, I ain't heard nothing about My Honey making you no guardeen over him, to be saving him no chairs.

FEW CLOTHES: The first of my knowing it too. *(General agreement)*

DICEY: How come every time I open my mouth all you all got to jump down my throat? I got friends in Mulberry that wouldn't spit on this old low-life-ted place. I friends with Miss Ella Wall. She could buy all the trash in this place and sell 'em. In fact she could pay for 'em and give 'em away.

STEW BEEF: Oh, is that who you cracking off of? Ella Wall is a used-to-be. Good gun, but she done shot.

DICEY: *(Jumping to her feet angrily)* Who? Who you talking

about?

STEW BEEF: Aw, sit down! What you hollering "who" for? Your feet don't fit no limb

> *(There is the sound of a guitar offstage and the voice of My Honey singing.)*

MY HONEY:

> Had a good woman, but the fool laid down and died. (There is a stir in the place at the sound.)

SOP-THE-BOTTOM: Here come old My Honey now! *(There is a stir of anticipated pleasure.)* He can evermore pick that box.

> *(My Honey enters upstage right, with his hat set recklessly, his guitar around his neck and strumming.)*

STEW BEEF: Do that thing, My Honey! Have a fit! You got a fitten place to have it in. *(He creates a pleasant stir as he walks slowly down towards center stage.)*

DICEY: *(Jumps up and offers the chair she has been holding)* Have some set down. I been saving this chair for you Baby Boy.

MY HONEY: *(Unpleasantly affected by her too intimate address, halts and recoils)* Baby? Boy? How big do men grow where you come from?

DICEY: I mean youse my boy.

MY HONEY: *Your* boy? My mama is dead. *(He starts to turn away, left)*

DICEY: *(Still trying to save face as she sees the grins on the faces of the men)* Set down and play me something on that box.

MY HONEY: Don't believe I cares to set down just at present. I ain't tired the least bit. And my box ain't tuned to play nothing in particular.

> *(He crosses to where Stew and the others are grouped around the table. Some sit on the benches, some in*

tho chairs.)

STEW BEEF: Where Lonnie at?

MY HONEY: *(Looks elaborately in all of his pockets.)* Don't
believe that he's here.

LAURA B: *(Laughing)* You crazy thing!

STEW BEEF: But sure enough. You always be's together.

MY HONEY: *(Seriously)* That's what I want to know my own
self. I figured he might have come on here. He's acting
kind of funny and I wanted to find out what was the
matter with him.

BOX CAR: Aw, Lonnie is a man just like me. I ain't going
to waste no breath asking about no jar-heads. What I
wants to know is, where is that pretty little doll baby
from New York? How come you ain't scorching her
tonight?

MY HONEY: I ain't got no deeds to Miss Leafy.

BOX CAR: *(Happy)* Tell a blind man something! If you can't
do no good, git out the way and give somebody else a
chance.

MY HONEY: *(Soberly)* Suppose us don't handle her name
so careless like. Anyhow, her and Big Sweet will be on
afterwhile. They putting they trunks on they backs
tonight and they tray on they heads. Shoved me and
Lonnie on out. Said they had to git dressed particular.
(Smiles pleasantly to himself) Don't know who they
gitting dressed so for.

STEW BEEF: But you hope it's you. *(Comes around the table
and begins to rub My Honey all over his chest to the
amusement of the others.)* Good gracious! *(Snatches his
hand away as if he got burned)* Poor My Honey! His
heart is about to burn a hole in his undershirt.

MY HONEY: *(Snatches away and backs downstage, fending
his teasers off)* Git away from me I don't want no
mens feeling all over me, like I was a woman. Gwan!!
(Worried) Wonder where Lonnie is sure enough?

SOP-THE-BOTTOM: Oh, don't you worry about Lonnie.
He's all right. Bet he's off somewhere having one of his
visions. Nothing don't worry that Lonnie. He's just like
High John de Conquer. Don't care what trouble it is.
He can always find a way.

LAURA B: That's the truth, now. Just listen to Lonnie talk
awhile, and he can make your side-meat taste like ham.

(Somebody begins to hum)

Troubles will be over, Amen
Troubles will be over, Amen
Troubles will be over, when I see Jesus
Troubles will be over, Amen.

DO-DIRTY: That's old Lonnie's song, all right.

LONNIE: *(Steps in the door and stands. He has a wild look
in his eye, and a fixed smile on his face.)* Yeah, this
old Lonnie. *(Advances from right to left a few steps)*
Otherwise, Old Peter Rip-Saw, the Devil's High Sheriff
and son-in-law! Hello, people!8

*(There is a great gust of welcome, but all look at him
curiously.)*

LAURA B: Whats the matter with you, Lonnie? You got a
grin on you like a dead dog in the sunshine.

LONNIE: *(Coming to center stage)* Who said anything
was the matter with me? Nobody ain't heard me
complaining is they?

STEW BEEF: Naw, but anybody can see you looks like you
been drug through hell on a buzzard gut.

MY HONEY: *(Goes to Lonnie and takes his arm.)* What's
wrong? You know you can git the last cent I got, and if
you needs any backing up otherwise, you know so well
I'm already dressed to die standing by you.

*(General clamor from the men to the same effect.
Lonnie drags the table a little away from the group*

*by the wall towards center stage and stands leaning
heavily on it with both hands while he laughs and
laughs without mirth. My Honey stands looking at
him and listening for a moment then shoves a chair
up behind Lonnie.)*

MY HONEY: Why you don't stop that laughing? You know
you ain't tickled.

LONNIE: *(Drops loosely into chair)* Naw, I ain't tickled. *(Puts
his hand in the side pocket of his jumper-jacket)* I got a
letter. Yeah man, somebody done wrote me a letter.
(Laughs) And I'm so outdone, till I just opened my
mouth and laughed.

*(The place breaks into a big hum. Everybody is
conjecturing and wondering. Curiosity and sympathy
are mingled. It goes on and gets higher. Dicey falls all
over herself in a happy, gloating laugh.)*

BOX CAR: *(Angrily)* What you laughing at, Dicey? This ain't
your fun.

DICEY: Do I have to tote a coffin in my pocket because
Lonnie is feeling sad? Everybody don't have to cry at
one time. Nobody round here don't cry when I cry. I
cries all by my own-self. How come I can't laugh the
same way? *(She bursts into loud, taunting laughter)* Aye,
Lord! A heap sees, but a few knows. God don't love
ugly.

BOX CAR: Well He must be ain't got a bit of use for *you.*

DICEY: Maybe He ain't. Maybe He's just like you. But that
don't stop me from having my proper amount of fun
when them that goes for pretty, and you all washed up
so much, gets put out doors. *(She laughs gloatingly all
over herself.)* Oh, me! I sure got something funny to tell
Ella Wall when she gits here.

*(They all look at her in an unfriendly way, and
gather round Lonnie in an attempt to soothe him.)*

LAURA B: Lemme go git you a piece of that fried rabbit we had for supper, Lonnie.

MY HONEY: Would you choose a piece of barbecue?

SOP-THE-BOTTOM: How about a big drink of likker? That will make you forgit anything you got on your mind.

LONNIE: Naw, I thank you. I done had all I want to eat, and likker won't do my case no good. Naw, I thank you.

> *(They all look from one to the other in puzzlement, and Lonnie picks up the deck of cards and begins to fumble with it aimlessly.)*

STEW BEEF: Did you and the Bossman have some words?

LONNIE: *(Nervously lights a cigarette)* Naw. And I don't never expect to have no words with him, long as I stay here, neither. He may be lying, but he make out he can't git along without me.

BOX CAR: And he told that right. Youse the best man on the job, without a doubt. *(They all agree to that.)*

LONNIE: I tries to do what's right.

STEW BEEF : So it's something else, and look like you could tell us whats wrong? Did I hurt your feelings?

LONNIE: Oh, no. Not to give you no short answer, but this don't come before nobody but me. If my heart is beneath my knees, and my knees is in some lonesome valley crying for mercy where mercy can't be found, its just me. No help can come to the place where I'm at.

LAURA B: *(With deep feeling)* I reckon us all knows the feeling of that. Everybody is by theyselves a heap of times, even when they's in company.

DO-DIRTY: So what can you do? Just open your mouth and laugh.

STEW BEEF: Aw, we been sad long enough. Let's git up a skin game and laugh.

> *(He reaches for the deck of cards, but Lonnie clutches*

them to him and shakes his head.)

SOP-THE-BOTTOM: *(Fishing another deck out of his pocket)*
Here, I got a deck. Let's git on the other table.

BOX CAR: *(Grabbing for them)* Is they star-back?

SOP-THE-BOTTOM: *(Showing them)* Sure.

BOX CAR: That's all right then. I don't want nobody
carrying the cub to me for my money I done worked
for.

SOP-THE-BOTTOM: *(Arrogantly)* Aw, man, I don't have to
cheat you when I can beat you. *(Coaxingly to Lonnie)*
Come on man, and git in the game.

LONNIE: You know I don't much gaming nohow, and
tonight more especial, I don't.

SOP-THE-BOTTOM: Come on, My Honey.

MY HONEY: You know my money ain't going on no cards.
Chew my tobacco and spit my juice. Save my money
for another use.

> *(The crowd moves to the other card table noisily, and
> My Honey begins to pick absently on the box. Lonnie
> keeps his seat and fumbles with the cards. The pianist
> notes that My Honey is chording "Daisies Won't
> Tell" and joins in. As the game is being organized,
> the crowd sings it first spottily, and then intensely
> on the chorus. All of the men except Lonnie and My
> Honey are in the game. Tho women stand around
> behind them vary interested and rooting for their
> own men. Lonnie is doing something with the cards
> that interests him. Dicey rocks her hips exultantly
> over to the game and looks on. My Honey starts that
> way, but on seeing Dicey going, he turns and walks
> towards the piano and sits on the seat. The pianist
> has gotten up.)*

PIANIST: *(Hurrying across to the game)* Gimme a card.

SOP-THE-BOTTOM: *(Dealer)* I'm ready to deal out your
cards.

BOX CAR: *(Stops him abruptly)* Don't deal me none. I want to scoop one in the rough.

SOP-THE-BOTTOM: That will cost you a dollar. *(He offers the deck to Box Car and he selects one far down in the deck and turns it down beside him and places a dollar on the card.)*

SOP-THE-BOTTOM: *(Deck in hand)* All right you pikers, I'm dealing. *(Looks all around the table and stops abruptly)* I don't see no bets down. It's a quarter. Put your money on the wood and make the bet go good. And then again, put it in sight and save a fight.

> *(All put down a quarter. Few Clothes gets his from Bunch, who goes down in her stocking to get it on his request by gesture. They are all set.)*

STEW BEEF: Let the deal go down, Sop-The-Bottom!

ALL: *(In chorus)* Let the deal go down!

SOP-THE-BOTTOM: *(Sings)*

> When your card gets lucky, Oh, partner!
> You ought to be in a rolling game.
> Let the deal go down, boys!

ALL: *(In chorus with harmony)* Let the deal go down!

> *(Sop-the-Bottom turns every card off the deck with deliberation and hits it on the table with a smack. All eyes watch eagerly to see who "falls.")*

SOP-THE-BOTTOM:

> I ain't had no money, Lord, Partner! *(Card smacks)*
> I ain't had no change. *(Card smacks)*
> Let the deal go down, Boys! *(Card smacks)*

ALL: Let the deal go down!

SOP-THE-BOTTOM: *(Turning another card and looking around the board)* That's you, Stew Beef! You head-pecked shorty! Pay off!

STEW BEEF: *(Shoving in money and card)* I can't catch a thing tonight. Can't even catch nobody looking at me. Gimme another card.

SOP-THE-BOTTOM: *(Takes one from the discard)* Here! Take this Queen. It's clean.

STEW BEEF: *(Positively)* Aw, naw! Gimme another card. I don't play them gals till way late at night.

> *(Sop-The-Bottom hands him another card. Stew puts down another quarter and the game goes on.)*

SOP-THE-BOTTOM:
> I ain't had no trouble, Lord, Partner!
> Till I stoppod by here.
> Let the deal go down, Boys!

ALL: Let the deal go down!

SOP-THE-BOTTOM: That's you, Few Clothes! Pay off!

> *(Few Clothes does so sadly)*

Here, you want another card?

FEW CLOTHES: *(Feeling in his pockets)* I'm clean as a fish, and he been in bathing all his life. *(Looks around at Bunch suggestively)* Bunch, lemme have another two-bits.

BUNCH: Naw! You wasted up seven dollars pay night skinning. You gimme this to keep, and I'm a-going to do it too.

FEW CLOTHES: I worked for that money. How come I can't spend it like I please?

BUNCH: Naw! You wouldn't have doodly-squat if I leave you have your way. Naw!

SOP-THE-BOTTOM: Lady people sure is funny about money. *(To the table)* I'm raising the bet. Another two-bits. I likes long sitters and strong betters. Put down! My pockets is crying for your money.

> *(The others all put down another quarter.)*

DICEY: *(Putting down money)* Four bits on Box Car's nine!

STEW BEEF: *(Looks around and sees that Dicey is directly behind him and has her foot on his chair.)* Take your foot off my chair, Dicey! You holding me down.

BOX CAR: And a dollar my nine is the best.

SOP-THE-BOTTOM: *(Covers it)* Let the deal go down, boys.

ALL: Let the deal go down!

> *(Big Sweet enters left, followed by Leafy Lee. Big Sweet has a new hair-do, and is dressed very becomingly if a little loud. Leafy looks very chic in a low-priced silk dress.)*

BOX CAR: *(Leaping up from the table)* Look a-yonder! Whooeee! *(Slams his hat down on the floor in pretended ecstasy)* Must be a recess in Heaven – all these little ground angels out and walking around.

SOP-THE-BOTTOM: *(Also jumping up)* Big Sweet, youse sharp! You so sharp in that dress, that if you didn't have but one eye, I would swear that you was a needle.

MY HONEY: *(Advancing quietly to meet them with a chair)* Miss Leafy, Ma'am, also Ma'am, will you be so condescending as to stoop without bending, and have this chair?

> *(Big Sweet and Leafy advance leisurely to center stage, smiling and conscious that they look well.)*

BOX CAR: *(Seizing a chair)* Miss Leafy, you don't want that old nasty chair My Honey got. Take this here nice one I got for you, Miss Leafy.

LEAFY: *(Accepting My Honey's chair with a self-conscious smile)* I thank you, but I reckon this one will do. I wouldn't want to deprive you. *(To My Honey with a sweet smile)* You sure I ain't depriving you?

MY HONEY: *(Overcome)* What would I look like setting down with er, pretty ladies standing up? *(There is a howl from the crowd.)*

BOX CAR: Listen at old bashful My Honey! Done found his
tongue.

STEW BEEF: Yeah, he's getting on some stiff time.

SOP-THE-BOTTOM: Big Sweet, you got to accept this chair
from me. The rest of these jar-heads is scared to tell
you how pretty you is on account of Lonnie. *(Throws
Lonnie a pseudo-challenging look)* Me, I ain't got Lonnie
to study about. I'll fight him about you right here and
right now.

BIG SWEET: *(Casts an adoring look at Lonnie)* Oh, you
bad, eh? You must be the guy that killed Jesse James.
(General laughter)

SOP-THE-BOTTOM: I hates to tell you how really bad I is.
I'm so bad till my spit turns to concrete before it hits
the ground. *(General laughter)*

Fact is, I'm worser than that snake that was so poison
that he crawled up and bit the railroad track, and he
was so poison that it killed a train when it come long
past. *(Great shout of laughter)*

STEW BEEF: *(Laughing)* Stop your lying, Sop!

SOP-THE-BOTTOM: *(Chuckling)* Man, I ain't lying.

STEW BEEF: Naw, you done quit lying and gone to flying.
*(Gets behind Big Sweet's chair and bends over her
confidentially)* But all joking aside, Miss Big Sweet. You
evermore looks good tonight. You got on drygoods! It
would take ten doctors to tell how near you is dressed
to death.

BIG SWEET: *(A concerned look at Lonnie)* Much obliged
for your compliments, but you all go on and woof at
Leafy. I done heard all them lies too many times.

BOX CAR: That's right you is. So us can just tell Miss Leafy
how much us loves her. *(Tries to suppress a grin)* 'Cause
then that will be the truth. Miss Leafy, is your little
feets resting good in My Honey's no-count chair? You
better git up and take mines.

MY HONEY: Oh, she's doing all right where she is.

BOX CAR: Oh, it'll do in a rush. But what you reckon a pretty girl child like she is would want with your old chair when she can git mine? Take my chair, Miss Leafy. This is the first time I had a real good look at you, but I declare, already, I would rather all the rest of the women in the world to be dead than for you to have the toothache.

> *(There is a room-wide howl at the big lie and the audacity to tell it.)*

SOP-THE-BOTTOM: Man, how come you don't quit your lying?

BOX CAR: *(Suppressing a grin)* That ain't no lie. Miss Leafy, if that ain't so, God is gone to Tampa, and you know He wouldn't fool around a place like that. *(They all laugh, and this time Box Car laughs himself.)* Take my chair and show those no-count jar-heads who you really love. *(Laughter)*

SOP-THE-BOTTOM: *(Pretended disgust)* What you want to waste up the girl's time woofing at her for? Why you don't give the girl something to prove how much you love her? *(Tenderly to Leafy)* Miss, just tell me what it is your little heart crave and desire. I sure will git it for you. Course, I aim to give you a passenger train just for a sort of remembrance – *(A howl of laughter)* And then I aims to hire some mens to run it for you.

DO-DIRTY: *(Shoves Sop-The-Bottom roughly aside)* Git away, Sop! A passenger train! Is that all you aims to give a pretty girl baby like this? A little old passenger train? Miss Leafy, I aims to buy you one of them big oceanliners, and then I aims to buy you a ocean of your own to run it on. *(Scornfully)* Passenger train!

BOX CAR: Some these mens around here is too cheap to live. *(Sighs heavily and rolls his eyes up)* My people, my people! *(Laughter)*

DO-DIRTY: *(Shoving in between Leafy and Box Car)* Miss

Leafy, Old Maker didn't give you all them looks you got to be talked to any which a way. Youse something special. You hear these jigs woofing at you and telling you about all they going to give you, and they don't even know how to talk to a girl like you.

BOX CAR: Come on! Come on! Pick up your points.

DO-DIRTY: Oh, I'm going to pick 'em up.

LEAFY: *(Smiling in the spirit of the game)* And how would you talk to me, Do-Dirty?

DO-DIRTY: You just ask me something and see. *(He makes an ornate gesture of getting ready to answer.)*

LEAFY: Mr. Do-Dirty, are you having a good time tonight?

DO-DIRTY: *(Screws his face all up in a grimace, that is meant to be very ingratiating and pleasing)* Yes ma'am. *(The crowd howls as he does his act. Then he comes out of it)* That's the way to talk to a pretty girl like *you* with all that Nearer My God to Thee hair. *(Makes a gesture of combing long, silky tresses)* If they answers you any other way they is sassing you. *(Laughter)* That's how come you ought not to be setting in that old chair My Honey stuck under you. *(Offers chair)* Move into this nice setting-chair that I got for you.

LEAFY: *(Laughing)* Reckon I'll have to humor you, Do-Dirty.

MY HONEY: *(Rushing forward with a gesture of restraint)* No, no, Miss Leafy. Don't move out that chair I give you. *(He is very earnest about it, and it is noticed by all.)*

STEW BEEF: Look like old My Honey done got thunder-struck by lightning. *(Looks at My Honey's face seriously)* Don't move out his chair for goodness shake. It will throw him into a three-weeks spasm.

DICEY: *(Thrusting into the center of the group)* How come she can't move? My Honey needs that chair more than she do. He got to set down to play, ain't he?

MY HONEY: *(Quickly to defend Leafy)* Aw, she ain't keeping me from setting down if I wants to. I can play if I wants to, but there ain't no compellment about it. Just set and rest yourself, Miss Leafy. I loves to stand up anyhow.

> *(There is a tense feeling and silence for a minute. Everybody looks to Lonnie.)*

LONNIE: Aw, table that talk. Leafy can set in any chair she will or may. They all belongs to the Bossman. If My Honey feels to stand up and let her set, that's his privilege. No need for all this who-struck-John about it.

STEW BEEF: *(Indicating Dicey)* That's what I told her.

DICEY: *(Significan'tly)* Some folks better sweep around they own door before they go trying to clean around mine. They got plenty to worry about they own self.

> *(She throws Lonnie a triumphant look, and then purses her mouth in a knowing way. All look at Lonnie to see if that is the answer to his strange behavior.)*

BIG SWEET: *(Crossing to Lonnie happily and with self assurance)* What you setting off by yourself for, sugar, like youse somebody throwed away?

> *(Lonnie lays out the cards carefully, looks up at her briefly then down again without speaking.)*

SOP-THE-BOTTOM: *(Worried, but trying to be light)* Oh, leave the man alone. Maybe he's just dreaming up something like he always do.

STEW BEEF: It can't be that, 'cause he always dream laughing. Something to make everybody feel good. He ain't laughing now, and none of us don't feel right.

SOP-THE-BOTTOM: Maybe it's something deep this time. He might be way out on Ether's blue bosom somewhere travelling around. Then he going to come

back and tell us something to make our work seem
easy, and our burdens seem light.

DO-DIRTY: Sure is the truth. This old saw-mill job seem
just like New York with Lonnie around. I wouldn't stay
here a day if he was to leave. *(General agreement with
this.)*

DICEY: *(Laughs)* If some folks would mind they own
business instead of meddling with mine, they wouldn't
be in the fix they's in.

MY HONEY: Aw, you always saying something nobody don't
want to hear!

BOX CAR: *(To Dicey)* Shut up!

DICEY: *(With hand thrust suddenly into dress pocket)* You
better come shut me up, then you'll know its done
right. My shutters ain't working so good.

BOX CAR: Keep on cackling when Lonnie feel bad and I
will.

DICEY: I wish to God you would put your hands on me. I'll
cut everything off you but quit it.

BOX CAR: Aw, don't be so public. Draw that knife and I'll
draw my gun. *(Ominously)* And my gun don't lie to
me. I'll shoot till my gun jumps the rivets.

BIG SWEET: *(Turns impatiently from her observation of
Lonnie)* Aw, you all stop that racket in my ear!

BOX CAR: Well you make old ugly Dicey leave me be.
Looking like some old phantassle!

DICEY: If I'm ugly, God made me ugly.

BOX CAR: That's a lie! God ain't never made nobody ugly.
They gits that way they own self. Thinking evil.

BIG SWEET: Hush!! I got to see about Lonnie. It's something
wrong with him. *(Tenderly)* Whats wrong, pudding-
pie? You ain't going to keep nothing from *me*, I know.

> *(Lonnie looks carefully at the arrangement of cards,
> but does not look up at Big Sweet who tries to get into
> his line of vision.)*

PIANIST: *(Begins to play softly and sing)*

> I'd rather see my coffin come rolling in my door
> Than to hear my baby say she don't want me no
> more.

BIG SWEET: Lonnie, why yow! You ain't even told me if I look good in my clothes or not.

> *(Piano keeps on in undertone. Lonnie picks up a card and regards it intently. Everybody crowds about him and Big Sweet. There is a dramatic wait, then Lonnie begins to read the deck.)*

LONNIE:

> Ace means the first time that I met you.
> Deuce means there was nobody there but us two.
> Trey means the third party – Charlie was his
> name.
> Four means the fourth time you tried that same
> old game.
> Five means five years you played me for a clown.
> Six means six feet of earth when the deal goes
> down.
> Now, I'm holding the seven spot for each day in
> the week.
> Eight, means eight hours you shebaed with your
> sheik.
> Nine spot, nine hours I worked hard every day.
> Ten spot, the tenth of every month I brought you
> home my pay.
> The Jack, that's Three-Card Charlie (Sensation)
> who played me for a goat.

And the queen, that's you, Pretty Mama, also trying to cut my throat. *(Rises to his feet)* The king, that's me, old Lonnie, and I'm going to wear the crown. So you better be sure your ready when the deal goes down! *(There is a moment of stunned silence as Lonnie and Big Sweet stand facing each other.)*

DICEY: *(Breaks into raucous laughter which convulses her)* Whatever goes over the devil's back is bound to buckle under his belly.

> *(People are so intent on Big Sweet and Lonnie that they do not notice Dicey's antics, so she desists. Big Sweet approaches and tries to take Lonnie's arm, but he jerks away.)*

BIG SWEET: What make you mention Three-Card Charlie?

LONNIE: *(Hurt and belligerent)* Because you make me do it, that's why. That bed-bug!

BIG SWEET: Bed-bug? Even so, what is Charlie being a bed-bug got to do with you and me?

LONNIE: *(Vehement)* That is all he is, the scoundrel-beast, a bed-bug. *(Mimics stoop – shouldered posture)* He is flat, he crawls, he bites in the secret of darkness, and he stinks!

BIG SWEET: *(Bewildered and alarmed)* Is you done gone crazy? What the hell is the matter with you?

LONNIE: I'm a straight man, and believe in doing right. So, I ain't Lonnie got no time to fool with you, and neither take up no time with you. I'm going down to the railroad station and grab the first thing smoking.

> *(There is a general sigh and cry of dismay from all. Leafy thrusts through and faces Lonnie.)*

LEAFY: What *is* done got the matter with you, Lonnie?

LONNIE: I'm hurted. I'm hurted to my very heart. *(Bows his head)* I loves Big Sweet, but she can't snore in my ear no more.

STEW BEEF: *(Desperate)* Lonnie you can't go off and leave us like that.

LAURA B: Him and Big Sweet been gitting long too good to bust up and fall out.

BUNCH: It makes us all feel bad. What would us *do*?

> *(There is a general feeling of helplessness and dismay.*

Big Sweet, resolute, steps forward, waving the others back. She raises Lonnies chin and forces him to look at her.)

BIG SWEET: Don't you all worry. Lonnie is just talking, for some reason or another. *(To Lonnie)* You ain't through with me Lonnie Price.

LONNIE: *(Trying to resist her)* Oh, yes I is through with you. Why you think I can't quit you?

BIG SWEET: *(Growing confidence)* Because you belonged to me when they lifted you out of your cradle, and you going to be mine when they screw you down in your coffin.

LONNIE: Still and all, how come I can't git through with you?

BIG SWEET: *(Sensing his yielding)* Because I'm a damned sweet woman and you know it, too. *(Kisses him tenderly, which he does not resist.)* Now, tell me what I done.

DICEY: *(On edge of crowd)* What she done, she been doing that.

(There is a general snarl from the crowd which has been anxiously watching the progress of agreement with expressions of hope and pleasure.)

SOP-THE-BOTTOM: Hush up!

MY HONEY: *(Intense)* I wish thunder and lightning would kill you!

BIG SWEET: *(Gestures for quiet)* Tell me, Lonnie, what is I done?

LONNIE: What is you done? You done fooled me. You done cut the ground from under my feets. You done put out the sun and muddied up all the water in the world. You done took off all my dreams. You done stuck my foot in the mire and clay, so I can't fly no more. You done drove off the Great Crow.

(There is a sob and a sigh from the crowd.)

BIG SWEET: I never meant to do nothing like that to you.
Tell me how I done it. *(She is deeply moved.)*

LONNIE: *(Looks at her searchingly)* You and Charlie been
playing me for a fool. *(He explodes on 'fool'.)* And I
don't intend to put up with it no more. I didn't choose
you for that. Never no more.

BIG SWEET: No *more*? You got to have *some*, Lonnie, before
you can have *more*. And you ain't had none up to now.

LAURA B: *(Very partisan)* Somebody done told a big old
sway-back-ted lie. Big Sweet ain't harmed a soul.

BIG SWEET: Lonnie, I don't know as yet where you got this
mess from, but it certainly is a lie.

LONNIE: I got a letter right here in my pocket say you been
giving him my money. Say you been meeting him
down in Mulberry.

BIG SWEET: *(Indignant)* That's another lie! *(Suddenly
remembers and begins to laugh)* Shucks! I thought you
was mad with me about something. I did meet Charlie
once, but it wasn't nothing.

LONNIE: Nothing? You mean meeting another man on me
ain't nothing? *(He shoves her away from him again.)*

BIG SWEET: *(Smiling and hugging him again)* That was way
year before last.

LONNIE: That don't excuse you none. Year before last I was
working for you and bringing you home my pay just
like I got it from the man. Just like I been doing ever
since.

BIG SWEET: But, pudding-pie, what evil have I done? Since
some old sea-buzzard had to go tell a lie on me, I
reckon I better tell you how it was.

LONNIE: And you better git it fixed, too.

BIG SWEET: Baby, you know old Charlie always did have a
pick at me.

LONNIE: That I know is so. But you always made out to me

you didn't want him.

BIG SWEET: And I done neither. Never did. Well, about two years back, he took to picking at me, and sending me messages how he love me so hard, and all that money he had in his pocket was for me, till I got up a real good feeling for Charlie.

LONNIE: *(Groans)* Do, Jesus!

BIG SWEET: So one time when he begged me so hard, I thought I might as well go down there and git all that money he had for me.

> *(Lonnie groans and almost collapses on table, but Big Sweet makes him sit up again.)*

BIG SWEET: Wait a minute, sugar. Lemme finish telling you how it was. So I went down to Mulberry, and met him where he told me to come. He was there waiting with his hair all slicked down and everything. Soon as my toenails crossed tho doorsill, I told Charlie, "Gimme what you got for me." He look like he didn't git the right understanding because he come telling me about all the love he had for me. So I asked him plain, "Is you got anything besides yourself?" *(Emphatic with rage)* And baby, you know that mink didn't have a dime to cry. When he told me that, honey, you know that good feeling I had for Charlie took and left me right then and there, and I ain't had it since. I turnt right 'round and come on home to you.

LONNIE: *(Jerks her roughly to him)* I dare him to send you any more messages. I'll give him a straightening if he do.

BIG SWEET: *(Drops down in his lap and begins to fondle him.)* Which one would you rather believe – your baby, or that old lying letter?

LONNIE: I rather to believe *you*, Baby. I loves you harder than the thunder can bump a stump.

BIG SWEET: *(Snuggles down, and Lonnie's hand unconsciously begins to caress her legs.)* You see, sugar, I didn't fly hot and go accusing you when I found out that Ella Wall was sending for you all the time like she been doing for the last longest.

LONNIE: You don't need to worry about Ella Wall and no other woman God ever made. You got the keys to the kingdom.

STEW BEEF: *(Triumphant)* There now! The mule done kicked Rucker!

BIG SWEET: *(Hands on her hips, self-assured and smiling)* What I put on you, brother, soap and water won't take off.

LONNIE: All right, I admits to the truth. You done put me on the linger. And I even went so far as to ask you for your hand. How come you won't marry me like I asked you to?

BIG SWEET: *(Recoils in hurt)* Now, *my* feelings is hurted, Lonnie.

LONNIE: I don't see how come. I been good to you as any man could be and I'm asking you to be my wife. I aims to go with you and stand by you till I press a dying pillow.

BIG SWEET: And I loves you just as hard as you love me. But, Lonnie, you want us to be running and gitting married like common folks. Us got this big love that nobody ain't never had before. Us don't have to run to the courthouse and git papers and witnesses to prove if we is guilty. Us got that big-feeling love for one another. If I go dragging you to the white folks, it won't look like I believe what you say. I ain't never going to leave you, and I don't aim to let you leave me, neither. So what we got to act scared about?

LONNIE: *(Happy)* I'm mighty glad to hear you say we is never to part, baby. I just figured me and you ought to make a example out of ourselves for Leafy and My Honey and the rest of these folks round here.

BIG SWEET: Oh, it's going to be plenty marrying going on round here first and last. *(She looks pointedly at Stew Beef and Few Clothes.)* Some of these womens is been good to they mens, and they going to git ast-ed for they hands. Things got to be different on this job.

BUNCH: Lord knows it's time. I ain't seen a marriage on this job since I been here, and that's going on seven years.

BIG SWEET: It's going to be plenty marrying going on pretty soon now. This place got to be fitten for somebody like Leafy to live in.

STEW BEEF: How come you can't lead off, then?

BIG SWEET: Don't try to do as I do. You do as I say do. Most of you all won't tell the truth. Just like I told Leafy – she ain't to believe a thing you all say after ten o'clock at night, and nothing you promise no time on payday. I know you. Youse a gang of minks. I ought to know you. I done summered and wintered with you, ain't I? And then again, I hauled the mud to make you. I know just exactly what's in you.

FEW CLOTHES: But, Big Sweet, these womens –

BIG SWEET: I don"t want to hear it. If you will hang after 'em you going to marry 'em. You going to ask for *hands*. Not cans.

LONNIE: And me and you can stand on the floor with each and every couple, can't we, baby? See the thing well done.

BOX CAR: I reckon we better start considering, if that's the way its going to be. But it sure is taking a lot of fun out of payday.

STEW BEEF: *(Sighs heavily)* Just 'cause you shack up with a woman now, you got to give her money. Umph! Umph! Umph!

SOP-THE-BOTTOM: It's hard, but it's fair. *(Looks at Leafy)* I might as well git married now and git used to things.

LONNIE: *(With an air of command and finality)* Yeah, the time done come when big britches got to fit little

Willie. *(Takes Big Sweet's arm affectionately)* Now, I can dream some more. Listen! I hear the drums of High John de Conquer. I can fly off on the big wings. I can stand on ether's blue bosom. I can stand out on the apex of power. Nobody can beat me doing what I'm supposed to do, and nothing can't keep me down. I got my wings. I rides the rainbow.

> *(He stands exalted, and his mood touches all. The faint throb of a distant drum permeates the silence, and gradually draws nearer. First Lonnie smiles beatifically, than good humor and laughter spreads over the place.)*

STEW BEEF: Lonnie, youse a pistol! You can make anybody feel good. You can make a way out of no-way, and hit straight with a crooked stick.

BIG SWEET: That is how come I ever loves Lonnie. *(To Lonnie)* Come on, let's we go home and get our night rest.

LONNIE: *(Eagerly)* That's the very corn I wants to grind. *(Big Sweet rushes towards exit, right, downstage.)* I got to speak to you pointedly about your hand.

> *(They stride towards exit, with the others clapping time with their hands, and exit. The others come out of the mood and begin spreading over the place.)*

BOX CAR: *(Passing Dicey puts his hand on her head)* Well, Dicey, you took and laughed too quick. Big Sweet and Lonnie didn't bust up like you was hoping.

DICEY: *(Snatching away)* Keep your old nasty hands off my head! I ain't got Big Sweet and Lonnie to study about.

SOP-THE-BOTTOM: Oh, yes you is. You was cackling to beat the band, and urging it on. That's how come I don't like you – always for a fuss.

DICEY: Oh, nobody on this job don't like me nohow.

BOX CAR: Look like you don't want nobody to like you, the

way you do.

DICEY: Yes, I do too. I wants folks to like me just like anybody else. That's how come I likes to visit down at Mulberry. Ella Wall, and two three more likes me fine down there.

LAURA B: That's the place you ought to live, then Dicey – where folks friends with you. How come you don't move down there?

DICEY: Naw, I ain't going to move down there nothing of the kind. They will turn against me too. *(Musing)* It's a funny thing – them that don't know me good is just crazy about me, but them that knows me well ain't got no use for me at all.

STEW BEEF: *(Chuckling)* Maybe it's because they know you. *(There is a spontaneous burst of laughter.)*

DICEY: *(Instantly riled)* That's right! Laugh! Like a passle of jackasses, You just wait till I see Ella Wall and my other friends. You'll be laughing out the other side of your mouth, then. *(She starts furiously towards left exit. At the door she halts.)* I'll give you something to cackle over – you self-conceited dogs! *(She vanishes out of the door instantly. There is a light sprinkle of laughter after her exit.)*

STEW BEEF: Let's dance this thing off. Play that piano, boy! I feels like a waltz. Miss Leafy, can I scorch you round the hall?

LEAFY: *(Hugging herself as if with cold, perches on the side of the table and looks nervously about her)* Not just now. Dicey – the way she looks at me – she gives me the weak-trembles.

BOX CAR: *(Crosses to table and stands admiring Leafy)* Pay it no mind. Dicey been talking about cutting up everybody for the last longest. She ain't crazy sure enough to think anybody is going to let her cut 'em and do nothing. Pay it no mind.

LEAFY: *(Still nervous)* You sure about that, now? The way

she looks at me, nothing in the drugstore would kill me quicker than she would.

MY HONEY: *(Trying to get closest to Leafy)* I wouldn't stand round and let her hurt you, even if she had that in mind.

LEAFY: *(Not too sure)* I hope you know what you talking about.

BOX CAR: Let's table this talk on Dicey and open up the house for new business. *(Diffidently)* My Honey, is Miss Leafy your best-goodest lady friend?

MY HONEY: If you want to know who going to scoorch Miss Leafy home tonight, I'm doing it. Anything else you want to know there she is, ask her! She can tell you what she want you to know.

SOP-THE-BOTTOM: Oh, you don't have to git mad because somebody also want to talk with the lady. She's a much-right, ain't she? Much-right for me as she is for you.

MY HONEY: There she is. Ask her your own self.

BOX CAR: *(Diffident)* Miss Leafy, which would you ruther be, a lark a-flying, or a dove a-setting?

SOP-THE-BOTTOM: He mean would you ruther be married or single?

LEAFY: *(Bridling)* Oh, you done asked me a hard question, Box Car. It all depends.

BOX CAR: Depends on what?

LEAFY: *(With an under-eye at My Honey)* It depends on whether I was in love or not. If I was in love, I would want to be a dove a-setting like Big Sweet. If I wasn't in love, I would choose to be a lark a-flying like I been doing.

BOX CAR: Now, we gitting deep. Is you seen anybody around here up to now that you figger you could nest with?

MY HONEY: Oh, leave Miss Leafy alone! She don't want to be bothered with you into her private business.

BOX CAR: I can't pick no box, My Honey, but I got a right to talk, ain't I? Good Lord! I'm looking out for my own self. I ain't breaking into none of *your* arrangements, is I? *(Turns back to Leafy)* You ain't answered me yet?

LEAFY: *(Sits thoughtful)* Well, and then again, I can't say. *(The piano begins a waltz, and the couples begin to dance.)* But I did have a dream last night. *(My Honey strolls over to the piano and stands. Box Car and Sop get partners and dance.)* No, it wasn't true. It was just dream. He came right into my room last night. The moonlight was tropic-white. He kissed me. He pressed me there on my bed. But it was just a dream. A shadow thrown by the moonlight. *(Sings)*

> The moonlight came into my room
> With his laugh
> With his light
> With his loom.
> He brought your face so near to me
> I could feel
> I could touch
> I could see
> I could seem
> I could dream in the spell of the moon.
> In my room
> Ah, the moon!
>
> It was the full moon with his light
> That brought you
> And brought love
> In the night.
> He wove your wish right into mine.
> With a kiss
> That was bliss
> So divine
> Made you near
> Ever dear, ever true – Ah that moon!

In my room
Ah, the moon!

*(The dancers keep on waltzing softly as Leafy sings
in a sort of picturization of her dream desires, there
on the edge of of the table. My Honey approaches her,
puts down his guitar. She steps into his arms and they
waltz into the crowd as the curtain falls.)*

SCENE 2.

SCENE: *One month later. Interior of Big Sweet's house. Raw,
unpainted lumber with rafters and uprights showing.
Furniture whole, but cheap. The decor, garish. Bright-
colored calendars and advertisements nailed on walls.
Watermelon-pink curtains at the two windows. White
iron bedstead in one corner with clean, starched lace
trimmed pillowslips, and a cheap, slazy silk spread. Three
kitchen chairs and a cheap wooden rocker with coarse lace
antimacassar.*

*At the rise, it is early night, and Big Sweet is in a loose
wrapper arranging her hair for the street. She sings a
light song as she dresses, She puts on her street shoes and
stockings, adding proudly a pair of beribboned red garters.
A silk dress is laid out on the bed, and she throws off her
wrapper to put it on. But she whiffs under her arms,
reaches over over on the window sill and gets her wash
cloth and wipes again, dusts herself with talcum, and
arranges the dress carefully to go over her head, without
wrinkling.*

LONNIE: *(Bursts in, his face lit up with happy excitement)*
Sugar! Sugar! What you reckon? *(He grins delightedly.)*

Old My Honey done got it out at last!

BIG SWEET: *(Dress still in her hands)* What?

LONNIE: He done got up the nerve and asked Leafy for her
hand. They's going to git married sure enough!

BIG SWEET: *(Glorified)* No! Well, the old slow thing got it
out at last, eh? I sure is glad.

LONNIE: Yeah, and everything is going to be up to time,
too. Bought license, a finger-ring and everything. Ain't
that something?

BIG SWEET: *(Pulling dress over her head)* When did you find
it out?

LONNIE: He just told me a while ago at the commissary. I
come quick as I could to let you know. I wouldn't take
a play-pretty for that.

BIG SWEET: Me neither. I'm so glad for Leafy. The poor
thing wanted My Honey so bad, and look like the fool
never was going to ask her. So bumble-tongued! I felt
like zotting him over the head two three times.

LONNIE: He was scared she wouldn't have him. So pretty,
and from New York and everything. But look like he
done talked up a breeze now. Everything is copasetty.

BIG SWEET: *(Smiling)* That sly little hussy! She must of
knowed he was due to ask. No wonder she went off
from here around sundown dressed to death. Where
they at now?

LONNIE: Down at the cafe. Eating ice cream out the same
spoon and grinning at each other like two glad dogs in
a meat house.

BIG SWEET: *(Laughs heartily)* They's in heaven now, baby.
They can't help it.

LONNIE: And My Honey done bought out the place with
chocolate bars, and I reckon done started on the
chewing gum by now.

(They both laugh heartily, but proudly.)

BIG SWEET: *(Fully dressed)* You wasnt much better when

we first got together. *(Crosses and kisses him lightly)*
Remember that first time down behind the saw-mill?

LONNIE: Aw, quit bragging on yourself! You knowed right
then you had done laid me under conv_ction. And you
meant to do it too.

BIG SWEET: Of course I did. I seen right away I was going
to love you. Man, I throwed you some waves the ocean
ain't never seen. *(Lonnie gives her an affectionate shove
and slaps her on her hips.)* And I hopes that Leafy do
the same by My Honey.

LONNIE: You women always setting 'round figuring out
how to take the undercurrents on some man. But us
likes it, though.

BIG SWEET: But Lonnie, not changing the subject, us can't
let Leafy and My Honey go get a house and live all by
theyselves.

LONNIE: Why not? They'll be man and wife then, and he'll
have all privileges. You can't -

BIG SWEET: Oh, I ain't talking about that. Them two will
starve to death if we leave them do like that.

LONNIE: Like what? My Honey makes good money all the
time.

BIG SWEET: Leafy is crazy about singing and dancing and
she will forgit all about cooking something to eat. And
My Honey he's carried away with picking that box and
he won't think to say nothing to her about it. They'll
sit round and starve just as stiff as a board. *(Both
laugh.)*

LONNIE: Oh, I don't know. When that big gut reach and
grab that little one, they'll scrabble up something to
eat.

BIG SWEET: But it would be more better if they stayed right
here with us.

LONNIE: *(Delighted)* You do git hold of the *best* notions!
They got to stay right here. Anyhow, they going to be
going to New York before long if Leafy have her way.

She'll die the death of a doodle-bug if them folks in New York don't hear My Honey play that guitar.

BIG SWEET: Oh, yeah. She done talked my ear-flaps down about how famous My Honey will be when he gits up there. Somebody of note like Booker T. Washington. She claim I and you ought to go up there and sing for money too. *(Laughs)* She must figure them white folks up there is crazy – paying folks good money just to sing.

LONNIE: She swears they does it, though. Maybe white folks ain't as smart as some folks thinks they is. Paying out good money to folks for having they fun. *(Chuckles)* I hope I meets up with some like that.

BIG SWEET: Well, us got money in the post office. If Leafy and them go up there, or if things was ever to go wrong round here, us could go up there and look around.

LONNIE: We could, at that. *(Gets up hurriedly)* The skitter man is ill-sick in the hospital.10 Got to go put somebody else on the job till he gits better. *(He hurries to door and opens it.)* I'll be looking for my ground-rations tonight. *(He exits quickly.)*

BIG SWEET: *(Calls after him)* Okay, Papa! I'll meet you at the Jook. *(She smiles to herself as she rubs powder on her face with a rubber sponge.)* What I tell that lie for? I know I ain't particular about going to no New York. I likes it here. I done come to be something here. I got Lonnie, and everybody puts they dependence in him and me. Its nice. Wonder who wrote that mean letter to Lonnie? Sure do wisht I knowed. I'd fix 'em.

(There is a loud rapping at the door.)

BIG SWEET: *(Listens)* Is that him doubling back? He must think I'm going to run off sure enough. *(Calls over her shoulder.)* Come on back in Lonnie. I know it ain't nobody but you.

(*The door is thrown open roughly and the Quarters
Boss enters, with his pistol hanging loosely in his
hand. Big Sweet stares at him in surprise. He shoves
his hat far back on his head, and with legs apart
stands looking Big Sweet over sternly.*)

Oh, er, was you wanting to see Lonnie about
something?

QUARTERS BOSS: Naw, I come here to –

BIG SWEET: Oh, you wanted to see me.

QUARTERS BOSS: I don't want to see you half as bad as the
sheriff do, I reckon. (*He pauses to let that sink in.*)
Vergible Thomas wasnt able to go to work today.

BIG SWEET: (*Off hand*) He don't do too much work no day.

QUARTERS BOSS: (*Losing his temper*) Never mind about how
much work he do. I been told that you jumped him.

BIG SWEET: They told you right.

QUARTERS BOSS: Ain't I done told you and told you about
stomping people and knocking 'em around?

BIG SWEET: (*Calm*) Vergible brought that on his own self. I
told him to hush his mouth. Talking all under folkses
clothes and a whole lot of dirty, slack talk.

QUARTERS BOSS: (*Sneering*) Now, ain't that just too bad?
Slack talk in sawmill quarters! Humph! Well, I aims
to put a stop to you bulldozing these quarters. You act
like you're some lord-god sitting on a by-god. Doing
just as you damn please! Do you know you done kilt
three men since you been on this job? THREE MEN!

BIG SWEET: (*Nonchalantly*) I know it. I kilt 'em my own
self, didn't I? (*Boss almost explodes with anger, but
cannot find words. Sits in rocker and makes herself
comfortable*) And not a one of them minks died a
day too soon, neither. They was low and mean and
bulldozing, and had done kilt folks they own selves.
They wouldn't do for theyselves – they wouldn't do for

nobody's else. They ought to been dead ten thousand years, the no-count things!

QUARTERS BOSS: So you mean to keep your meanness up, eh? Keep it up, and see what happens to you, then. The Judge down to Bartow told me the last time you was there for a killing, that the very next time you come up before him for a killing, he was going to go hard on you. He's going to lay ninety days on you in the county jails.

BIG SWEET: *(Undisturbed)* Getting tough in his old age, eh? I bet you when lightning strikes him, it goes off through the woods limping.

QUARTERS BOSS: Smart eh? Well, you done done your last big talk around here. Folks been bringing me news about your doings for the last month or so. I got plenty on you now. I git sick and tired of some coming to me telling me how you runs over folks. Well, one person will tell me things, anyhow. I'm telling you, you got to leave off this job.

BIG SWEET: *(Stunned)* Me leave here?

QUARTERS BOSS: Yes, you leave here. And no later than next payday. *(He strides sullenly to the door.)*

BIG SWEET: *(Hard to comprehend the blow)* You mean I got to go? I - or, whats that you said?

QUARTERS BOSS: *(At door)* You heard me what I said. By next payday. *(He slams the door hard and is gone.)*

BIG SWEET: *(She is stunned and disorganized. She gets up slowly and moves about aimlessly. Finally, she sinks on the side of the bed with her hands in her lap.)* But how can I leave here? I won't have no home no more. Be like I was before. Just on the road, somewhere. *(Overcome)* No! No! I just can't leave. I'm somebody now. Folks needs me. I can't go off feeling like nothing no more. And everybody here will feel like nothing again when me just sawdust. Some more sawdust piled up like that behind the mill with the rain and the storm beating on it. *(She clenches her hands and suppresses a sob.)* Poor Lonnie! He's going to follow me off and he ain't never going to be satisfied no more. *(In helpless appeal)* Jesus! *(Begins to chant)*

Jesus, Jesus, Jesus, Jesus, Jesus!

(She sings the melody with a distant drum rhythm under her. Then the strings in the orchestra take up the melody while she talks and chants against it.) I ain't nothing. None of us ain't nothing but dust. Sawdust. Piled up round the mill. What is left over from standing trees. Sometimes, when Lonnie talks, the sawdust shines like diamonds, and glints like gold. Then the light goes out, and we are dust again. Dust from God's Big Saw. *(Sings)*

Jesus, Jesus, Jesus, Jesus, Jesus.

(She gets hold of herself and the music fades. She gets up and goes resolutely to the door.) Lonnie said meet him at the Jook. So I'm going and laugh and dance and sing. *(Quick exit.)*

SCENE 3.

SCENE: The following night. Interior of the jook. At the rise, Sop-The-Bottom, Box Car and Do-Dirty are at the dice table playing. The pianist is playing, but in an experimental manner. Bunch and Laura B are sitting against the wall to the left, conversing in low tones and laughing quietly. Stew Beef and Few Clothes are in the center of the floor chatting inaudibly.

BOX CAR: *(To Sop-The-Bottom)* Six is your point.

DO-DIRTY: Two bits you don't six.

BOX CAR: What's your come-bet?

FEW CLOTHES: *(Shoving Stew affectionately and laughing)* Aw, man, I wouldn't believe that lie if I told it my own self.

STEW BEEF: Yeah it is so. Monkeys can talk when they want to. *(Laughs.)*

FEW CLOTHES: Youse crazy! *(Laughs)* After that, I'm going to coon some with your old woman. *(Lifts voice as he goes to card table.)* Come on, Laura B, let's coon.

LAURA B: *(Getting up briskly and going to table)* All right, I'll play you.

FEW CLOTHES: *(Braggadocio)* You reckon you know the game?

LAURA B: *(Bragging)* If I ain't a coon-can player, I'm a 'leven card layer.11 *(Shoves the deck towards Few.)* Strip it! *(Chants)*

> Before I'll lose my rider's change. I'll spread short deuces and tab the game.

(Few Clothes offers her the deck to cut. She shoves it back in disdain.)

LAURA B: Deal! I don't cut green wood.

BUNCH: *(Coming over to watch)* Naw, no need to cut a rabbit out when you can twist him out.

LAURA B: That's right. *(Sings)*
> Give my man my money to play coon-can
> He lost all my money but he played his hand.

(Stew Beef wanders over to dice game.)

SOP-THE-BOTTOM: *(Starts Singing)*
> Oh, Angeline! Oh, Angeline!
> Oh, Angeline, that great, great gal of mine.

(The four about the table form a quartet and sing.)

And when she walk, and when she walk
And when she walk she rocks and reels behind.

You feel her legs, you feel her logs
You feel her legs then you want to feel her thighs
You feel her thighs, you feel her thighs

(Leafy enters downstage left, locked arms with My Honey, both are radiant.)

STEW BEEF: *(Seeing them enter)* Shhhhh! Here come Miss Leafy. *(The song ceases instantly.)* How you do, Miss Leafy? Hello My Honey.

> *(Both respond and stroll towards piano. Box Car, Sop-The-Bottom and Do-Dirty all regard Leafy with hungry admiration as she swishes along with My Honey.)*

BOX CAR: *(Turning completely from the game)* Oh, will I ever? Will I ever?

MY HONEY: *(Over his shoulder)* No, you'll never, no, you'll never! *(All laugh at this passage.)*

BOX CAR: Well, you sure can't keep me from hoping.

MY HONEY: *(Rests his guitar on piano and turns. Laughs good natured.)* That's right. I can't keep the sight out of your eyes, but I sure God will keep the taste out your mouth. *(Takes Leafy's arm again.)* Come on, sugar, lemme find you a good seat.

> *(They head downstage.)*

BOX CAR: *(Half in fun, half serious)* You don't care if us walk behind you do you, whilst you scorch Miss Leafy to a chair?

MY HONEY: *(Laughing)* You can walk behind and wish all you want to.

> *(Box Car, Sop-The-Bottom, and Do-Dirty leave the*

> *table and fall in behind Leafy and My Honey with*
> *the most yearning and beseeching expressions in face*
> *and body and follow them along.)*

BOX CAR: *(Feigning utmost desire) Oh*, I wish it was me!
DO-DIRTY: *(Same business)* Oh, don't I wish it was me!
SOP-THE-BOTTOM: Lord knows, I wish it was me!
BOX CAR, SOP-THE-BOTTOM AND DO-DIRTY: I wish it was me! I wish it was me!

> *(They follow My Honey and Leafy all around the*
> *room in a parade lamenting, while the others laugh*
> *at the show. Finally, My Honey and Leafy shoo them*
> *off and sit down.)*

DO-DIRTY: *(To Sop and Box Car)* Oh, well, look like he got us barred. We done let the 'gator beat us to the pond. We might as well give up.
SOP-THE-BOTTOM: Yeah, My Honey got the business. *(To My Honey)* When you all figger on jumping over the broomstick? I know Big Sweet ain't going to stand for no commissary license.
MY HONEY: We don't want none. We going to do it up brown.
STEW BEEF: Yeah man, he got them license in his pocket right now. I done seen 'em myself.
LAURA B: Yeah. And we done fixed up to give 'em a big woods dance and all. Just waiting for Big Sweet to make the arrangements.
BUNCH: This marriage is got to be fine. Its the first one, and it will be setting the style for the rest of us.
FEW CLOTHES: *(Groans)* I reckon nothing can't stop the rest of you womens after this one come off.
BUNCH: That's right. Me and you is going to marry. You heard what Big Sweet said.
STEW BEEF: *(Looking at Laura B)* And I guess I'm dead on the turn.
LAURA B: If you expect me to do for you anymore.

STEW BEEF: Well, we better give My Honey a big send off. Plenty to eat and drink, and cut big Jim by the acre. Then they will do the same by us. Anyhow, this one got to be fine. It's the first one to come off since here on this job I been. I'm gitting so I likes the notion.

LAURA B: It's about time.

> *(Big Sweet enters upstage, right with Lonnie. She is greeted with enthusiasm.)*

LONNIE: How ye folkses!

BIG SWEET: *(Coming down to center stage and looking all around her)* Well, people! I thought you all was teaching Leafy some more songs.

STEW BEEF: Leafy ain't got her mind on no singing. Look at her.

LEAFY: *(Coming out from under a long kiss)* Yes, I do want to know some more songs, too.

BIG SWEET: *(Seriously)* And I want you to learn all there is just as quick as you can. *(Meaningly)* It might git so you wouldn't be here to learn no more.

LEAFY: Why?

> *(Everybody looks puzzled.)*

BIG SWEET: Oh, you just might not be here that's all. *(To the room)* You all learn Leafy some more.

STEW BEEF: We done learnt her about all we know. Me and Laura B was just saying we couldn't think up no more. Lonnie, how about that thing you and My Honey was messing with today down in the swamp?

LONNIE: Oh, if she wants to learn it, we can do the best we can. Come on My Honey, and git in quotation with the piano so we can show the girl.

> *(My Honey rushes to piano and gets guitar. A chord or two is struck and Lonnie begins.)*

Mama, Mama, who is Jack?

Where's his horse and where is his shack?
Was he true a sawmill man?
Did he skin and play coon-can?

(Drums dominate)

This is the house that Jack built.
This is the malt that lay in the house that Jack
    built.
This is the rat that ate the malt, that lay in the
    house that Jack built.
This is the cat that killed the rat that ate the malt
    that lay in the house that Jack built.

*(All begin to join the rhythm, clap hands stomp with
the drums.)*

This is the maiden all forlorn
That milked that cow with the crumpled horn
That tossed the dog that worried the cat
That killed the rat, that ate the malt
That laid in the house that Jack built.

(Drum interval.)

MY HONEY:

    This is the cock that crowed in the morn
    That woke that priest all shaven and shorn, etc.

(Drum interval.)

BIG SWEET:

    Oh, this is Jack with his hound and horn, etc.

(Drum interval.)

LEAFY:

    Oh, Mama! Mama! Look at sis
    Out in the yard trying to do that twist.
    Come in here, and I mean now!
    You're trying to be a rounder

But you don't know how.
Let your Mama show you.

Oh, this is the horse of the beautiful form
That carried Jack with his hound and horn, etc.

*(The others have worked up to a high pitch and are
on their feet for the most part, dancing, clapping, etc.
to the drums.)*

This is Sir John Barleycorn
That owned the horse of the beautiful form
That carried Jack with his hound and horn
That caught the fox that lived under the thorn
That stole the cock that crowed in the morn
That woke the priest all shaven and shorn
That married the man all tattered and torn
That kissed the maiden all forlorn
That milked the cow with the crumpled horn
That tossed the dog, that worried the cat
That killed the rat, that ate the malt
That lay in the house that Jack built.

*(Every "that" is accented with drum and voice. The
drums continue and finally die away like the end of a
rainstorm.)*

BIG SWEET: Did you git that one, Leafy? Git it right?

LEAFY: *(Happily)* Oh, yeah. I got it good. And I like it too.

BIG SWEET: *(Very subdued)* As I before said, git all you can
just as quick as you can. I might not be here always to
see to things.

LONNIE: You been saying that all day. What you mean by
that?

> *(Big Sweet, with her eyes down, hesitates, while all
> hang on what she might say in explanation. Dicey
> enters downstage, left, with a triumphant flourish
> with Ella Wall, who has the air of a conqueror and*

struts towards center stage.)

Sop-The-Bottom: Ella Wall, Lord! Hi there Ella!

Ella Wall: *(With a flourish)* I'm folks.

Dicey: I'll say youse folks. You was folks up in Middle
Georgia before you ever come to Polk County. Youse
folks in Mulberry, and youse folks in Lofton. Fact of
the matter is, youse folks whereever you go.

> *(Ella Wall has advanced to center stage confidently
> expecting Big Sweet, Leafy, and Lonnie who are still
> there to give way. She is brought to a halt when she
> sees that Big Sweet does not move, and the others take
> their cue from her. Ella stops abruptly as she comes
> against them. She halts and looks Big Sweet up and
> down in a sneering way.)*

Ella: Hello, there, Big Sweet. Look like you got changing
clothes, now.

Big Sweet: It do look like it, don't it?

Ella: You sure done improved up from what you used to
be. I knowed you when you was just as naked as a jaybird in whistling time.

> *(She laughs excessively and Dicey joins her in the slur
> by laughing.)*

Big Sweet: *(Quietly)* You sure telling the truth, Ella.
(Cruelly) But that was before I got the man that
you was trying to git. Lonnie don't let me want for
nothing. Every payday I sits on my porch and rock and
say, "Here come Lonnie and them."

Ella Wall: Them? What them?

Big Sweet: *(Arrogantly)* Them dollars! You hear me. You
ain't blind.

Ella Wall: Lonnie? I just let you have him because I seen
you was in need. I can git any man I wants.

Lonnie: Excepting me. Not since I come to know Big
Sweet anyhow.

SOP-THE-BOTTOM: *(Woofing)* Pay Lonnie Price no mind, Ella. What you care about him when you can git me? If you handles the money you used to handle about ten years back and let me spend it like I please, I'm yours any time.

(There is a big laugh and Ella is taken aback.)

DICEY: Who? Ella don't have to give no mens her money. They gives her. She's just like the cemetery. She ain't putting out, she's taking in.

BIG SWEET: *(With a catty smile)* I see you got something too, Ella, that you didn't used to have.

ELLA: What is it? *(Displays her hands full of cheap jewelry)* I always had jewelry and things.

BIG SWEET: *(Indicating Dicey)* You got you a yard dog now to do your barking for you.

BOX CAR: *(Pretending sympathy for Dicey)* Aw, aw! Big Sweet, what make you play so rough? Dicey, I wouldn't take that if I was you.

STEW BEEF: *(Egging the fight on)* Now, what you want to try to start something for, Box? You know Dicey ain't going to get on Big Sweet. Not unlessen she's braver than I figure her out to be.

ELLA: Dicey don't have to act scared. She got somebody to back her up.

BIG SWEET: I ain't looking for no trouble, but if anybody pay their way on me, God knows I'll pay it off.

(A yell of expectant excitement.)

BOX CAR: Of course now Dicey is going to back her crap.

DICEY: *(Afraid)* Us come in here for pleasure. Us didn't come here to fight. *(With a knowing leer)* And then again, I don't have to be fighting and carrying on. Some folks that's around here thinking they got the world by the tail ain't going to be here long. Then everything will be nice. *(She looks venomously from Big*

Sweet to Leafy.)

LEAFY: If you're talking about me, I'm in the be class – be here while you're here, and be here when you're gone.

LAURA B: *(Proudly)* Listen at little crowing!

LEAFY: Yeah, I'm getting married to My Honey, and it won't be long, either, and it ain't no help for it. I got more right here than you have. *(Beams up proudly at My Honey)* I got a *husband* on this job.

> *(Dicey, full of hate and frustration, instantly puts her hand in her pocket. Everybody sees the gesture and grows tense.)*

BIG SWEET: Don't you pull no knife in here. I dare you to even take it out! And Ella Wall, you don't belong on this place at all. The Bossman said *particular* he didn't want no stragglers on the premises. Git on out here and take your yard dog along with you. Git!

ELLA: *(Shows hot resentment in her face, but looking around she sees nothing friendly in any of the faces. No possible help.)* I'm going, but I'll be back. Your time now, but it will be mine after while. Come on, Dicey.

DICEY: *(As they retrace their steps)* Hanh! Big Sweet won't be here long. *(Laughs gloatingly)* Nobody didn't tell me, but I heard. Then other folks *(pointedly at Leafy)* can be straightened out.

LONNIE: Big Sweet can stay here just as long as she please, and go when she gits ready.

DICEY: *(At door)* That ain't what the Quarters Boss say.

> *(She and Ella exit laughing triumphantly. A profound silence settles over the place.)*

LONNIE: Now, what you reckon that Dicey mean by that? *(He looks at Big Sweet questioning)*

STEW BEEF: I sure dent know.

BIG SWEET: *(Sighs)* Oh, you all leave me be. *(She drags over to the table, left and drops down in a chair. She sits a moment gloomily.)* It's another song I got to teach you, Leafy. It ain't got no laughing in it, but I reckon you got to learn it. Help me out on it, My Honey, much as you can. *(Begins to sing to herself, gradually swells.)*

Ever been down, know just how I feel
Ever been down, know just how I feel
Been down so long till down don't worry me.

I wonder will he answer if I write
I wonder will he answer if I write
I wonder will he answer if I write.

Well you may leave and go to Hali-muh-fack
But my slow-drag will bring you back
Well, you may go, but this will bring you back.

(She gets an ovation as she ends first chorus. As she begins second verse Lonnie moves in closer as My Honey moves closer in his enthusiasm of playing.)

LONNIE: *(Crosses and puts his arm about Big Sweet's shoulders)* It's something wrong. Why you don't tell me what it is?

BIG SWEET: *(Breaks down)* You so nice. I didn't want to hurt your feelings.

LONNIE: *(Commanding)* Tell me what it is.

BIG SWEET: Well, the Quarters Boss come to me last night right after you left and said I had to leave. *(This stuns everybody.)*

LONNIE: *You* leave? What he mean by that?

BIG SWEET: Said somebody been coming to him saying I makes all the trouble around her. Said I had to leave – no later than payday. *(A deep gloom settles over the place.)* And that's how come I tell Leafy to do the best she can whilst I'm here, so her and My Honey can git gone. Somebody is liable to hurt her when I'm gone.

MY HONEY: I begs to differ with you – not to give you no short answer – but Leafy got me behind her.

BIG SWEET: I know, and I don't doubt you one bit. But you have to be on the job all day long, and a whole heap could happen in that time. Folks can steal her.

LAURA B: Some lowdown jig been toting lies to the white folks on Big Sweet. That's what's the matter.

LONNIE: Wish I was sure who it was. I sure would hang for 'em.

STEW BEEF: Me too. *(General chorus of agreement.)*

BIG SWEET: *(Idea)* Maybe it was the same one that wrote Lonnie that lying letter on me. You still got it, Lonnie?

LONNIE: *(Fooling in his pockets)* Maybe I is. Done most forgot I had it. *(Pulls out a crumpled letter written in pencil and hands it to Big Sweet.)* I always thought I didn't have no sense, and every time I thinks about the fuss I had with you, I know it.

BIG SWEET: *(Unfolding letter and scanning it)* This letter say its from Three-Card Charlie, turning me some humble thanks for the spending-money I sent him. *(Looks all around amazed.)* He must be crazy! I ain't never sent him dime one.

BOX CAR: When was it wrote?

BIG SWEET: Oh, little better than a month back.

BOX CAR: Then, Charlie sure never wrote it.

LONNIE: How come he didn't? It would be just like the dirty mink to try to git my baby away from me.

BOX CAR: Because Charlie been dead to my knowing for more than over a year. Woman killed him in Savannah.

LONNIE: Sure enough?

BOX CAR: I know it for a fact. I was there. Remember I quit here and was off a couple of months. Seen her when she stabbed him. He sure did die.

LONNIE: *(Hugs Big Sweet impulsively.)* Well, well!

BOX CAR: So if Charlie wrote you that letter, things must be different down in hell from what it used to be. They didn't used to send out no mail from there.

LONNIE: This don't say hell. It say, Mulberry, Florida.

BOX CAR: Maybe they done took in Mulberry for a new addition, but I ain't heard nothing about it. I knows the place well.

SOP-THE-BOTTOM: Hush your lying, Box Car! How you know anything about hell?

BOX CAR: Don't tell me, man. I don't say in one place like the rest of you all. I gets around.

LONNIE: So now, us know that Charlie ain't wrote no letter back. Wonder who?

BIG SWEET: And went and lied on me to the Quarters Boss?

LAURA B: Aw, you know nobody done it but Dicey. Nobody else on the job would want to hurt you.

MY HONEY: Sure. She's trying to hit a straight lick with a crooked stick. She figger she can git to Leafy if you is out the way. And she don't love me to all of that, neither. She just hate to be outdone.

LONNIE: Well, I reckon she will move off with Ella now, so —

LAURA B: But you heard both of 'em put out they brags that they will be back with help.

BIG SWEET: *(Resigned)* I reckon they will have they swing. Everything will be back like it used to be.

LONNIE: But you can't go.

BOX CAR: Nobody here want you to go no where, do us? *(A general protest against her leaving.)*

BIG SWEET: But the man done told me that the Company would rather have my room than my company. *(Sighs heavily. General desperation and gloom)*

LEAFY: *(Almost in tears)* I'm the cause of it all.

BIG SWEET: In a way you is, and then again you ain't. All you done was come here and put words to the feeling I already had. I ever wanted things to be nicer than what they was. Ever since I been with Lonnie, more especial.

STEW BEEF: But My Honey and Leafy is gitting married.

We going to cut Big Jim by the acre when that come off. Big woods picnic and everything. Who is going to general our business for us if you ain't here?

BUNCH: Nobody can't do nothing right on this place without you. What *will* us do if you ain't here?

BIG SWEET: Do like the folks over the creek, I reckon. Do without.

LONNIE: *(Pulls out a chair and drops down in it backwards and sits in gloomy thought.)* I reckon you all know that if Big Sweet has to go, I don't aim to be here another minute. Tain't nothing bad about Big Sweet at all. She got plenty good friending in her if you let her be.

BUNCH: We all knows that. LONNIE: *(Face hard)* Something is wrong 'round here if somebody like Big Sweet can be told to go. Somebody trying to drive her.

SOP-THE-BOTTOM: And it sure ain't clean.

MY HONEY: *(Most dejected)* Everything was going along so good. Big Sweet doing the best she could to make everything nice –

LONNIE: What is we? We ain't nothing. We didn't come from nothing. We ain't got nothing but the little wages we makes. Look like then us ought not to be bothered with trouble. That's for big, rich folks that got their many pleasures. Why we got to have troubles too? *(A harmonic, vocal chant whispers under him and gets a little stronger as he talks.)* Where is these quarters nohow? Wild woods all around and the mill in the middle. *(As if in sudden discovery)* We's in a cage! Like a mule-lot down in a swamp.

BIG SWEET: *(Takes lead in chant and puts softly sung words to chant and the others follow her. Humming)*

> I got my hands in my Jesus hands
>
> *(With Chorus)*
>
> I got my hands in my Jesus hands.

LONNIE:

>Panthers in the swamp.
>Moccasins round your feet all day.
>Standing in water.

>*(Chant grows intense but not loud. More fervent)*

>Trees falling on men and killing 'em.
>Saw liable to cut you in two.
>Sundown, nothing but these quarters to come to
>>and keep on like that until you die.

>*(Chant dominates the pause with repetition of Jesus, Jesus, Jesus, Jesus, Jesus.)*

>Its something wrong.
>But what can we do?
>You don't know and I don't know, so I can't tell
>>you. Just moving around in the cage.

>*(The chant comes out in the open, while Lonnie sits and looks off into space.)*

BIG SWEET: Sawdust, even if it do shine sometime.

>*(The faint whisper of distant drums comes and Lonnie begins to smile more and more. The others watching Lonnie's face begin to smile too, as the drums become more audible.)*

LONNIE: *(Smiling and chuckling)* What make me talk so disencouraged like? Old John de Conquer would know how to beat the thing. *(Chuckles broadly)* Shucks! High John could git out of things don't care how bad they was, and finish it off with a laugh.

>*(The drums are very pronounced now, and some pat their feet, and in other ways accent the rhythm of the drums.)*

> Big Sweet ain't going nowhere. That Quarters
> Boss ain't got no stuff for me. If he got to listen to
> everything that old Dicey say –

LAURA B: Every lie she make up and tell.

LONNIE: I'm going to make my left-here now.

> *(Chorus of "and we're going when you go"!)*

STEW BEEF: One day after you leave, there won't be a soul
in the quarters.

LONNIE: And I'm going to be the one to tell the Big Boss
my own self. The man can wait till he git the straight
of things, or else we all can go. If the Boss ruther for
him listen to lies than for us to do his work, then we
still can go. *(A great cheer goes up.)* Tomorrow will tell
the tale.

*(The prayer-chant for victory takes up again. Getting to his
feet dramatically.)* Something ought to be like we want it.
We ain't got nothing. We ain't never had nothing. Our
folks ain't left us nothing. *(Chant dominates for a moment.)*
Six feet of earth when the deal goes down. *(Chant)* And we
ain't never milked for much.

> *(Chant over drums is repeated and variated until
> curtain.)*

CURTAIN

ACT THREE

SCENE 1.

SCENE: *Following Saturday night. Interior of Dicey's shack.
At the rise, the shack is empty. It is of the same crude
construction as Big Sweet's house, but little has been done
here to relieve the raw, unpainted lumber and careless
structure. The bed is lumpy and covered by a worn,
faded quilt. There is a small iron heater in the corner,
downstage right. It needs polish. The bed is across the
center of the wall upstage. Two or three shoddy dresses
hang against the door, which is left. A cheap suitcase is
under the edge of the bed. The thin curtains are only half,
and hung on strings that sag. Two unpainted kitchen
chairs and a goods box covered with newspaper complete
the furnishings of the room, except for a chipped slop-jar
in the corner behind the door.*

*There is no one in the room at the rise. One hears a key
thrust hurriedly and nervously in the door, then Dicey
opens the door and fairly leaps inside, looking back over
her shoulder as she enters.*

DICEY: *(Shutting the door quickly and locking it.)* I don't
reckon nobody seen me come in. *(She turns on the light
above her head and looks all around the room furtively.)*
Better git all ready before Nunkie git here for me.
*(Pulls suitcase from under bed, puts it on the bed and
opens it.)* Don't want to forget a thing. When I leave
here this time, this place won't never see me no more.

(She takes down the clothes from the door and hurriedly folds them into the bag. Picks up a cheap comb with some of the teeth missing, a box of talcum, and puts them in. Keeps looking about to miss nothing.) They can have this little old furniture. I can't tote it nohow. Crip owed the man for it anyhow. Let 'em git it. *(She suddenly remembers the package that she brought in and eagerly grabs it and packs it.)* Lord, I sure don't want to forgit my regalia! Got to have that with me tonight. *(Rushes to head of bed and lifts the corner of the mattress and takes out a "hand," a small bundle about three inches long sewed up in red flannel and regards it fondly.)* Wouldn't that be awful if I was to go off and forgit my Mojo? *(Regards it gloating.)* It was fixed for me to conquer and overcome. Big Sweet don't need to think she got no stuff for me – not with the help I got. *(Thrusts it deep into her bosom and smiles.)* The voodoo-man and Ella Wall say it will sure do the work. *(Sees the small, cheap mirror on the improvised dresser and takes it and carries it to the bed. Starts to pack it, then sits down on the bed and studies her features in the glass. Feels her hair first, then passes her fingers over her face in concentration in the mirror.)* How come I got to look like I do? Why couldnt I have that long straight hair like Big Sweet got, and that Leafy? They own looks like horse's mane, and mine looks like drops of rain. *(Feels disgust, self-pity, then resentment.)* And these mens is so crazy! They ain't got no sense. Always pulling after hair and looks. And these womens that got it is so grasping, and griping, and mean. They wants everything – and they gits it too. Look like they would be satisfied with *some*! Naw, they wants it all. Takes pleasure in making other folks feel bad. *(Hurls mirror into bag face down and slams it shut.)* How come I got to be a swill barrel to take they leavings? *(In utter revolt)* Things ought not to be that way. What do they do more'n me? I wish

they all was dead! Wish I could cut 'em and mark 'em
in they faces, till they all looks worser than me! They
acts like they thinks the world is made just for them to
strut around and brag on theyselves in.

*(She leans against the bed post and thinks aloud
on life and what it has done to her and comes to
her conclusions. During the lament. a dance group
interpets Dicey's despair.)*

Pretty women! How I hate their guts!
This talk about equality is nuts.
Have *I* got an equal chance
With anything that's wearing pants?
I'll tell the world, and Georgia too, tain't so.

(Examines herself in mirror.)

My looks is just a heavy load
That sends me down a lonesome road
And *no one* cares the way I have to go.

(Looks again in glass and sighs.)

I ain't a woman in a way
Where men have anything to say
Of love, and tenderness, and such.
I'm just another kind of mule –
A bad exception to a rule
So what I feel don't seem to matter much.

(Conversational outburst of outrage at inequality.)

What did the white folks do to Big Sweet for shooting
them men? Nothing! Naw, with that hair and them
looks, she could kill a thousand and they wouldn't
care.

Yeah, a pretty gal can kill a man
And never sleep a night in can

They'll give her back her gun and let her go.

But let an ugly gal like me
So much as cripple up a flea
And they will build a new and better jail.

The judge and jury'll sit in state
And ponder grimly on my fate
And give me time, I've never seen it fail.
They won't try me by no law books.
They'll see the crime right in my looks
And sentence me according to my shape.

There'll be no mercy on the bench
I'll get a look that's meant to lynch
Good riddance for a trashy, ugly ape.
If Leafy Lee would shoot me dead
And weigh me down with red hot lead
It will be only a regrettable mistake

But if I scratch her yellow skin
It is a deathly, mortal sin
They'll put me in the chair and let me bake.
No, it ain't right, and it ain't fair
Cause I ain't got that skin and hair
I wasnt born the way I ought to be.

I'm on the outside looking in
So don't expect to see me grin
And laugh the way that pretty women do.
I have to scramble for a kiss
When they get all this married bliss
The men, the world, and Heaven too.

So I feels mean, and I get sad
I tries to laugh, but I ain't glad.

I often curse the day that I was born.
I build some lovely dreams at night
Then see them killed in broad daylight
And all my tender feelings laughed to scorn.

I sure can't help the way I'm made
And so, when all is done and said
I'm just a victim of relentless fate.
I got big love, that I can't give.
I got a life still I can't live.
Just all dammed up and turning into hate.

I hate the women through and through
Who get the things that I want, too.
I wouldn't like 'em, even if I could!
And women thwarted, just like me
Thought up those fires in hell, in glee
So come on, Evil! Be thou now my good!

*(Takes her knife out of her pocket, feels the edge
carefully, and begins to whet it grimly on the edge of
the stove. Stops and tests it on her thumb, and whets
again vigorously. Sings briefly.)*

Get your razor 'cause I got mine
Feel mistreated and I don't mind dying –

*(There comes a swift, but stealthy, insistent knocking
at the door. Dicey halts whetting abruptly, looks
scared but on guard, wonders whether to open door or
not, but as the knocking begins again, she hears the
voice of Nunkie frightened outside.)*

NUNKIE: *(Offstage)* Dicey! Dicey! Let me in here! *(Dicey,
relieved, hurries to door, turns key and opens it partly.
Bursting past her into the room.)* What you keep me
out there knocking for? Somebody could have cut my
throat.

DICEY: I didn't know if it was you or not. Somebody could
have seen me coming in.

NUNKIE: Oh, they don't know –

DICEY: I bet they does, too. Lonnie – 'course I don't expect
no more out of him. Big Sweet must got him fixed. He
believe what she say all the time. It's a hidden mystery
how she got him so tied up. And that Quarters Boss,
he ain't nothing. Made out he was going to run Big
Sweet off, but you see she's here right on.

NUNKIE: *(Outdone and depressed)* Oh, you didn't tell him
like I told you! If you had of made it bad enough -

DICEY: *(Hotly)* Yes I did too! I made it real distressing. But
look like it don't do no good at all, no matter what you
say about her.

NUNKIE: *(Glum)* I sure hopes we git her good tonight. Ella
Wall say it will. She say they don't last when she hold
that kind of dance on 'em. *(Animated)* Lord, if it work
like she say! We dance on 'em and they all stand there
in they tracks and can't move. Just like statutes! *(Happy
anticipation)* And whilst they standing there and can't
move at all, we go in on 'em with our knives and ruin
'em! I takes Big Sweet first one.

DICEY: And I takes that Leafy Lee. My Honey too. I hates
him now just as bad as I used to love him. All I want
to do is to git them two good. Then I'm long gone,
like a turkey through the corn.

NUNKIE: We better be fast. Just in case, you know. Big
Sweet might be able to move some, and if she do –

DICEY: Didn't Ella say they won't be able to move atall? Just
like they made out of wood till we git through, and be
out and gone.

NUNKIE: *(Not too assured)* Yeah, but voodoo don't take on
some folks, 'specially if they got this straight hair. It
ain't got nothing to tangle in. Us better dash in and
do what we got to do, and light out. After me and Ella
gits Big Sweet, hack all of 'em a lick or two and git

for Mulberry. *(Imagines he hears a sound outside and is frightened)* What's that? *(They both listen for a while.)*

DICEY: I reckon it wasn't nobody. They all down in the woods not far from where we going. *(Face goes grim.)* My Honey and that Leafy thinks they going to git married.

NUNKIE: *(Restless)* You ready? Come on let's git out of here. I don't want to git hemmed up in here.

DICEY: Me neither, as far as that is concerned. But they all off down there carrying on over My Honey and Leafy.

NUNKIE: *(Very nervous)* Ella and them is waiting on us. Come on. Where your things?

DICEY: *(Indicates suitcase on bed)* There everything is. You tote it while I put out the light and lock the door.

NUNKIE: *(Grabs up the bag and hurries to the door.)* Hurry up.

DICEY: *(Takes a few more whets with her knife.)* In just a minute.

NUNKIE: *(Hand on door knob)* Aw, make haste!

DICEY: *(Tests knife edge and is satisfied. Smiles and puts it in her pocket, and moves to the light.)* Don't crack that door till I outen the light. Then wait for me. Its more better for both of us to step out at the same time. *(She turns off light and goes softly towards the door.)* I don't see to my rest what My Honey want with that Leafy nohow.

NUNKIE: Tain't nothing wrong with her. She sure is pretty, now.

DICEY: I can't see where at. She's too poor. She ain't got no meat on her bones at all. And My Honey, he's kind of rawbony too. I bet you when they gits in the bed together they bones sound like a dishpan full of crockery.

NUNKIE: *(Outside)* Aw, come on!

(The door closes softly, and the key is turned in the

lock. Curtain.)

SCENE 2.

Scene: *An hour later, the same night. A clearing deep in the woods. The clearing is small, and freshly cleared. Brush hurriedly cut away. Wall of tropical growth around. Big trees, hung with Spanish moss. Glistening leaves, trailing vines, and bright flowers. Lush. Upstage center is a rude seat covered with a symbolic cloth like a throne. Before it is a short length of log for a footstool. The drums are against the shrubbery, right. In the center is a miniature coffin with a circle of candles about it.*

At the rise, Ella Wall in full ceremonials is seated on the throne. Two men naked to the waist stand on either side of her with a gourd rattle, highly decorated, in each hand. A red candle is fixed to Ella's headdress and is alight. There is a small white candle fixed to the back of each of her hands. All of the others wear lighted candles also. The dancers are ranged around the clearing in a circle. Two women downstage right and left have no candles on their hands. They have cymbals poised to play. The men with the rattles have their arms uplifted tensely, waiting for the downstroke. The drums are playing the introduction. All the dancers have their hands extended toward the throne. The right hand is drawn back stiffly, while the left is extended full length, palms down, with knees flexed. They hold this pose rigidly while the drums mount and Ella begins to make rhythmic motions as she sits. The gourd-rattles take up and the "rattling men" beat a counter time on the back of the drums. Ella steps down to the drums and begins to dance.

ELLA: *(Chanting)* Ah, minni wa oh! Ah, minni wa oh!

DANCERS: *(Beginning to dance)* Say kay ah, brah aye!

ELLA: *(Dances to coffin, makes some liquid movement of her upper body.)* Yokko tekko! Yokko tekko! Yahm pahn sah ay!

MEN: Ah yah yee-ay! Ah, yah yee-ay! Ah say oh!

ELLA: *(A vigorous solo about the coffin. Comes to dramatic pause.)* Yekko tekko! Ah pah sah ay!

> *(Up to now, the dance has been mostly movements of the upper body.12 Posture dancing. Now it mounts. Ella is dancing solo against the Corgo of the group. They circle the coffin in a wide circle as they dance with hands stiff at the wrist, palms down. Ella begins to sing and they fall in behind her.)*
>
> Hand a-bowl, knife a-throat
> Rope a-tie me, hand a-bowl
>
> *(Drums and rattles have mounted to furious pitch.)*
>
> Hand a-bowl knife a-throat
> Wangingwalla, knife a-throat
> Hand a-bowl, knife a-throat
> Wango doe-doe, fum dee ah!
>
> *(The dance reaches a frenzy. Some leap over the coffin. Others do other steps. Ella dances furiously in their midst. Now their movements blend with hers. Now the others are more background for her. At the climax, suddenly every candle is blown out and in the dim light, the dancers depart silently to the throb of the diminished drum tones. Curtain.)*

SCENE 3.

SCENE: *Woods, picnic grounds. This clearing differs from the*

other only in that it is larger and shows signs of long use.
A rude table has been contrived by laying long boards on
saw-horses. An old tree stump is downstage center. A few
wooden boxes are scattered around the edges for seats. A
quilt or two have been brought along to sit on. These too,
are along the edges, so that the main clearing is left for
movement. Just beyond the clearing, upstage left, a crude
dressing booth has been erected of palm fronds. Several
large market baskets covered with colored table cloths and
towels are under the table. They have the refreshments in
them.

At the rise, Bunch, Laura B and Maudella are
fussing around the table unpacking baskets, setting out
the pans and dishes of foods, and tasting things here and
there as they work. My Honey is seated on the stump, with
Few Clothes squatting on the ground beside him. Both
have their instruments and are playing. All the men are
grouped around the musicians harmonizing "Georgia
Buck."

LONNIE: *(Singing)*

Oh, Georgia Buck is dead!
Last word he said
I don't want no shortening in my bread.

CHORUS:

Is that you, Reuben?
Is that you, Reuben?
And they laid poor Reuben's body down.

MY HONEY:

Oh, rabbit on the log, ain't got no dog
How am I going git him?
Lord knows!

CHORUS:

> Is that you, Reuben?
> Is that you, Reuben?
> And they laid poor Reuben's body down.

STEW BEEF:

> Oh, Reuben had a wife.
> Swapped her for a Barlow knife
> And they laid poor Reuben's body down.

CHORUS:

> Is that you, Reuben?
> Is that you, Reuben?
> And they laid poor Reuben's body down.

LAURA B: *(Admiringly)* Now, listen at Stew! *(Beaming at his cleverness)* That's the biggest fool!

STEW BEEF: *(Acknowledging the compliment,* Being ah fool never kilt nobody. All it do is make you sweat.

LAURA B: *(Even prouder)* Didn't I tell you he was crazy?

STEW BEEF: Did you cook that stew beef and bring it with you like I told you? I'm gitting peckish. *(Rubs his stomach.)*

LONNIE: Me too.

FEW CLOTHES: *(Starting to get up hurriedly)* Let's eat!

LONNIE: Big Sweet and Leafy say you ain't supposed to eat before a marriage. After the couple stands up is when you eats.

STEW BEEF: My Honey, go ahead and git your marrying done so we can eat. My biggest gut feel like it done dwindled down to a fiddle-string.

(They all get up and look towards the table.)

LAURA B: Naw. Big Sweet said not to touch a thing till after the marriage.

BUNCH: *(Heaping up a pan of fried chicken)* These mens!

They sure favors they stomachs. If Judgment Day was
to come, Few would expect me to fix him a bucket to
carry along.

LAURA B: Stew Beef is just the same. He ever love beef stew.
Look like I can't never fill him up. Just like Eating-
Flukus – eat up camp meeting, back off of association
and drink Jordan dry.

LONNIE: Look like the thing to do is to git the marrying
done. You ready, ain't you, My Honey?

MY HONEY: *(Nervous, but trying to be casual)* Just as ready
as a meat axe.

SOP-THE-BOTTOM: Turn 'round here let's see how you look
in your new suit. *(They all scatter back in a rough circle
around My Honey and look him over from head to foot.)*
You looks fine, man. Any gal ought to be glad to git
you, looking like that.

STEW BEEF: That suit is ready! Believe I'll git me one like
that. Laura B, you want me in a double-breaster like
My Honey got on when we jump over the broomstick?

LAURA B: *(Bridling)* Yeah. You would look good in it, all
right.

LONNIE: 'Course My Honey look good. I picked out that
suit for him to stand up in. *(Looks to table)* Maudella,
run back there and see if Big Sweet done got Leafy
dressed.

MAUDELLA: *(Hurrying towards booth)* Yessir.

LAURA B: Oh, don't worry the gal. It takes time for dressing
for gitting married.

LONNIE: You women and your dressing! *(Sighs)* But I
reckon us men just have to put up with you. We can't
git along without you. But you sure got funny ways.

*(The women protest this but the men laugh in
agreement.)*

STEW BEEF: Lonnie, you acts slow and everything, but you
sure knows a heap. Always saying something deep.

(Big Sweet enters with Leafy all dressed in white with a veil. Big Sweet is holding the veil up from the grass with one hand, Maudella is walking behind and admiring Leafy with open mouthed wonder. Leafy advances slowly with a nervous smile and downcast eyes. All the men gaze at her with awe and admiration. My Honey stares in awe, then takes a step or two towards her and stops as if approaching an altar.)

BOX CAR: *(More brazen, walks nearer and stands and admires)* Lord! I could lick icing off of that all day long.

LONNIE: Leafy, you looks like a glance from God.

(My Honey advances slowly as Big Sweet looks at her handiwork and beams.)

MY HONEY: Baby. *(Swallows hard)* Baby, you looks too good to walk on the ground.

LEAFY: Much obliged for your compliments. *(They start to hold hands.)*

LONNIE: *(Looking around)* Now, where is that preacher? He was here just a while ago.

SOP-THE-BOTTOM: *(Indicates the woods)* Oh, he stepped off a piece. Be back after while.

BIG SWEET: *(Fussing with the wreath)* Hold on a minute. I needs another hairpin right here. *(Turns to hurry off)* Be back in just a second. Want to catch that up a little more.

(She darts off and disappears into the booth. My Honey takes Leafy's hand and they stand there smiling and swinging hands without speaking.)

DO-DIRTY: This marrying business is nice. Us could have been having fun like this all the time, but we didn't have no sense. If Big Sweet and Lonnie hadn't of told us, we wouldn't know.

STEW BEEF: That's a fact. You just wait til next month when me and Laura B stand up. We going to have –

FEW CLOTHES: Man, but me and Bunch is going to really break it up. She's going to have a dress like that and I'm going to be togged down in a suit and white shoes and everything. Lonnie, you sure done started something.

>   *(Preacher enters upstage, left on a run, with his eyes wild and popping. He stumbles to center stage with his mouth working, but no words come out. They look at him for a moment in astonishment. But Maudella cries out and points upstage left as Dicey leaps out into the clearing with her knife drawn. Her entrance is like the spring of a lioness. She is only a few yards off and behind My Honey and Leafy who are looking at each other.)*

DICEY: *(After her initial spring, stops dramatically, with her knife in hand and takes in the situation gloating. She has all the manner of a lioness ready to charge.)* Well, I told you I would be back, didn't I? *(Leafy gives a little cry of helplessness. My Honey, whirls, leaps in front of Leafy instinctively and hold his guitar like a shield. The group is struck dumb for an instant. Everyone is frozen in their tracks. Dicey laughs, wringing herself from her hips.)* You can't do nothing. Youse planted in your tracks. I'm going to cut you all in your face. *(Venomously as she crouches)* Slice you too thin to fry. *(Gestures to the woods behind her)* I got plenty help to do it with.

>   *(She advances slowly, knife poised and laughing. Suddenly, Ella and Nunkie run on to the edge of the clearing behind Dicey.)*

BIG SWEET: *(Enters hurriedly. Is brought up short by the tableau and gets set to spring, at the same time yelling)* Lonnie! Stew!

> *(Her cry and movement bring everybody alive,
> and they rush to the charge. It also affects Dicey
> profoundly and she leaps back in fright.)*

DICEY: *(Backing up in betrayed horror of her situation)* They
ain't 'sleep! They can move! *(It is a bitter accusation of
Ella who is also retreating.)*

ELLA: *(Dazed and terrified by the danger, and astonished
by the failure of her magic, leaps back and looks at the
onrush in unbelief.)* Make it to the hard road! Dicey!

> *(They all turn and flee pell mell through the woods.
> The men start to pursue, but Lonnie halts them.)*

LONNIE: Stop! Box! Stew! My Honey! All you all! Stop!

BOX CAR: *(Unwilling)* They will make they git-away!

LONNIE: Naw, they won't. Listen to me, now.

MY HONEY: We got to make it so they can't come back,
Lonnie.

> *(There is a shot offstage right and a loud voice cries
> "Halt!")*

QUARTER BOSS: I said "halt!" I'm shooting to kill next time.

BIG SWEET: The Quarters Boss!

LONNIE: That's what I'm trying to tell you all. He knowed
we was going to have this picnic down here, and you
know he's always hanging around close enough to hear
what go on.

LAURA B: That sure is so. Soon as you make the least noise,
here he come.

LONNIE: That's what I knowed. Its better for him to handle
'em than for us. You know they ain't coming back now
– Not for years to come.

BIG SWEET: Won't that be nice and fine?

LONNIE: And another thing, when I got to talking to
Pringle and the Big Boss about Big Sweet going off, I
took and told 'em not to listen to everything they hear.
Just be around and see for theyselves who was stirring

up trouble and who wasnt.

LAURA B: *(Laughs)* Dicey was so glad to git to Pringle to talk, she got plenty chance to talk with him all she want to tonight.

(All laugh.)

STEW BEEF: Yeah, but she don't much no talk with him tonight.

LONNIE: Oh, poor Dicey was all right as far as she could see.

BIG SWEET: But she couldn't see no further than from the handle of a tea cup 'round the rim.

LONNIE: Maybe she done the best she knowed how. It wasn't her fault.

BIG SWEET: Well whose fault was it then?

LONNIE: Nobody's exactly. Her mama's womb just played a dirty trick on her when she borned Dicey. That's all. *(They laugh, but lightly.)*

PREACHER: *(Mopping his face from fright, but getting control)* I seen them folks a-coming while I was out there.

LONNIE: I could tell you had seen something, but I couldn't know what. You ready to go to work?

PREACHER: *(Assuming his official manner)* If the bride and groom will take the floor.

(He advances toward them pompously as Big Sweet arranges the couple center but a little upstage.)

LONNIE: This is more like my dream. *(Musing)* Things is going to be better now. Folks everywhere will look upon us more. Us can make things more better all around. *(Unconsciously begins to hum, and the others drift in.)*

> Troubles will be over, Amen
> Troubles will bo over, Amen
> Troubles will be over, when I see Jesus

Troubles will be over, Amen.

*(Preacher takes his stand before My Honey and Leafy,
opens his book dramatically, and begins to perform
the ceremony in pantomime. The singing goes on and
the audience only sees the motions of the marriage
and the movements of lips.)*

I see the lighthouse, Amen
I see the lighthouse, Amen
I see the lighthouse, when I see Jesus
Troubles will be over, Amen.

PREACHER: *(Triumphantly)* I now pronounce you man and
wife. Salute the bride.

*(A shout of joy breaks out and everybody rushes up to
kiss Leafy and congratulate My Honey. Box Car, Sop-
The-Bottom and Do-Dirty kiss enthusiastically. My
Honey pulls Do-Dirty away.)*

MY HONEY: That's enough, Do. You only supposed to kiss
a bride in a manner of speaking. You ain't supposed to
taste it at all.

DO-DIRTY: Aw, man don't be so selfish! You can git your
little old kiss back when I gits me a wife. *(Starts to kiss
Leafy again, but My Honey grabs him.)* Man, I likes this
thing. Tain't going to be no time at all before I'm going
to be asking a gal to gimme some hand.

SOP-THE-BOTTOM: Give Lonnie credit. He sure do think
up some nice things.

LONNIE: I got another notion right now.

SOP-THE-BOTTOM: What is it?

LONNIE: *(Getting a head start towards the table)* Let's eat!

*(The men all break for the table except My Honey,
who leads Leafy over tenderly and self-consciously.)*

BIG-SWEET: *(Presiding at distribution of plates)* One at a

time! One at at time! Like gamblers going to heaven.
It's plenty for everybody.

LONNIE: *(Stepping back from the table with his plate.)*
Ummmmm! This is nice! Chicken purleau!

> *(Strolls over to the stump with his plate and sits
> down and eats a few mouthfuls. As the others get
> their plates, they scatter from the table and sit about
> laughing and talking happily. My Honey and Leafy
> go sit on a a quilt with their plates and she feeds him
> with her fork.)*

MY HONEY: This is love, baby, with the sun and the moon
thrown in.

LEAFY: That's right. Everything! With the sun and the
moon thrown in.

BIG SWEET: *(With her plate in her hand)* Everybody got
what you want?

ALL: Yes, indeed!

BIG SWEET: Well, all right now. I'm going and set down by
Lonnie. Come on Bunch and Laura B Let's sit down
by our men folks.

> *(They cross to their places, down contentedly and all
> begin to eat.)*

LONNIE: Just like I keep telling you all, you can git what
you want if you go about things the right way. *(Pets Big
Sweet on the ground beside him.)* Now, I can fly. Everything
is going to be just fine.

> *(There comes the sound of the mystic drums. They all
> listen. Lonnie smiles in his peculiar way as the drums
> grow in volume. They smile, they laugh, then begin to
> sway to the drums.)*

I ride the rainbow, Amen
I ride the rainbow, Amen

> *(A huge rainbow descends. They all scramble on*

board, plates in hand, and take seats. Lonnie in the very center with Big Sweet on one side – My Honey and Leafy on the other, keep singing.)

I ride the rainbow, when I see Jesus
Troubles will be over, Amen.

(The rainbow begins to rise as the verse is repeated. The rainbow rises slowly and the curtain begins to descend at the same time slowly.)

CURTAIN

Endnotes

1. Original text reads "de heuvof."
2. Carrie's re-entrance (necessary for her lines later in the scene, on p. ___ [35 in first pages]) is not indicated in the original.
3. Original text reads "Jim."
4. The lyrics to the spiritual "Downward Road is Crowded" was not included in the typescript.
5. The Black Bottom dance originated in New Orleans in the late 1910s and achieved widespread popularity during the mid-1920s, being most notably featured in the George White Scandals in 1926. Perhaps because of its popularity, the song is not included in the typescript. If one were to produce the play, one might use Jelly Roll Morton's rendition of "The Black Bottom Stomp" (1919).
5. September Morn (1912), a painting by Frenchman Paul Chabas, won the Medal of Honor at the Paris Salon of 1912, but became infamous in the United States a year later when it was shown in a Manhattan art gallery. Showing a nude young woman standing in the middle of a stream, the New York Society for the Suppression of Vice considered it far too risque for public display and ordered it to be removed. The gallery owner refused. The ensuing controversy assured its indelible imprint in the American

mind's eye. Over the next decade, the image appeared on postcards, figurines, calendars, and even clothing. And, as we see here, the "September Morn pose" became a common sight gag in popular drama of the 1910s and 1920s. The painting currently hangs in the Metropolitan Museum of Art.

De Turkey and de Law

1. Original text reads "Lour." (p. 117)
2. Places in church reserved for those leading congregational responses. (p. 137)
3. Original text reads "heavy-hipted." (p. 144)
4. A kind of revolver. (p. 146)
5. "Diddy-Wah-Diddy": slang for "a faraway place"; "Ginny-Gall": a suburb of Hell. (p. 148)
6. Original reads "Davie." (p. 151)
7. Original reads "I have studied jury and I know ... " (p. 152a)
8. Original reads "bought." (p. 159)

Cock Robin

1. Original reads "The Bull"; name changed because Sparrow is also referred to as "Bull Sparrow" in the typescript.
2. The Palmer House, a luxury hotel in Chicago, was noted for having an all-black staff. Stavin' Chain (Wilson Jones), a boogie woogie and blues musician from Louisiana, was active throughout the first few decades of the twentieth century and subsequently immortalized in such songs as "The Stavin' Chain Blues" (Big Joe Williams) and "Winin' Boy Blues" (Jelly Roll Morton, later sung by Janis Joplin among others). The line is probably an allusion to "Winin' Boy Blues" ("Pick it up and shake it like Stavin' Chain"). The next line, omitted in this edition, is a stage direction reading "Boston tune: Oh te dee tat a de ta a putzy wanza."

Heaven

1. When the South Fork Dam failed on May 31, 1889, over 2,200 people in the town of Johnstown, Pennsylvania, perished. It remains to this day one of the worst natural disasters suffered in American history.

Bahamas

1. The typescript is marked out with pencil scribbles up to the "seaman's chorus" on p. ___. [p. 85 of 1st pages]
2. The song "Don't You Hurry, Worry with Me" is not included in the typescript. A song with the same title was recorded by Alan Lomax is included in Deep River of Song: Bahamas 1935, Vol. 2: Ring Games and Round Dances (Rounder Records, 2002). The reference to "pee vee voo" is unknown.
3. This line and the following one from the Emperor are struck out in pencil on the typescript.

Poker!

1. This play contains many similarities to Jook in Cold Keener. It's possible that they were simply different versions of the same play, as Hurston had a propensity for recycling her material.

Woofing

1. See p. ___ of Jook in Cold Keener for a possible rendition of this song.
2. See p. ___ of Jook in Cold Keener for a possible rendition of this song.

Forty Yards

1. The typescript includes the following lines after the curtain:
   Lincoln's Prayer:
   Ah, ah, they shall not ah pass us

Lord, Lord, Lord, Lord

They shall not pass us, Ah-h-h-h.

SPUNK

1. The rest of this song is not included. [p. 198]
2. The lyrics of this song, as well as many others in this play, are not included in the typescript. [p. 198]
3. Since Blue Trout has not exited earlier in the scene, dialogue and/or stage directions will need to be added in order to preserve continuity. [p. 203]
4. The typescript names this girl Palmetto. [p. 206]
5. Prior to the scene description, Hurston has included the following note: "Conjure scene cannot be fully put on paper. Must be done in direction." [p. 230]
6. Original text reads "kiering." [p. 233]
7. The first verse is not included in the typescript.

POLK COUNTY

1. Workers on a turpentine camp slash the bark of trees in order to collect gum.
2. The following animal sequence is a stylistic anomaly in what is otherwise a solid piece of realism. It is hard to imagine that this scene would have survived if the New York production had gone forward.
3. To cheat by arranging to get a winning card.
4. A popular folk-hero. Most stories cast him as a slave from Africa who outwits characters such as Ole Massa, God, or the Devil with great joviality.
5. Sweetheart Soap is the brand name for a common perfumed soap. Octogon Soap is a harsh lye soap.
6. A version of "Cold Rainy Day" is included in Meet the Mamma. [check this]
7. Slang term for a promiscuous woman. It comes from the

nickname of a species of gecko that was believed to have venomous toes.

8. Probably a reference to Peetie Wheatstraw, a blues recording artist of the 1930s, who called himself "the High Sheriff from Hell" and "the Devil's Son-in-Law."

9. Original reads "ear-laps."

10. Someone who drives a heavy tractor.

11. An early form of rummy.

12. Referring to the type of loa or spiritual ancestor that is conjured in a voodoo ceremony or in this case, a man possessed by a loa.

apprentice
house

Apprentice House is the future of publishing...today. Using state-of-the-art technology and an experiential learning model of education, it publishes books in untraditional ways while teaching tomorrow's future editors and publishers.

Staffed by students, this non-profit activity of the Department of Communication at Loyola College in Maryland is part of an advanced elective course and overseen by the press's Director. When class is not in session, work on book projects is carried forward by a co-curricular organization, The Apprentice House Book Publishing Club, of which the press's Director also serves as Faculty Advisor.

Contributions are welcomed to sustain the press's work and are tax deductible to the fullest extent allowed by the IRS. For more information, see www.apprenticehouse.com.

Student Editors (2004-05)

Jeffrey Bradley '05
Christine DeSanctis '05
Elizabeth Didora '05
Michael Hilt '05
Lauren Galvin '05
Marion Goodworth '05

Morgan Hillenbrand '05
Patricia McNamara '06
Kathleen Nagle '05
Kerri Reilly '05
Erik Schmitz '07